No Country for Migrants?
Critical Perspectives on
Asylum, Immigration, and
Integration in Germany

Studies in Critical Social Sciences Book Series

Haymarket Books is proud to be working with Brill Academic Publishers (www.brill.nl) to republish the *Studies in Critical Social Sciences* book series in paperback editions. This peer-reviewed book series offers insights into our current reality by exploring the content and consequences of power relationships under capitalism, and by considering the spaces of opposition and resistance to these changes that have been defining our new age. Our full catalog of *SCSS* volumes can be viewed at https://www.haymarketbooks.org/series_collections/4-studies-in-critical-social-sciences.

Series Editor
David Fasenfest (Wayne State University)

Editorial Board
Eduardo Bonilla-Silva (Duke University)
Chris Chase-Dunn (University of California–Riverside)
William Carroll (University of Victoria)
Raewyn Connell (University of Sydney)
Kimberlé W. Crenshaw (University of California–LA and Columbia University)
Heidi Gottfried (Wayne State University)
Karin Gottschall (University of Bremen)
Alfredo Saad Filho (King's College London)
Chizuko Ueno (University of Tokyo)
Sylvia Walby (Lancaster University)
Raju Das (York University)

No Country for Migrants? Critical Perspectives on Asylum, Immigration, and Integration in Germany

Wilfried Zoungrana

Haymarket Books
Chicago, IL

First published in 2019 by Brill Academic Publishers, The Netherlands.
© 2019 Koninklijke Brill NV, Leiden, The Netherlands

Published in paperback in 2020 by
Haymarket Books
P.O. Box 180165
Chicago, IL 60618
773-583-7884
www.haymarketbooks.org

ISBN: 978-1-64259-356-3

Distributed to the trade in the US through Consortium Book Sales and Distribution (www.cbsd.com) and internationally through Ingram Publisher Services International (www.ingramcontent.com).

This book was published with the generous support of Lannan Foundation and Wallace Action Fund.

Special discounts are available for bulk purchases by organizations and institutions. Please call 773-583-7884 or email info@haymarketbooks.org for more information.

Cover design by Jamie Kerry and Ragina Johnson.

Printed in United States.

10 9 8 7 6 5 4 3 2 1

Library of Congress Cataloging-in-Publication Data is available.

For Zéphorah Yennenga

Contents

Acknowledgements   IX
Abbreviations   X

Introduction   1

1 **The 2015 German Refugee Crisis as an Event**   11
  1 From Political to Metaphysical: Multiple Conceptualizations of the Event   13
  2 Syria: The Supernumerary of an Evental Site   28
  3 Undecidability and the Edge of the Void   39
  4 Interventional Gestures   43
  5 Transcendental Arrangements   46

2 **An Abbreviated History of Germany's Migration Discourses and Policies**   49
  1 Historiographical Omissions and Sociological Exclusions   50
  2 Bismarck, *Leutenot*, and the Early Securitization of Migration   52
  3 Weber and the Empowerment of Nationalistic Audiences   59
  4 Of C2, 3P, and Muddling through: Regulating Securitized Migration   64

3 **Soft and Hard: Power, Asylum, and Germany**   91
  1 Soft Power Meets Asylum   92
  2 The 'Objective' Soft Power of a Reluctant Hegemon   94
  3 The Duality of Soft Power on Asylum   97
  4 Hard and Economic Power in Migration Control   106

4 **On Language, Integration, and Pedagogy**   111
  1 Language, Structuralist Linguistics, and Integration   116
  2 The Language Testing Regime and Its Discontent   120
  3 Challenges in Acquiring German as a Second Language, and Integration   123
  4 Toward Radical Perspectives on the Pedagogy of Integration   133
  5 Jacotot's Method and Secondary Language Acquisition   140

5 **Civilization-Culture-Character: the Plateaus of the 'Clash Rhizome'**   151
  1 Civilization in the Clash Rhizome   153
  2 The German Reception of the Clash of Civilizations   159

    3 Culture in the Clash Rhizome   169
    4 Character between Affects and Late Modernity and Capitalism   176

6 The "Deep Story" of the Elder Son   181
    1 The Prodigal Son in the Biblical Narrative   185
    2 The Younger Son's Revolutionary Wager   187
    3 The Father and the Cost of Humanitarian Largesse   188
    4 Exit, Voice, Loyalty, and the 'Anger and Mourning' of the Elder Son   189

7 '*Muslim Girls*' and '*Muslim Men*': Cursory Notes on Entangled Subalternities   194
    1 *'Muslim Women'* and Epistemic Violence   200
    2 Migration and (Post) Colonial Path Dependency   202
    3 *'Muslim Men'* and a Critique of Patriarchal Reason   204

Bibliography   209
Index   239

Acknowledgements

I have to start by thanking my awesome wife, Dina. From giving me advice on layout issues to taking care of our newborn baby, so I could work on this book, she was as important to this book getting done as I was. Thank you so much, Cheifu.

I'm eternally grateful to my parents and my siblings Fabrice, and Irène for their constant encouragements. Likewise, I am indebted to my in-laws who stood ready to provide any help they could.

I am indebted to David Fasenfest who gave to me the opportunity to reflect and elaborate on the issues presented in this book and to the editorial team at Brill for publishing the outcome of this process.

I am also grateful to Mark Anyorikeya Amaliya, Elza Hermann, Diana De Fex Sierra, Aline Mugisho, Malek Harbaa, Emmanuel Gómez Farías Mata, Mohammed Alhaj Kanama, Jana and Silas Domrös, Sandy Gieske, Michelle Randow, Szilvia Schaefer, who stood by me during different stages in the planification and writing of this book. Thank you for your friendship.

Last but not least, to all those Syrian, Iraqi, Eritrean, Afghan refugees, and migrants in Germany I have encountered in the last four years inside and outside the German language classroom and who have broadened my horizon on issues of asylum, migration, integration, and are the raison d'être of this book: Thank you.

Abbreviations

3P	Public Private Partnership
AnkER	*Ankunfts-, Entscheidungs- und Rückführungszentren* (AnkER stands for arrival centers for asylum seekers, decision on asylum applications, and repatriation of rejected asylum seekers)
AQIM	Al-Qeada in Islamic Maghreb
BA	*Bundesagentur für Arbeit* (Federal Employment Agency)
BAMF	*Bundesamt für Migration und Flüchtlinge* (Federal Office for Migration and Refugees)
BMZ	*Bundesministerium für wirtschaftliche Zusammenarbeit und Entwicklung* (Federal Ministry of Economic Cooperation and Development)
C2	Command and Control
CAH	Contrastive Analysis Hypothesis
CDU	*Christlich Demokratische Union Deutlschlands* (Christian Democratic Union of Germany)
CEAS	Common European Asylum System
CEFR	Common European Framework of Reference for Languages
CFSP	Common Foreign and Security Policy
ISB	*Staatsinstitut für Schulqualität und Bildungsforschung* (State Institute for School Quality and Educational Research)
ISF	Internal Security Forces (Mali)
CIA	Central Intelligence Agency
CSS	*Collège Sahélien de Sécurité* (Sahelian Security Council)
CSU	*Christlich-Soziale Union in Bayern* (Christian Social Union in Bavaria)
EC	European Communities
ECOWAS	Economic Community of West African States
EUCAP	EU Capacity Building Mission in Mali
EUTM	European Union Training Mission
FDP	*Freie Demokratische Partei* Deutschlands (Free Democratic Party)
FIT	*Front Islamique Tunisien* (Tunisian Islamic Front)
G5S	*G5 du Sahel or G5 Sahel* (Security Cooperation Group emcompassing five Sahel countries: Burkina Faso, Chad, Mali, Mauritania, and Niger)
GDR	German Democratic Republic
GIA	*Groupe Islamique Armé* (Armed Islamic Group)
GNI	Gross National Income
GSPC	*Groupe Salafiste pour la Prédication et le Combat* (Salafist Group for Preaching and Combat)
ICG	International Crisis Group

ISIS	Islamic State of Iraq and Syria
MINUSMA	*Mission multidimensionnelle intégrée des Nations Unies pour la stabilisation au Mali* (United Nations Multidimensional Integrated Stabilization Mission in Mali)
MSA	Modern Standard Arabic
MUJWA	Movement for Unity and Jihad in West Africa
ODA	Official Development Assistance
PCI	*Partito Comunista Italiano* (Italian Communist Party)
Pegida	*Patriotische Europäer gegen die Islamisierung des Abendlandes* (Patriotic Europeans against the Islamisation of the Occident)
PLO	Palestine Liberation Organisation
POW	Prisoner of War
PSI	Pan Sahel Initiative
SCPR	Syrian Center for Policy Research
SPD	*Sozialdemokratische Partei Deutschlands* (Social Democratic Party of Germany)
TSCTI	Trans- Saharan Counterterrorism Initiative
TSTI	Trans-Saharan Counterterrorism Initiative
TWAIL	Third World Approaches to International Law
UN	United Nations
VBIED	Vehicle-Borne Improved Explosive Device
WMD	Weapon of Mass Destruction
ZPD	Zone of Proximal Development

Introduction

There is in the canteen (generally referred to as *casino*) of the state parliament of Berlin, the *Abgeordnetenhaus*, a massive oil on canvas triptych, *"Die Öffnung der Berliner Mauer"* by Matthias Koeppel, who is undoubtedly the painter of the Opening or Fall of the Berlin Wall. He painted the triptych between 1996 and 1997; the left and right parts of the imposing triptych are each 220 × 320 cm, the middle part measures 440 × 400 cm. Images, John Berger had argued, more than any "other kind of relic or text from the past can offer such a direct testimony about the world which surrounded other people at other times. In this respect images are more precise and richer than literature. To say this is not to deny the expressive or imaginative quality of art, treating it as mere documentary evidence; the more imaginative the work, the more profoundly it allows us to share the artist's experience of the visible (1972, p. 10)." Following Berger, Koeppel's triptych is a direct, historical testomony not only to those like me who had not witnessed this historical moment, but also to the more priviledged, who also witnessed the event. It is certainly not fortuitous that Koeppel revived the genre of history painting. History painting had arguably lost its priviledged status by the late nineteenth century, and was thought to have been dead by some art historians, but history painting's subjects still continue to inspire artists (see Hart, 2015).

The first time I caught sight of Koeppel's painting was when I took a group of adult German language learners to the *Abgeordnetenhaus*, to get in touch with a political institution of the *Land* they were living in and discuss with an MP. During the guided tour, we came to the famous casino where the triptych hangs. Of course, some saw the ideal background for a selfie. When the selfie-takers had moved from the picture, a Colombian graduate, a Chadian academic, a (stateless) Palestinian born and raised in Syria, an Afghan asylum seeker stood in front of the triptych, facing it, scrutinizing it. I wondered for a while how they were seeing the picture but ultimately took the picture of them contemplating Koeppel's triptych and kept on making other pictures of the guided tour.

As I was busy making pictures, Amir (I changed the name), the stateless Palestinian, turned to me and asked whether it was the late chancellor Helmut Kohl, the chancellor of the German reunification, giving an interview in the middle part of the triptych. Amir had arrived in Germany in 2015 as a stateless refugee from Syria. He identifies himself as Palestinian, but was born in Yarmouk, a Damascene suburb, mostly inhabited by Palestinian refugees and their descendants. You would think that identifying a massive chancellor like

Helmut Kohl, who was 1.93 m tall should not be particularly difficult. Yet, it is not that straightforward. Nearly two thirds of the space of the triptych are covered by the sky, the trademark of Koeppel. People, the protagonists of the Opening of the Wall are depicted in the lower thirds of the pictures and not only politicians are depicted, but also ordinary scenes that Koeppel observed during the opening of the Wall. Furthermore, he has not depicted the facial traits of the key protagonists in a photographic manner. Amir's was a commendable interest in the political history of his host country.

Local, federal politicians, and ordinary citizens are recurrent in the triptych. The left part of the triptych depicts the scene of the night of the 9th of November 1989, where the border passage on the *Invalidenstraße* was opened. Such an historic moment generates chaos. Then ruling (West-) Berlin mayor Walter Momper is portrayed on the right corner of the picture, regulating the traffic with a megaphone.

The second part of triptych depicts the occupation of the Wall segment in front of the *Brandenburger Tor*. There is a scene where Helmut Kohl, whom Amir had recognized, attends to the media. But there is also Willy Brandt, the chancellor of the *Ostpolitik*, rushing into the frame from the left-hand side, as if to claim his historical role in the build-up to this event. Both Brandt and Kohl have had their struggles with immigration. Brandt put an end to the recruitment of foreign workers (so-called *Gastarbeiter*) in 1973. In the 1980s, Kohl proclaimed Germany was not an immigration country (*Deutschland ist kein Einwanderungsland*), planned to halve the number of foreigners (mostly Turks) through multiple pecuniary incentives. He did not succeed in his enterprise but Germany might still have an ambivalent relation to immigration.

In the third part of the picture, Koeppel portrays the lifting out of the first wall segment on the Potsdamer Platz in the early morning of November 12, 1989. The prominent politician in the frame is then Federal President Richard von Weizsäcker, greeting an officer of the GDR border troops. All these scenes take place under Koeppel's munitiously painted sky. Art historian Stölzl had remarked that Koeppel's colors, despite all the gray in the background, radiate, sparkle and sometimes even scream. They are real and surreal at the same time. In painting the Opening of the Berlin Wall, Stölzl thinks, Koeppel could have – for superior reasons – used more optimistic color or at least raised the contrast between gray (German division) and color (German future) (Stölzl, 2014, p.13), Koeppel stuck to his many shades of grey. Just as he chose the genre of history painting to pain an event that would be thought to mark the end of history!

Koeppel likes portraying the sky – or heaven if you prefer (both words translate as *Himmel* in German), but rarely in a deep blue sky. He has a dazzling command of cloud formation patterns that impresses meteorologists and pilots (See Wehry and Ossing 1997). But when he paints the Fall of the Berlin Wall, which he has seen firsthand and chronicled, he does not yield to the simple jubilatory mood one would expect. His *'two-third' Himmel* keeps the serenity or pesssimism of the intellectual and watches carefully what humans do under the sky, at times seeming to make a parody out of humans' actions. Art historians have trouble classifying the work of Koeppel; his work can be romantic and realist, utopian and concrete at the same time.

There are ways of seeing and "[t]he way we see things is affected by what we know or what we believe" (Berger, 1972, p. 8). If I had expanded on Koeppel's triptych, it is because, it – in many instances from the trivial to the methodological – illustrates the case of migration to Germany and the overall project of this book.

Koeppel is a migrant to Berlin. He left his native Hamburg for (West) Berlin. Both were part of West-Germany and so this type of migration did not seem problematic. It was more a case of internal mobility. Koeppel's artistic output is mostly about Berlin, itself a city of migration. Recent statistics evaluate the numbers of yearly newcomers to Berlin at 30,000 to 40,000. The overwhelming majority of these newcomers are foreigners: European migrants, and refugees. Only a slight number are Germans from the other 15 *Länder*. That was for the trivial part.

The Opening of the Berlin Wall in 1989 is first and foremost a story of uneffective command-and-control migration policies. The GDR built the Berlin Wall in 1961 as a desperate attempt to the curve the flight of refugees to West Germany. The 3.6 m-tall and about 160 km-long wall did not deter candidates to immigration into the more prosperous, liberal, democratic, and social-capitalist West Germany. Worldwide, this migration pattern has not completely changed: phantasies of stringent migration control still dominate the imaginary of proponents of a command-and-control steering model of migration. In the case of the two German countries in the Cold War (FRG and GDR), a totalitarian regime in the GDR financed and built a wall, shot its own citizens before they could reach the other side of the Wall. Today, this pattern has been reversed in international migration control. Dictators are paid or incentivized to prevent their citizens from migrating into the prosperous Europe or the so-called West and across the pond, a democratically-elected president is pressing for a Wall to keep out his southern neighbors. Estimates put the death toll of the Berlin Wall between 140 and 245 so-called *Maueropfer*, victims of the Berlin Wall. Restrictive migration policies reduce migration to a life-and-death-game. Democratic countries do not shoot people down from walls in the manner the GDR did. The task has been tacitly outsourced to dictators, non-democratic or unstable regimes. Where these regimes fail to prevent their citizens for emigrating, the Mediterranean Sea takes over. Human beings fundamentally believe in the singularity or their own fate. Death on the Wall or in the Mediterranean Sea did not deter the next candidates to attempt the impossible. Sometimes, the Wall or the Sea were less terrifying than what they were fleeing from.

Koeppel's triptych is also a story of hope, of history repeating itself, under new aspects, with new protagonists under his dramatic sky. It yields itself almost to a Pasolinian interpretation. Pasolini had re-interpreted the biblical St. Paul, using dynamic equivalences to recreate the key scenes of St. Paul's conversion, first missionary travels, thus adapting it to the historical context of the 1970s. If one were to attempt such a Pasolinian contemplation of Koeppel's triptych, the storyline would go as follows: the time is September 2015. Merkel, Kohl's former protégée, casts in the role of her former mentor, as the Chancellor of the second border opening. Walter Momper stands for the numerous communal and regional politicians that have sprang in to provide accommodation, and basic services to the refugees and manage an extraordinary humanitarian situation in the heart of Europe. Joachim Gauck is the von Weizsäcker of this 'second German border opening,' concerned with the rash integration of the refuges for the sake of public safety. The large numbers of Syrian refugees from the 2011 Arab-Spring-revolution turned Civil War under the counterrevolution of the Syrian regime, Afghans, so-called economic migrants from Albania and other south-east European countries, or North and Sub-Saharan Africans are the 'East-Germans,' who risked their lives by assaulting the Wall. The plot would not be dramatic if it does not include the mixed signal of Germany's unilateral foregoing of the Dublin agreements that unleash the exodus from Hungary and the aftermath of what one could call the 2015 German refugee crisis.

But Koeppel's triptych is also to me an allegory of the relationship between theory and praxis, the (meta-) theory of clouds, seemingly removed, that few have taken the time to engage with and use to make sense of the political, the social among all phenomena that happen under the sky. Koeppel brings the sky and the people in a frame, the laborious and studied sky occupies two-thirds of the picture but is not disconnected from the ground, and the people on it. There is a horizon where they meet, where the seemingly remote sky encounters the earth. We all have our relationship to theory. Some would have reduced the sky to a third of picture, brushed it more or less superficially, and dispensed of the bunters of specific cloud formations, then consecrated most of their energy to the depiction of the main figures in the painting. After all, they could argue, people opened the Wall, not the sky! Others still would have

INTRODUCTION   5

left out the sky altogether or painted the sky and the earth in two different frames, or reversed the order, the earth coming before the sky. In their opinion, the sky would have no meaningful relevance for the depiction of this historical moment. Others would keep the sky, as in Koeppel, but painted it in brighter, more positivist colors and not in the relatively sober colors of Koeppel. Then, there are those who would depict the sky and earth in a dialectic relationship, define the horizon where they meant, or devoted their energy to finding the liminal spaces between the two.

As a student, I have always tried to pay attention to (meta-) theoretical and critical questions in theory and how they translate into praxis. Very often, I have heard people say theory was no more relevant and wished for sheer empiricism, and neo-positivist forms of knowledge gaining. Contemplating Koeppel's triptych, I get the sense that the sky makes the picture. Without the laboriously painted sky, one does not get the dramatic and intellectual sense the picture transmits. But unlike Koeppel, I am unable to paint and have only a modest command of art history.

Yet, the reader will notice that I spend some time depicting my own variation of Koeppel's sky: introductory discussions on chosen theories, approaches to highlight specific aspects of migration. The wider theoretical debates at times occupy nearly a third of the chapters and are followed by the practical application I make of these theories to the German context. To be sure, theory and empirics are never neatly separated, and they aren't either in the following chapters. They intersect at specific points, move and constantly readjust their horizons. In each frame, I chose the theoretical toolkit that I see fit to convey the aspects of migration I witnessed or would like to discuss. I have different frames (chapters) where (in my poor imiation of Koeppel) I portray my take on specific aspects of migration. I will not really be in measure to ground why I chose certain aspects and not others. And indeed, they are certainly more aspects that I omitted which could/should have been included. The reader would get the sense that although the seven chapters are closed in themselves and could exist independently from one another, they are nonetheless united through the fact that they approach general questions of migration in Germany. Likewise, the critical approaches I employ vary from chapter to chapter. At times I have needed to subvert existing non-critical theories and bring them to bear upon the phenomena I analyze. This collection of chapters aims to critically contribute to ongoing debates about migration, integration, and xenophobia in Germany since the massive arrival of refugees in 2015. Set against the backdrop of Germany's bold yet highly controversial political decision to open its borders to Syrian refugees, the volume aims to realign this watershed with the broader post war historical narratives of migration to explain its exceptionality both as an event and transformative force on the migration-integration discourse. The book is inspired by the author's personal experience and is written from the vantage point of my engagement with international relations theories, public policy, critical theory, and subsequent professional experience as a lecturer within the German refugee integration policy. Although the respective chapters address separate emerging themes of the migration debate through the application of theories from social science and international relations, they are structurally interwoven and interconnected.

Chapter 1 is on the 2015 German refugee crisis and the geophilosophy of the event. The chapter opens with a discussion on political and metaphysical conceptualizations of the event. It discusses non-causal relations and compositional dependence in Kim, Davidson; non-event and fake events in Baudrillard, the edge of the void, discursive events respectively in Badiou, Foucault, and Deleuze. I evaluate the different theories considered in terms of how they can be used to make sense of the refugee crisis. In the second part, I apply mostly Badiousian categories to the 2015 refugee crisis. The Event, in Badiou's thought interrupts the course of history and is not "preceded by any sign, and catches us unawares with its grace, regardless of our vigilance." (Badiou, 2003, p. 111) Badiou's claim that the event is not preceded by signs is not a negation of the possibility to explain events through economic, political, or social categories. However, it translates the impossibility to reduce or justify the event through numerable factors. The incapacity of the *Event* to justify itself, the radicalism of reactions to the *Event*, and its revolutionary effects provide interesting points to analyze the German refugee crisis since 2015. But also contingence, locality, retrospectivity, intensity of appearance, and connectivity contribute to make sense of Event in Badiou's thought. The multiplying connections reach back to the Euro-crisis and the reform of migration policies. These combined causes could explain the massive influx of refugees in 2015. The financial crisis that shook countries like Spain, Italy, and Greece have reduced refugees' destinations to a few countries, namely those which at their the core, withstood the crisis rather well and offered to refugees a chance to restore their own economic well-being or simply a shelter of the war. Analysts often tend to reduce asylum-seeking to the simple search of a safe shelter. The category of the *Event* will ultimately help to make sense of the shifting coordinates in the political and social landscape of Germany, the reinvigorated debates on populism and antisemitism.

Chapter 2 focuses on the history of migration policies. It opens with observations on historiographical omissions and sociological exclusions on migration into Germany. These omissions reflect in a 'presence-absence paradox' of the migrant that those interested in migration research in Germany have noted. Although the country has been *de facto* an immigration country not only since 1949 but way back in the nineteenth century, political discourse and practice have long denied this fact. I follow Herbert's history of immigration to Germany for chronological and factual accuracy. I then offer a framework, a typology to make sense of the country's migration policies. Bismarck's policy on the *Leutenot* after the foundation of the Reich in 1871 is an early case of a securitization discourse of migration. I discuss Weber's role in the empowerment of nationalistic audiences within the securitization theory. Securitized discourses of migration have produced three types of policies: command-and-control (C2) ones, public-private partnership (3P) approaches for migration regulation, and muddling-through-policies. C2-policies are recurrent in nationalistic, imperialistic and Nazi migration policies, but also in contemporary political programs of the Far Right. Roughly speaking, the periods between 1885–1890/1, the 1914–18 WWI era, Nazi-Germany (1933–1945) far-right anti-migration showcase a C2-approach to migration control. Public-private-partnership migration control in this chapter is a model of migration steering where the political and economic aspects conjointly regulated by the state and private sector stakeholders. Wilhelmine Germany between 1890 and 1914 offers an early illustration of this model. In this model, nationalistic groups, foreigners' recruitment agencies, and the state through its police apparatus conjointed regulated the influx of migrants, and internal policing migration. Muddling-through policies are policies caught between humanitarian commitments, demographic imperatives, economic conjunctures, and soft power considerations. They further oscillate between the integration of aliens, a tolerated stay for the rejected asylum applicants, between letting the migrants settle and deporting them. It does not follow any specific imperative and constitutes the fertile ground for far-right anti-immigration discourses and phantasies of C2-approaches to thrive on.

In Chapter 3, I contrast Germany's posture as a reluctant Hegemon with its increased global attraction through the concept of soft power and hard power and the role they play in regulating international migration into Germany. I suggest that there are two forms of soft power: a desired one, one associated with international prestige and a less-desired one: the attraction of asylum seekers and migrants. Germany possesses both forms of soft power. The imperative of regulating migration also has hard-power dimensions. Germany's military involvement in the Sahel region, economic incentives provided to the countries of origin of 'unwanted' migrants show that the country is recurring to these two forms of power to regulate immigration.

Chapter 4 is on language, integration, and pedagogy. It opens with informational background on state-financed language courses and integration courses for migrants and specific asylum-seekers in Germany. I then go on to make sense of language as a central instrument in the integration policy. I follow a Bourdieusian reading of Sausurrian linguistics and introduce the alien, the foreigners in the language and integration regime. From here, I move to the second part of the chapter where I try to make sense of the results of refugees/foreigners in the language integration test. In the second part of the chapter, I draw from my experience as a lecturer in integration classes and language acquisition to highlight some of the challenges faced by adult migrants learning German. In the public opinion, failing to succeed in language tests are quasi-systematically perceived as caused by laziness, ungratefulness, and social parasitism. But as I intend to show, the wider picture is somehow more nuanced. In the third part of the chapter, I introduce radical pedagogy into thinking about language teaching and integration. I analyze how – by reworking Ivan Illich's *Deschooling Society* – integration in a society does not simply emanate from language textbooks. I also look at Rancière's Jacotot and Paulo Freire. I examine the claim of 'universal intelligence' by Jacotot in the context of foreign language acquisition as well as his conception of auto-didactical learning. It does not only contrast current methods in language teaching. Language learning and teaching take the dimensions of intellectual emancipation. In Freire, I find that his *Pedagogy of the Oppressed* is not only a piece of critical, pedagogical methodology or the reservoir of critical concepts such as the banking concept of education or cultural invasion. I argue that there is more to Freire's book that the aspect mentioned earlier. I re-interpret his book as a personal missive to the refugees who fled oppression to find refuge in Germany. Freire seems to have much to say about their struggle, their present condition and the prospect of their integration in the German society.

In Chapter 5, I look at civilization, culture, and character as the plateaus of the 'clash' rhizome. I suggest that the metaphor "rhizome" can be applied to make sense of the clash of civilisations/ cultures on the meta-sense. It is a discourse that appears on different plateaus: the international, national, and indeed personal or individual. The different planes connect together and are the sites where the discourse of clash can be observed. Huntington posited in the 1990s that the clash of civilizations would remake the world order. The chapter starts with a discussion on his initial thesis, engages with the German reception of Huntington's thesis. I review the German reception of the clash of civilizations in the writings of Kai Hafez, Udo Steinbach, Bassam Tibi, and the speeches of Roman Herzog. I then move to analyze culture in the clash rhizome. I analyze the concepts of *Leitkultur*, *Verfassungspatriotismus* in the context of discussions on the national 'culture' and increased immigration. In the last part of the chapter, I address 'character' as another site where the clash rhizome reaches. Both civilizational and cultural essentialist neglects the character, a site where the clash regime is played out. I suggest that 'character' is caught between human affects, the effects of late capitalism.

Chapter 6 discusses the paradoxes of the renewed xenophobia since 2015 in a context of growing right-wing extremism through the Biblical parable of the prodigal son. I argue that told from a secular perspective, the parable would fit appropriately as a humanitarian tale. A distraught people calling for help after losing their 'inheritance' and with no shelter and a good Samaritan rescuing them without first trying to inflict additional humiliation on them or lecturing them on the perils of hazardous revolutions. But to catch the dramatic sense of the parable, one needs, I think, to redirect the spotlight to the third character of the story: the elder son, the 'faithful' one that has to cope with a new situation his father singlehandedly designed. The elder son was confronted with three options – to adapt Hirschman's typology – in his situation of dissatisfaction: exit, voice or loyalty. In the exit option, the elder son would be expected to leave his fatherland (homeland or *Heimat*) and emigrate to show his dissatisfaction. Alternatively, he could remain faithful and accept the father's authority and decision as a (benevolent and compassionate) patriarch. These two options are radical: extreme, maybe (over-)reaction on the one hand and uncritical submission despite dissatisfaction on the other hand. The rise of right-wing populism in post-2015 Germany is a voiced protest to the perceived magnanity of Merkel's humanitarian asylum policy. US sociologist Hochschild's book *Strangers in Their Own Land* on the Tea Party and the rise of populism in the USA might be also be read as a study of the elder son's complex. White workers who were arguably patiently waiting in line to see their American dream fulfilled, believed to be witnessing migrants/refugees and others break the rules and enjoy multiple privileges. I argue that the Far Right manifests traits of perceived emotional deprivation of the elder son, and try to inscribe the rise of right-wing extremism in the framework of a third-way reaction between exiting (the homeland) and uncritical submission. I then proceed to discuss the sociopolitical functions of strategies of positive self-representation, and nationalistic othering.

Chapter 7 is a take on subaltern studies and the Muslim migrants. I read Sineb El Masrar's 2010 *Muslim Girls* and her 2018 *Muslim Men* through the prism of what I name entangled subalternities. As in most chapters, I start with a discussion on theory; postcolonial theory and subaltern studies in this concluding chapter. I then move on to re-interpret El Masrar's two books as a form of postcolonial critique. To be sure, El Masrar would not see herself as an academic critic, even less a subalternist one, nor does she attempt to appropriate the vocabulary of subaltern/postcolonial studies. Her books nonetheless echoe concerns of subaltern studies and at time transcend them. Moreover, she transcends the simple dichotomy of the subalterns and subalternizers and point to epistemic violence from the host society and complicity with the migrant community in reproducing subalternazing structures. For example, the male Arab migrants/refugees are depicted as 'subalternizers' who deprive women of their autonomy. The discourse further views interaction between Arab men and their wives as being fundamentally a relation of oppression. Procreation, childrearing, religious symbols, or household dynamics are systematically viewed through the lens of the oppressive Arab macho. In addition to the label of the domestic macho, the male Arab migrant is himself subalternized as a criminal or terrorist threat and a (burden) to the state. And then, there are the cases where Arab women are not only subjected to mysogyny within their community of reference but also to epistemic violence within the host society that El Masrar denounces. Furthermore, she might indirectly participate in the reproduction of patriarchal structures of domination, as El Masrar further suggests. Entangled subalternities go beyond simple dichotomies of oppressed/oppressor and show that political and social emancipation is a holistic, multi-level societal task.

CHAPTER 1

The 2015 German Refugee Crisis as an Event

What is an event? What are its characteristics or what causes it? More theoretically, when did (critical) theory take interest in the event? Keucheyan had located the beginings of the 'event' in critical theory within the passage from structuralism[1] to poststructuralism in the 1960s.[2] However, it is nonetheless important to recognize that the question of the 'event' recapitulates to a certain extent the multiple theoretical perspectives in philosophy itself. It has been addressed by analytical and continental philosophy alike, constructed under the prism of logical positivism with its emphasis on causation (Hume),

---

1 Deleuze might have provided one of the primary intellectual histories of structuralist thought. The title of his contribution *Á quoi reconnaît-on le structuralisme?* echoed the interrogation, *A quoi reconnaît-on l' existentialisme?* of Sartre that was being challenged by structuralism. His text starts with the question 'Who is a structuralist?' He leaves the question unanswered and did seem to side with the mainstream, which regarded Roman Jakobson, Claude Lévi Strauss, Lacan, (and to a certain extent) Michel Foucault, Althusser or Barthes as structuralists. He locates the beginnings of structuralism in linguistics. He then went on to identify the criteria by which to identify structuralist thought. The typology derives from his systematic interpretation of the methological approaches of structural across different fields. His first criterion to recognize structuralism is its rapport to the symbolic (*le symbolique*). Human thought has been conceptualized – prior to structuralism – as a dialectic game between the real and the imaginary. Structuralism is for him the refusal to confuse the symbolic with the imaginary or the real, thus consecrating the symbolic as independent category that transcend the terms of this dichotomy. The second criterion refers to the position of the symbolic (*local ou de position*). The elements of a structure have no extrinsic designation or intrinsic meaning. They are not located in in real or imaginary places, in a properly structural space. The third criterion is about the differential relations and the singular points, the reciprocal determination and complete determination (*le différentiel et le singulier*). The fourth criterion is the operation of differentiation performed by a differentiator (*le différenciant, la différenciation*). Put together, symbols (or one should better translate them as signs) represent a structure, an ideal repertory, where the actualization follows exclusive directions. The fifth criterion states that the differentiated symbolic elements are organized in series (*sériel*). Further criteria deal with the role of the subject in structuralist thought. Deleuze contends that structuralism does not do away with the subject, but splits it and distributes it systematically from one location to another. The subject is thus nomadic (See Deleuze, 1973, pp. 299–335). For further treatments of structuralism, *See* Sturrock 1979, Assiter 1984.
2 Structuralism and poststructuralism dwell in a relational dependence and one needs to pay closer attention to their properties to differentiate them. Structuralism mainly purported to unlock the structures of the human condition and provide objective knowledge of the social realm by recurring to systematic, quasi-scientific methods. Posstructuralism rejects stable concepts, and stress the multiplicity of meaning.

conceptualized in Wittgenstein's and Heidegger's work, viewed through post-structuralist lenses (Baudrillard, Badiou) and at times echoed Plato's epistemological distinction between truth and knowledge. Analytical philosophers have taken different routes to come to terms with the event. The main avenues in analytical philosophy to conceptualize the 'event' have been to analyze the event in relation to (material) objects, properties and propositions (Zacks and Tversky, 2001, p. 7). Pianesi and Varzi offer a relatively extensive typology of the conceptualization of the event in the analytical tradition. They categorize the metaphysical approaches to event depending on whether they view events as universals or particulars, treat them "as 'thick' (concrete) or as 'thin' (abstract) entities," and lastly according to the degree of reality they ascribe to events.[3] Theorizing events according to properties can be equated with a theorization of events as universals. It is a theorization that does not treat events as entities but as properties of moments or intervals of time (as in Montague) or as a time-independent state of affairs as in Chisholm (Pianesi and Varzi, 2000, p. 6). Recurring events (the rising of the sun every morning) are thus called generic events or event type (ibid.).[4] Pianesi and Varzi observe that the characterization of events as recurrables as in Montague and Chisholm provide a semantics to voice familiar events of the everyday such as missing a train connections twice or taking the same walk every evening (ibid.). This theorization nonetheless becomes unsustainable once one admits that some events are particulars as in a Quinean theory of events. Quine's theory does not proceed from properties but from (natural) objects. It does not distinguish objects from and events and collapse them "into a single category of four-dimensional entities, and the problem of explaining our event talk extends to the problem of explaining our

---

3   The distinction between universals and particulars is for Pianesi and Varzi an absolute distinction, which does not admit matters of degree. Events categorized as universals refers to things that can "recur or be instantiated at different places and times." Particulars happen at a specific place and time (2000, p. 5). The distinction between thick (concrete) and thin (abstract) conceptions of events is not an absolute category. For them, "[a]n event is thick to the extent that it prevents other events from occurring in the same place at the same time. Some theories impose maximum thickness; other theories (the majority) allow for the possibility that distinct events occur in the same place at the same time, though the degree to which this is possible is a matter of controversy (Pianesi and Varzi, 2000, p. 5)." Theories that portrays events as basic entities are treated by Pianesi and Varzi as eventist theories. Those theories take "events to be basic entities, entities to be included in the basic ontological inventory. Others deny existence to events in favour of 'ontological parsimony,' arguing that every seemingly event-committing statement can in principle be paraphrased in terms of event-neutral statements. And between these two extremes (the eventists and the eliminativists) there are those who avoid the language of reduction while also denying that events and objects are coordinate and equally basic (ibid.)."
4   For Montague's conceptualization of the event, see Montague, 1969; For Chisholm, see 1990.

talk of ordinary entities *tout court* (ibid., p. 8)."[5] In other words, talking about an event presupposes the readiness to discuss similar ontological questions as with objects, since events are spatially and temporally bounded as objects are. Pianesi and Varzi find fault with the 'spatiotemporal boundaries' of Quine's theory of events. They posit that, for certain events, it seems preposterous to posit "the existence of a determinate spatiotemporal boundary. *Where* exactly did John catch a cold? *When* exactly did the industrial revolution begin? *What* exactly are the spatiotemporal boundaries of an event (ibid., p. 10, italics in the original)." It follows from this simple overview that theories of the event are more or less indeterminate and provide different heuristics to recognize and conceptualize occurrences as such. But this apparent indeterminacy and vagueness should not preclude a deeper engagement with the event. As such, it is certainly not a useless digression to attempt an in-depth survey of some of the conceptualizations of the event and assess their possible relevance for the analysis of phenomena in the political and social realm.

1 From Political to Metaphysical: Multiple Conceptualizations of the Event

In this subpoint, I look at the key tenants of selected relevant approaches to the event. The main aim of this panoramic overview is to interrogate the multiple conceptualizations and usages of the event and assess their commonalities and differences.

1.1 *Kim on Events: Non-causal Relations and Compositional Dependence*

Jaegwon Kim has arguably written one of the most influential theories of the event that approach the event from the point of view of properties as stated above.[6] Drawing from Hume's four constituents (constant conjunction, contiguity in space and time, temporal priority, and necessary connection) in relation to causation,[7] Kim went on to outline a typology of the properties of the event (s) based on the differentiation between determinism and causation. He sees his theory of the event as simultaneously building on and transcending

---

5 On Quine's theory of event, see Quine 1960.
6 Kim's concept of the 'constituent objects' to denote the change in relations in on objects or the other has been served for Shoemaker to develop his concepts of 'constituent properties' and 'constituent times' (Shoemaker, 1980, p. 109). Zacks and Tversky have drawn among others on Kim's work on the events and its properties to analyze the event and its structure in perceptual psychology (2001, pp. 3–21).
7 See Hume (1986 [1739]).

causation. His point of departure is Hume's relations of causation whose constituents his extensively reviews. The Humean first constituent (constant conjunction) is for Kim a property of "generic events," events that are poorly individuated and which provide no clear meaning within "spatiotemporally bounded individual events" (1995, p. 3) and thus failing the test of causation for Kim. For a philosopher who avoids studied obscurities and favors clear language,[8] Kim fails to provide the reader with examples to substantiate the limitations of constant conjunction.

The second constituent of contiguity, he argues, yields itself better to temporal events than to spatial events. Temporally contiguous events tend to overlap but the notion of spatial location becomes "fuzzy and indeterminate" when applied to events. Kim prefers instead to apply spatial contiguity to events and provides some examples to exemplify his points. One of his examples involves Socrates and his death in prison. When Socrates died in the prison, so Kim, his wife Xantippe became a widow and their three sons became fatherless. These are three events which simultaneously took place so that the temporal contiguity (to the point of complete overlapping) is guaranteed but the example does not satisfy the condition of contiguity of space so that Kim wonders where exactly did these latter events (the widowing of Xantippe and the loss of the father in the case of her sons) take place? (1995, p. 3) The temporal contiguity of the three events are obvious since the moment of Socrates's death marks simultaneously the change in marital status, the loss of the father and certainly many more events. The spatial locations of the changes operated by these events are understandably indeterminate.

Kim skips the analysis of the third constituent (temporal priority), which suggests that he sees no ground for contestation. For the fourth constituent, the "controversial idea of necessary connection," (1995, p. 4), Kim thinks that it should readily better be applied to grammatical propositions, events, and objects in the *de dicto* sense than in the *de re* sense.[9] For Kim, Hume fails to explicit the causal relations that determine events and states and makes the case for what he referred to as "relations of 'dependency' or 'determination' between events and states" (p. 22). Kim identified the so-called "Cambridge dependence" and agency dependence as two sorts of ways in which an event is non-causally determined by another. There is a case of Cambridge dependence when the property "true" of an object changes over time so that what is true at

---

8 See Kim, October 2000.
9 For a deeper explication of the *de dicto* and *de re* propositions in event theory, see Pianesi and Varzi, 2000, p. 14.

a particular time is false at another (ibid., p. 29). The agency dependence refers to the situation where in a pair of actions that are being considered, one action is done by doing the other (p. 30).

Causal relations between events are sometimes achieved in compositional dependence, a concept Kim coined to denote the way in which an event is determined by its constituent events (ibid.). His concept of event composition argues that events are interrelated in various ways that can produce determination relations (ibid., p. 32). Kim unfortunately rather refrains from an in-depth analysis that could have provided a typology of compositions and the type of correlations between events they invoke. Moreover, the concept of compositional dependence seems to suggest a possibly human agency while at the same excluding arbitrariness, anarchy or randomness in the constellations of particular events. In the case that a human agency is responsible for the compositional dependence between events, what would be the political implications of such a gesture? Unfortunately, Kim does not expand on what seemed to be a promising concept. His main aim in reviewing Hume was mainly to alert to alternative ways to conceive the relation between events beyond causation. After an extensive review of the Humean categories, the discussion of non-causal relations between events, Kim went on to suggest a definition of individual events as having three unique constituents. An event, in Kim's taxonomy would count as such if it combines the three constituents or variants of constitutive object, constitutive property and time, which he codified respectively in the formula $[x, P, t]$ (ibid., p. 35). The fundamental question with Kim's formula is whether events can be reduced to the properties or variants theory that he outlined or as to what could count as a property in a relevant sense since there seems to be according to critics, no clear demarcation heuristics (Pianesi and Varzi, 2000, p. 9). The second question is the extent to which Kim's concepts yield themselves to a world-political analysis. In the course of his two main essays on the event, he has used examples from history – the death of Socrates, the assassination of Brutus, or killings as actions, i.e. a subclass of events (Kim, 1995, p. 49), – and a number of down-to-earth examples to substantiate his proposition. But rarely does the analysis go beyond the explication of the logical or sometimes semantic contents even if the author assures that we are surrounded by a multitude of events. The merit of Kim's theory of the event (despite the indeterminacy of his spatial and temporal categories) is his transcendence of pure causation in the analysis of event. His treatment of contingence and determinism in events, his concept of compositional dependence are interesting concepts that can be used to talk about the event whether one subscribes to his overall philosophy of the event or not.

1.2 Davidson on Language, Truth, Meaning, and Events

Davidson presented events as constituting "a fundamental ontological category" in themselves (2002, p. 180). For him, ontological and even metaphysical assumptions about the event are *sine qua non* conditions to make sense even most of our common talk (ibid., p. 162). Ontological assumptions (for example taking truth as the central primitive concept) are important to make sense of propositions, circumvent semantic paradoxes in language and detail their structure. To paraphrase Davidson, asserting for example, that a particular person fell from the ladder and died is less an explication of the cause the death of the falling person from the ladder than the case of a sentence expressing a condition of truth for other sentences (ibid., p. 151). Falling from a ladder does not necessarily imply death. Likewise, the event of the death of Caesar in the hands of Brutus or the death of Socrates in prison (two of the examples that occur in Davidson's and Kim's discussions of events), can generate numerous sentences that a priori refers to the same events. The question is whether the sentences will be describing the same event or rather represent several individual events. In Kim's theory of the event that I depicted above, truth was guaranteed if there is a correspondence in the sentences between the particulars of the event and their relations (ibid., p. 170). For Davidson, "events are identical if and only if they have exactly the same causes and effects. Events have a unique position in the framework of causal relations between events in somewhat the way objects have a unique position in the spatial framework of objects. This criterion may seem to have an air of circularity about it, but if there is circularity it certainly is not formal (ibid., p. 179)." Davidson has sometimes more or less anticipated and rebutted critiques of the circularity of his theory of event. The most important aspect in his theory nonetheless resides certainly in his crossing his theory of event and the truth procedures to test the latter ones and survey any eventual special effects. Davidson has published on language, truth and meaning and made a noted contribution to Tarski's convention theory of truth by extending the former's truth conditions and applying them to natural languages. If Tarski analyzed the concept of truth through the concept of meaning, Davidson believed, as he himself claims, that truth is a central primitive concept and that detailing truth's structure can help to get to meaning (Davidson, 1991, p. xiv). Davidson has been impatient with theories of truth that make use of meaning as entities or those that introduce correspondence between objects and predicates or sentences and argues instead that it is possible from a finite set of axioms to prove, for each sentence of the language to be interpreted, a theorem that states truth conditions for that sentence (ibid.).

Davidson employs a similar argumentative logic to his theory of the events. He does not view causes as necessarily individual events but reverts to their underlying assertions and denials to determine if a specific event is particular or not (Davidson, 2002, p. 180). Particulars are events that do not have repeatable properties. For him, it is through the semantic analysis of the utterances on an event that one can specify the properties of an event and determine their underlying logic.

If, as I argued, there is a similar pattern in the argumentative logic of Davidson's theories of truth and event, then it begs the question of whether or under which conditions an event or accounts thereof can be regarded as true. An event in the social, political or even scientific realm is *par excellence* an occurrence that generates multiple accounts. How does one make sense of these multivariate accounts if one dismisses correspondence theory or reference theory as approaches to truth? How does one determine a finite set of axioms for an event or outline its truth conditions? Do these categories make sense in the interpretation of events? Or to take it a step further, what makes an event true? When is it possible to say that an event has happened and does the simple utterance that something happened suffice to make an event true? These rapprochements are certainly no more than semantic simulations and extrapolations to Davidson's theory but can help make a theoretical transition to the more discursive approaches to the concept of the event.

1.3 Baudrillard on Non-events, Events, and Fake Events in Times of Globalization

Baudrillard has touched on the issue of events sometimes directly through his essay on *Events and Non-Events* or indirectly through his premonitory and post-9/11 reflections on terrorism in the collection of essays titled *Spirit of Terrorism*, or more superficially in his comments on media and the society of the spectacle in the age of globalization. It is by gleaning through these disparate writings that one can try a collage of a theory of event(s) or at least attempt a typology of the events in Baudrillard's thought.

He seems to posit a period of 'event strike,'[10] or dearth of event that could be said to roughly run between or slightly before the Fall of the Berlin Wall in 1989 or even earlier and the terroristic attacks on the Twin Towers in September 2001. For Baudrillard, the dearth of meaningful political or social movements that has set in since then represents a period of accelerated globalization towards the monotony of the end of history. But the end of history Baudrillard

---

10   See for instance Baudrillard, 1992.

sees is not the triumph of democracy Fukuyama envisioned but the uncontested domination of a hegemonic world order where (global) events are the sum of their probabilistic causes and the choreography of their dramaturgic script. In the world order dominated by the major 'global events,' i.e. the death of Lady Diana, FIFA World Cups, the release of blockbusters and similar events with a global repercussion are viewed by Baudrillard as *non-events* or *fake events*. What makes these events fake? Are they fake simply by virtue of not being overtly political or for pertaining to popular culture?

Fake events are utterly globalized, broadcasted, staged events that are non-political and subscribe to the status quo of the (hegemonic) world order instead of challenging it or subverting globalization (which is negatively constructed in Baudrillard's thought). To extend Baudrillard's thought, only acts of subversion and resistance would qualify as 'real' events. As Baudrillard puts forwards, the domain of the non-events is "a realm where events no longer really happen, thanks to their production and diffusion in 'real time' – but rather lose themselves in the void of information. The information sphere is like a space that, once events have been emptied of their substance, recreates an artificial gravity and returns the events to circulation in 'real time.' Once divested from history, events are thrown back onto the transpolitical stage of information (2007)." In the realm of the no-events, to recoup Baudrillard's essay *In the Shadow of the Silent Majorities*, the masses becomes a spongy, opaque and simultaneously translucent referent that "absorb all electricity of the social and political and neutralise it forever (1983, pp. 1–2)." The social is portrayed as a simulation and where "the social is a simulation, the only likely turn of events is that of a brutal *de-simulation* – the social ceasing to take itself as a space of reference (p. 71, emphasis in the original)."

The (real) event in Baudrillard's sense is a brutal de-simulation of the social and per extension of the political that disturbs the world hegemonic order through its exceptional and fulgurating occurrence. The event breaks with "the fastidious linkage of the news in the media, but which for all that are not the reappearance of history, nor the reappearance of a real irrupting at the heart of the virtual (as has been said of 9/11). They are not events in history, but beyond history, beyond the end of history. They are events in the system that ends history (2007)." Events happen ex-nihilo, are unforeseen. The event has quasi-miraculous properties. It can be violent but is not simulated. Baudrillard is intellectually fascinated by terrorism not as the threat of use of violence (which would certainly be no more than simulation) but the actual use of violence to political, anti-hegemonic aims. Terrorism as an event combines his ingredients for the perfect event and to a certain extent represents the brutal de-simulation that his 1983 essay somehow conjured. For him, "with the attacks on the World Trade Center in New York, we might even be said to have before us the absolute event, the 'mother' of all events, the pure event uniting within itself all the events that have never taken place (Baudrillard, 2012, p. 3)." It is not sure whether violence needs to be a permanent feature of the event but it is already clear that the evocation of brutality and his poorly nuanced reflections on terrorism could lead to think that he uncannily apologizes terrorism. Baudrillard's ambiguous fascination towards revolutionary violence is reminiscent of a Fanonian or Sartrean defense of terrorism in the Algerian war of liberation. Baudrillard contrasted events to non-events but a critical look at the 'mother of events' that for him is the paragon of events, is also subject to the properties he critiqued in non-events. 9/11 was not only staged (carefully planned), designed, and executed so as to produce the maximum symbolic impact by the choice of the target and the quasi-cinematographic special effects the crashing produced. It is a destruction done using, to paraphrase Audrey Lorde, the tools of the master. But in Baudrillard's understanding, terrorism is the event and (preventive) counterterrorism stands for the model of non-event and its negation of the political and the social.

After the invasion by the US and their allies in Afghanistan and the more controversial intervention in Iraq, Baudrillard tweaked his conceptualization of the non-event to include so-called counter-terroristic operations. The non-event is no more the monotony toward the end of history (Baudrillard, 1983, pp. 1–2) but is transformed into a "domain of perpetual change, of a relentless actualization, of an incessant succession in real time, from whence this general equivalence, this indifference, this banality which characterizes the degree zero of the event (ibid., 2007)." The post- 9/11 conception of the non-event resembles now an autopoietic system that has banished revolutions. It is "[a]s in a machine that has perfected itself, in a system too-well integrated, there are no more crises, only malfunctions, flaws, lapses, aneurysms. Meanwhile, the event is something other than an accident. It is a symptom, an episodic malfunction, an anomaly in the technical (or natural) order that can eventually be prevented: today's whole politics of risk and foresight (ibid.)."

Baudrillard's theory of the event is relatively circular in the end. It is banal and miraculous, triumphalist and defeatist. At the beginning was the non-event. Then came the event *ex nihilo*, as Baudrillard claimed, to challenge the hegemonic (world) order. And the non-event was restored again through the securitization of the social and political and the surveillance apparatus used on the dormant masses he fustigated in his earlier writings. The effects of the miraculous event Baudrillard prophezied have faded away and despair has set in again. Maybe Baudrillard could have avoided the void of despair in his circular theory if his focus was not on big-scale (actually quite spectacular) events or non-events. His obsession with the negation globalization represents, has prevented him from paying attention to the multiple, unsung sites of resistance both in the Global South as in the North, where (non-violent) resistance from below happens and hegemonic order(s) are being contested.

1.4 Badiou on Events on the Edge of the Void, and Intervention

Badiou has arguably written one of the most extensive and impressive treatments of the event. His theory of the event which is recurrent in two imposing works, *Being and Event, Logics of Worlds*, and to a smaller degree in his work, *Théorie du Sujet*. It combines the logic(ist), semantic, and mathematical approach of analytical philosophy with the discursive praxis of a more continental approach to philosophy.[11] The conditions of the emergence of his work on the theory of the event were, as Badiou claims, not very favorable. He characterized the 1980s (*L' Être et l' Événement* [*Being and Event*] appeared in the French original in 1988) as a period of general intellectual regression, where the philosopher was reduced to being a maidservant of a brand of moral philosophy masquerading as political philosophy.[12] Badiou did not believe that the task of philosophy was to laboriously provide sophist defenses of democratic values or arguments for the incommensurability of cultural values. One senses in Badiou the kind of intellectual boredom and desperation that similarly affected Baudrillard with regard to the 1980s. Where Baudrillard made the translucent and amorphous masses responsible for this situation of political and social non-events, Badiou found fault with the ambient philosophy of the time. Surprisingly, the 1980s were to end with the unforeseen or unpredicted event of the Fall of the Berlin Wall, which ironically will subsequently introduce a period of autopoietic stabilizations made of globalized fake events for Baudrillard. Badiou's impatience with culturalist and universalist theories of truth has led him to suggest definitions of truth, and subject that he directly predicates on 'the event.'

---

11 In *Being and Event*, Badiou deals with the properties, the condition of emergence of the event after discussing the ontology of being. *Logics of Worlds* appears as a substantiation of the theories of events he already outlined in *Being and Event*. But Badiou examines in greater detail the subject, truth and the dependences between these concepts in *Logics of Worlds*. *Théorie du Sujet* is Badiou's early treatment of the subject, which he would refine and extend in the two works mentioned above.

12 In Badiou's words, "philosophy was reduced to being either a laborious justification of the universal character of democratic values, or a linguistic sophistry legitimating the right to cultural difference against any universalist pretension on the part of truths (Badiou, 2005, p. xii)."

The Badiousian concept of the event is a particular occurrence that breaks with an existing order, allowing truth to spring forth out it. The truth in turn, engenders the militant subject, who tacitly pledges or – better said – manifests an active fidelity (or should one say allegiance) to the event of truth that generated it (Badiou, 2005, p. xiii). The birth of truth and the militant subject takes place on the *evental site,* which designates an *abnormal multiple,* a *supernumerary* (of more or less aleatory arrangements and elements) detached from a wider *situation,* and located (spatially and/or temporally) on the *edge of the void* (Badiou, 2005, p. 175). The evental site is a point in a non-natural or historical situation (ibid., p. 177), where a multitude of non-apparent circumstances conglomerate to facilitate the emergence of the count-for-one event.[13] It is certainly not a stretch of Badiou's thought to represent a war, a social movement as historical situations as they represent extraordinary and not natural situations. Nonetheless, Badiou is keen to maintain a clear distinction between the evental site and the event itself. The site can represents different fields as, in Badiou's own example, the working class, artistic tendencies or scientific impasse(s). These sites do not necessarily produce events since sites are simply the material or metaphysical conditions for an event but not necessarily their cause or trigger. Confusing the site of the event and the event itself is for Badiou a fallacy caused by deterministic or globalizing thought (Badiou, 2005, p. 179).[14] The site is a set of different elements or circumstances inside a given situation that are not always visible (Badiou's *abnormal multiple*), that are located in an (il)legal, spatial (geographical borders for example) or temporal (the sheer incertitude of waiting qua waiting) void or maybe an aleatory combination of any of these three elements since Badiou does not explicitly disprove of any such combinations or conceptualization of the void. Conceptualizing the edge of the void as a legal void is reminiscent of similar concepts such as Agamben's bare life, where the subject is stripped of conventional human rights protection and reduced to a (bare) biological body. Maybe a crucial difference between Agamben's concepts of bare life and the state of exception

---

13 Events are not facts in Badiou's theory. A fact is for Badiou, a natural or neutral situation of global value whereas the event is local (2005, p. 178)." It is not sure whether by global is a vocabulary substitute for the more controversial lexeme 'universal' and whether events are strictly local. In *Logics of Worlds,* he added a further distinction between facts and events: "[A]n event is a site which is capable of making exist in a world the proper inexistent of the object that underlies the site. (2009, p. 452)."

14 Even if Badiou does not refer here to Kim's work which he might not have been aware of, he somehow directly contradicts Kim's concept of compositional dependence which asserts that deterministic relations can exist between events by virtue of the events being contiguous to each other in a dependence relation (*See* Kim, 1995, p. 22).

as compared to Badiou's *edge of the void* resides in the fact that primarily for Badiou, in the evental site, not all multiples of the situation are on the edge of the void (ibid., p. 176) and secondarily Badiou goes beyond the bio-political to include scientific, cultural, social, and political sites as possible generators of events. It follows that impasses provoke a condition of undecidability for the event which doubly evokes the edge of the void while purporting to interpose itself between the void and itself (ibid., p. 182).

The (retrospective) consecration of an event qua event is performed through the double gesture of *recognition* and *interpretative intervention*. The latter declares "that an event is presented in a situation; as the arrival in being of non-being, the arrival amidst the visible of the invisible (ibid., p. 181)." It predicates a subjective agency that recognizes and resolves the condition of undecidability of the event by interpreting it out of the underlying web of the multiple and supernumerary elements pertaining to the situation. But intervention does not necessarily takes the form of subjective operations. It can take the form of time (p. 210) or be superfluous (p. 218).

The fidelity is the after-effect of the (subjective) intervention (p. 219). Badiou defines the fidelity in event as "[...] the set of procedures which discern, within a situation, those multiples whose existence depends upon the introduction into circulation [...] of an evental multiple. In sum, a fidelity is the apparatus which separates out, within the set of presented multiples, those which depend upon an event. (p. 232)" The effects of an event do not stop with the production of the subject or a truth. In *Logics of Worlds,* Badiou ascribes to the event the property of changing "the transcendental arrangement [*dispositif*] of a world (2009, p. 311)" and altering objectivity (2009, p. 222).

He further claims that it is not possible to anticipate the effects of the transformations that a particular event may produce. Even if the event provokes a rupture of the present and unpredictably alters the transcendental arrangement of a world (in the future), it will be wrong, in Badiou's term to posit a separation between a past and a future of the event since the event theoretically contains both (2009, p. 282). There are some similarities between Baudrillard's and Badiou's concepts of the event. Both view the event as a rupture, a miraculous, *ex nihili* appearance. In Badiou's, the event is not only of a political nature. It can be cultural, scientific or social. In Baudrillard, it has to challenge the fundamental arrangement of the hegemonic order. In Badiou, it needs to transcend the organizational *dispositif* of the count-for one order. What are the transcendental arrangements an event can possibly alter? Does the alteration affect the locality of the evental-site that gave rise to the event in the first place? It is possible to envision that a scientific event for example (born in the evental site of a scientific impasse) has the potential to alter domains beyond the confines of its original conditions of emergence. The resulting transcendental alteration may affect the societal, political, and/or economic dispositif of a world and constitute for Badiou the difference between a true event and a false one.

1.5 Foucault and Deleuze on Events: Discursive Events and the Geophilosophy of the Event

Foucault's conceptualization of the 'event' arises from his engagement with the archeology of discourses and aims to challenge traditional representation of events qua fixed corporeal objects and the properties and relational systems established by the historiographical traditions he wants to challenge.[15] He posits that traditional historical analysis has been concerned with working causal successions, continuity, totality, periodization, and systems of relations between events or series of events (Foucault 1972, pp. 3–5, 7). With the growth of knowledge and the accumulations of events, traditional history did not only distinguish between important and less important events, but paid attention to the duration intervals (short, mid-term, long) and the frequency "rare or repetitive events" (ibid., p. 8). Foucault portrays the historian in the classical historiography as an editor or director who cuts, removes or structures through analysis the disparate material of multiform events and using what one could term a 'temporal fix' to come to terms with discontinuous events (p. 8). This historical practice assumed well-defined spatio-temporal,

---

15   It has been argued, as I have noted in the introduction to this chapter, that the turn to the 'event' as an analytical category took place in or could be dated back to the transition from structuralism to poststructuralism, and Foucault was one of the precursors of this analytical turn (Keucheyan, 2014, p. 170). One should however be wary of what Foucault himself has called "the search for silent beginnings, and the never-ending tracing-back to the original precursors" and instead pay attention to the *"displacements and transformations* of concepts [...]; they show that the history of a concept is not wholly and entirely that of its progressive refinement, its continuously increasing rationality, its abstraction gradient, but that of its various fields of constitution and validity, that of its successive rules of use, that of the many theoretical contexts in which it developed and matured (1972, p. 4, emphasis in the original)." What makes the search for silent beginnings dubious is not that the genealogy of a concept or approach may reach far further back in time than what the historian of ideas may have chosen to set as the reference time frame to examine the emergence of a concept or an event. The trouble is that such a search conceals more than it reveals, assumes false continuity where the focus should be on surveying the discontinuous and the rifts. But not every aspect in the traditional approach is problematic. The search for the silent beginnings can shed light on the compositional dependence between approaches and their implications for the concept being studied. Seen from this perspective, structuralism and poststructuralism dwell in a relational dependence and one needs to pay closer attention to their their properties to differentiate them.

homogenous, analogous, symbolic properties that needed to be exemplified (ibid., p. 9). To make sense of Foucault's characterization of the old method, let's consider the following example: two countries (Country A and Country B) are waging a war in the 21th century. An historian working on that particular event in what Foucault sees as the traditional analysis, would suppose that there was an initial event (an act of aggression most likely) that ignited the war and from there establish a causal property between the event of the act of aggression and the ensuing war and its casualties. Moreover the historian may want to inscribe the war within a series of variant duration of ethnic, cultural, colonial, religious or mercantile hostilities that constitute the build-up to the war. The historian could also look for analogies in the stratified archives of human history in the near past or reach further back as the antiquity. The vast archives of written human history being considerable, the historian is sure to find somewhere something that helps fix the temporal exception of the war and re-arrange to fit the continuity of history. This is a very simplified rendition of Foucault's analysis as the historian could claim Foucault himself offered a reductionist treatment of events by the historians. To transcend traditional analysis, Foucault proposes to renounce the search for a 'secret origin' and the 'already-said (ibid., p. 25).' He does not want to treat event as spatio-temporal objects or trace them back to a quasi-mythological beginning. He instead turns to language to collapse the linguistic statements on the event with the event itself, paradoxically treating the event as unique but repeatable, transformable (ibid., p. 28). Foucault has nevertheless not totally renounced the search for properties. It seems as if he has given up a kind of search for Humean four constituent on causation, to exemplify in the manner of Kim's property exemplification in the analytical philosophy of the event, modes and systems of relations beyond causation, analogy, hierarchy and so on, not between the events *per se*, but between the (recorded) statements on the events. In his words, he wants to

> […] be able to grasp other forms of regularity, other types of relations. Relations between statements (even if the author is unaware of them; even if the statements do not have the same author; even if the authors were unaware of each other's existence); relations between groups of statements thus established (even if these groups do not concern the same, or even adjacent, fields; even if they do not possess the same formal level; even if they are not the locus of assignable exchanges); relations between statements and groups of statements and events of a quite different kind (technical, economic, social, political). To reveal in all its purity the space in which discursive events are deployed is not to

undertake to re-establish it in an isolation that nothing could overcome; it is not to close it upon itself; it is to leave oneself free to describe the interplay of relations within it and outside it.

    ibid., p. 29

Discursive events are fluid, not foreclosed (p. 30) and the analysis of "[a] discursive formation, then, does not play the role of a figure that arrests time and freezes it for decades or centuries; it determines a regularity proper to temporal processes; it presents the principle of articulation between a series of discursive events and other series of events, transformations, mutations, and processes. It is not an atemporal form, but a schema of correspondence between several temporal series (ibid., p. 74)." So far, it is possible to identify three pillars in the Foucauldian analysis as opposed to what he characterized as 'traditional analysis': discursive events, discursive formation, and archaeology.[16] Each of his pillars renounces causation, periodization, favors contiguity and breaks with the teleology of the traditional approaches Foucault took aim at. Archeology is nonetheless a sphere where the property relations between discursive events are exemplified and different levels of analysis identified. Foucault seems to have a predilection for negative definitions. He painstakingly tries to tell what his subject matter is not so that one has to mind the passage from negative to positive definition in order not to miss the gist of his thought. The reader who engages with his *Archeology of Knowledge* would have understood the centrality of the event to Foucault's methodology through the multiple demarcation attempts the author made. What is an event for Foucault? Here is one of most-quoted excerpts of the *Archeology of Knowledge* that

---

16   Archeology contains the two aforementioned pillars: discursive events and discursive formation even if Foucault does not establish any hierarchical relation between them but rather seems to assign to them similar tasks. For him, "Archaeology also reveals relations between discursive formations and non-discursive domains (institutions, political events, economic practices and processes). These rapprochements are not intended to uncover great cultural continuities, nor to isolate mechanisms of causality" (ibid., p. 162)" and "[i]nstead of considering that discourse is made up of a series of homogeneous events (individual formulations), archaeology distinguishes several possible levels of events within the very density of discourse: the level of the statements themselves in their unique emergence; the level of the appearance of objects, types of enunciation, concepts, strategic choices (or transformations that affect those that already exist); the level of the derivation of new rules of formation on the basis of rules that are already in operation – but always in the element of a single positivity; lastly, a fourth level, at which the substitution of one discursive formation for another takes place (or the mere appearance and disappearance of a positivity). (ibid., p. 171)."

encapsulates in negative multiple layers Foucault's definition of the basic unit of discursive practice:

> [a]n event is neither substance, nor accident, nor quality nor process; events are not corporeal. And yet, an event is certainly not immaterial; it takes effect, becomes effect, always on the level of materiality. Events have their place; they consist in relation to, coexistence with, dispersion of, the cross-checking accumulation and the selection of material elements; it occurs as an effect of, and in, material dispersion. Let us say that the philosophy of event should advance in the direction, at first sight paradoxical, of an incorporeal materialism.
> ibid. p. 231

Foucault urged the philosophy of the event to advance to an incorporeal materialism[17] and Deleuze seems to heed his call. In Deleuze's assemblage theory of the event, events are not only properties and qualities of material objects, but also the immaterial elements of the production of sense. The *pure event* represents the atomic particle of his theory of the event and is already a cluster of pure events. It is a kind of unequal and asymmetric Janus-faced event that eludes the present and collapses the past and the future together in its (self) actualizing fluidity (Deleuze, 1990, p. 1; Berressem and Haferkamp, 2009, p. 11). One of the faces of the event in this arrangement points towards 'states of affairs' (as opposed to bodies) and the other towards propositions (where sense resides) and sense and event are ultimately the same thing in Deleuze's thought (Deleuze, 1990, p. 167).

The site of the event is a border and not a hypothetical depth that has to be searched for (Deleuze, 1990, p. 9), a "problematic field" where events are deployed singularities (ibid., p. 56). Singularities can be situated both in physical objects or human beings and are the site of disruption. They "are turning points and points of inflections; bottlenecks, knots, foyers, and centers; points of fusion, condensation, and boiling (ibid., p. 52)." A transformed, fused, or condensed singularity can engender "the event which is ideal by nature, and its spatio-temporal realization in a state of affairs (ibid., p. 53)." Deleuze's typology of events further includes concepts as incorporeal events of pure sense without spatiotemporal coordinates (Deleuze and Guattari, 1994, pp. 21, 144), "conceptual personae (ibid., p. 110)." What is one to do with the event? Deleuze and

---

17 Deleuzians have pointed out to the 'oblique reference' to Deleuze's 'incorporeal materialism' in Foucault (Berressem and Haferkamp, 2009, p. 7).

Guattari suggest a turn to a geophilosophy of the event that comprises two gestures:

> One consists in going over the course of the event, in recording its effectuation in history, its conditioning and deterioration in history. But the other consists in reassembling the event, installing oneself in it as in a becoming, becoming young again and aging in it, both at the same time, going through all its components or singularities.
>
> ibid., p. 111

Deleuze and Guattari provide a name for the engagement with the event from the point of view of the observer: geophilosophy. It is of course possible to find similarities between their concept and Foucault's archeology of discourses. But not all gestures they outlined can be performed. It is partly due to the age of the event, whether one can observe its multiple singularities over an expanded spatio-temporal plane.

1.6   Concluding Remarks on the Conceptualizations of the Event

The treatment of the 'event' and its conceptualizations offered above are in no way exhaustive as the reader would have noticed and certainly could have not also done full justice to the complexities of the concepts of the event presented above. I tried to establish a dialogue between the analytical and continental traditions in the philosophy of event, between the metaphysics and politics of events. I reckoned with the missed dialogue opportunities and pointed to some observed commonalities between the frameworks highlighted above. The overview mainly aimed at extracting from the multiple varied thoughts on the events conceptual tools, operative vocabulary to come to terms with the event of September 2015. In the variety of conceptualizations of the event, one can broadly identify 10 different axioms or tendencies in the treatment of the event both in the analytical as in the continental traditions. There is no chronological order in their appearance and the different theorizations may combine their strands of these axioms. The first tendency is the rejection of simple and direct causation (as Hume posited them) and the attempt to explicit properties or relations between events that go beyond causation. Kim's property exemplifications and concept of compositional dependence in the analytical tradition or Foucault's archeology of events in the continental tradition can be seen as attempts to transcend causation. The second tendency is the rejection of chronological periodization between past/present/future, before/after or temporal boundaries for events and instead to present them as Janus-faced reality, simultaneously facing the past and the future but absent from the present (as in Deleuze) or to constantly pay attention to the actualizations of the event in the present (as in Foucault). The third tendency is the semantic turn. It brings together truth, meaning, and language to bear on events. Some take truth as a prerequisite to talk of the event (Davidson for example), for others the truth arises from the event and constitutes its subjects that in turn plead allegiance or fidelity to it (as in Badiou), or see truth or better sense as the event itself (as is the case in Deleuze). The fourth tendency is a meta-theoretical turn, which arises partly from the semantic/linguistic turn. This tendency is exemplified in Deleuze's geophilosophy of the event and in Foucault's archeology of discourse formation. They take the interest for the event as far as to engage with the historiographical records of events and the construction of the event in scientific or philosophical discourse. The fifth tendency is a philosophical or cultural tendency that treats concepts in philosophy and their emergence as event (as in Deleuze and Guattari). The sixth tendency is the political turn to the event. It transpires mostly in French theory and in the writings of the generation that was influenced by the events of May 1968. In Badiou, the event produces a militant subject that adheres to a truth. In Baudrillard, the absence of real events leaves the masses dormant, translucent and apathetic. The sixth tendency is also a personal turn in the event. Through it, the body becomes a possible locus of physical, mental or spiritual events in the form of transformations. The theorization of the conceptual personae as an event in Deleuze is a point in case. In Badiou, the site of amorous or spiritual events can be said to be located in the person. The seventh turn is a post-modern or radical turn. It is utterly political and does not hesitate to challenge boundaries. Baudrillard's treatment of terrorism as violent de-simulation of the social or the anti-hegemonic properties he assigns to 'real' events is example of his radical take on the event. The eighth turn is an epistemological one. In it there are true events and fake events, as in Baudrillard, or ideal or pure events as in Deleuze. The ninth tendency is the (re-)turn to a form of the transcendental. In Deleuze, it is an 'impersonal transcendental field,' an immanence and in Badiou it is the 'Greater Logic (Badiou, 2007, p. 37).' The tenth tendency is the turn to the paradoxical. Deleuze identifies multiple series of paradoxes about the event in his *The Logic of Sense*. The recourse to the paradoxical is also recurrent in Foucault and Badiou.

2   Syria: The Supernumerary of an Evental Site

How does one apply a theory of event? The theories considered above make meaningful contributions to make sense of different events and their properties, independent of their metaphysical or political orientation. Nonetheless, when it comes to the analysis of 'real' world problems, the approaches to the 'event' that I termed political theories of the event seem to have a comparative advantage over predominantly metaphysical theories of the event, which were mostly seen in analytical philosophy. Of all the theorists considered above, Baudrillard has drawn attention to the role of the media in the globalization of the event. Most of the mediatized events are for Baudrillard probabilistic, staged, fake events or simply did not take place as he argued about the Gulf War (1995). Baudrillard would have certainly not argued that the Syrian civil war did not take place and "[i]n this sense, the gravity of the non-event [...] is even greater than the event of war: it corresponds to the highly toxic period which affects a rotting corpse and which can cause nausea and powerless stupor. Here again, our symbolic defences are weak: the mastery of the end of war escapes us and we live all this in a uniform shameful indifference, just like the hostages (1995, p. 24)." To be sure, we [external observers] still lack any capability to intervene but the Syrian case does have element of a non-war as "*the absence of politics* pursued by other means. Non-war is a terrible test of the status and the uncertainty of politics, just as a stock market crash (the speculative universe) is a crucial test of the economy and of the uncertainty of economic aims, just as any event whatever is a terrible test of the uncertainty and the aims of information (ibid., pp. 30–31)." A war or a revolution is indeed a speculative undertaking. Nonetheless the Syrian war would not count in his framework as a fake, mediatized event, even if those days of September 2015 where thousands of asylum seekers from war-torn Syria and other countries were allowed to pass without restrictions through the border to Germany and Austria after being stuck in Hungary were largely echoed by the media. It was not an event that could be put in the black box of a recurring, staged, controlled, globalized and apolitical event. It was neither a non-event where Baudrillard's usual suspect, the US as an oil-craving hegemonic power, had the lead role. How to make sense of the Syrian war and the refugee crisis beyond Baudrillard?

Analyses of the refugee crisis in the media privilege disparate explanations, relying on some form of causational relations between political decision-making, survival instincts, and war. It was for instance argued that a tweet of the Federal Office of Migration and Refugees (BAMF)[18] unilaterally suspended

---

18 According to a collective of Journalists from *die Zeit*, "[m]ore than 150,000 refugees had been officially registered in Hungary by the middle of August. But two weeks ago, something changed. On August 25, Germany's Federal Office for Migration and Refugees (BAMF) sent out a tweet, 134 characters long, saying that Germany was now accepting

the Dublin convention procedures for all Syrian refugees sent a false signal towards the refugees who henceforth refused to claim asylum in the EU-countries on the Balkan route. But such a proposition would not satisfy the conditions of truth and meaning (for an event), as in Davidson, since the tweet could have had different consequences or even could have gone unnoticed. In other words, there is no unequivocal sense in which the tweet could be the cause of the massive influx of refugees Germany witnessed in 2015.

One could further posit that news outlets tend to favor direct causation in the reconstruction of the build-up to a particular event, building considerable time-limes and highlighting key-stories of a particular event (See Aljazeera, 2018). For a chronological retrospective point of view, the days from September 4–6, 2015 are the chronicles of a foretold loss of control (Blume et al., August 2016). Blume and his colleagues emphasized the ill-preparedness of the German government, ambiguous signals and the repercussions of the crisis on inner political debates. Their accounts are focussing on building a repertoire of causes that led to the crisis, situate the responsibilities and work out the implications for future policies.

Alternatively, one could instead bring the tweet in a kind of compositional dependence with other factors and posit a deterministic relation between the elements of this cluster. From this perspective, it would follow that the initial tweet, the EU's lack of anticipation, busied with the Greek debt crisis or simply neglecting the voices of its periphery (Spain, Italy or Greece) accustomed to keeping Europe's outer gates from refugees and other migrants are elements that stood in a deterministic arrangement to each other and as such created the conditions for the eruption of the refugee crisis.

There is nonetheless the need for a deeper account of the crisis, of the set of circumstances that gave rise to it, and their implication for a political theory of the event. There are – in the list of political theories of the event sketched above – different theoretical tools to help the critical scholar make sense of the German refugee crisis not as an epiphany or catastrophe moment, but in order to interrogate its singularity, work out the deeper compositional dependence of the event. These critical approaches outlined above could help one interpret the refugee crisis as a fake, globalized, or true event in Baudrillard's radical approach to the event. The test question in Baudrillard's framework would then be whether the refugee crisis challenges the hegemonic world order, wakes up the masses from their political slumber and (violently) operate a de-simulation

---

unregistered refugees from Syria – and since then, people have been refusing to register in Hungary. Instead, they are showing the tweet to police on their smartphones and insisting that they want to continue onward to Germany (Blume et al., August 2016)."

of the social. Can one conceptualize Germany as a hegemon in the manner of the US? Which kind of de-simulation of the social could possibly be identified as in the humanitarian gesture of Germany? Would the reinvigorated racism and of right-wing extremism combined with the demise of democratic parties qualify as a (violent) de-simulation of society? It would certainly not count as such. Baudrillard's theory of the event might be too radical to be applied to analyze events that display a greater complexity in their internal sequencing.

Another option would be to turn to Foucault to attempt an archaeology of the discourse formation of the refugee 'crisis,' problematize it and interrogate its obvious categories. Badiou's theory of the event offers more analytical categories for the analysis of the refugee crisis that hit Germany than the competing frameworks. Scholars have reverted to his theory mostly to make sense of different social movements and revolutions. At times, the application of the framework to the analysis of political crises may sound celebratory, as proving the 'event-ness' of a particular social-occurrence represented an award for revolutionary subjects. In this line, many events have come to be analyzed through the Badiousian framework of the event. The UK mass revolts in 2011, the Arab Spring or the 1989 Caracazo in Venezuela have been presented as events (Robinson 2014). In his writings, Badiou himself mentions different political events: the Paris Commune, the French and Russian Revolution, and the Chinese Cultural revolution in the 1960s and most recently the Jasmine revolution (Robinson 2014). Robinson argues that the 'grammar' of Badiou's theory can be applied to different event eruptions but he cautioned against enumerating long list of events. The ultimate test of whether a particular social eruption qualifies as an event is its effects on the transcendental organisation of discourses in a society (ibid.). In addition to this cautionary note, there is maybe the possibility to engage with and apply Badiou's theory without special revolutionary expectations or pithing in a binary opposition different entities against each other or celebrating the triumph of a weaker side against a stronger one. In applying Badiou's framework to the Syrian crisis/ German refugee crisis, I hope to show how Badiou's framework allow for a contiguous reading of the relational dependences between two occurrences and simultaneously surveying the explanatory potential of some of Badiou's categories.

Central to Badiou's concept of the event, is the eventual site. The site is local and presides over an existing ideological, economical, and political order. It is the count-for-one situation. If the state of the situation is such that it favors the inclusion and membership of all or most of its elements, then the likelihood of an event bursting in this scene is thin. When members of a situation feel deprived, excluded from the dominant order and/or perceive discrepancies between their particular situation and the situation of the "existent order and the stress points within that same order, [then] there is the greatest likelihood of its coming under pressure from elements excluded by the count-as-one (Norris, 2009, p. 112)." If the theory of the event was a pure theory of political revolt and change, than it would certainly share some of the assumptions of deprivation approaches to revolutions and crises. But Badiou's conceptualization of the event, as noted earlier, transcends the political.

Following Badiou's category of the evental site, Syria could be identified as the evental site of the refugee crisis that shook Europe back in September 2015. What made Syria, "once known as the kingdom of silence (Yassin-Kassab and Al-Shami, 2018, p. x)," the site of the latter refugee crisis, and what multiplicities did it conceal? Pre- 2011 Syria was the home of multiple ethnic and religious groups[19] and was ruled since the 1970s first by Hafez Assad and then by his son Assad. When the latter assumed power in 2000, he promised a transformation of Syrian political life. He employed the rhetoric of liberal democratic discourse, spoke "of greater transparency and accountability, of shaking up the bureaucracy and fighting against corruption (ibid. p. 17)." Assad was nonetheless keen to point that his was more an economic than a political opening. As Yassin-Kassab and al-Shami argued, Assad's words resonated with a democracy-thirsty public sphere that established number of forums (*muntadiyat*) to debate reform ideas (ibid.). In repeated statements, intellectuals called for an end to the martial law and the state of emergency in place since 1963, political pluralism and rule of law (ibid., pp. 17–18). The Syrian regime first tolerated these the discussion forums before denouncing and infiltrating them and ultimately arresting and incarcerating some of the leaders of these discussion groups (ibid., p. 20). What was known in 2000 as the Damascus Spring turned into a perpetual winter of persecution and torture for political opponents (ibid., pp. 23–34). The economic and social record of the regime has not been better either. For Yassin-Kassab and Al Shami, Bashaar's economic reform was a "perestroika without a glasnost, Chinese- style- but Syria was no China (ibid., p. 30)." In a report by the Syrian Center for Policy Research on Syria before the beginning of the Revolution in January 2011, the researchers stated:

> Syria suffered from institutional bottleneck because of the inefficiency, lack of transparency and accountability, and the absence of political participation by all population. These conditions triggered developmental distortions such as low productivity, weak societal participation in the development process, and increased inequality as the expansion of crony capitalism diverted attention from the people's aspirations and their

---

19   See Yassin-Kassab and al-Shami (2018, p. 2).

need for inclusive human-centered development. The applied development policies adopted by different Syrian governments caused deterioration in the relationship between the population and their natural, socioeconomic, cultural, and institutional environment.
SCPR, 2016, p. 7

The political and social ontology of Syria prior to the outburst of the war was an evental site that comprised multiple ingredients that could make for an explosive situation and a refugee crisis. The Shia- Sunni hegemonic divide between Iran and Saudi Arabia, its political excrescences and vested interests in Syria, the quasi dictatorial regime and corruption of the Assad clan, the (post-)colonial arbitrary heritage of the 1916 Sykes-Picot Agreement and the French colonization, bad governance, the flaws of the Baath Party and Pan-Arabism, political estrangement and disinterest from different segments of the populations, the phantasies of fundamentalist Islam, despotism, unemployment and economic slumber are among others inconsistent multiples in this eventalsite. The compositional dependence between these elements is aleatory and the configuration of this set is certainly not unique or typical to pre-crisis Syria. They are numerous elements of the eventalsite of the Syrian civil war that were present or recurrent in other countries caught in the turmoil of the Arab Spring (Tunisia, Egypt and Libya) and also in those where the state managed to steer away from it (Yemen, Jordan, Saudi Arabia). This is certainly a further reason why metaphysical or even political theories of the events that posit deterministic or causal relations are limited in their hermeneutic power.

In order to further grasp the relational dependence and consequences not only of the Syrian war but also of the refugee crisis in Europe, one needs to add to the multiple connections of a political analysis of Syria, the Euro-crisis and the reform of migration policies to the event-site. These combined elements help make sense of the massive influx of refugees in 2015 to Europe and especially to Germany and Austria. The financial crisis that shook countries like Spain, Italy, and Greece have reduced refugees' destinations to a few countries in Europe, namely those which at its core, withstood the crisis rather well and offered a chance to restore a modicum of dignity and economic welfare or at least to shelter themselves from the war. Analysts often tend to reduce asylum-seeking to the simple search of a safe shelter and lose sight of the economic dilemmas tied to war and its effects.

The description of the Syrian case could also be applied to several other countries in which an oppressing count-for- one-situation where a state exhibits legitimacy and representation deficits. A state that excludes systematically members of the population from political, economic, and social participation is indirectly laying the foundation for a Badiousian event. There is however no direct deterministic relation between the existences of an evental site on the one hand and the eruption of an event on the other. In Badiou's words:

> The confusion of the existence of the site (for example, the working class, or a given state of artistic tendencies, or a scientific impasse) with the necessity of the event itself is the cross of determinist or globalizing thought. The site is only ever a condition of being for the event. Of course, if the situation is natural, compact, or neutral, the event is impossible. But the existence of a multiple on the edge of the void merely opens up the possibility of an event. It is always possible that no event actually occur.
> BADIOU, 2005, p. 179

How can one then conceive of the event as a temporal rift, a disruption if the advent of the event in such a situation cannot be predicted? The event, in Badiou's thought interrupts the course of history and is not "preceded by any sign, and [uses] to catch us unawares with its grace, regardless of our vigilance (Badiou 2003, p. 111)." Badiou's claim that the event is not preceded by signs appears as a negation of the possibility to explain events through rational economic, political, or social categories. It is not Badiou's attempt to deny the possibility of a heuristic of event formation and eruption. It is more an illustration of his skepticism toward causation as a property of the event. He wants to keep the possibility of transcendental, surprising, miraculous intervention(s) that sets the elements of the evental site in motion. He is not the only theorist who is impatient with such postures. Foucault, as discussed in the subsection above, thought that the search for causation relations is a tool of traditional historical analysis. Through it, the historian tried to eliminate the discontinuous from the event and re-inscribe it in a continuous historical time. An explanation gesture that takes its departure from this point would disenchant the event, negate its specific forces, and leaves it as a weak, probabilistic event. As such, Badiou presents the event as a quasi-miraculous occurrence in order to circumvent the dilemma of bounded rational explanations. Foucault's approach to this dilemma would be to investigate the archeology of the discourse formation of an event to gain different insights and work out relational dependence between events. A Foucauldian analysis it seems, – because of its underlying predilection for *longue durée* – requires historical distance, archives and the accumulation of discourses. Badiou's framework is in comparison less demanding. Its main thrust is the axiom of the impossibility to reduce or justify the event through the numerable factors located in its site. His categories can nonetheless provide deeper analysis of contemporary challenge without assuming an intensive archival work on discourse on the one hand and avoiding the circularity of causation and event on the other hand. From this perspective, it seems that Badiou's framework is more appropriate to analyze the German refugee crisis.

The incapacity of the *event* to justify itself, the radicalism of reactions to the *event*, and its revolutionary effects provide interesting points to analyze the German refugee crisis since 2015. But also contingency, locality, retrospectivity, intensity of appearance, and connectivity contribute to make sense of the event's eruption conditions in Badiou's thought. To this end, one needs not to necessarily yield to a miraculous account of the eruption of an event and instead try to introduce revolutionary subjects as ferment or combustible of the evental site (at the onset of event) and not only as a produce of the event. It can, of course be discussed whether such a gesture is guaranteed in Badiou's framework. Badiou has not been consistent, as observers noted, with the trigger of the events. At times, he seems to attribute the eruption of an event to pure chance, at other times he treats it as a creation of nothingness or the product of a structural necessity (Robinson, 2014). It seems, however necessary, to think about avenues to integrate (non-) state actors or other forms of human agency as a trigger of transformative operations on the evental site. A positive spill-off of such a gesture would be that the trigger agent could be another demarcation criterion between the natural and the historical event. Badiou posited that "there are no natural events, nor are there neutral events. In natural or neutral situations, there are solely facts. The distinction between a fact and an event is based, in the last instance, on the distinction between natural or neutral situations, the criteria of which are global, and historical situations, the criterion of which (the existence of a site) is local. There are events uniquely in situations which present at least one site (Badiou, 2005, p. 178)." Can one conceive of the trigger event as a further demarcation between the natural and the historical event, facts and events? Without the intervention of a being-qua-agency, it would be difficult to conceptually demarcate a natural catastrophe, which can be localized, supernumerary, inconsistent and affect the transcendental arrangements a situation from another historical event that happen to showcase similar constellations of the evental site. For instance, the 2011 tsunami in Japan has significantly altered the discourses on nuclear power in Japan as in some Western countries but the tsunami would still count as a natural event, a fact. The category of a sentient, historical (non-) state actors might be necessarily to fill in the theoretical gap between the arbitrary, inconsistent configuration of the evental site and the eruption of the event. To be sure, some academic discourses, especially in international relations, have long hesitated before internalizing the role and impact of non-*state* actors in world politics.[20] The main reason was a lasting focus on states as the primary subjects of international law and relations. The international order was thus conceived as anarchical and states are competing for survival and power in this order. There have since been theoretical shifts that are reckoning with the role of NGOs, MNCs, and violent terrorist groups in global governance, and world politics and steering away from assumptions of a purely anarchical system. Badiou seems to collapse non-state actors together in the supernumerary event site and assigns to them the same valence and contingency as non-material conditions or truth procedures. Perusing on Badiou and scientific discoveries as events, Norris believed that "[...] on Badiou's account there is room – indeed a strictly indispensable role – for the subject as involved in the production, discovery or progressive emergence of truth though not in any sense that could possibly set it *apart from* or *over against* those procedures that constitute the methodology of the formal sciences (2009, p. 235, emphasis added)." To be sure, non-state actors are indeed a wide category and can include armed or non-armed groups, NGOs but also human subject who can trigger events. Those non-state actors are not necessarily an intellectual consciousness breeding lofty ideas about History and may a priori not be aware that they are triggering an event with national or sometimes international dimensions, if one were to posit an 'Invisible Hand' of History operating through humans. They are the working class, the colored ethnic minorities of the French *banlieus*, oppressed sexual and cultural minorities, refugees, migrants and the possible intersections between these categories. On the surface, the affects of these non-state actors such as feelings of injustice and exasperation as in the case of Mohamed Bouazizi whose self-immolation on December 17, 2010 triggered the Jasmine Revolution in Tunisia, or teenage impetuousness as in the case of Gravilo Princip, the underage Bosnian Serb nationalist whose act of murder on Archduke Franz Ferdinand of Austria and his wife triggered the First World War or in the case of Syria, Naief Abazid, whose graffiti with the message "It's your turn, Dr. Bashar," on February 16, 2011 would "improbably set in motion a chain reaction of events that continue to rock the Middle East – and the world (MacKinnon, December 2016)." The initial trigger can also include inappropriate reactions by other subjects pulling back towards the status quo of the ex-ante existing order. 'Measured' and 'appropriate' responses from the state can quench, contain or delay the volatility of the evental site. This could also partly explain why some regimes 'survived' the Arab Spring

---

20 For a conceptualization of non-state actors in world politics, see: Arts, Noortmann & Reinalda, 2001; Halliday, 2001; Josselin and Wallace, 2001, p. 6; Siles, 2000; Hutter, 2006.

(partly through timely reforms, concession of co-option of oppositional figures) while others were engulfed in it. 'Unmeasured' reactions can accelerate the decomposition of the inconsistent multiples of the site. For this operation as well, I posit a human subject. Atef Najib could be seen as such a *state* actor in this particular sense. His sociopathic reaction to a committee of elders in Syrian Daraa who came to negotiate the liberation of the graffiti kids (Naief Abazid mentioned earlier and some of his friends) held and tortured by a branch of the Syrian internal intelligence agency *Mukhabarat* was certainly a missed opportunity at de-escalation and the preservation or restauration of the status quo.[21] It further introduced "a nonnegotiable rift between the sociopolitical orders as viewed from a legitimist, reformist or social-democratic perspective (Norris, 2009, p. 8)." The nonnegotiable rift is the point of radicalization of the position of the actors involved on the evental site.

State and non-state actors generally pull in different directions and can engineer different outcomes for their side. Their actions set in motion the aleatory arrangements of elements located in the evental site and make the event possible. They are simultaneously part of the inconsistent multiples of the site and nonetheless preserve their own singularity. Singularity takes here an additional meaning. It is the existential belief of the (non-)state actor in its singular immanence and fate, its rejection of the current practices of the status-quo, its disobedience to the oppressing order, its voicing of demands. It is this belief in situational and existential singularity that ignites or prevents the ignition of the evental site. Najib and Abazid in the Syrian crisis, acting for their respective sides, are singular in that their actions could have steered the outcomes of the conflict towards their expectations. This short theoretical disquisition could prove a constructive addition to Badiou's theory of the event. He focused on the resistance of the revolutionary subject and the counter-insurgency of the *state* to guarantee the status quo as well. The transfiguration of the subject is conditioned by the outcome of the revolutionary and counter-revolutionary processes on the evental site. There is a quite oblique rapprochement one is tempted to make after considering the case of Naief Abazid, the naïve and accidental revolutionary of the Syrian war/revolution. He claimed that when he was brought to the local branch of the Syrian internal intelligence agency to be interrogated, he saw a sign on a wall, which read: "Those who enter here are missing. Those who leave are newborn (MacKinnon, 2016)." The signpost suggested that any suspected dissident the agency arrested underwent (certainly through torture) a renewal of the inner operational code

---

21 Najib allegedly told the elders to 'forget about your children. Go have new kids. If you can't, send us your wives and we will get them pregnant for you (MacKinnon, 2016).'

almost akin to the experience of conversion in Christian redemption doctrine.[22] Naief Abazid and his graffiti friends were celebrated as heroes after they were released from the torture dungeons of the Assad regime to join the fight for the reversal of the status quo. But were the crowds right in celebrating the graffiti kids turned revolutionaries? MacKinnon answers in the negative and ponders:

> Without Naief's act of teenage impetuousness – and the Assad regime's violent reaction to it – would the extremist caliphate have been declared? Would the refugee crisis be on the scale it is now? Would the United Kingdom – spurred by campaign posters of streams of refugees heading north – have voted to leave the European Union? Would the anti-immigrant message of Donald Trump – who has spoken, without evidence, of possible "Trojan horses" among the Syrian refugees accepted into the United States – have resonated quite so deeply with the American electorate?
> MACKINNON, 2016

The eventual site with its multiple abnormalities is located on the edge of the void. The actors or the subjects through their actions can tip the re-arrangement of the aleatory elements towards their preferred expectation or the void. They are certainly never in the position to gaze into the depths of the void and predicate their actions on the insights they would have gained. This may partly explain why some contemporary theorists circumvent direct causation and examine alternative systems of relations between objects. The consequences of the Syrian war as an event can bring one to reflect about tenses in events. Badiou's preferred tense is the future anterior -actually a grammatical conjugational category available in the French language that has dynamic equivalents in some other Indo-European language- which he applies to the tense of an event. The future anterior is the 'will-have-been' perspective (Norris, 2009, p. 230), which assigns signification to names "when [a] situation will have

---

22   Paul the Apostle, who considered himself the 'prisoner of the Lord' (Ephesians 4: 1, KJV) after his encounter with the Immanent Being, exhorted his brethren to put off the 'old man' and be 'renew in the spirit' (Ephesians 4: 23, KJV). Not only is the revolutionary aiming to put off the old order and create a 'new man' (sic), but the counter-revolutionary also though their apparatus of counter-insurgency aims to convert the dissident member into a newborn person.

appeared in which the indiscernible-which is only represented (or included)-is finally presented as a truth of the first situation (Badiou, 2005, p. 398)." The event is a future in perfection. But the event can also be argued to be more of an indeterminate tense than a future anterior. It includes different fragments of the conjugated tenses and modes. In the indicative, it is foremost a future hope, a realizable utopia. It the conditional, it is the interplay of elements in a compositional dependence that influences the outcome of the event. In the subjunctive, it is the mutation of a promising evental situation into a disillusioned present and a nostalgic past. Erupted events or events under completion can exhibit the properties of these protracted tenses. Their idiosyncrasies are hidden from the subject when they set the evental site in motion and sometimes also from the analyzer when they attempt a geophilosophy of the event. The ultimate outcome sometimes can be the past anterior of the edge of the void.

3 Undecidability and the Edge of the Void

In the subsection above, I posited that the arrangements of the inconsistent multiples in pre-Civil War Syria could be analyzed within some of the Badiousian categories. I stressed that the presence on the evental site is a compositional dependence between the aleatory and multiple elements and does not systematically determine the onset of an event. I posited that a form of agency is needed to make sense of the transformative operations on the site that will then retrospectively be regarded as an event. I suggested that the inclusion of a non-state actor in the framework could provide the missing link between the arrangement of the site and the eruption of the event. However, I did refrain to hastily call the (still ongoing) Syrian war or revolution an event, a true event in Badiou's sense. There are two main reasons for this posture. The first is that (as of 2018) the Syrian conflict is still an ongoing civil war with uncertain outcomes. It would then be more of a divinatory exercise than a critical analysis to extrapolate at this point on the end of the war. Secondly, for Badiou, an event is an event, a true event, when it challenges, reorganizes the transcendental organization of a situation. This concretely means that one should assess the outcome of an event in terms of the reversal of the order that existed before the event, the inclusion of the excluded categories in the count-for-one situation. From this perspective, the prospects of the Syrian war are also unclear. The disillusion of the triggering subjects of the revolution, the evolving protracted nature of the conflict, the paralysis of the international community, do not seem to encourage optimistic expectations of the outcomes of the Syrian war. Nonetheless, I tried to engage with the conflict and reconstruct some of the Badiousian categories on the assumption that there was more to the Syrian conflict than a teleological assessment of its qualities as an historical event. Now, I am to try to provide an explanation of how the Syrian revolution (an erupted but unfinished event as of now) could be brought in a compositional dependence with the refugee crisis and the arrival of nearly a million of refugees (not only but mainly from Syria) to Germany in September 2015. How can one arrive at a more or less satisfactory Badiousian explanation of the refugee crisis? For such a purpose, it would be necessary to construct the refugee crisis as an independent event, indeed the real event in Badiou's sense. This move would presuppose the identification a local evental site, the multiple on the site and the edge of the void and all the relevant categories. The Syrian war, which was analyzed above, would qualify as the evental site at the edge of the void. This approach grants for the possibility to reckon with the compositional contiguity of the Syrian Civil War and the refugee crisis and construct the latter an event as ensuing from the first. The Syrian Civil War would constitute – together with other multiples – the event site for the refugee crisis. The first approach although legitimate does not do justice to the compositional interrelation between the two situations. The second approach gives us the leeway to highlight the edge of the void as a productive hermeneutic concept. In Badiou, the evental site is contiguous to the edge of the void. In 2015, the year of the refugee crisis, the Syrian civil war entered its fourth year. Revolutionaries and the excluded members who sensed in the eruption of the event an opportunity to do away with the existing order, Baachar's regime, were slowly being disillusioned. It is a delusion nurtured not only by the longevity of the conflict, but also by the undesirability and poverty of the alternatives (ISIL and its gruesome politics) that a reversal of the state of the evental site would possibly imply. It was arduous for the actors who triggered the conflict to maintain fidelity to the event. In fact, some of the protagonists of the onset of the Syrian civil war, celebrated as heroes in 2011, later fled to Germany and have lost most of their illusions (MacKinnon 2016). As the Syrian revolution was taking the characteristic of longevity (meanwhile in its eight year), and the site of multiple protracted sub-conflicts through the game of alliances (the Iran-Russia-Syria-alliance versus Free Syrian Army, Turkey versus the Syrian regime, nationalistic Kurds versus ISIS, US versus ISIS, etc.), the geographical expansion of the conflict(s) to nearly all major provinces in the country, the persisting intensity of the conflict, the conditions of life in Syria could without exaggeration be described as the edge of the void. Protracted conflicts in so-called failed states or fragile states are humanitarian edges of the void. Consider for example the following analysis:

> When widespread destruction and indiscriminate targeting become central to the means and method of armed conflict in protracted conflicts, people suffer severely. The humanitarian consequences of armed conflict – like displacement, impoverishment and a lack of access to basic services – can become entrenched, even if the pattern of violence is sporadic rather than constant. Damage that goes unrepaired, lost livelihoods and continuing protection risks mean that humanitarian consequences continue to affect people for a long time.
> ICRC 2016, p. 11

A protracted conflict is situated at the edge of the void. It suspends legal orders and silences the voice of the 'gentle civilizer of nations,' as Koskenniemi characterized International Law (IL) (2004). As a gentle civilizer, he remarked, international law is after all a rather 'fragile structure (ibid., p. 440),' which suffered from the asymmetrical relation between the political and the legal. Whereas there seems to be a priori no limits to the justiciability through international law, "States refused to bring their grievances to third-party settlement – in particular if they appeared to deal with their 'vital interests' or 'national honor.' (ibid., p. 441)"

The attempts to define the political in ways amenable to a legal settlement or intrervention were not concluding, because 'the political had no fixed substance (ibid.).' Anything that mattered to the State can take the property of the political. The unsuccessful attempts by the UN through special prosecutor Carla Del Ponte to sue the Assad's regime for charges of war crimes have once again demonstrated the embeddedness of justice in political procedures and will. Syria's non-ratification of the 2002 Rome Statute of the International Criminal Court, its political ties to veto-power Russia are to be taken into account in order to make sense of the hitherto limited resources of international action against the Syrian warring parties. Badiou's framework does not foresee the settlement of events through legal interventions. The event, once erupted, aims at the reversal of the existing order of the state. 'State' in Badiou can designate the political state. Dealing with a breeding revolution is perceived as a matter of honor and vital interest by the challenged State. The excluded members of the state and located on the edge of the void look up to IL and international organizations to find respite only to witness how the principles of *jus in bello* are more or less willfully ignored by all sides in the war. Civilian infrastructure, means of subsistence, water provision, and sanitation are attacked and destroyed, leaving the excluded multitude closer to the edge of the void. It is also the systematic violation of human rights, the unbridled display of oppressive and retaliatory violence (ICRC, 2016, p. 15). The SCPR provides data to picture the humanitarian void of the Syrian crisis:

> The crisis has led to a dramatic rise in the mortality rates. The crude mortality rate increased from 4.4 per thousand in 2010 to 10.9 per thousand in 2014, accounting directly and indirectly for the death of about 1.4 per cent of the total population. Childhood mortality reached about 11.4 percent, and women's deaths reached 12 per cent of the total deaths due to the crisis. This report estimates the crude mortality rate at 10.8 per thousand in 2015. With the increase in the mortality rate, life expectancy declined significantly for males and for all age groups, especially the younger ages, where a male's life expectancy at birth retreated from 69.7 in 2010 to 48.2 in 2014 and 48.4 in 2015. The decline of life expectancy was less acute among females because of the lack of direct engagement of hostilities; female life expectancy at birth decrease from 72 years in 2010 to 64.8 years in 2014 and 65 in 2015.
>
> SCPR, 2016, p. 9

The fragile structure of IL and the complex international community have not improved the fate of Syrians. The controversial doctrine of the responsibility to protect did not find use. Migration or exodus more or less imposed itself as a necessary course of action for more than 5 million Syrians.[23] It would be wrong to assume that migration and internal displacement suspends the void. The

---

23   Syrian policy researchers present the forced migration of Syrians outside of their country as a necessary evil: In their words: "Despite knowing that their dignity and rights might be abused in some countries of asylum and migration, many Syrians were forced to leave the country as a result of the deteriorating social and economic situation, widespread violence, and insecurity. They have seen their humanity and dignity squandered, while losing hope for a just and fair solution to the conflict. According to the population survey in 2014, the first receiving state of Syrian refugees is Turkey, where the share of those who migrated to it reached 37.5 per cent of the total number of Syrian refugees. Lebanon comes second, as it received 35.6 per cent of the Syrian refugees; 14.1 per cent of refugees headed to Jordan, 4.8 per cent to Egypt, and 4.6 per cent to Iraq. The numbers of migrants increased, but at a slower pace than in the first years of conflict. Most people capable of travel had left already. The results show that about 32 per cent of migrants went to Lebanon, 18 per cent to Turkey, and 16 per cent to the Gulf countries (SCRP, 2016, pp. 10–11)." Forced migration can be said to be the consumption of the exclusion of the members of the situation from the existing order, the consequence of the failed reversal of the order.

difficult conditions in refugee camps in Jordan and Turkey, the uncoordinated responses of the EU to the crisis have not significantly altered the situation of the refugees. In a more critical perspective, The Turkey-Greece-Balkan route was not an exit from the situation and when, on June 17, 2015, Hungarian Prime Minister Viktor Orbán announced his country will build a fence along the Hungarian-Serbian border, citing European law as the basis for his decision (Blume et al., August 2016), he was simply cementing the edge of the void, the Syrians never really escaped from. Life for the refugee was still bare, deprived of political rights, as in Agamben conception of bare life (1998), or precarious, disposable as in Butler's characterization (2004).

4   Interventional Gestures

'Intervention' is, like most concepts in Badiou's vocabulary, polysemous and ambivalent and productive maybe because of these contradictory properties. It is used in Badiou's writing both in a meta-theoretical sense and at times in a political sense. Both senses are contiguous. The meta-theoretical conceptualization of intervention with relation to the event is akin to the recognition of the properties of an event operated from outside the situation by an observer. It is a form of recognition that implies the designation of the multiples of an evental site and relating them ultimately to an event (Badiou, 2005, p. 202). It may seem that intervention is the gesture of the analyzer, the historiographer who upon examination of the elements of the evental site decides that a particular event belongs to a situation. It is a hermeneutic intervention, a recognition of a shift, the dawn of a new era or the disruption in an existing order. Without their intervention, an event might go unnoticed and unrecorded. Intervention is the director's cut, the historian identifying the discontinuous and who having surveyed the situation and the conditions of the multiples, concludes that the elements of a particular event are part of a particular situation. There is, from that perspective, no event, if there is no recognition and naming intervention. The intervention, one is tempted to argue, invents the event even if the historiographical gesture is posterior to the event itself. This form of intervention assumes a clear subjectivity that puts the event in *circulation*. In Badiou's words:

> It is just as certain that if no intervention puts it into circulation within the situation on the basis of an extraction of elements from the site, then, lacking any being, radically subtracted from the count-as-one, the event does not exist. In order to avoid this curious mirroring of the event and

the intervention – of the fact and the interpretation – the possibility of the intervention must be assigned to the consequences of another event. It is evental recurrence which founds intervention. In other words, there is no interventional capacity, constitutive for the belonging of an evental multiple to a situation, save within the network of consequences of a previously decided belonging. An intervention is what presents an event for the occurrence of another. It is an evental between-two.
 ibid., p. 209

The analysis of the refugee crisis that shook Germany in 2015 that was attempted here would count – according to the framework presented above – as a form of (discursive) intervention. I designated the elements of the evental site which I located within the Syrian civil war that broke out in 2011 following an act of teenage impetuousness and a state's inappropriate reaction to this original act. We argued that because the Syrian revolution/Civil War is still ongoing and with uncertain outcomes as to the re-arrangement of the transcendental political organization, it could not be presented as a true event in Badiou's sense. One would have to await the end of the conflict and in retrospect assess whether and to which extent the transcendental arrangements of the site have been altered. Only after then is it possible – in accordance with Badiou's category – to speak of the Syrian war as event. I posited an evental recurrence between the Syrian revolution and the refugee crisis and outlined the network of consequences that establish the compositional dependence between the two occurrences. The Syrian event and the refugee crisis are facts; the interpretational gesture performed here is the intervention that presents a quasi-event (the Syrian civil war) as the consequence of another event (the 2015 German refugee crisis). As Robinson argued, reflecting on Badiou, "[a]n intervention is a way of naming or analysing an Event without denying its evental nature. It saves the Event from disappearing by attaching a name to it. And it avoids denying its evental nature by choosing a name which is not simply the name of a part of the existing situation (2014)."

When one has decided to call the massive arrival of refugees to Europe an event, one is performing an interventional gesture. But it does not entail a denial that this refugee crisis interpreted as an event is a part of a much greater reality or situation. The event exists in a compositional dependence with European migration policies, the civil war, the erosion of social infrastructure, the precariousness of life in refugee camps in Turkey, the rise (and fall) of the Islamic state, the turf war between regional hegemonic powers, both on security and religious grounds. All these aspects are part of the situation from which the crisis emerged in 2015. Deciding to name the refugee crisis (an aspect of the overall situation) as event does not disservice the other aspects or reduce the interpretation field. The refugee crisis includes these multiple aspects. Naming the refugee incidentally redeems these aspects from being forgotten, since the interventional gesture captures and freezes the event and the inconsistent multiples that composed it.

But there is another meaning to intervention in Badiou's theory, an aspect that is predicated on and derived from the meta-theoretical intervention. One could term it the political theory of intervention. In it, the subject is endowed also with an *interventional capacity* (2005, p. 203). But it does not interpret event with the distance of hindsight but impacts the situation from the outside. It is a kind of *deus ex machina,* which is simultaneously subtracted from the void and can intervene in it. It is indeed a radical theory that is more perceptible in *Logics of Worlds*. The interventional capacity which he outlined in *Being and Event* can be contrasted with the "'right of intervention': legal, international, and, if needs be, military (2009, p. 3)" in *Logics of Worlds*. The political theory of intervention is radical; it is a scission, a division that puts asunder "the social world into different camps – those for and against the Event. There is no space here for any middle ground. There is also no space for distanced sympathy for an Event. And there is no space for debate with opponents. In many ways, Badiou is advocating the creation of strong dualisms and absolute social antagonisms. Those who embrace the Event should simply reject and fight those who oppose it (2014)."

It is a conception of revolutionary intervention that negates the possibility of compromises and neutrality, and measure. It is intrinsically militant. But there is more to Badiou's radical conception of intervention than the politics and revolutions he originally had in mind when he outlined his theory. The second theory of intervention that one can extract from Badiou transcends revolutionary, liberational and anti-imperialist wars. It is readily more applicable to interventions at the edge of the void, since Badiou endows the intervening subject with the capacity to use legal, international (which could mean diplomatic) and military means. This theory of (political) intervention is tied to the theory of (meta-theoretical) intervention highlighted above in that an intervention at the edge of the void would retrospectively be interpreted as such when it exhibits the specific properties of intensity, excess, non-regulation, or outrageousness.[24] When the refugee crisis broke out in 2015, some observers wondered why Germany decided to welcome so many asylum seekers

---

24 The refugee crisis hit the Merkel government unprepared. "On August 19, the government had already increased its prognosis for the number of refugees it was expecting in 2015 to 800,000, four times as many as in the previous year – but no additional preparations

whereas countries like France or Canada fixed a quota for asylum seekers they want to welcome. Tibi for example posited a German special way to explain the decision of the German chancellor to welcome so many refugees in 2015.[25] Badiou's framework seems to suggest that it is exactly the characteristics of excess, intensity, controversy (within the populace) that give to Merkel's decision, Germany's humanitarian *intervention* its evental quality. Merkel's controversial decision[26] followed with the pessimistic attitudes towards it are the elements that make the crisis an event in Badiou's framework. An event is not necessarily the outcome of a rational policy policy approach. It dwells in the realm of the extraordinary, of speculative faith. It is carried by the euphoria it set in motion. Moreover, one should remember that Badiou is impatient with moral philosophy. As such, his approach is unapologetically radical and seems to be able to put up with the controversy it generates.

5   Transcendental Arrangements

Badiou's ultimate 'test' to determine whether a particular occurrence qualify as an event is the assessment of the degree to which the potential event has effected the transcendental arrangements or disposition of the situation, of the world from which the situation arises. Badiou assumes that said worlds are governed by transcendental laws, reflected in the observable order of things. The eruption of the event "perturbs this world's transcendental laws, on the observable unruliness in the appearance of objects, on the nature of the trace

---

followed. Neither did anything happen after Merkel promised during her summer press conference in Berlin on August 31 that, 'we can do it' (Blume et al., August 2016)."

25   For Tibi, the extreme is a recurrent characteristic of the German mindset. He mentioned the French president who welcomed a maximum of 30,000 Syrians. In his words, the German Chancellor, on the contrary, absorbs 1.5 million refugees and even then refuses to introduce an upper limit. This is a special way, as it is for the Germans. In a discussion in die Welt, an artist told this to the Jewish journalist Henryk Broder: "We are Germans, we cannot have normality." Broder asked, "Why not?" The artist said, "We murdered the Jews." Broder said: "I am a Jew and I would like to live in a normal country (Tibi, July 2016, my translation).

26   Most journalists characterize Merkel's border's opening as a controversial one. It was one "that will divide the country – a division that remains to this day. The rift cuts through families, clubs, companies and editorial staffs: How much immigration can we handle? Where are the people from that we are accepting? Are there any potential attackers among them? What about our security? Above all: Did Angela Merkel encourage the people to come or would they have arrived anyway? (Blume et al., August 2016, my translation)."

wherein the vanished event endures and, finally, on what is capable of incorporating itself into the present under the sign of this trace (2009, p. 69)." Badiou does not characterize any political conflict as an event. In *Logics of Worlds*, Badiou refrained from characterizing the revolt of the Mohawks against the municipality of Oka as an event. For him the revolt "does not transform the transcendental evaluations; it presupposes them, insofar as it too appears in the world. We will therefore maintain that the Mohawk revolt, rigorously conceived as the relation between the object 'the Mohawks' and the object 'Quebecois administration,' only elicits the appearance of objective existences that are already there, even if – and this is one of the reasons for the revolt – this existence is minimized or belittled by its official counterparts. Equally, we will say that the internal differentiations deployed by the violent incidents and their outcome – on the side of the Mohawks as well as on that of the different tendencies within the administration – are legible on the basis of the relation, but are not created by it (ibid., p. 311)." Badiou's 'event policy' is quite restrictive and certainly could be applied to scientific, cultural, and amorous events as well. I had already made the case above that the Syrian Revolution/War that was still ongoing could be treated as an event in Badiou's sense. One would have, as stated earlier, to await the end of the conflict and survey the alterations of the transcendental orders to decide on its 'eventness.' Robinson found Badiou's downplaying of the Mohawk's revolt rather unfair. He argued that the revolt had 'evental effects' since it galvanized the claims of the indigenous and increased their visibility (2014).

The arrangements of the transcendental arrangements bring mostly subjects to the foreground. Subjects can be political, cultural, amorous or scientific in Badiou's typology. The subject can be the excluded from the situation, the count-as-one, who gain (revolutionary) subjectivity and reorganizes the state of the situation. In the French revolution, the sans-culottes are the revolutionary subjects that emerged after the transformation of the situation. This is the type of subject that comes to mind when one think of the event. But there is also in Badiou the reactionary/reactive political subject that arises to oppose the revolutionary momentum. A new order, a transcendental intervention, a reorganization of the situation also set in motion unsupportive forces that intend to re-reverse the situation created by the event. In Badiou's words, "[t]he reactive subject carries the reactionary inventions of the sequence (the new form of the resistance to the new) into the heart of the people [*le peuple*] or of people in general [*les gens*]. For a long time, this has taken the name of *reaction*. The names of reaction are sometimes typical of the sequence, for instance 'Thermidorian' for the French Revolution, or 'modern revisionists' for the Chinese Cultural Revolution (Badiou, 2009, p. 72)." The arrival of refugees (a putative event) has created a 'situation,' and unleashed opposition from elements of the populace "between the phenomenal persistence of a world and its evental rearrangement (ibid., 2009, p. 79)." In Germany, the country that welcomed approximately more than a 1 million refugees since the summer of 2015, the coordinates of the political and social have been fundamentally shifting. The enthusiasm of the early days, the euphoric welcome by Germans of the refugees, the optimism – maybe best encapsulated in Merkel's "*Wir schaffen das*" (we can do it) – has given way to a growing xenophobia, and a reinvigorated right-wing populism that stirred up Germany's 2017 federal parliamentary elections. Merkel survived her humanitarian feat in the 2017 federal elections but has since nuanced her original stance, seeming at times to concede that those September days were an exception to her political operational code. There would not be another generous border opening, she assured, as if to assuage some right-wing sympathizers in her party and the ill-defined crowd of anxious Germans. Meanwhile agreements were reached with Turkey to contain refugees and deny them further passage to Germany. For the refugees now in Germany, integrating in the German society is not being an easy task. Terrorist attacks, homicidal acts committed by refugees despite their statistical relative proportions, prejudice against Islam have not contributed much to further their case. But there seems to be an additional way to include these aspects in Badiou's theoretical framework. He also outlined a typology of the affects "that signal the incorporation of a human animal into a subjective truth-process (ibid., p. 86)." At first sight the affects Badiou theorized make sense when applied to the revolutionary subjects. The desire for a decisive discontinuity coupled with an anxiety of the discontinuous, courage, justice are the subjective modalities of the journey (ibid., p. 86). What are the affects that signal the incorporation of reactive subject in an event? Is it not the fear of the discontinuity that the event introduced, the desire for the familiar, the phantasies of the nostalgic pre-order? What consequences can the affects of the reactive subject have? Badiou offer concluding words on the fundamental indeterminacy of the events. In his words, "[t]he real difficulty is to be found in the following: the consequences of an event, being submitted to structure, cannot be discerned as such. I have underlined this undecidability according to which the event is only possible if special procedures conserve the evental nature of its consequences. This is why its sole foundation lies in a discipline of time, which controls from beginning to end the consequences of the introduction into circulation of the paradoxical multiple, and which at any moment knows how to discern its connection to chance (2005, p. 211)." Maybe, at the end, time is the event.

CHAPTER 2

An Abbreviated History of Germany's Migration Discourses and Policies

There is a 'presence-absence' paradox that those interested in migration research in Germany quickly notice: although the country has been de facto an immigration country, political discourse and practice has long denied this fact. In 2004, the country bundled different legal texts into a more comprehensive *Zuwanderungsgesetz*, an immigration law.[1] But not only politics 'excluded' the migrants. It seems, as Bommes in his 2006 contribution *Migration and Migration Research in Germany* noted, that migration has not been a "major topic in the core of the various disciplines of the social sciences in Germany nor has it been addressed by major social theorists as a central challenge for theory-building (Bommes, 2006, p. 163)." Bommes went on to offer a typology of German migration research from WWII onwards. The first research tradition Bommes identified was concerned with returnees, ethnic German refugees, returning to Germany after the lost WWII or expelled from Eastern European countries from the late 1940s to the 1950s. This strand of migration research was cathartic, "a means to cope with irreversible outcomes of the national catastrophe (ibid., p. 164)." It was a 'research program' concerned with the questions of integration and incorporation of the expellees.

The second research paradigm emerged in the late 1950s to the early 1980s and coincided with the expansion of the welfare state, the recruitment of foreign workers, and the political and social context created by the events of 1968 (ibid., p. 169). This research paradigm started, as Bommes further argued as a *Gastarbeiterforschung* (research on guest workers), before being renamed into *Ausländerforschung* (research on foreigners) and rebranded as 'general migration research (ibid., p. 170)' in the 1970s and 1980s. The third research paradigm arguably emerged after 1989 and represents the institutionalization of migration research (ibid., p. 184). Of the main topics of the research program as highlighted by Bommes, religion (i.e Islam), the cost of migration seem to be the most novel features (ibid., 192–196). Migration research has since been an expanding field of research and has expanded its thematic portfolio to include security, perceived cultural values, and racism.

---

1   I will analyze the context of emergence of this law and situate it within the overall migration policies of Germany in the last part of this chapter.

In this chapter, I want to attempt an interdisciplinary or multidisciplinary approach to Germany's migration policies. Contrary to Bommes, I take a more extended *longue durée*-approach to migration in Germany in the sense that I take the late nineteenth century into account in my analysis of migration. As such, I follow the history of migration and interrogate the fault lines using approaches from critical theory. I also interrogate Weber's contribution to the securitization of migration. I then proceed on to offer a typology of German migration policies from the nineteenth century to the present. I identify a command-and-control approach, a public-private-partnership approach to migration regulation, and a general muddling-through approach to migration control. I further argue though there are renewed talks roughly since 2016 to pass a new immigration law (*Einwanderungsgesetz*) as opposed to the 2004 *Zuwanderungsgesetz*, to attract skilled labor in Germany, there is no guarantee that this will put an end to the overall muddling-through migration policy of Germany after 1945.

1   Historiographical Omissions and Sociological Exclusions

The chaotic German twentieth century has cast a long shadow over its nineteenth century. Paradoxically, few centuries in the German past yield more insights about its contemporary age than the nineteenth century, as Görtemaker already noticed (1989, p. 5). Görtemaker compiled one of the seminal textbook works on the German nineteenth century and located in it the source of German modernity. The ideals of the Enlightenment, the 1789 French Revolution at the turn of the eighteenth century, the revolutions of 1830 and 1848/1849, the constitutional developments, the formation of organized political parties, the industrialization and the emergence of the labor movement, the rise of nationalism and territorially bounded nation states laid the groundwork for the German present (1989, p. 5). Görtemaker's historical account is not a people's history of the nineteenth century but rather focused, as he claimed himself, on the 'great' topics, an outline of the lines along which the century developed.[2] To be fair, he has included not only excerpts from foundational texts of the

---

2 To be sure, Görtemaker's textbook also featured a chapter on the social consequences of industrialization, the structural transformations, the wretchedness of the workers, child labor in industries and mines, as well as the degrading housing conditions in urban centers that early capitalism brought to the proletariat (Görtemaker, 1989, p. 175). It is in this early hotbed of social consequences that capitalism undoubtedly started inventing itself as a dynamic, adaptable system that is in a position to internalize the negative externalities of its unbridled exploitation drive. It also overcame the original skepticism against the steam engines, constantly turning its crises into growth opportunities.

Enlightenment or first-hand historical accounts of workers' testimonies on the beginnings of industrialization, the rural exodus, the influence of Marx and Engels on workers' union or the introduction of welfare policies through the 'reactionary progressivism' of Bismarck.

The rapid industrialization process had caused the rural exodus from the agrarian eastern part of Prussia to the expanding industrial Ruhr area (Görtemaker, 1989, p. 176). The flight to the urban cities was accompanied by the growth of the urban industrial centers. At the turn of the nineteenth century, two cities in Germany (Berlin and Hamburg) had a population of more than 100,000. At the creation of the German Reich in 1871, already eight cities numbered more than 100,000 people in population and 65% of the Reich population lived in rural communities (ibid., pp. 176–177). The industrialization process converted peasants into urban workers, transformed family bonds, and used child labor. In this burgeoning history of the proletariat in the early industrialization, Görtemaker does not expand on the migrants and their contribution to the development of German capitalism or the dilemma between economic interests and nationalistic endeavors, or the contribution of Polish seasonal laborers. He had warned, as mentioned earlier, that his contribution would concentrate on the 'great' topics. As such, one could get the sense that for Görtemaker, migration in nineteenth century Germany was not considered as a 'great topic.'

There have been nonetheless historical accounts that tried to restore the excluded subjects from 'big' historical recounting, drawing attention to lesser-known aspects of German history and the lines of developments of migration in the country. Such attempts at a tentative people's history, as I would like to call them, should not be considered as footnotes to the mainstream of historiographical works but considered as restoring the formative importance of the migrants and other under-theorized subjects. Such a people history could survey, based on the historiographical data, the paradoxical relational dependences between the construction of Germany as a nation-state and the history of migration and its contribution to the stabilization of the labor force in Germany. The population movement in the nineteenth century is not only the rural exodus from rural communities towards the growing industrial centers in the Ruhr area Görtemaker one-sidedly described. It was firstly a story of German emigration that culminated between 1846/47 (shortly before the onset of the 1848 revolution) and 1857/59. An estimated 1.3 million Germans emigrated after having worked in the factories of the urban centers to gather enough financial resources to support an emigration to the US, the favored destination of 92% of the German emigrants back then (Herbert, 2001, p. 14). A people's history of migration is also a history of the migrants from Poland into Germany to fill the void left by the rural exodus described above. The *Leutenot*, the term used to describe labor shortage in the 1880s, occurred in a context of the imagination of the German nation-state, the catching-up process of German industry with its European competitors Great Britain and France, whose industrialization process were well advanced while the multiple German states lacked a comprehensive tariff union. The reaction of the eastern landowners to the shortage of labor force in Germany was to step over to recruit workers from contiguous former Polish regions, then occupied by Austria and Russia. For the landowners, this was an obvious and cheap course of action for their shortage in man power (ibid., p. 15). These economic interests however collided with the political endeavors of the new Reich of the consolidation of the German identity (*Festigung des Deutschtums*) and the reduction of the Slavic influence (*Zurückdrängung des slawischen Einflusses*) of governmental bodies and lobby groups in the eastern provinces (ibid.). The recruitment of the Polish workers and the nationalistic opposition defined the field of tension that would henceforth, according to Herbert, characterize the stakes of migration policy in Germany. The nationalistic anti-immigration groups feared political agitation from Polish workers that were being recruited from outside and a vested belief in the cultural superiority of Germany over Slaws. The Polish Kingdom had been divided between the German Reich, Austria, and Russia (ibid.). The imagined community is constructed as limited nation, with finite – even though elastic borders – that is without the pretension of including the whole of mankind as proselytizing monotheistic religions sometimes purport to (Anderson, 2006, p. 7). For the German nationalists, the construction of the German identity was only possible through the exclusion of the Poles, whose political entity was dismantled by the imperialist ambitions of the Germans, Russians and Austrians. Efforts had been made to 'germanize' and absorb the Polish 'barbarians' on the occupied German side but the Russian and Austrian Poles were considered as a threat. The acquisition of workers from the occupied Russian and Austria territories by German landowners was a motive of concern for the nascient nation-state. The sovereignty of the nation seemed only guaranteed when the 'barbarian' Poles were kept outside the gates of the Reich. There was no 'policy on barbarians,' that could be applied on those Poles without infringing the territorial sovereignty of competing occupying powers.

2 Bismarck, *Leutenot*, and the Early Securitization of Migration

There have been recently numerous publications on securitization and migration.[3] But the association of migration with insecurity is certainly not a

---

3 See for example, Kaya, 2009; van Munster 2009, Watson 2009.

discursive novelty (Watson, 2009, p. 15). Securitization as a practice has not originated within the post-9/11 War on Terror, or the nuclear deterrence policies of the Cold War area. The historical construction of walls around cities, the introduction of passport systems, visa requirements are among others proto-examples of security practices in international state relations.

The study of securitization has been a growing sub-field in IR theory since the 1990s. Since then, world events, and globalization has provided it with opportunities to extent his conceptual toolkits. In the profusion of possible securitization issues in world politics, the theory has been searching for ways to define, delineate and demarcate security questions from non-security ones. It interrogates the rationales behind the selective conceptualizations of particular issues as security problems and not others, as well the translation of security discourses into policies and the relations between politics and security (Balzacq, 2011a, p. xiii). Meta-theoretically, there are two main avenues to arrive to securitization theory. Issues can be approached from a philosophical, poststructuralist or from a sociological perspective (ibid., 2011b, p. 1). Philosophical approaches to securitization attribute a magical power to language, which bring realities in being by the simple virtue of evoking them. The magical power of language to conjure up realities emanate from its performative property. It transcends the simple dichotomies of 'true' and 'false.'

Compared to the former approach, the sociological approach emphasizes the embedment of securitization discourses in social contexts, practices, and power relations. It posits that those discourses take place in strategic, pragmatic processes that occur "within, and as part of, a configuration of circumstances, including the context, the psycho-cultural disposition of the audience, and the power that both speaker and listener bring to the interaction (ibid.)." For Balzacq, the sociological approach yields a richer account and analytical categories to come to terms with the emergence, formation of securitization discourse that a purely philosophical, nearly tautological outlook on securitization. His definition of the sociological approach reflects the ambitions of the theory to cover as exhaustively as possible different levels of analysis and simultaneously accounts for the interaction and interdependence of these levels. In Balzacq's words, "securitization as an articulated assemblage of practices whereby heuristic artefacts (metaphors, polity tools, image repertoires, analogies, stereotypes, emotions, etc.) are contextually mobilized by a securitizing actor, who works to prompt an audience to build a coherent network of implications (feelings, sensations, thoughts, and intuitions), about the critical vulnerability of a referent object, that concurs with the securitizing actor's reasons for choices and actions, by investing the referent subject with such an aura of unprecedented threatening complexion that a customized policy must be undertaken immediately to block its development (2011b, p. 3)." Balzacq's definition is in a sense an attempt to reciprocally fertilize structure and agency through affects and teleology. His analytical categories are broad enough to be empirically applied to the analysis of securitization discourses but Balzacq is keen to issue warning on methodological dilettantism (See ibid., pp. 31–50).

There is between the duality of approaches presented by Balzacq, the possibility to suggest or simply to combine the sociological analysis with a historical reading. The majority of the approaches to migration as security threat dwell on the contemporary surface. Here, I want to suggest that the context of the nineteenth century Germany presented a situation where migration was securitized. I try to apply the central categories for a process tracing as highlighted by Balzacq and survey the possible fault lines and substantiate the implications of such a move. An issue can only be characterized as an instance of securitization only if it highlights the centrality of an audience, the co-dependency of agency and context as well the dispositif of the structuring forces of practices.

2.1 The Centrality of an Empowering Audience

I had introduced in the subsection above the context of the German nineteenth century. An unusual conjunction of multiple events had seen the German Reich inventing its national community, while at the same catching up industrially with other competing European nations and eventually joining the scramble for Africa. The rural exodus of workforce from the eastern, agricultural provinces to the burgeoning western industrial centers has created a situation of manpower shortage that landowners intended to fill. This shortage was soon known as the *Leutenot*. I argued that whereas the category of an audience is not unproblematic, there is need to break the singularity of the audience and account for the plurality of audiences in a securitization process. Theoretically, this differentiation can ultimately be included in the conceptualization of the 'empowering audience' that sustains the move of the securitizing actor. Considering the question of the *Leutenot*, it is possible to posit a plurality of 'audiences' in the question of migration securitization and highlight some of their vested interests. Accordingly, the first 'audience' is represented by the agricultural owners, at the search of affordable manpower that incidentally could be recruited from the Russian and Austrian-occupied Polish territories. They did not construe the migration as a threat to Prussian security. They were actually obfuscated and saw the migrants from the occupied territories as harmless people who came to Prussia to earn their bread and should not to be seen as security threats to the security of Prussia (Herbert, 2001, p. 16).

The second 'audience' are the nationalist Germans who the saw the acquisition of foreign workers from the occupied territories as potential agitators that were going to endanger the construction of the German identity and the stability of the Reich. Theirs were, one would assume, the apprehensions of the populist and racist ideologies of nationalism. But Anderson had suggested that in order to make sense of nationalism, one should not align it "with self-consciously held political ideologies, but with the large cultural systems that preceded it, out of which – as well as against which it came into being (Anderson, 2006, p. 12)." Accordingly, the 'self-consciously held political ideologies' of *Deutschtum*, 'German identity' in the novel German Reich should be read in conjunction with or against "cultural systems," that represented "taken-for granted frames of references (ibid.)." The emergence of the nation-state, Anderson argued, happened against the background of the decline of religions and dynasties as primordial frames of references. It was not only the demise of religion as a frame of reference that propelled the emergence of the nation-state. Sometimes the 'transition' took the form of a direct confrontation, or of a *Kulturkampf*. Bismarck feared that the adepts of Ultramontanism in the Reich, who weighted the political directives of the Pope more that of the political power of the nation-state would constitute a hindrance to the new secular, political sovereignty of the Reich. The chancellor attempted to crush the *Zentrum*, a political party with Ultramontanist leanings, in his *Kulturkampf* before cooperating with the party after 1878 (Görtemaker, 1989, pp. 274–275). In 1870, one year before the creation of the German Reich, the First Ecumenical Council of the Vatican under Pope Pius IX, had defined the dogma of Papal Infallibility. This prompted the chancellor to demand from the 'political Catholics' an undivided and total recognition of the political authority of the Reich within its borders (ibid., pp. 276–277). The nation-state in the German Reich did not grow from a chronological superseding of an assumed decline of a religious, and moral power, but emerged from confrontations and compromises between national, monarchic authority and supranational, Papist moral and political authority. As for the dynastic community, Anderson had already pointed to the fact that "many dynasts had for some time been reaching for a 'national' cachet as the old Principle of Legitimacy withered silently. While the armies of Frederick the Great (r. 1740–1786) were heavily staffed by 'foreigners,' those of his great-nephew Friedrich Wilhelm (r. 1797–1840) were, as a result of Scharnhorst's, Gneisenau's and Clausewitz's spectacular reforms, exclusively 'national-Prussian'(Anderson, 2006, p. 22)." To summarize and insert the digression above into the securitization discourse of the *Leutenot*, the 'second audience' identified above was recapitulating the conflicts between religious authority and modern concept of national sovereignty as well as early efforts to define a 'national people' that accompanied the emergence and the consolidation of the nation-state in the nineteenth century. This 'second audience' of anti-immigrant nationalists could eventually, in the framework of securitization theory, be seen as the 'empowering audience.' For Balzacq, the empowering audience must satisfy the following criteria: (a) direct causal connection with the securitization issue, (b) ability to enable the securitizing actor to adopt measures in order to tackle the threat. In sum, securitization is satisfied by the acceptance of the empowering audience of a securitizing move (2011b, pp. 8–9). Positing a 'direct causal connection,' as Balzacq suggests, can prove a tricky endeavor. As the discussion of the event in Chapter 1 has shown, causation, especially direct causation is a contested philosophical category to deal with. It demands an explication of time, space categories to establish a relation between two 'events' or 'entities.' Both analytical and continental traditions tend to subscribe to variants of compositional or relational dependence to establish a causal or deterministic link or introduce an actor that sets the foyer of disparate and multiple elements within an evental site in motion. The background of the nationalist endeavors, the *Kulturkampf* (s) against Papal authority and internationalist labor movements are an in a compositional dependence with the securitization move that can be a deterministic outcome of the arrangement of these elements. But there seems to be further fault-lines in the relational dependence between the securitizing actor and the empowering audience. Balzacq seems to posit the securitization actor as the source, the initiator of a securitizing discourse that is ultimately validated by an audience that, from the top of the situation, performs the securitization move. This view would be valid if applied to the *Leutenot*, as the historical account by Herbert, for example would suggest. But there are no contraindications to positing a bottom-up approach to securitization in which the securitizing actor opportunistically intervenes in a security discourse brought into circulation by an audience and enacts policies in order to affirm their legitimacy.

The second assumption to pronounce the securitization of a discourse is the co-dependency of agency and context. The performative dimension of a discourse emanates from "a combination of textual meaning – knowledge of the concept acquired through language (written and spoken) – and cultural meaning – knowledge gained through previous interactions and current situations. Thus, the performative dimension of security rests between semantic regularity and contextual circumstances (Balzacq, 2012b, p. 11)." The *Schlesische Volkszeitung* was considered the mouthpiece of landowners and industrial entrepreneurs in Silesia who employed Polish workers from the dismantled and occupied territories. It deflated the idea commonly held in public opinion that Polish workers were displacing German citizens who were then forced to emigrate. In an excerpt that Herbert quoted, the newspaper, the *Schlesische Volkszeitung*, rhetorically asked whether the Slavs were rolling over Prussia like an avalanche (*lawinenenartig über Preußen*) so that the powerful *Prussia* (*das mächtige Preußen*) and the reunited German Reich were now shaken in its foundations (*in seinen Fundamenten erschüttert*). The newspaper's response to its own rhetorical question was to argue that the handful of Polish were after bread and means of subsistence that it was impossible for them to endanger the security of Prussia (*die Sicherheit Preußens gefährden*). Any claim to the contrary, was according to the paper, so absurd, that it could not earnestly be considered (Herbert, 2001, p. 16).[4] It follows, that the newspaper was trying to 'de-securitize' the question of Polish migrants by extracting it from the discourse of political agitation, terrorism and aimed ultimately to promote a laborist discourse on the migration of the Polish. For the securitizing actor, the discourse on the necessity of cheap and wilful Polish migration for agriculture was a Trojan horse into the sovereignty and security interests of the state. Such an actor emphasizes the priority of the political above the economical and to a certain extent – the humanitarian. Hence, for Bismarck, "we could not admit that the need for workers from the border regions is more important than the political and national dangers (*die staatlichen und politischen Gefahren*) inherent in the Polonization (*die Polonisierung*) of a large part of the Prussian population. In spite of all acknowledgment of agriculture as the most important of all trades, we hold it to be a lesser evil that specific regions suffer from a shortage of labor than that the state and its future suffer [from the consequences of an unchecked migration](quoted ibid., 2001, p. 17, my translation, emphasis added)."

This is certainly the appropriate point to introduce the third assumption on the *dispositif* and the structuring force of practices. 'Un-securitization' actors

---

4 The German idiom *'davon kann die Rede nicht sein,'* used by the newspaper or its variant *'davon kann keine Rede sein,'* both used in everyday language, can be translated into English as 'that is not what this is about,' or 'not to be in the offing,' or 'there is no talk of it' or 'there can be no talk of it' depending on the contexts of locution. It does not simply mean – as in the confines of the semantic- the demarcation or exclusion of a topic from questions that are not in a direct relational dependence to it. Pragmatically, the grammatical composition of the idiom negates ultimate the possibility of speech *'die Rede.'* 'Davon' is the pronominal adverb set up from 'da-' and the preposition 'von,' plus the modal verb of possibility 'können' conjugated in the third (in)person (al)singular (the pronominal es), the noun substantive *'die Rede,'* and the copula *'sein.'* The pronominal adverb 'davon' perform here an anaphoric function, establishing a back reference between a subject matter previously evoked and a present issue. In the newspaper's excerpt (See Herbert, 2001, p. 16), 'davon' refers to the construction of the Polish migrants as a security threat. The noun substantive *'die Rede'* can mean 'talk,' 'speech,' or 'discourse.' Thus to use the idiom *'davon kann keine (nicht die) Rede sein'* is not simply to argue that a particular conversational contribution is off-topic but to exclude it altogether from the realm of 'speech,' and discourse.

and securitization actors compete in a contested field, which "consists of practices which instantiate intersubjective understandings and which are framed by tools and the habitus inherited from different social fields. The *dispositif* connects different practices (Balzacq, 2011b, p. 15)." A securitization intervention is determined by the intersubjective contentions and arbitrations where the power relation more often than not tips in favor of the securitization actor. The securitization actor empowered by an audience is simultaneously alienating parts of the wider audience. The securitization is the calculus of the opportunity costs of defeating un-securitization moves. Bismarck's refusal to view migration as a purely economic or humanitarian issue and his regulative interventions caused some protests from the agricultural employers, which largely remained without major political consequences for him. Herbert suggested that the agrarians did not withdraw their political support to the Chancellor following his move to securitize the Polish migration to the eastern provinces. He locates the reasons thereof in the relative low number of Polish migrants that were actually recruited and which did not cause a critical revenue loss for the farmers.[5] The second reason was that prior to the industrialization and the growth of the industrial centers in the Ruhr area and the rural exodus it caused, the eastern agricultural provinces were facing an overabundant offer of manpower. In 1886, the conjectural phase in the agricultural employment numbers, did not offer solid grounds to vehemently oppose Bismarck's anti-immigrant policies (Herbert, 2001, p. 17). The securitization move is essentially a regulatory move. In Balzacq's conceptualization, the "regulatory tools seek to 'normalize' the behavior of target individuals (e.g., policy regulation, constitution, etc.). Policy instruments of this sort thus aim to influence the behaviors of social actors by permitting certain practices to reduce the perceived threat; by prohibiting some types of political activities which are transformed into a menace; by promoting certain perceptions of threat – e.g. since 2002 almost all of the documents on illegal migration and asylum (in Western countries) have a strong connection to terrorism (Balzacq and Carrera 2005; Balzacq et al. 2006). (Quoted in Balzacq, 2011, p. 17)." Bismarck set in motion so-called *Ausweisungsverordungen,* deportation decrees between 1885 and 1891 to come to term with his perceived dangers of migration. Under them, all non-naturalized Polish in the four eastern Prussian provinces, who numbered

---

5   Herbert does not provide statistics on the number of Polish workers employed in the eastern agrarian provinces. Between 1871 and 1910, the number of foreigners in the German Reich increased from about 206,000 at the founding of the empire (0.5% of the total population) to 1, 259 million in 1910 (1.9%) (2001, p. 25).

ABBREVIATED HISTORY OF GERMANY'S MIGRATION DISCOURSES 59

around 40,000, a third of them Jews, were to be deported. New immigration was prohibited and Polish married to German wives were to be expelled together with their spouses (Herbert, 2001, p. 17).

A securitization gesture that one-sidedly intervenes in an intersubjective security dilemma cannot be a sustainable course of action since it neglects the concerns of some audiences. Bismarck's securitization did not address the interests of the agrarians and the demand for cheap labor grew. There was, as Herbert noted, nothing left but to reopen the closed borders and give the Russian-Polish and Galician workers access to the Prussian farms again (ibid., 2001, p. 21). In November and December 1890, new decrees that purported to negotiate and unify the economic and security interests came into being. Thereafter, for a period of three years, Polish workers from Russia and Galicia were admitted to the agricultural and industrial estates of the Prussian eastern provinces. However, this was only valid for the unmarried, in order to prevent the sedentarization of families. Above all, however, this approval was limited to the period from 1 April to 15 November and by introducing a waiting period, according to which the Polish workers had to leave Prussia after the end of the winter season, the anti-Polish *Abwehrpolitik* 'defense policy' also catered to the need of the eastern provinces (ibid., p. 22).

3 Weber and the Empowerment of Nationalistic Audiences

There is a comment in Anderson's *Imagined Communities* on the paradox between "the 'political' power of nationalisms versus their philosophical poverty and even incoherence. In other words, unlike most other *isms*, nationalism has never produced its own grand thinkers: Hobbeses, Tocquevilles, Marxes, or *Webers* (Anderson, 2006, p. 5, emphasis added)." But there is a sub-paradox to Anderson's paradox, that even if national*ism(s)*don't produce top-notch thinkers on their own, they nonetheless excel at recuperation, subversion, and co-option of grand thinkers. Aditionnally, some 'grand thinkers' – that would not necessarily identify themselves as utterly nationalistic – seemed to have underestimated the implications of their theoretical gestures and political interventions for militant nationalistic agendas. In both cases, nationalists develop subtle and direct ways to compensate the philosophical poverty and emptiness Anderson highlighted at the expense of naïve thinkers. But how did Anderson come to think that Weber was not a grand thinker of 'nationalism.' Maybe Anderson never got acquainted with the writings of Mommsen in the 1980s who "exposed a side of Weber little known until then – a figure whose political ideas epitomize the illiberal nationalism of Wilhelmine Germany (Kim, 2004, p. 8)."

To be sure, the point here is not to explain paradoxical notions of nation and nationalism or rescue Weber from his critics. Weber has had ambivalent encounters with the non-German and the non-Western to justify the postcolonial flagellation he is sometimes submitted to (see for example Boatcă, 2013, p. 57). I would like to spare Weber another flagellation and instead look at him from the perspective of securitization theory. The social scientific work, the partisan publications, and speeches of Weber on the Polish questions are relevant to understanding the securitization of migration in the German Reich in the end of the nineteenth century. As such and for this subsection, we would like to revisit Weber's take on the *Leutenot* and identify the ambivalent points that were recuperated by nationalist xenophobic propaganda far beyond the controversies in postcolonial theory about the excluding gestures in Weber's and his belief in the superiority of the German model or 'race.'[6]

There is – considering securitizing discourse – a need to locate the role of the intellectual(s) in the production of securitizing discourse. Since Foucault and Said's Orientalism, social scientific knowledge cannot be treated as unproblematic, neutral knowledge, but needs to be read in the political contexts of their emergence, and the hidden (imperialistic or nationalistic) agendas they overtly or covertly sustain. But it is not the orientalist or postcolonial attack of Weber that can yield novel insights into early proto-securitization of migration. It is the interrogation of the impact of Weber's intellectual output on migration in the debate on Polish migration and the extent to which they provided the intellectual legitimacy for anti-immigrant call for radical anti-migration

---

6 Weber's liberal apologists such as Kim have lamented that the reception of Weber's social and political theory has been conditioned by an exclusive attention to his partisan journalism and public speeches. Kim then pleaded to incorporate Weber's theoretical contributions to assessing his legacy. But Kim has in mind the seminal work by Mommsen who posited that Weber's two "icons," politics and scholarship should be conjointly read and not treated as separate. He argued for instance for the incorporation of Weber's comparative sociology of religion in the analysis of his treatment of the non-Europeans and to analyze Weber's "sociological concepts of bureaucracy, charisma, and nation" within Weber's scholarship in general. Kim does not deny Mommsen's claim that in Weber's political value system, expediency "was measured by serviceability to the enhancement of German national power. National imperialism was the ultimate political value Weber subscribed to consistently throughout his career, and all other values and institutional commitments were subject to it [...]. Weber shifted the focus in his proposal for the German political reform from a liberal parliamentarianism to a charismatic Caesarism. The new focus, if not its inevitable outcome, falls within the parameters of Weber's political thought, which were delimited by the abandonment of liberal modernity and sanctification of irrational nationalism. (Quoted in Kim, 2004, p. 10)."

policies. As such, I consider two contributions by Weber, his 1893 Speech *Die ländliche Arbeitsverfassung* (The Condition of Rural Labor) and his 1894 essay *Entwickelungstendenzen in der Lage der ostelbischen Landarbeiter* (Developmental Trends in the Situation of the East Elbian Farm Workers) as important to reconstruct his main arguments on the Polish question. Most of Weber's work is not only at the interface between politics and academia, but between social 'scientific' knowledge and policy-making. And at a time where academics (IR scholars for instance) complain about the irrelevance of their sub-field to (foreign) policy makers,[7] Weber's paper would certainly have qualified as policy-relevant by modern standards. It apparently does not use abstruse jargon, impenetrable mathematical models and could certainly speak truth to power. His essay is based on collected data and has clear policy recommendations. But Weber's case also shows that policy-relevant research can be entrapped in unacknowledged and unquestioned ideological allegiances that can overshadow the most brilliant scholarship.

Weber's analysis of the agrarian sector in Prussia arguably contains brilliant insights. At the onset of his *Entwickelungstendenzen*, Weber identified the organization of work in the agricultural sector as the biggest challenge for large farming estates in modern Prussia. He noted that the fluctuating labor demands were met by two categories of workers: permanent and seasonal workers. But Weber was not introducing in a new typology of workforce. He claimed he used the prevailing distinction between permanent and seasonal workers in those days and builds his take on this duality. Permanent workers were local Germans, contractually bound to and usually living on the estate. The seasonal workers were mostly paid in money and regularly brought from 'outside' as 'foreign' workers and then kicked out (*abgestoßen*) when they were no more needed (Weber, 1988 [1894], p. 447).[8] The local German workers are in Weber's

---

7   Nye had complained in an article in the *Washington Post* titled *Scholars on the Sidelines* that "scholars are paying less attention to questions about how their work relates to the policy world, and in many departments a focus on policy can hurt one's career. Advancement comes faster for those who develop mathematical models, new methodologies or theories expressed in jargon that is unintelligible to policymakers (2009)." For a discussion of Nye and the replies to his original article, see Zoungrana, 2017, pp. 55–56.

8   The employment of the Polish in the Prussian agricultural sector can be seen as an early illustration of the labor market segmentation. Bauder traces the origin of the theory in Marx's distinction between variable capital and constant capital. Labor was in Marx's equation, as Bauder expounded, a 'variable capital' while the 'means of production' represented constant capital. Labor was deemed a variable because workers' employment depended on economic conjunctures (See Bauder, 2006, pp. 19–20). Applied to the Prussian agricultural sector, the division between primary and secondary segments takes an additional ethnic touch. In the developing industrial estates, most German locals were mostly employed in the primary

imaginary, situated on a higher level of cultural sophistication than their 'foreign' counterparts, better fit to survive the rudest conditions of rural life. This distinction was so natural for Weber that he did not seem to be utterly scandalized by the differences in treatment between local and foreign workers, their diverging housing conditions, and the underlying exploitation by unaccountable agrarian magnates. A further and less obfuscating diagnosis operated by Weber is the paradox in modern agricultural practice in the relation between workforce and new agricultural technologies. The introduction of mechanical processes and machines did not reduce the demand for human labor force in agriculture (or industry) as it was anticipated. For Weber, it lead on the contrary, to a shift within the structure of the workforce: the reduction of permanent workers (i.e. Germans), and the increase in the demand of temporary workforce (i.e. foreigners) (ibid., p. 496). One gets the sense, reading Weber here that the nascent agrarian capitalism had already discovered a proto-form of flexible labor regime where labor was simultaneously desirable and disposable, and the Poles were willful servants to this regime.

Weber lamented the lift of the Polish ban (*Polensperre*) in 1890, a policy that deported Poles from the eastern provinces and banished further Polish immigration: a radical policy that the Reich ultimately repelled and replaced by a stringent *dispositif* of multiple management and control tools for migrants as highlighted in the subsection above. I argued earlier that a unilateral securitizing move in a situation of competing interests was most likely to be unsustainable. The deportation of Poles, the travel ban clashed with the interests of the magnates who overturned the policy. Weber would have wished for the travel ban to be maintained because its lifting brought a crossing to the East, namely Saxony (the so-called *Sachsengängerei*) not only of Poles but Russian Poles and Galicians who were in his eyes seen as potential agitators and threats to the stability of the nation-state. Weber estimated the number of 'these foreign nomads' as he calls them, in the four border provinces at about 30,000 a year. The evocation of this number seems rather to serve alarmist purposes and conjure up a demographic threat. Weber seems to equate the lifting of the travel ban to a deregulation of migration to the eastern provinces, which simply was not the case. Weber's national preference leads him to divest the Polish migrants of any positive qualities. Weber ascribed the agrarians' predilection for Poles on the agrarian estates to their purported docility, their poor qualification and frugality as employees. For Weber, landowners enjoyed the

---

segment, lived on the estate and enjoyed extended privileges. The Polish seasonal workers on the contrary occupied the secondary segment, where labor was intensive, rudimentary and at times dangerous. Nonetheless, they were laid off during the winter months.

boundless power they exerted on the Poles: they could dispose of them at any time and nearly for any reason. They used the Poles as a weapon in the anticipated class war, directed against the awakening self-consciousness of the (German) workers (Weber, 1988 [1894], p. 501). But Weber did not expand on or substantiate the economic incentives that made foreign workers economically more attractive to landowners. Herbert had emphasized that the substantial cuts in social benefits, quasi inexistent work invalidity policies, insufficient health insurances, the cheap labor of migrant women and children are factors that influenced the decision of landowners to prefer male migrant workers (Herbert, 2001, p. 29). It would not be an exaggeration to state that Weber did not see the Poles as workers at all and the self-consciousness he describes was a category beyond the reach on the Poles. They are demographical, cultural, and political dangers to the German societies (Weber, 1988 [1894], p. 503). Weber's thesis that Poles displaced and replaced Germans in the eastern provinces because of their low cultural development, was quickly recuperated in the public discourse. Knoke, a disciple of Weber argued that "German workers were completely at the mercy of the Foreigners' assault/invasion (*vollständig schutzlos dem Ansturm der Ausländer preisgegeben*) [...] As the survey of the *Verein für Sozialpolitik* showed, sedentary workers were displaced by the foreign workers [...] German workers were not only threatened economically, but also physically by the foreigners' unhygienic lifestyle and ignorance of business operation rules (quoted in Herbert, 2001, p. 27, my translation)." It is difficult to overlook the militaristic vocabulary used on unarmed subjects. A depiction of migrants as an economic and biological hazard now sustained a nexus of social-scientific, nationalistic-tainted knowledge. The statistical data gathered by the *Verein for Sozialpolitik* were used to cement ideological prejudices. Knoke is not the only follower to heed Weber's call for the absolute exclusion of the Russian-Polish workers in the German Eastern province. Militant nationalistic groups soon brought into circulation the slogan 'Germany to the Germans' (*Deutschland den Deutschen*). Weber's message further resonated with Pan-Germans and colonial enthusiasts (ibid., p. 29).

Weber's 'self-proclaimed' apologist Kim argued that Weber's scholarship and partisan intellectual output were meant for two distinct yet overlapping audiences: scholars and bourgeois.[9] It is possible, to side with Weber's apologist

---

9   In Kim's words, "[Weber] first addressed his fellow scholars; at issue was the value-neutral pretension of the study of political economy. Using his earlier investigation of the East Elbian problem as an example, Weber pointed out that, in terms of the Darwinian law of adaptation and survival, the Polish displacement of German agrarian laborers in East Prussia was perfectly justifiable; the Poles simply proved to be a stronger "race" when it came to the competition for survival. From the perspective of allegedly value-neutral political economics, which

that Weber primarily sought to address these audiences. But it is equally valid to claim, considering Weber's treatment of the Polish question, that these were the relevant audiences to preach nationalistic messages to. Anderson noted that the "energetic activities of [...] professional intellectuals were central to the shaping of nineteenth-century European nationalisms (2006, p. 71)." The professional intellectuals are not only the army of philologists, grammarians who elevated vernaculars to standard national languages, thus paving the way to nationalism. It could also include sociologists, political scientists or the wider university and schools in general, whose progress "measures that of nationalism, just as schools and especially universities became its most conscious champions (quoted in Anderson, 2006, p. 71)."

4 Of C2, 3P, and Muddling through: Regulating Securitized Migration

Securitizing discourses produced three types of migration regulation policies in Germany. They are not chronologically neatly delineated. At times their properties may seem to overleap or repeat themselves even in the contemporary discussions about migration. The typology includes command-and-control (C2) policies, public-private-partnerships as well muddling-through approaches. C2-policies have mostly been favored by nationalistic, imperialistic and Nazi migration policy makers, but are also recurrent in contemporary assertions by hardliners of migration policy. One could thus roughly assert that the periods between 1885–1890/1 discussed above, the 1914–18 World War era, Nazi- Germany (1933–1945) reflect far-right parties' and anti-migration hardliners' wish for command-and-control approach to migration regulation.

Public- private-partnerships are a tacit or direct union of different stakeholders to regulate migration. In Wilhelmine Germany, between 1890 and 1914, a model of partnership between state, nationalistic groups, foreigners' recruitment agencies governed the regulation of migration. In the progressive migration regulation model of the Weimar Republic, workers' trade unions were included in the management of migration.

Muddling-through policies refer mainly to post-WWII migration policies and could be argued to reach to the present age. They are policies caught between the demons of the xenophobic past, the contingencies of economic

---

Weber identified with social Darwinism, political intervention into this economic problem on behalf of German *Kultur* could not be legitimated scientifically. Nor could it properly account for the motivation behind the emigration of the German population, since the reason was far from being dictated by the naturalistic law of survival (Kim, 2004, p. 145)."

conjunctures and world politics, international humanitarian duties, and demographic challenges. One of the major properties of these policies is their unsustainability. This steering approach used (in the past) economic incentives to encourage so-called guest-workers to return to their home countries. In the comtemporary era, it oscillates between the will to integrate aliens, and the deportation of asylum seekers, whose asylum claims have been rejected.

4.1 The Command-and-Control Approach to Migration Policy

In Wilhelmine Germany and following the portrayal of the Poles and other seasonal workers as threat to the Second Reich stability, a number of policies were enacted, to come to terms with the perceived security threat. With hindsight, it is possible to identify these policies as a case of a traditional approach of command-and-control (C2).

The concept of command and control (C2 or CAC) finds its origins in military defense practice. It is a theory of information flow, hierarchical chains of command, centralized decision-making process, and steered by a commander.[10] In regulation theories, c2 designates the ability of a government to impose standards and back them with criminal sanctions (Baldwin, Cave, and Lodge 2011, p. 106). It is opposed to regulation models that privilege economic incentive to nudge people into a desired behavior. In C2, the state is an ultimate (benevolent) observer and commander that influences the behavior of economic and societal actors through legislation.[11] The approach is currently discussed in environmental policy on questions of legal standards, benchmark and compliance control.[12] In an age of globalization, the presence of non-state actors has influenced the C2-capabilities of the state in policy-making. NGOs, for example, are not likely only to be the initiator of (environmental) policies, but the data collectors and compliance controllers of enacted legislation. From the point of view of the regulating state actor, C2 evokes action-taking, as

---

10   In defense practices, two main approaches to C2 compete. In so-called traditional approaches, the focus is, as Builder, Bankes, and Nordin argue, on information hardware; diagrams are indispensable for the C2 framework. The commander was arguably an idealized, well-informed decision-maker. Newer approaches, as the one by Builder, Bankes, and Nordin, focuses "not on the sufficiency of bandwidth, interoperability, information overload, and stocks, flows, filters, and transformers, but on the cognitive processes of the commander (Builder, Bankes, and Nordin, 1999, p. 4)."
11   In economics, the 'commander' is responsible for "the setting of standards within a rule, it often entails some kind of licensing process to screen entry to an activity, and may set out to control not merely the quality of a service or the manner of production but also the allocation of resources, products, or commodities and the prices charged to consumers or the profits made by enterprises (Baldwin, Cave, and Lodge 2011, pp. 106–107)."
12   See Hunter, Salzman, and Zaelke (2002); Holling and Meffe (1996).

caring for the security of the populace by condemning certain forms of behaviors (ibid., p. 107). But C2 has been attacked on the grounds that it is ultimately subject to capture, over-regulation, legalism, and enforcement deficits (ibid., pp. 108, 110).

In Wilhelmine Germany, the C2 approach to the perceived threat of Polish workers took legalist forms. The Prussian government, as Herbert recounted, overrode the economic interests of the agrarian magnates and issued a series of regulations to reduce the immigration from Polish workers through mass expulsions between 1885 and 1890 (2001, p. 17). Wertheimer noted that "[w]hile German laws granted aliens some protection, they also provided states with a means of driving them out [...]; German states had the right to expel aliens for engaging in criminal activities or for endangering "public interests" and "security" (1987, p. 60)." Through the legal provisions for alien expulsions, the Reich was intruding on the managerial decisions of the agrarian magnates that relied on the affordable labor of the migrants. One could wonder, why the German state responded so radically to the threat they perceived and hardly considered any other options. Were there no alternative courses of action to deal with 'criminal' and 'dangerous' foreigners? A possible answer to this question emerges from the legalism entrenched in C2-approaches to regulation. In the C2 framework, state actors tend to "respond to particular problems or tragedies with general, or 'across-the board,' rules and solutions. This gives the appearance of 'doing something about that sort of thing' (2011, p. 108)." It follows that C2-policies can "be too narrow or too broad in scope. They may, accordingly, fail to cover conduct that should be controlled, or else may constrain activity that should be unrestricted (ibid., p. 110)." The mass expulsion policies of Poles and other aliens deemed as "threats" to the stability of the empire backfired as they clashed with economic interests.

The early nineteenth century state policy on migration can be contrasted with contemporary analysis on neo-liberalism and state policy. As Bauder as noted, "[i]t would be erroneous to believe that state policies and practices respond blindly to national and international business interests. Rather, states seek to protect their own geopolitical interests, associated with foreign affairs, electoral politics, and other political concerns (Bauder, 2006, p. 25)." Bismarck's thrust against the agrarian landlords shows that politics is not systematically or directly subservient of economic interests, as the popular conception tends to suggest.

Following Castells, Reich among others, Bauder has argued that the segmentation of the labor market is a divide-and-rule strategy of capital to undermine the welfare state and increase the competition between workers. Furthermore, he argued, that applied to immigration policies, "temporary labor migration programs, and the recruitment of international migrants into the secondary labor market segment can be perceived as divisive strategies, driving a wedge between the unity of workers (ibid., p. 21)." During the consolidation of the political power of the Reich, it was not so much capital that intended to undermine the unity of laborers through a segmentation of the labor market than politics itself. It was Bismarck, who, having tried vainly to crush the workers' party through police force ultimately introduced welfare policies to alienate the workers form the workers' union. Writing on Bismarck and social legislation, Görtemaker noticed that Bismarck was smart enough to understand that the workers' problem[13] could not be solved by police repression alone. He therefore sought to destroy the workers' party and at the same time to win over the workers to the state through a far-sighted and exemplary social policy, a positive counterpart to his struggle for social democracy (1989, p. 293).

The migration policy during World War One was another instance of C2 approach to migration. It represented a shift away from a competing model of multi-stakeholder approach to migration regulation.[14] The shift was

---

13   What Görtemaker terms the '*Arbeiterfrage* [workers' problem]' (of Bismarck) has its genealogy in the founding of the Social Democratic Labor Party at the Eisenach Congress in 1869 and its renaming as *Sozialdemokratische Arbeiterpartei Deutschlands* [Social Democratic Workers Party of Germany] in 1870. Founding members August Bebel and Wilhelm Liebknecht had called for a national political organization of the German working class with a corresponding, adequate power base. But the party was no particular political risk, as Görtemaker commented. But for Bismarck, the solution of the labor question could not be left to a party. Furthermore, he had already negotiated in 1863/64 with Lassalle the introduction of universal suffrage and state welfare, in order to win the Socialists for a social kingship and at the same time to dissuade them from the idea of a social-liberal coalition. Bismarck sensed that with the increasing industrialization, the emergence of a powerful labor party would be unavoidable, unless counteracted by social reforms from above and at least slowing down their growth. The Gothaer program, like the Einsenacher program before it, was completely revolutionary. A free state and a socialist society were called for, as well as the elimination of all social and political inequality. After an assassination attempt on May 11, 1878, Bismarck finally decided that the time had come to crack down on the Social Democrats. A plumber named Hödel had fired revolver gunfire at Wilhelm on the *Unter den Linden* street in Berlin, but without hitting him. This was the trigger for Bismarck to start persecuting the social democrats (Görtemaker, 1989, p. 286).

14   Before the outbreak of the war, Germany was using a public-private partnership that emphasized a circular mobility of the imported workforces. This pre-war migration model was based on the distribution of risks and dangers between the major stakeholders. For the Reich, it was important to avoid the permanent settlement of migrants and consolidate its Germanness – that excluded much needed but undesired foreigners- of its political order. The allocation of fixed-term visa tied with the obligation to return gave the political the assurance that imported workers would not settle in the country.

exemplified in the lifting of the obligation to return (to their home country) imposed on aliens and instead keep them on German soil for the duration of the war. As such, 300,000 Russian-Polish workers were barred from returning to their homes and factually forced to work in Germany. This has prompted Herbert to speak of a qualitatively new element in German migration policy (2001, p. 87). Herbert opposes two views on the forced labor of aliens during WWI: forced labor as an authoritarian solution to the labor problem and the stage-approach to migration policy. According to the first approach, which Herbert attributes to historians such as Friedrich Zunkel, forced labor translated the prioritization by the government of the military and economic necessities of the war at the expense of the rights and freedom of the seasonal workers. The second approach, which Herbert calls Marxist, sees forced labor as a gradual change in migration policy.[15] For this strand of research, the decision for forced labor was taken before the break of the war but could not be enforced due to safeguards and limits to the exploitation of the foreigners (ibid.). As Wertheimer had noticed, Prussia did guarantee their aliens and the vexations even if ultimately the government could expel foreigners it deemed dangerous (1987, pp. 16–17). But it is equally plausible that the reason for forced labor was foremost strategic. It did not make much military sense to repatriate able-bodied workers while attacking their homeland. Accordingly, they were given the status of civilian prisoners, were not allowed to change employers, leave their employment place or return to their homeland (Herbert, 2001, p. 92).

---

15 Herbert has in mind researchers like Elsner and Lehmann who looked at German immigration policies since the constitution of the Reich in 1871 throughout to the twentieth century through the lens of imperialism. Elsner and Lehmann followed Lenin's 1913 article on capitalism and labor immigration to represent Germany as an imperialist country. Lenin had referred above all to the United States, which since the nineteenth century was at the forefront of those countries that were importing large numbers of workers, depriving the world of the most energetic, able-bodied workers, At the same time he (Lenin) emphasized Germany, which gave its own workers, transformed into a country importing labor (1988, p. 5). For them, since the beginning of its existence, German imperialism has sought to recruit workers abroad and in their home country or in Germany. The extent of employment of foreigners as well as the forms and methods of foreigners' policy changed over time. They depended, among other things, on the given economic and political and political situation, on the strength of the working class and on the possibility given to the ruling class (ibid., p. 6). Elsner and Lehmann's main thrust is to show that -contrary to some bourgeois authors- as they claim without naming them, who only want to attribute the employment of foreigners in imperialist countries to the shortage of labor, the ruling class did not simply go for labor. Theirs was a parasitic exploitation of lesser-developed countries made possible by the status of legal bareness of the imported migrants (ibid. p. 8).

Amidst this divergence of views, there seems to be a consensus to characterize the prohibition towards Polish workers to return to their home countries as a case of forced labor. For Herbert himself, paying attention to the issue of forced labor yields insights about connecting factors and elements of continuity regarding pre-war foreigner policy and the predispositions of foreign policy makers and the German society as a whole. The experiences that were made during the First World War with foreigner employment and forced labor constituted the blueprint for the National Socialist foreigners' policy in the Second World War (ibid.). It is estimated that between 1914 and 1918, about 2.5 million POWs fell into the hands of the warring German Reich – a huge reservoir of labor in the face of extraordinary labor shortages –, although their employment opportunities were limited by the Hague Convention to areas not directly related to the war industry (ibid., p. 88). They were accordingly mostly employed in the private industry. But this was not enough to make for the labor demands of the German economy, also following the departure of Austrians and Italians that were primordially employed in the industrial sector. The Third Reich recurred to the recruitment of Eastern Jewish workers to fill the vacancies left by the departed Austrian and Italian workers and thus sustain the war economy (ibid., p. 99).

To be sure, and as Herbert recounts, in the 1880s, Eastern European Jews who were subjected to arbitrary oppression by the Czarist authorities and multiple pogroms, chose to migrate to more liberal Western countries, preferably to the US. It is estimated that more than 3.5 million Jews immigrated mostly to the United States between the 1880s and 1930s. As a rule, the emigrants' route passed through the German overseas ports; and the transit migration in Prussia had already prompted an agitation of anti-Semitic formations directed against Eastern Jews that were considered strange and sinister as well as the suspicion of the Prussian authorities (ibid., p. 99). Herbert estimated that in total, some 30,000 Eastern Jewish workers came to Germany in the course of the war, voluntarily or forced. At the end of the war, therefore, about 100,000 Eastern Jews lived in Germany, around 80,000 of them as workers (ibid., p. 102). Jewish-Polish workers were viewed in the German population as particularly suitable carriers and 'disseminators' of typhoid and other infectious diseases. The characterization of Jews as propagators of epidemics, especially typhoid, should henceforth become an integral part of anti-Semitic agitation during the second world war. It also served to legitimate the deportation and the murder of the Jewish population of Eastern Europe (ibid., p. 102).

Altogether, forced labor was a relatively expensive affair for industrial entrepreneurs. Since the foreigners were at least nominally paid the same salary as the German workers (in order to prevent the dismissal of Germans and their replacement by foreigners), the costs of recruitment, transportation, accommodation, security personnel, increased considerably (ibid., p. 116). But whether or not one decides to look at forced labor from the viewpoint of authoritarian economic policies or imperialism, both perspectives would fit a C2-approach to migration regulation. Indeed imperialist and authoritarian economics overlap. In C2-approaches, the sovereign is factually endowed with the right to expel or to keep the alien according to their whims or economic demands. The alien is a workforce supplement, usable and disposable at the same time.

In World War II, Germany experienced another case of C2-approach to migration. The Third Reich had already sensed a shortage in workers' manpower in the war economy and undertook to conclude agreements with Italy and some other states for labor exchange. By the mid-1939, agriculture employed about 37,000 Italians, 15,000 Yugoslavs, 12,000 Hungarians, 5,000 Bulgarians, and 4,000 Dutchmen. Already here, however, there were also considerable thoughts on security concerns on the German side (Herbert, 2001, p. 125). Nazi-Germany recourse to aliens to gain additional workforce was primarily to preserve the exclusion of women from power. Although high officers of the Economic and Armament Office were convinced that women can be skillful and competent factory workers (just as men), the regime refrained from employing women because such a policy would have contradicted the anti-feminist ideology of Nazism which mainly limited women to procreation and child-reading (ibid., p. 130). But the employment of foreigners, especially in agriculture, where they were particularly urgently needed, had the 'ideological' disadvantage that German food was being produced by strangers (ibid, p. 131), a prospect that certainly did not please the Nazis. It may also be that the employment of women would have led to significant wage increases for female workers, which for economic and ideological reasons could also not be desired by the regime (ibid., p. 130). Ultimately, the recourse to foreign labor was the easiest way to make cheap labor available to German companies for war plans.[16] After Nazi Germany invaded Poland, it issued orders in 1940 to transport nearly one million workers to work in the factories and agrarian estates. At least 50% of the imported workers had to be women (ibid., p. 132). Foreign

---

16 It is difficult to overlook the parallels between this Nazi policy and Bourdieu's juxtaposition of "the deliberate creation of a "global reserve army of labor" through international neoliberal policies (Bauder, 2006, p. 5)." Business elites in neoliberal economies tended to privilege an emigration composed of disposable, temporary, single workers with no families and no social protection (like the French sans papiers) ideally suited to providing the overworked executives in the dominant economy with the cheap and largely feminine services they need (ibid, p. 40).

migrants were subject to arbitrary killings in the last days of the Third Reich (ibid., p. 181).

Can one conclude that C2-approach to migration is *passé* since the regimes that applied them have receded in history? As an overall statist approach to migration, C2-approach seems to be a relic of a distant past.

But as far-right inclined individuals, political parties seem to call for a hardliner approach to migration regulation, one could advance that command-and-control phantasies of migration policies may have not died.

The post-WWII German history is replete with such phantasies, which at times masqueraded as scientific knowledge. For example, the Heidelberg Manifesto of June 17, 1981 reconnected to the *Volkish* theories of the 1920s and 1940s to portray migration not only as a political threat but also a threat of social and cultural alienation. It conceived of cultures as biologically and cybernatically closed systems passed on genetically and by traditions (Herbert, 2001, p. 239). There is here a seeming argument of an incommensurability of cultural systems used to claim a cultural and racial segregation. It did not deny that the Muslim Turkish migrants have a 'culture.' It argued instead that so-called Muslim and migrants' culture in general are intrinsically different from Europe's. Behavioral scientist Irenäus Eibl-Eibesfeldt introduced a notion of competition between cultures where procreation was the comparative advantage of the so-called 'ethnic cultures.' Therefore, he concluded, the higher birth rate of foreigners in the long run will inevitably lead to the downfall of the Germans. Eibl-Eibesfeldt built stringent dichotomies between homogenized cultures, German culture (the here) and the ethic cultures (there). The binary differences encompass religious differential lines (Christians vs. Muslims), gender (emancipation vs. women's submission), and social dynamics (decadence of the family model vs. tight family order). Pointing out to the possibility of biological and cultural repression does not ultimately entail racism in Eibl-Eibesfeldt's self-reflection, especially if he is keen enough to point to the fact that Muslim migrants were 'first' invited just as Poles in the nineteenth century. For him, the difference between the Koslowskis, Miloczyks and Zylinskis on the one hand and the Turkish migrants on the other hand was merely that the Poles came from the same European culture as their German working colleagues. In the true sense, the only inhibiting factor to their integration was language. Eibl-Eibesfeldt is oblivious of the securitization discourse that accompanied the 'importation' of Polish workers, the stringent C2-regulation regime imposed on them that ultimately ended in forced labor during WWI. The responsibility for the failed integration lies on the part of the migrant that were not willing to settle 'here' permanently and tacitly refused to mingle with the locals. Eibl-Eibesfeldt's conclusion was that, whoever still believes that Turks can live with us like Germans, forgets that Turks are only human; a people with a different culture (Quoted in ibid., pp. 240, 259). Ultimately, in the 1980s, political discourse discovered culture. Minister of Labor Zimmermann emphasized in particular the cultural difference between Italians, who faced had comparatively few access restrictions to Germany, and Turks: "The Turks come from a different culture and on a different scale. It makes a huge difference whether I have here 1.7 million Muslims in front of me, who in reality do not want to become German citizens, but enter with the recognizable will to earn money here and then go back again (quoted in ibid., p. 253)." In a Cologne appeal against a misanthropic foreigners policy, many intellectuals and politicians turned against the foreign policy measures of the Kohl government in general and especially against luring out or pushing out foreigners with the help of the return bonuses (ibid., p. 254).

The portrayal of culture as a closed system, a kind of prison from which the individual cannot free themselves, the neglect of the plurality of Islam and Islamic cultures, were recurrent assumptions not only in the discourse of migration deniers like Eibl-Eibesfeldt. It surprisingly also featured in progressive defenses of the migrants. The reason was that since the early 80s, Islam was increasingly perceived as a political threat after the revolution in Iran. Scholl-Latour for example presented the Turks as doubly alienated: "The Turks living in Germany are deprived by the anti-religious military dictatorship in Ankara, but here they feel that they have broken from an underdeveloped society into a world of soulless consumption, many of them are now anxious to find the roots of their identity, self-affirmation in the glorification of Islam, which was denied them in the foreign, often hostile environment (quoted in ibid., p. 260, my translation)."

4.2 *3P Approach to Migration Regulation*

I term 3P-approaches to migration approaches that show parallels with a public private partnership (3P) cooperation model between the state and non-state actors for the provision of certain services. In the 3P approach, a multiplicity of actors tacitly or directly team up around the state to design migration policy regulation. To be sure, my conception of the 3P approach to migration regulation is not far from the key tenets of the regulation school. As Bauder noted, looking at labor, a regulation-school perspective "entails rejecting the notion that labor is a pure commodity and the myth that labor markets self-regulate through the wage mechanism (2006, p. 16)." He reintroduces 'social regulation' through a re-reading of Marx, Marshall, Polanyi and others. Bauder further argues, "that social practices and institutions, including the state, connect people to the labor market, assign workers to occupations, manage labor at the workplace, and create the conditions for the reproduction of labor. Social processes and institutions regulate labor markets, not as a mere fine-tuning exercise to an otherwise self-regulating market but in a fundamental and constitutive manner (ibid.)."

When Bismarck's migration policy was repelled under the pressure of agrarian magnates, a new model of migration regulation emerged. Patriotic circles, agrarian employers and the Prussian state conjoined their expertise(s) to simultaneously provide agricultural workforce, guarantee state security and satisfy local nonmigrant workers. Michael Piore's linkage of segmentation to labor migration makes sense within a 3P-approach to migration and/or labor regulation. For him, "migrants are recruits in the *labor reserve army*. The flow of migrants into the cyclical, secondary segment of the labor market helps secure the jobs of nonmigrants [i.e. local Germans] in the primary sector. Thus, migration enables the nonmigrant population to escape being used as expendable labor in the secondary labor market. The use of migrants as secondary labor indeed provides "a reason why [nonmigrant] workers, as well as their employers, might have an interest in the continuation of the migration process (quoted in Bauder, 2006, p. 20, emphasis and square brackets added)." Foreign workers were the employment safeguard for the local workforce.

The 3P model is also a model of the distribution of risks: the risk of shortage of manpower for the agricultural sector, the perceived foreign policy risk and the nationalistic interests of the bourgeoisie. For the state, aliens constituted a risk for the construction of a homogenous nation. The aliens were perceived as uncultured, biological hazards who were fundamentally inferior to the Germans.

Two frameworks compete here to make sense of the construction of risk in the management of aliens in Wilhelmine Germany. The first framework is Beck's conceptualization of risk in the context of 'second modernity.' For Beck, "[t]he discourse of risk begins where trust in our security and belief in progress end. It ceases to apply when the potential catastrophe actually occurs. The concept of risk thus characterizes a peculiar, intermediary state between security and destruction, where the perception of threatening risk determines thought and action (2006, p. 63). In Beck's, risk is better understood constructively and one should survey its contextual materializations (ibid., p. 64). His constructivist-realist approach to risk locates risks in the middle ground between factual statement and value claims or conflate both in a materialization of risk (ibid., p. 65). Beck further argued that modernity is a project of social and technological control by the nation state and the risks are the unintended consequences of this political and sociological project of the nation-state (ibid., p. 67). There are two fault lines when one empirically contrasts the conjunction of risks in the Reich in 1890s. First, there was the perceived, constructed political risk associated with the presence of aliens on the German territory. But there was another risk, more factual, mathematical, that stated a risk of economic downturn in the agricultural output if the import of cheap labor was not guaranteed. An alternative framework to make sense of risk in the nation-state is through a sociology of risk as derived from the governmentality approach of Foucault. Governmentality emerged from the sixteenth century onwards in Europe, when governments developed and introduced multiple techniques for economic regulation, measures of public order, and general rules of hygiene to enhance the life of their citizens (Foucault, 1984, p. 278). Armies of experts, scientists designed the economic management tools "to organize around them [the citizens] an apparatus which will ensure not only their subjection but the constant increase of their utility (ibid., p. 279)." Arguably, Wilhelmine Germany had internalized most of the governmentality techniques and applied them both to the domestic population as well as the foreigners. There was, as I have noted above, a reluctance in enforcing safety rules for alien workers, the control of children's labor or insurance policy. As such governmentality in Wilhelmine Germany was (to state the least) relatively discriminative. The alien populations were seen as a danger, a political risk by the Prussian government. Their absence was a risk to the nascent liberal economic order. One is yet to make sense of the role of the non-governmental actors, patriotic groups in helping the state deal with the 'dangers' or risks the Poles and other aliens represented (without paying great attention to the potential differences between the two concepts as of now). I argue that one has to posit a public-private partnership where these three afore-mentioned state and non-state actors share the risks involved both in the presence and absence of foreigners.

In Wilhelmine Germany, the economically advantageous sugar beet cultivation was labor intensive and depended on the import of cheap, foreign, willing manpower. There ensued a competition not only between statist interests and farmers but between farmers to acquire and maintain cheap labor force (Herbert, 2001, p. 18). Polish seasonal workers exploited the competition between the landowners to improve their social and economic conditions by offering their services to the highest-bidding employers or quitting unprofitable jobs (ibid., p. 32). The Prussian government feared that an unregulated system for the recruitment of foreign workers after the mass expulsions and the travel ban for Polish workers between 1885 and 1891 would potentially get out of control. As the same, it became clear that a unilateral C2-approach prohibiting the acquisition of alien workforce would damage the economic interests of its farmers and lead to a legitimacy loss. The novel approach to solve this dilemma was the centralization of the recruitment process of the migrants to curve the informal recruitments at the Prussian-Polish border regions. The commercial and labor contracts that were signed there were described in public opinion "as trade in human flesh and an unbearable cancer [*Handel mit Menschenfleisch und unerträglicher Krebsschaden*] (ibid., p. 33)."

There was apparently more to the 'trade in human flesh' than a simple metaphor. The recruitment of workers through agents was akin to slave auctions.[17] For the workers recruited through the *Centralstelle zur Beschaffung Deutscher Ansiedler und Feldarbeiter* [Central office for the procurement of German settlers and field workers], it was a situation of double deprivation. They could no more offer their services to (highest-bidding) employers of their choice and the signed contracts bound them with one employer for the duration of their stay, where they were housed in unhuman conditions and most likely to be subjected to physical ill-treatment by the employer or his officials (ibid., pp. 36, 40). The surveillance interests for aliens by the state curtailed the rights of the farm workers to change their employers (ibid., p. 43).

For the local workers, foreign workers did not represent competition but "a working class of the second degree" [*Arbeiterschicht zweiten Grades*] (ibid., p. 48), an "economic buffer, [...] a safety valve for the continuous employment of the locals" in times of crisis (ibid. p. 50). Restricted legal rights ensured that aliens were fired in negative economic conjunctures. Furthermore, discriminative application of safety policies, insufficient insurance coverage and poor unionist organization accounted for the precarious condition of the foreign workers (ibid., p. 50). Indeed, and drawing from Bauder, it is possible to conceptualize this labor force as unfree labor, a labor which provided "a low-cost, disciplined, and flexible foreign workforce in the secondary labor market (2006, p. 22)." The state for its part intensified its surveillance of the aliens through an extensive apparatus of policies (Wertheimer, 1987, pp. 16–17) and applied a very restrictive nationality that selectively nationalized some aliens, denied citizenship to other aliens with no criminal records and who resided in the Reich for a longer period of time (Herbert, 2001, p. 68).

---

17 Herbert quoted a testimony on how the recruitment market functioned at the Prussian border in Neuberun: "Beyond the Prussian border in Neuberun, many workers are now being held by these agents or subagents, and are mostly left in the lurch. Deprived of all means, ignorant of the official language and unable to avail themselves of any legal remedies, these people are placed under the control of other agents and are formally placed in a market that bears the lowest characteristics of a true human market. The workers are tested for their physical strength and stamina; the strongest and most resistant are hired by the farmers or agents appearing in Neuberun [...] the rest left in the market quite helplessly (2001, p. 34, my translation)."

The migration regulation in the Weimar Republic could also be qualified as a multi-stakeholder approach to migration regulation. The lost war, the rising of trade unions, unemployment and the 1929 crisis are factors that softened the C2 approach to migration regulation before and during WWI. For Marxist historians Elsner and Lehmann (1988, pp. 101, 105–106), the ruling circles in Germany had to take account of the changed balance of power between them and the working class after the lost world war. The state monopoly system reduced the number of employed foreign workers and modified its policy towards the foreigners. The social situation of the workers was improved in comparison to their condition in the pre-WWI area, not least because of the demands raised by the German workers' movement.[18] Policy makers sought to reduce Germany's dependency on labor importation and at the same time encourage the sedentarization of German agricultural workers through a process that was branded as inner colonization. For example, SPD leaders pursued a policy of domestic primacy. It used the November Revolution's recognition of collective bargaining and the lack of a naturalization law to reduce the employment of foreign workers during the massive post-war unemployment. As Elsner and Lehmann commented (ibid., p. 148), social reformists have campaigned for a more restrictive migration policy. These reformists saw the foreign workers as labor usurpers, wage dumpers, a threat to their working and living conditions rather than as mates of the same social class or co-proletarians. They focused on enforcing the primacy of Germans in the labor market, actively participated in the implementation of the licensing procedure, and the rationing of imported rural agricultural workers. Nonetheless, as Elsner and Lehmann positively emphasized, the reformists committed themselves to equal pay of the foreigners.

After WWII, the German Federal Labor Office, political parties such as the SPD and CDU, trade unions contributed to the design of migration policy and regulation. The Labor Office was keen to regulate the competition between the companies as the search for labor forces increased and began to manifest in

---

18 Elsner and Lehmann have identified two main currents in the labor movement that prevailed in the international and German labor movement. Since the pre-war period, class struggle played out in the relation of labor movements to the question of foreign migrants during the Weimar Republic. The two opposing basic positions, i.e. the class struggle and the conquest of political power by the proletariat, had expressed themselves in the different positions on the migrant workers' question (Elsner and Lehmann, 1988, p. 146). As such, the labor movement on the one hand spoke out against immigration and emigration bans, against expulsions; on the other hand, however, restrictions were endorsed, such as the right of the state to restrict or prohibit immigration in times of economic depression or to protect public health (ibid., p. 147).

wage concessions towards the employees. Their thrust for an external additional labor supply was meant to counteract this development. The political parties were concerned with a 'full-employment' of the locals before the recruitment of foreign labor force. The trade unions advocated that foreign workers were to be fairly treated in terms of employment, participation to collective wage bargaining, and social protection, in order to prevent (with regard to German workers) wage-absorbing effects (Herbert, 2001, p. 203). As such, when the German-Italian recruitment agreement was concluded in 1995 in Rome, these concerns have been largely taken into account. The recruited workers were guaranteed extensive rights: the payment by tariff for the duration of the contract, the provision of a suitable accommodation. Moreover, applications for family reunification should be considered when the applicant could provide a proof of adequate housing (ibid., pp. 203–204).

Seen from this perspective, the recruitment of foreign workers has a participative dimension that qualifies it to be considered as a model of concerted approach to migration regulation. But it also contains elements of an evolutionary approach to solving labor problems in Germany. Undoubtedly, the importation of foreign workers since the nineteenth century had created a path dependency to resolving the labor shortage in Germany. No radical or revolutionary approaches to the labor shortage problem has been extensively pursued or developed. This does not mean that there was no qualitative shift in migration policies. Indeed there is no point in comparing the authoritarian, nationalistic or imperialistic migration policies of Wilhelmine Germany or the Third Reich with the progressive migration policies of the Weimar Republic of post-War World II. Later, however, post-WWII migration policies evolved into muddling-through policies. In the next subsection, I expand on muddling-through migration policies.

4.3 *Muddling through – Policies in Post-WWII Germany*

Lindblom introduced the concept of 'muddling through' to denote incrementalism in policy-making. Policies are enacted not on a revolutionary basis, but rather on an evolutionary one, are constantly updated with the growth of information at the disposition of the policy-maker. It contradicted the illusion of rational decision-making and instead advanced the idea that policies happen in context of limited knowledge and foresight. Ultimately, 'muddling through,' is the 'science' of managing quasi-chaotic conditions. 'Muddling through' is at times the combination of multi-stakeholder approach to solve a labor force issue. At other times, it tends "to follow a trial and-error approach, evolving in a manner that benefits capital and production. Despite the complexity and ambiguity of migration and settlement processes, it is undeniable that international migration influences the manner in which economies and labor markets operate (Bauder, 2006, p. 15)."

Here I want to make use of the metaphor of 'muddling through' to make sense of migration policies in Post-WWII Germany beyond the participative elements I outlined in the subsection above. The regulation of migration was simultaneously caught between contingency and economic opportunism. There was no legal or ideological framework that could guarantee the continuity of C2-approaches to migration as they were practiced to varying degrees before 1945. Herbert had argued that the integration of the returning refugees and displaced people (DP) was essential for the economic recovery which would have not been possible without this labor force.[19] But the influx of refugees was not at first a subject of jubilation and they were as well social concerns (housing and work) as well cultural (the different cultural background of the refugees) (Herbert, 2001, p. 196). It is estimated that by 1950, around 8.5 million displaced persons (so-called *Vertriebene*) from East Europe, eastern and Soviet-occupied zones had arrived in the Federal Republic, and their number continued to rise. Their return would prove a valuable workforce compensation for the gap created by war casualties and the return of foreign workers after the war (ibid., p. 195). When the 1948 currency reform and the Marshall plan triggered the economic recovery in the three Western zones, Germany was able to address the labor shortage that set in as early as the 1950s.

The integration of the returnees has not proved an unsurmountable challenge as originally feared. There were crucial differences between their condition and the situation of previous foreign workers. They were ethnic Germans who mostly spoke German so that many legal or linguistic problems could not be posited. Moreover, the DPs represented a heterogeneous group and had suffrage rights. As such they were an important voters' group. It is estimated that the DPs constituted around a quarter of the German population by 1960 (ibid., pp. 196, 199–200).

The returning German refugees had helped fill the gap of war casualties and departed foreign DPs but were ultimately not enough to satisfy the labor demands of the reinvigorated German economy. Soon they were talk of contracting foreign workers. The decision to contract foreign workers instantiates a muddling-through between alternative approaches such increasing the internal mobility of unemployed workforce within Germany (with the risk of housing shortage), accelerating the technological rationalization (to decrease the human labor demand) or further women's employment (deemed family-wise

---

19   I use here the term DPs and refugees interchangeably.

undesirable) or increasing working hours (risk of trade unions' veto) (ibid., p. 204).

4.4 Path Dependency in Foreigners' Recruitment

It is not only the recourse to foreign workers that outline elements of a muddling-through policy. The path dependency to earlier migration regulations is reflected in the traditional employment of foreigners in unqualified jobs with particularly heavy, dirty, dangerous or generally unpopular work (ibid., p. 225). Political scientist Knut Dohse emphasized that in the 1950s the re-enactment of the Foreigners' Police Regulations of 1938 [*Ausländerpolizeiverordnung*] and the Ordinance on Foreign Workers [*Verordnung über ausländische Arbeitnehmer*] of 1933 repeated the regulatory instruments and rigid provisions of National Socialist immigration legislation (quoted in ibid., p. 205). The Federal Republic concluded recruitment contracts for workers with Italy (1955), Spain and Greece (1960) and later with Turkey (1961), Morocco (1963), Portugal (1964), Tunisia (1965) and Yugoslavia (1968) (Butterwegge 2005).

I view the recourse to past policies as a consequence of the path dependency of previous migration policies rather than a conscious effort to reproduce totalitarian migration policies. Germany was muddling through between poorly processed fascist migration policies, and present economic demands. In muddling through approaches, short-term economic demands predominate over human and social considerations. The workers are reduced to (cheap) bare labor power, human buffers to absorb economic shocks and that could be disposed of in negative economic conjunctures. As such, when economic growth was challenged in the 1970s by the Oil crisis, the employment of foreigners was called into question. The employment of around 2.3 million foreigners was deemed unprofitable through cost-benefit analysis (ibid., p. 227). Foreign workers with predominantly low qualifications were particularly affected by the structural crisis in the steel and metal sector, the construction sector or the textile industry since the mid-1970s (ibid., p. 237).

The turning point in policy in this sense was reached in the course of 1973.[20] In his government's policy declaration in January 1973, Chancellor Brandt considered that the absorption capacity of the German society was exhausted and

---

20 Bauder applied a labor segmentation theory to make sense of "[t]he use of migrants as secondary labor helps explain the cyclical demand for migration and immigration. Demand exists until the cyclical and seasonal jobs in the secondary labor market are filled; demand declines in periods of economic slowdown. For example, Germany's guest worker program aimed to fill labor shortages in the secondary labor market during the post-WWII recovery period and recruited millions of international migrants from southern Europe, the Balkans, and Turkey. On the eve of the recession following the oil crisis of

that the focus should be henceforth on social stability. Subsequently, on November 23, 1973, the further influx of guest workers from non-EC countries was completely cut off through recruitment freezes. According to the experience of 1967, the government and the Federal Labor Office hoped that this would lead to a noticeable decline in foreign employment, since they assumed that 200,000 to 300,000 foreign workers would freely return to their home country each year (ibid. p. 228).

The calculus of a recruitment stop had not worked; the number of foreigners in Germany did not decline, but on the contrary increased. All signs indicated that more and more foreigners wanted to stay in the Federal Republic for a longer period of time, if not permanently. They fetched their families, moved from the dormitories into (cheap) accomodation, their savings rate fell, their consumption rose, and the ties to the homeland became looser, especially among the children of the guest workers, the so-called Zweite Generation (ibid., p. 232). Within a few months, it became apparent in the Federal Republic of Germany that with the unchecked rise in the number of foreigners in recent years, long-term, cost-intensive, socially explosive and morally serious problems had emerged, both in public and among political leaders (ibid., p. 233). Henceforth, migration policies were to muddle through an ambient migration denial, which I explicate in the following sub-point.

4.5   *Muddling through in Migration Denial*

Despite the multiple encounters of Germany with migration, political discourse denied the phenomenon of migration when it argued that Germany was not an immigration country. Being an immigration country was pictured as being like the USA or Canada or even France or Great Britain. Even if Germany's relatively short colonial history has not particularly influenced the German population (which largely remained homogenous), the country has nonetheless relied on 'invited' or forced Polish migration from its industrial development in the nineteenth century to the world wars in the twentieth century. From the historical perspective, the migration denial meant in reverse that the country could only predominantly conceive of migration as solicited, controlled, and forced. The democratic orientation of post-WWII would not permit that the authoritarian, nationalistic, and imperialist migration policies of Wilhelmine or Hitlerian Germany. The return of Germans expelled from Eastern Europe after WWII was portrayed more as a homecoming experience or reunion rather than a massive influx from foreigners. These returnees were

---

1973, 2.6 million guest workers were employed in West Germany. With the emergence of the recession, the recruitment of international migrants ended (2006, p. 21)."

German nationals, endowed with voting powers and did not showcase feared cultural differences. When the *Wirtschaftswunder* (economic miracle) demanded cheap labor power, a participative-public-private approach was developed in the recruitment of foreign workers after WWII. It proved to be more an evolutionary than a revolutionary approach to migration.

The foreigners's policy guideline of the Federal Republic since 1974 has been a quagmire. It was more backward-looking than forward-looking. Its mantra was the integration of the existing foreigners but was resolved to prevent further influx of migrants. This concept of "integration on revocation [*Integration auf Widerruf*]" created a particularly difficult situation for the second generation of foreigners in Germany: the children were to be integrated into the German school system, but on the other hand they were not not lose contact with the culture of their parents' homeland, so as to keep open the return option. The consequences were bilingual illiterates who did not speak the language of their parents or their classmates, who were accordingly socially isolated and barely qualified to work (quoted in ibid., p. 238).

The reluctant integration of foreigners translated the hope that Turkish workers could be incentivized to return to their home country. When the newly elected Federal Chancellor Helmut Kohl made his policy statement on October 13, 1982, he emphasized that Germany was not an immigration country. This resulted in three objectives: (1) integration of foreigners living there; (2) the promotion of readiness to return and the prevention of further influx; (3) a significant shift in foreigners' foreign policy from the Federal Ministry of Labor to the Ministry of Interior stated that it was no longer social policy, but regulatory aspects in the foreground (ibid., pp. 249–250).

It quickly became apparent that a drastic reduction in the number of foreigners in the Federal Republic could only be enforced with drastic measures or what I have termed C2 migration regulation. In the context of post-WWII Germany, such radical solutions were neither humanitarian nor legally enforceable due to the international legal obligations of the Federal Republic (ibid., p. 251). The country was left with the realization that imported labor was now not as easily disposable as in the past. Max Frisch's famous quote, "We called for workers, and people came," encapsulates the disillusion of Germany's recruitment of foreign workers (Bauder, 2006, p. 104).

Germany was caught between the containment of migration and the structural change of the labor force demands. Whereas in the past from the nineteenth to the twentieth centuries, the labor market demanded low skill workforce, it was constantly demanding skilled labor in the IT sector. Starting from the 1990s, and despite the presence of more than 3 million unemployed in Germany, specific sectors were in need of skilled labor. To respond to this new situation, the country undertook in 2000 two initiatives that represent incremental changes in the general muddling-through approach to migration regulation. Both initiatives were launched in 2000. The first was a short-term initiative to address punctual labor needs while the second aimed at outlining a comprehensive immigration law [*Zuwanderungsgesetz*].

The first initiative was the introduction of a German Green Card. German Chancellor Schröder had announced during an electronic fair that Germany would be introducing a Green Card. There are of course similarities to the North American one but also crucial differences as well. The American Green Card included a permanent work and residence permit, including the option of naturalization. On the other hand, the German version only granted a temporary work permit of up to five years, provided that the foreign expert was offered a job by a German employer. It was therefore more akin to the American "H-1B" visa, which provides for a temporary immigration option for highly skilled workers in specialized occupations (Kolb, 2010). 20,000 such work permits were expected to be awarded, but after three years, less than 15,000 such work permits had been granted. Most immigrants came from Eastern Europe (35 percent) and India (27 percent). The majority worked in small and medium-sized companies, especially in Bavaria, Baden-Württemberg and North Rhine-Westphalia. The "Green Card" was only considered "moderately successful" since it failed its recruitment target (Lindner 2015).[21] Lindner's explanation for the limited success of the policy was obvious: the initiative was a response to an acute shortage in the IT industry, but while the regulation was being introduced, the so-called dot-com bubble exploded in March 2000, halting its hitherto rapid growth. Moreover, he argues, the 2000 German green card was uncompetitive. It did not provide for the possibility for naturalization. Furthermore, the German Green Card policy was "reflective of the German public's split over identifying itself as an immigration country and the disagreement over the direction of a future immigration policy (Bauder, 2006, p. 104)."

---

21 The follower of the German Green Card, the EU Blue Card was arguably more competitive than the German Green Card described above. It was introduced On August 1, 2012 in Germany. It was implemented under the European High Qualifications Directive and it was the first time that EU countries have introduced a common residence permit for highly qualified workforce from countries outside the European Union. The EU Blue Card is limited to a maximum of four years and can under certain conditions lead to a settlement permit. At the end of March 2015, almost three years after the introduction of the Blue Card, a total of almost 22,000 foreigners lived in Germany with this residence permit. Most of them are nationals from India (22 percent), China (9 percent), Russia (8 percent) and the USA (5 percent). A large part of them already lived in Germany before or had studied here. 47 percent of blue card holders work in so-called shortage occupations, such as engineers or doctors (Lindner, 2015).

In 2004, the Green Card regulation expired. Nonetheless, for Lindner (2015), it triggered a sustained debate: on the one hand, some audiences called for policies such as "children instead of Indians [*Kinder statt Inder*]" to be enacted, and on the other, Germany took a clear step towards becoming an "immigration country". In 2005, the *Ausländergesetz* [Foreigners' Act], valid since 1965, was finally replaced. It was followed by the *Gesetz zur Steuerung und Begrenzung der Zuwanderung und zur Regelung des Aufenthalts und der Integration von Unionsbürgern und Ausländern* [Act on the Residence, Economic Activity and Integration of Foreigners in the Federal Territory], in short *Zuwanderungsgesetz* [immigration law], which is still valid today. It allows, under certain circumstances, a permanent establishment permit for highly qualified people made clear legal provisions for the integration of foreigners. At the same time, migration policy remained ambivalent, a confusing accumulation of nearly 60 residence different titles. (ibid.)

The second initiative to design a sustainable immigration policy was Minister of the Interior Otto Schily's establishing in 2000 of an independent immigration commission. The panel gathered several migration experts and was led by Rita Süssmuth. The Commission proposed in its final report in 2001, an immigration model for skilled labor to supplement the local workforce with immigration. It argued that a sufficient number of (imported) young workers are needed to make the successful transition into the knowledge society. Their immigration model allowed for additional immigration models and aimed at a step-by-step replacement of the recruitment stops (enacted in 1973) through controlled immigration. It recommended the simplification of the complicated migration law to allow temporary and permanent immigration in order to reduce labor market shortages more quickly and attract skilled workers and highly qualified people into the country. This should be done on the basis of a concept based on the Canadian scoring system. The report further suggested the introduction of a uniform asylum law and procedure in the EU and language classes to promote foreigners' integration (Süssmuth, February 2016).

The recommendations of the Süssmuth Commission were in many ways incremental and novel.[22] They sought to put an end to the muddling-through policies and lay the foundation for an immigration law. The resulting law was

---

22   In her memoirs, Süssmuth affirmed that the commission was able to provide a wide-ranging analysis and fact-based stocktaking on immigration, combined with recommendations to the policymakers for dealing with refugees, including illegal immigrants. It also made suggestions on how to reshape the residence acts, further integration. One of the frameworks has been created for a reorganization towards a country of immigration with changed governance for qualified and highly skilled professionals on the basis of a points system (Süssmuth, 2015b, 136–137).

only passed in 2004 after tedious and very conflicting compromise attempts. Shortly after the adoption in the Bundesrat and the signing of the law by the Federal President Johannes Rau, a constitutional complaint was filed because of the voting procedure in the Bundesrat. The lawsuit was successful. It was not about content, but formal procedures (Süssmuth, 2015, p. 137).

But it is possible that the Commission overestimated the political readiness for a paradigm shift. A general lift of the recruitment stops was out of question for the conservative CDU / CSU. Assessing the proposals of the commission 15 years after the publication of the report, Süssmuth argued that even if some of the proposals of the commission are still up-to-date, they need to adapt to new challenges of forced migration with large flows of refugees. Most importantly, she found that it is still necessary to bundle the sometimes highly complicated immigration regulations into a clearly structured and comprehensible immigration law and called for a paradigm shift (Süssmuth, September 2015).

4.6 Muddling through into the Refugee Crisis

Since the mid-1980s, migration patterns into Germany have changed. Policy makers tried to come to terms with the rising number of asylum applications through deterrence policies. Herbert reminds that the number of asylum seekers, which had reached a peak in 1980, had fallen to less than 20,000 by 1983, but grew to over 100,000 in the second half of the 1980s (2001, p. 264). Indeed, asylum posed new challenges to migration policies: the right to asylum was enshrined in the German Basic Law (constitution).[23] However, and in order to achieve the desired reduction in the number of asylum seekers, procedures could be speeded up, the criteria for granting asylum tightened, the accessibility to the Federal Republic made more difficult. All these paths were taken in the following years in a series of legislative changes, albeit with little success.[24]

---

23   Some members of the Parliamentary Council (*Parlamentarischer Rat*) who wrote the German Basic Law had been persecuted by the Nazi regime and sought abroad.
24   As Butterwegge recounts, mostly right-wing extremists organized campaign-like protests. The protesters alleged, "mass misuse" of the constitutionally enshrined fundamental right to asylum (Article 16 of the *Grundgesetz* [German Constitutional Law] by economic refugees [*Wirtschaftsflüchtlinge*]). The attacks on refugee camps and the protests prompted politicians to react. Accordingly, on December 6, 1992 CDU / CSU, FDP and SPD agreed on the so-called asylum compromise. It severely restricted the fundamental right to political asylum and became effective on 1 July 1993. In 1993, the new Asylum Procedures Act (*Asylverfahrensgesetz*) and the no less controversial Asylum Seekers' Benefits Act (*Asylbewerberleistungsgesetz*) came into force. These form the basis of the asylum legal framework in Germany up to today (with further improvements introduced by by subsequent immigration laws) (Butterwegge 2005).

Structurally, there were problems in the asylum policy, according to Herbert. The classic definition of political persecution, as it was applied to political opponents during the Nazi dictatorship had changed. On the other hand, the Federal Republic of Germany was not allowed to send back refugees who were threatened with death and dangers in their home countries because of the provisions of the Geneva Refugee Convention. As a result, rejected asylum seekers in the Federal Republic could de facto still be tolerated on the gounds mentioned earlier (ibid., pp. 264–265).

The migration denial complex has not waned since. Pundits, experts and politicians try to distinguish between legal/illegal migration and asylum seeking. International law conventions bind countries to accept and process asylum claims while migration issues are mostly left to the discretion of the respective countries. This is the most used avenue these days for right-wing politicians to press for fast-track deportation procedures for rejected asylum applications. But at the heart of this move is a denial of the nodal point between asylum and migration.

Whereas fleeing from a war-torn country necessarily entails a humanitarian aspect, it is also often the case that refugees in the same flight look to restore or rebuild for themselves a modicum of economic stability. The (safe) countries passage on their flight route from Syria throughout the Balkans did not offer much of a chance to start a new life. The only viable option was to press further towards the arguably greener pastures in the heart of Europe. For this reason, the restrictive migration policies have led potential migrants to opportunistically rebrand themselves as refugees to access Europe. Refugees are (economic) migrants to a certain degree, not least because they chose the path to economically prosperous countries and wish to earn their living. Their dream is not to be cajoled into a golden cage of social welfare but the possibility to reconstruct a modicum of a living through a prompt integration in the workforce.

To be sure, muddling-through approaches to migration regulation are mainly steered from above. Those policies try to monitor global and transnational practices they no longer solely drove, as say in the nineteenth and the beginning of the twentieth century when C2 migration policies were predominant. Bauder has argued that "the agency of individuals, social groups, and institutions drive the processes we associate with globalization, international migration, and labor market regulation (Bauder, 2006, p. 7)." Not only migration research has to reckon with, as Michael Peter Smith argues, "the presence of myriad local and transnational practices 'from below' (quoted in ibid.)," but migration policies as well. After the refugee crisis in 2015, there have been a number of policies and actions from above to steer or limit the influx of refugees to Europe in general and the EU in particular. The deal with Turkey[25] and the closure of the Balkan route[26] have been policies by EU-countries and Germany to limit the influx of refugees.

Parallel to these efforts to control, a new discursive approach to the refugee crisis prevention and management has emerged and purports to get to the roots of the migration and exodus from poorer countries to the West (*Fluchtursachenbekämpfung*). The concept that was arguably first advanced by pro-migration and human-rights NGOs aimed at exposing the short-sightedness of unilateral, securitized approaches to migration regulation and emphasize the need to the causes of asylum seeking qua migration.[27]

While Chancellor Merkel tended to favor EU-wide, multi-lateral, concerted, deals, her Minister of the Interior was a partisan of a form of command-and-control approach to asylum-seeking. His *Masterplan Migration: Maßnahmen zur Ordnung, Steuerung und Begrenzung der Zuwanderung* [Masterplan Migration: Measures for the Organization, Control and Limitation of Immigration] made public in June 2018 represents more an inward-looking, indeed a command-and-control approach to asylum management. He advanced 63 measures to come to term with migration/asylum. Seehofer (2018) identified four main fields of action that are more precisely conceived of as geographies of

---

25   The EU-Turkey Refugee Agreement, also known as the Merkel Plan is a refugee containment plan between the EU and Turkey. It came into force on March 20, 2016. According to the agreement, refugees landing in Greece from Turkey should be sent to Turkey through 'an orderly process.' In return, the EU is to relieve Turkey of Syrian refugees. The mind behind this agreement has been said to be Gerald Knaus, the founder of a think tank named ESI. Knaus argued that Turkey must help the moderately conservative and social democratic governments in Central Europe. It could have no interest in the AfD or the FPÖ, right-wing extremist parties getting respectively stronger in Germany and Austria, or that France may soon be governed by the Front National. Then it would be anti-Islamic, pro-Russian parties setting the tone in Europe. It was thus in Turkey's interest that Merkel philosophy gets the upper hand, not the Orbán philosophy. The continuing rising number of refugees since September 2015 has increased the pressure on Merkel to act to contain the influx of refugees and migrants (Lau 2016).

26   The Balkan route refers to the main escape route through Greece, Macedonia, Serbia, and Hungary that refugees from Syria, Iraq and Afghanistan took to get to Western Europe. It was factually closed around March 2016 when Macedonia closed its border to prevent further crossing of refugees following the EU-Turkey to contain migration.

27   Trittin, politician from the green named bad governance, the competition for natural resources (among Africans), growing inequality, climate change, and arms export policies (of Westernized countries) as the major causes of refugee crisis (2016). It is difficult to contradict the diagnosis. But political praxis is divided between a multi-lateral, EU-wide concerted migration and refugee to address and redress the equalities that lead to forced migrations and a unilateral thrust.

anti-migration policy, where law and development politics combine to tighten the migration regime to Germany. These geographies include the countries of origin of asylum seekers and illegal migrants (*Herkunftsländer*), transit countries (*Transitländer*), the EU, and of course the domestic arena. The domestic field of action is further sub-divided in four areas: internal borders (within the Schengen area), legal procedures on foreigners and asylum seekers, integration and return (*Rückkehr*). The intentions of the Masterplan are clear from the preamble: to reestablish a system of *order* [*System der Ordnung*] through a clear limitation of immigration, the speedy deportation of rejected asylum seekers, the prioritization of aid in kind (*Sachleistungen*) instead of cash (*Geldleistungen*). Integration is only for asylum claimants that have good prospects of being granted asylum.

The Masterplan suggests an increased use of development aid as a tool of migration control especially for African and Maghreb countries and called for a development investment law [*Entwicklungsinvestionsgesetz*] that should guarantee private investment, development cooperation, new forms of technological exchange and vocational training (ibid., p. 5). It nonetheless fails to explain how the hierarchy between these areas of development aid will be articulated and seems to reduce development aid to migration control assistance.

The BAMF should offer counselling for so-called voluntary return consultation. The consultation should strive to offer unified, country-specific returnee programs. Rejected asylum applicants that are ready to return to their home countries should be offered the chance to take a vocational training in Germany prior to their return in their home country. This offer should not extent the residence permit in Germany but prepare the candidate for a new start in their home country (ibid., pp. 5–6). To this effect, the so-called *Beratungs- und Betreuungszentren* (advice and care center) are to coordinate qualification and re-insertion programs.

The Masterplan further suggests the creation of so-called secure places (*sichere Orte*) to prevent further migration to Europe and extend the capacities of the regions around the conflict areas. It is the quasi extra-territorialization of the migration management. These secured areas are to be created in North Africa (to welcome the refugees caught in Mediteranean Sea) and in the Sahel region. The Sahel region should serve as a shelter for refugees from conflicts regions. Through the help from the EU, these centers should provide a weirdly termed *robuste Sicherung* (robust security) and 'expectation management regarding the chances of success of continuing a journey to Europe' (ibid., p. 8). It proposes to train the border forces of the *Collège Sahélien de Sécurité* (CSS) in the G5-States in emigration prevention (ibid., p. 9).[28] Migration is securitized and criminalized and existing border plans and regional security cooperation initiatives are to be co-opted in European anti-migration plans. Frontex should evolve into a full-fledged European border police and accordingly staffed and the extension of the geographical patrol areas. Under point 23, the Masterplan proposed the development of a standard model for a European Center of Receptions [*Erstaufnahmezentren*]. A German initiative should develop a German standard model of a hotspot. The Masterplan seems to suggest that this will ensure the transferability to other regions if necessary (ibid., p. 11).

In point 27, the Masterplan aims for the rejection of asylum seekers who have already been registered in another EU country and the Common European Asylum System [*Gemeinsames Europäisches Asylsystem* (GEAS)]. Under point 32, arguably the most controversial of the measures the Minister of Interior: the AnkER. The acronym (which means 'anchor' in German) sounds like the promise of integration but is rather conceived as an optimization of the asylum procedure: AnkER stands for arrival, decision, repatriation [*Ankunfts-, Entscheidungs- und Rückführungszentren (AnkER-Zentren)*]. Different administrations (BAMF, BA, reception centers of the federal states, youth welfare offices, administrative court) would work together under one roof to ensure quick decisions on asylum claims and eventually facilitate the repatriation of rejected asylum claimants (p. 14). The complete asylum procedure should take place in the asylum centers and the involved administrative courts should be represented to speed up the legal process.[29] Measure 37 proposes the reduction of minimal age for taking of fingerprints at the time of completion of the sixth year of life (ibid., p. 17).

---

28   The G-5 was created in February in Nouakchott, Mauritania. Five Sahel countries: Burkina Faso, Chad, Mali, Mauritania, and Niger joined forces to tackle security and development challenges in the regions and confront the threat of jihadist organizations operating in the region such as AQIM, MUJWA, Al-Mourabitoun, Boko Haram. The *Collège Sahélien de Sécurité* (CSS) preceded the emergence of the G5 Sahel and was created in 2011 and officially launched in September 2012. It organizes seminars and qualifying trainees related to the areas of intervention of the G5 Sahel (See G5 Sahel Sécurité et Développement 2018, pp. 15–16).

29   The Masterplan aims to speed up the review of appeals in the asylum procedure and so that the enforceability of the deportation can be applied and wants to assess whether asylum seekers could be involved in court costs (Seehofer, 2018, p. 18). The overall optimization of asylum-based proceedings through the drafting a bill to relieve the administrative courts and speed up procedures and the increase of the staffing of the courts and participation of more judges, who are not yet employed for life, in judicial decisions (ibid., p. 17).

Seehofer's 'neo-C2 approach' applies pecuniary sanctions to asylum seekers that breach their duty to cooperate in the asylum procedure with the asylum services. To that extent, the Plan proposes the direct data exchange between BAMF and social transfer authorities. Moreover, it seeks to extend the maximal duration for lower-rate transfer to asylum seekers to 36 months. The current regulation sets the maximal duration to 15 months. Seehofer's plan is to delay the transition to higher-rate social assistance (under social law act SGB XII). While it applies sanctions, it also purports to allow asylum seekers to take up employment during the asylum procedure to structure their daily routine during the waiting period (ibid., p. 17).

The Masterplan has numerous measures to keep out or send asylum seekers out[30] but surprisingly little on how to successfully integrate the foreigners already living inside the country. From the total of 63 measures, only 9 refers to integration and most of them follow the C2 logic outlined above. Among the positive aspects are the calls to increase the quality of integration courses. But unfortunately it does not go beyond demanding the evaluation of courses to identify opportunities to further enhance the quality of the courses through control density of integration course (ibid., p. 19).

It arguably wants to promote a demand-oriented skilled labor immigration law, which should complement and better systematize the existing provisions in the Residence Act, as well as the implementation of accompanying measures for qualification recognition and administrative procedures, language acquisition and advertising abroad (p. 18).

The AnkER-Centers for accelerated asylum claim processing and deportation are deemed controversial in the public opinion Meanwhile a third *Land*, Saarland (in addition to Bavaria and Saxony) has rebranded its welcoming center into a AnkER center even without in fact knowing the extent to which the objectives formulated by the Masterplan have been achieved in the eight centers set up since the beginning of August. According to the Ministry of Interior, assistance will be offered to the *Länder* for the establishment of anchor centers (Bewarder, 2018). The reaction to the Masterplan's AnkER has been mostly skeptical. A consortium of professors have highlighted in a study for the *Mediendienst Migration* different fault lines in the plan. As such, Hess et al. (2018, p. 2) assert that the anchor centers are used for extensive insulation and highly

---

30   It even co-opts the visa regime as a bargaining tool to coerce states to readmit their nationals whose asylum claims have been rejected. It intends to do so through the so-call 'visa-lever.' This strategy is a generous granting of visas to states in the Global South only in the case of 'genuine willingness' to accept returnees. In Seehofer's plan, the visa lever is to motivate the countries of origin to improve their cooperation for the repatriation of rejected asylum seekers (Seehofer, 2018, p. 22).

strain the refugees, which will make their social and occupational integration more difficult. The authors seem to favor a municipality-led approach to the AnkER-centers. In recent years, they note, municipalities and initiatives have played a central role in the integration policy. The AnkER-centers ignore the importance of local support structures and are perceived as foreign bodies in the affected communities. In addition, they can provide a breeding ground for prejudice. Whether the asylum procedures in these centers are accelerated is also questionable. Above all, EU law calls for consideration of the specific situation of more vulnerable groups like women and children. Time will tell whether the Masterplan initiative will succeed in taking back control in migration question or simply be remembered as a desperate attempt to put an end to 'muddling-through' policies.

CHAPTER 3

Soft and Hard: Power, Asylum, and Germany

In Chapter 2, I looked at Germany's migration discourses and policies from a domestic and historical perspective. I argued that the endeavors to consolidate German identity and demarcate it from foreigners in the new-founded Reich in the nineteenth century were a case of early securitization discourse of migration. I went on to suggest that German migration policies oscillated between a command and control approach, and a public-private partnership in migration regulation between the foundation of the Reich in 1871 and WWII. I characterized post-WWII migration policies as mainly the outcome of a muddling-through between different imperatives- economic (roughly until the mid-1970s) and humanitarian (the increase of asylum applications from the mid-1980s onwards). After the 2015 refugee crisis, voices have been calling for a comprehensive immigration law (*Einwanderungsgesetz*) but there is no guarantee that this will end the muddling-through approach to migration regulation.[1]

In this chapter, I want to look at migration into Germany from an International Relations (IR) perspective. Specifically, I survey which role(s) projected soft and hard (economic or military) power would play or are playing in the regulation of international migration into Germany. I focus on the concept of soft power and its potential in making sense of Germany's appeal to migrants/ asylum seekers and its role in the intended re-orientation of the country's

---

1 Thym has outlined and reviewed three directions that a potential immigration law (*Einwanderungsgesetz*) could take. The first model is the SPD model of labor migration with a scoring system. Thym argues that although such a system is feasible, albeit he fears that such a concept of "immigration" does not conform to the public discourse and expectation on migration regulation. The public expects a holistic approach to the regulation of migration, whereas the scoring system is most likely to regulate economic migration into Germany. The second model Thym reviewed is the Greens' model of immigration. According to Thym, it proposes to bundle and rename the existing residence and immigration laws and tweak the content of these laws where needed. A forunner of this model is the 2004 immigration law (*Zuwanderungsgesetz*). The *Zuwanderungsgesetz* is a framework that bundled different laws (among others the residence law, nationality law and asylum law). Some were fundamentally reformed, but no permanent piece of legislation called immigration law established. The third approach Thym sees is for the federal legislature to provide a codification of the applicable laws in the form of a new, easily understandable "migration" or "immigration code." In all these cases, the potential for simplification will face the limits of European law (Thym, 2017, p. 362). Shortly after the completion of this chapter, the bill on the immigration of qualified immigration, the *Fachkräfteeinwanderungsgesetz* was passed on 19 December 2018.

migration policy. I review the Soft power index ranking of Germany and discuss its implications for a conceptualization of asylum-granting as a form of soft power. I further pay attention to how the projection of hard, military, economic power in international development cooperation, or international security management, play out in preemptive migration regulation.

1 Soft Power Meets Asylum

The term "soft power" was coined by Joseph Nye to describe the ability of a state to wield power in international relations via non-military means. In simpler words, "[i]t is the ability to get what you want through attraction rather than coercion or payments. It arises from the attractiveness of a country's culture, political ideals, and policies (2004, p. x)."

It is a conceptualization of power that goes beyond military might to include "soft" elements. Dominant (neo-)realist approaches to power in IR theory had outlined a number of countable, measurable, factors that account for the hard power or the ability to coerce other states into one's will.[2] As such, demography, geography, natural resources, economics, military force and social stability are criteria to gauge the hard (real) power of a country, territory, extensive natural resources, economic strength, military force, and social stability (ibid., p. 3). These aspects could prove to be a real advantage in classical, symmetrical warfare or in the bipolar context of the Cold War. The fall of the Berlin Wall in 1989 the collapse of the bipolar world order, the increased globalization, the rise of religious-fundamentalist terrorism, and ultimately the

---

2 The concept of power is a central to the discipline of international relations. The realist school of thought had defined power as the ability to coerce, threaten other states into a desired behavior (See for example Morgenthau, 1967, Mearsheimer, 2001; for a critique of neo-realist conceptualization of power, *See* Guzzini, 1993). Barnett and Duvall (2005, p. 40) have argued that there is a disciplinary tendency to associate power with realism and to work primarily with the realist conceptualization of power. They ascribe this state of affairs to the fact that rival theories have constituted their research programs by demarcating them from concerns of power or seeking alternative forms to power. As such, the theories of neoliberal institutionalists, liberals, and constructivists were geared toward a demonstration of the causal non-relevance of military and economic power variables in their explanation of empirical outcomes. Instead they relied among others on Digeser's *Four Faces of Power* and tried to offer a taxonomy of power that comprises compulsory power (direct control over another actor), institutional power (indirect control of actors over others), structural power (emerging from direct structural relations) and productive power (socially diffuses, intersubjective form of power) (ibid., p. 43). It is not clear where they locate soft power in their taxonomy.

mitigated results military post-2001 counterinsurgency actions have highlighted the limitations of hard power.

Nye's approach is to steer away from power that rests on coercion, threats, deterrence to an approach that emphasize co-option, public diplomacy and the dissemination of one's political and cultural values and models.[3] Soft power, as Nye sees it, then rests on legitimacy, moral authority, and ultimately acceptance. Applying his concept to the USA, he argued that when US policies are seen as legitimate by other states, the soft power of the country is enhanced (ibid.). According to Nye, the US has long had a great deal of soft power (through the Marshall Plan for Europe and the reconstruction assistance to Japan after WWII) and will need it to "obtain the outcomes it wants on trade, antitrust, or financial regulation" vis-à-vis the "European Union, Japan, China, and others (ibid., p. 4)."

Soft power emerges from "an attractive personality, culture, political values and institutions, and policies that are seen as legitimate or having moral authority (ibid., p. 6)." A country's soft power "rests primarily on three resources: its culture (in places where it is attractive to others), its political values (when it lives up to them at home and abroad), and its foreign policies (when they are seen as legitimate and having moral authority) (ibid., p. 11)." If cultural resources help produce soft power, Nye is keen to demarcate cultural resources from the soft power they sometimes help produce it. Soft power is the behavior of attraction (ibid.). As such, he identified the American way of life and Hollywood as cultural sources of American soft power. Thus, through culture, political values and foreign diplomacy, a country can enhance its image among its peers by leveraging their non-coercive power options. Like most concepts of international relations or law, its first addressees are primarily states but also ascribe to non-states actors such as NGOs or individuals a soft power.

But Nye's concept of soft power and his empirical application of the concept are not simply about the USA. He noted that "Britain and *Germany* rank ahead as havens for *asylum seekers*. France and Spain attract more tourists than the United States (though the U.S. ranks higher in revenues from tourism) (ibid., p. 34, emphasis added)." Attracting asylum seekers and tourists is a measure of soft power. Nye does not expand on why asylum seekers or tourists are a determinant of the soft power capital of a particular country. Neither does he seem to add a preference between asylum seekers and tourists. All that

---

3   Li (2018) has drawn attention to the hubris of soft power. The hubris brought by the belief in the potency and legitimacy of soft power was so great that tremendous hard power was deployed in its name. Soft power, he argued, is and will stay in an extension of hard power. For a critique of soft power on German perspective, see Joffe, 2006.

eventually transpires from the quotation above is maybe his disappointment that the US is not the uncontested leader in attracting tourists as well as asylum seekers. Moreover, he does not clarify whether asylum-seekers' attraction is an active policy pursued by these states, a conscious attraction and from where – according to his sources of soft power – this attraction emerged. The task now it would seem is to try to theoretically make sense of this attraction. Nye's concept of soft power seems to offer interesting categories to initiate an inquiry into this newly found status. What attracts the migrant/refugee to Germany? Is there a German dream that attracts asylum seekers/migrants? Do German culture and language account for the country's image? The chapter argues that the reasons for Germany's discreet charm owes considerably to its post 1945 and 1989 political values, its balanced foreign policy record and its efforts to carve a reputable niche as an eco-sensitive industrial nation.

2   The 'Objective' Soft Power of a Reluctant Hegemon

I want to suggest that there are different categories of soft power from the perception of the hegemon. There is the desired soft power, measureable and which appears in the indices. It yields international credence to a country's international diplomacy. It is a form of power that a priori is accessible to most countries and indeed more attractive to countries with negative past military experiences.

Germany, after WWII, focused on the reconstruction of its economic power and economic stability. If it was described in 1999 as the sick man of Europe, Germany had long evolved into one of the strongest and most stable economies not only in the European Union but worldwide. In the European Union (before the Brexit), Germany accounted for a fifth of the European Union's output and a quarter of its exports. It possesses important market shares in the automotive and software industries and many smaller German firms are global champions in niche markets (The Economist, June 15th, 2013).

If Germany aspired to wield any form of power after 1945, then it is certainly economic power.[4] It is a power Germany wielded already at the creation of the

---

4 The economic recovery was also the drive of Germany's migration policies and the recruitment in the country of foreign workers mainly from Mediterranean countries from the 1960s to the 1970s. For the recruited, it was primarily the personal economic prospects that brought them to Germany. There was certainly the belief that most guest workers would return to their home countries after having helped Germany to new economic heights. Instead, the second and third generations of the so-called guest workers have settled in and integrated into different spheres of the political, economic, and cultural life. It is possible that there

Eurozone. As the Economist (14 April 2018) recounts, "[t]he Germans insisted that it be modelled on the mighty Deutschmark and refused to entertain a "transfer union" channeling resources from Europe's austere north to its allegedly spendthrift south. Germany's politicians and central bankers stoutly defended the value of their country's currency, putting pressure on weaker economies such as France and Italy." These are more elements of economic coercion than the manifestation or use of soft power.

Another illustration of German economic assertiveness is arguably the country's stance in the recent Greek debt question. In the Greek debt crisis, Merkel and then finance-Minister Wolfgang Schäuble rejected outright debt relief, which was deemed by several economists to be the most sustainable relief intervention for Greece (Politico, 2017).

Otherwise, Germany seemed to have stayed faithful to its hands-off 'foreign policy' as the Economist described Germany's foreign policy (14 April 2018) especially in military affairs. Germany's post-WWII Constitution prohibited combat deployments of the armed forces. The prohibition was lifted in 1994. It enjoyed the military 'partnership' with the US via NATO to guarantee its security during the Cold War and for long there was no need to revise this approach. Although being Europe's largest economy, its defense spending fell short of the stipulated NATO target of 2% of the GDP of member countries. Its deficit in defense spending has been relentlessly criticized by the 45th President of the USA, Donald Trump, since his assumption of office in January 2017 (ibid.).

Notwithstanding, Germany has remarkable soft power resources. In the 2018 Soft Power 30 Report, Germany ranked third (with a score of 78. 87) behind the UK and France in the overall soft power raking. The Soft Power report combined quantitative data from government (accounting for 70% of the total score) with qualitative polling data (accounting for 30%) from the countries listed on the index. The qualitative data are gathered in seven different categories including culture, cuisine, foreign policy, liveability, luxury goods, friendliness, and tech products. The Soft Power 30 Index noted that the country has improved its performances in Enterprise[5] where it ranked 6th from 30 countries in the ranking. According to compilers of the report, the country is, "widely

---

were elements of a discreet charm that could eventually help explain, why most of the recruited 'guest workers' decided to stay in Germany after recruitments were stopped in the 1970s.

5 Enterprise as a sub-index in the Soft Power 30 refers to the relative attractiveness of a country's economic model in terms of its competitiveness, capacity for innovation, and ability to foster enterprise and commerce. The authors of the index are keen to demarcate enterprise from economic power, which they associate more with hard power (The Soft Power 30 Report, 2018, p. 33).

respected for the high quality of its advanced manufacturing sector and engineering prowess, which is prominently showcased at the annual Hanover Messe, as well as on roads, racing circuits, and railways around the world. Germany's ability to maintain a strong manufacturing base through technical skill and a practically-minded education system has seen it deliver admirably low levels of income inequality, low unemployment, and an all-round economic model envied by much of the world (The Soft Power 30 Report, 2018, p. 48)."

In the category of (global) engagement,[6] Germany ranked third behind France and the UK. The country has indeed a good network of 153 foreign embassies, 12 multilateral representations, 61 consulates-general and consulates offices and one representative office (Auswärtiges Amt, 2018). In 2017, Germany announced that it had achieved the target of 0.7 of the GNI for Official Development Assistance (ODA) with the help of a computational novelty. It added its expenditure on refugees. By adding the expenditures caused by the influx of asylum seekers in 2015, the federal state and its local governments could claim to have invested over 22 billion euros in development cooperation in 2016, an increase of 36 percent (BMZ, 2017).

Yet, some foreign policy analysts maintain, Germany is a dormant hegemon slow to assess and use its own voice in international affairs. The Soft Power Report for instance, had concluded that Germany needed to "rediscover its global purpose and voice quickly (2018, p. 48)" while leaving unanswered, how it should go about it.

On the culture sub-index, Germany ranked 4th. Admittedly, Germany faces stiff competition as it struggles to outperform the US (in film or music) and the UK (music industry, most visited art museums), or France (the most visited museum in the world and in the tourism sector) (p. 57). Nonetheless, one area where Germany is a heavyweight is in international soccer. It won four FIFA World Cups, the last one in 2014. If the ultimate measure of potential soft power is its perception through specific audiences (Nye, 2008, p. 34), then for soccer fans, Germany wields a disproportionate share of cultural soft power through soccer.

Germany was also ranked 2nd in the Report sub-index on education. It may eventually stand to benefit from Brexit in attracting more foreign students. In the category of Government effectiveness, Germany ranked eight. It is difficult to fathom what the specific categories under this sub-index category were defined. But for sure, Germany is one of the most stable and big Western

---

6   The engagement sub-index measures the reach and density of a country's diplomatic network and its involvement in major global challenges such as health, development and environment (ibid., p. 57).

democracies, which has hitherto managed to withstand the sweeping wave of right-wing populism.[7] Yet it has been hesitant to take responsibility on the supranational and international level on her own and constantly preferred to keep the position of the broker between the axes. Nonetheless this reluctant hegemon is exercising an attraction on many refugees and migrants that chose to brave their ways to the country.

Looking at the concept – which Nye has since tried to rebrand as smart power since softness sometimes implies weakness –, some political scientists have urged Germany to develop its soft power by combining its science policy with other areas such as foreign policy. While exploiting its Smart/soft power could prove to be a strategic area where the Central European country can excel, the country is still a reluctant hegemon.

3 The Duality of Soft Power on Asylum

Arguably, Germany's generous welcoming of nearly a million asylum seekers in September 2015 (which I analyzed as an event), elevated its reputation (based on Nye's framework,) to one of the foremost soft power countries surpassing the US in terms of being a destination attracting asylum seekers. However, such a proposition conflicts with the ambivalent relationship it has had with migration since the nineteenth century. In Chapter 2, I suggested that Germany's migration after WWII reflected more a muddling-through between different imperatives than a willful projection to attract asylum seekers/migrants.

The conceptualization and measure of power offered by most indices, as analyzed above do not inform upon the soft power preferences of countries. Put another way, they focus more on tourists than asylum seekers. The Soft

---

7 Merkel's border opening and welcoming of refugees does not reveal her Government's anticipation failure. The 2015 refugee crisis, as I argued in Chapter 1, is an unparelled historical event. From the point of view of government, its repercussions could be read on two main axis: On an international level, the refugee crisis has revealed once again the structural weakness of the EU, its internal dissensions as well as the failure of international organizations and community to respond to conflicts. But in Germany, the country that welcomed approximately nearly 1 million refugees since the summer of 2015 that the coordinates of the political and social have been fundamentally shifting. The enthusiasm of the early days, the euphoric welcome by Germans of the refugees, the optimism – maybe best encapsulated in Merkel's *"Wir schaffen das"* (we can do it), has given way to a growing antisemitism and xenophobia, and a reinvigorated right-wing populism that stirred up Germany's 2017 federal parliamentary elections. Merkel survived her humanitarian feat in the 2017 federal elections but has since nuanced her original stance, seeming at times to concede that those September days were more of an exception to her political operational code.

Power 30 Report's sub-index on Culture, which comes close to reflecting the human dimension of soft power (through sport and music, for example), does not include attraction on refugees as an analytical category. For this reason, these indices do no help to make much sense of the German attraction for refugees. In the following subsections, I provide some reasons why Germany has evolved into a haven for refugees.

3.1 The 'Gift' of the Parliamentary Council to Foreigners

When Germany's Constituent Assembly (Parliamentary Council) drafted the Basic Law (*Grundgesetz*), they included in it an article that will prove essential to Germany's asylum policy and its soft power attraction towards asylum seekers: article 16(2)2 of the German Basic Law (*Grundgesetz*), the country's Constitution. The provision by the Parliamentary Council of the right to asylum is derived from the experience of persecution during Nazism and exile by some of the members of the Council. For constitutional lawyer Kimminich (1972, p. 257), 'the right to political asylum' as enshrined in the constitution is one of the simplest, most unequivocal and most dignified sentences in the German Basic Law. According to Kimminich, the right to asylum as a subjective public right of each political persecutee was deliberately taken into the first section of the Constitution on fundamental basic rights. In their foresight, he continued, the founding fathers and mothers of the post-war Constitution elected not to attach any conditions to the right of asylum. By that, he meant that the constitutional right to asylum is not predicated on particular political or ideological views. And most importantly to keep in mind, it is also the only fundamental right that is solely applicable to foreigners on German soil, because Germans do not need it.[8]

To be sure, there are limitations to this general right to political asylum. Asylum claimants who enter Germany from a safe third country, for example through one of the six neighboring countries of Germany and other members of the EU are not eligible for asylum in Germany. The Basic Law restricted the right to asylum to cases of political persecutions. This could be interpreted to mean that the Constitution did not view the right to asylum has a mass migration provision to Germany. But the category of the political persecution is a broad one and leaves much room to interpretation as to what constituted

---

8   As such, and as Schuster has argued, the granting by the German Basic Law of the right to asylum echoed the emerging universality of liberal norms repressed and the desire for the preservation of the liberal character of the new Republic (2005, p. 184).

political persecution according to the 1949 Basic Law.[9] Furthermore, the 1990-signed Dublin Convention, the follow-up 2003 Dublin II Regulation, and the 2013-approved Dublin III Regulation substantiate and regulate asylum processes in the EU, splitting up the burden of processing of asylum application within the EU states.

Moreover, article 79 (3) outlined the conditions under which some provisions on the basic rights could be amended with two-thirds of the Members of the Bundestag and two-thirds of the votes of the Bundesrat (ibid.). This theoretically provides the framework (however stringent) for a modification of article 16, if ever political or societal will should steer toward that direction. But not only Germany's Constitution binds it to offer protection and asylum to foreigners who happen to claim it. Germany is also a signatory to the 1951 Refugee Convention Relating to the Status of Refugees. The 1951 Convention defines refugees as persons with a "well-founded fear of being persecuted for reasons of race, religion, nationality, membership of a particular social group or political opinion, is outside the country of his nationality and is unable or, owing to such fear, is unwilling to avail himself of the protection of that country; or who, not having a nationality and being outside the country of his former habitual residence as a result of such events, is unable or, owing to such fear, is unwilling to return to it. (Convention Relating to the Status of Refugees, 1951, art. 1)." Asylum seekers that are rejected under art 16(2)2 of the German Basic can still enjoy subsidiary protection if they can prove that their lives would be in danger in their country of origin. In such situations, the legal *jus cogens* norm of non-refoulement, compels states to keep within their borders anyone who might be might be endangered if sent back to their country of origin (Goldenziel, 2016, p. 582). As such, national, supra-national and international legal frameworks determine German asylum policy, a triple provision for the asylum seekers qua migrant.

Goldenziel had argued that international law for the most part does not protect migrants as it does asylum seekers (ibid., p. 579).[10] Looking at the

---

9 Arguing then that in its most strict sense, the right to asylum in the German Basic Law applied to people who were persecuted for political motives (and not because they were fleeing from war, poverty or climate change) would not be conclusive, as the political can encompass much of what threatens the livelihood of an individual.

10 This could partly help explain why asylum has mutated into the preferred immigration route into Europe and most particularly into Germany and also why asylum seekers in refugee camps in Turkey or Jordan decided to further migrate to Germany. Whereas fleeing from a war-torn country necessarily entails a humanitarian aspect, it is also often the case that refugees in the same flight look to restore or rebuild for themselves an economic stability. For some Syrian refugees into Germany in 2015, the (safe) countries on their

specific asylum provision in the German Basic Law, the 1951 Convention, the international *jus cogens* of non-refoulement, one can notice that domestic and international law protection for asylum seekers and refugees in Germany are relatively extensive. Indeed the 1948 Universal Declaration of Human Rights, the 1948-signed Convention on the Prevention and Punishment of the Crime of Genocide, the 1949 German Basic Law, and the 1951 Convention are in a temporal contiguity to the atrocities of Nazism in WWII. Marzower (2004, p. 380) had remarked that the protection of human rights implied a curtailing of a state's power over its citizens or subjects and wondered how then states nonetheless could group within the United Nations Organization to commit themselves to the defense of human rights against their domestic power interests. The usual explanations for the emergence of human rights, that Marzower renamed as the 'Eleanor Roosevelt' version and the 'Adolf Hitler's version offer both a morality tale, a tale of good triumphing over the evil through the courageous selflessness of a few committed individuals. In the Eleanor Roosevelt' version, the triumph of human rights is ascribed to the tenacity of visionaries such as Roosevelt herself, Raphael Lemkin and other early key activists after WWII. Their tireless activism had ultimately brought the powerful states to yield to the cause. In the 'Adolf Hiltler's version, the trigger for the post-WWII movement for human rights is the widespread revulsion at Nazi wickedness that galvanized the world into action. Marzower is not satisfied with none of these accounts. For him, the 'Eleanor Roosevelt' version conceals the ill fortune of earlier visionaries, like Andre Mandelstam, who in Marzower's terms labored in vain. It further conceals the political support those visionaries received from states and most importantly for Marzower, the supportive political context of post-war that gave visionaries the possibility to influence international politics. As for the 'Adolf Hiltler' version, Marzower argues that "the Holocaust as such was much less central to perceptions of what the war had been about in 1945 than it is today. And we still have to explain how those hard-bitten state bureaucrats, from the Kremlin to Whitehall, who had successfully resisted the siren-call of moral feeling in the past should now have succumbed (ibid., p. 381)."

Marzower's account of the 'strange triumph of human rights' revisits nineteenth-century Europe and introduces a longue-durée-perspective into

flight route from Syria throughout the Balkans did not offer much of a chance to start a new life. The only viable option was to press further towards the arguably greener pastures in the heart of Europe. For this reason, the restrictive migration policies have led potential migrants to opportunistically rebrand themselves as refugees to access Europe. Those migrants are (economic) refugees to a certain degree, not least because they chose the path to economically prosperous countries and wish no more than a chance to earn their living.

the emergence and triumph of human rights. Humanitarian and civilizational ideas evolved into meaningful instruments in the relations between the Great Powers after the defeat of Napoleon. To this extent, a set of constitutional principles including "a commitment to freedom of worship, and the abolition of religious and civil disabilities (ibid., p. 381)" was elaborated and bound the multi-nation Empires in Europe. After the dismantlement and the creation of new states, the recognition for these new states such as Romania was based on their adherence to the fair treatment of religious minorities within their borders. Later, the monitoring and guaranteeing of these provisions was entrusted to the League of Nations, rather than to the Great Powers themselves. This system for the protection of the group minority rights is, according to Marzower, essential to make sense of the turn to human rights after 1945. The League of Nations, although novel, failed because it did not challenge an earlier "Victorian tradition of Great Power paternalism, a paternalism that coexisted comfortably with both liberal Christianity and racism (ibid., p. 382)." From there, Marzower's account weaves the political role of the leaders of the winning Powers after the WWII as well the political activism of visionaries to account for the triumph of human rights in the post-War era.

Drawing on Marzower's refusal to view morality as the source for the triumph of human rights and Goldenziel's collapsing of human rights with refugee rights, I want to suggest that the rise and triumph of human/refugees rights after the war participated in the emergence and consolidation of asylum-granting as a form of soft power. Indeed, the history of international law and relations lends support to this view. Asylum-granting is an instrument of power politics between nations. It is the continuation of international politics by different means. By granting refuge to a fugitive, a European sovereign was not merely continuing a Christian, biblical tradition. It was asserting its territorial sovereignty and jurisdiction vis-à-vis other states as well as its (self-perceived) moral superiority of its political values. So when Grotius treats asylum as a possible cause of war between states and called for the extradition and punishment of (criminal) fugitive asylum seekers, he was articulating (in the core of his thesis) a political argument. As Price has argued, determining in the Grotian framework whether a fugitive should be extradited, punished or protected was no less a normative judgement about the political values and practices of the state of origin (and also of the receiving state). Accordingly, granting asylum implied the interference in the internal affairs of another state.[11] Building

---

11   Price has reviewed the approaches to asylum in the works of the major pioneers of international law in the seventeenth century. To be sure, Grotius's asylum framework was not only about the extradition and punishment of criminals. As Price argued, Grotius recognized a duty of hospitality to strangers and migration as a principle of natural liberty.

on Price, Goldenziel had argued that the provision of asylum through another state implies that individual rights existed beyond the confines of a territory and jurisdiction. When a human being exits their country of origin and seeks asylum in another country, the receiving state is simultaneously infringing on their own sovereignty by receiving the refugee and asserting their sovereignty and power vis-à-vis the country of origin (See Price, 2004, pp. 35–37, Goldenziel, 2016, p. 588).

This is the duality of soft power as applied to the asylum regime. On the outside, it is the projection of the receiving state's (superior) political values, i.e. the respect for human rights qua refugee rights. It is an ode to liberal, modern political values, a soft power mostly projected by a democratic, civilized self toward a barbaric, non-democratic other.[12] It is maybe in this sense that one can make sense of why Germany did not grant asylum to Edward Snowden in 2013 even if there was great repulsion in the German public sphere and politics for the NSA extensive surveillance system. Germany being a political ally of the US, arguably with comparable democratic values, it could not assert the

---

    A similar duty towards the foreigners was available into Pufendorf's duty of hospitality. Pufendorf reserved to states the right to select and preferably grant hospitality to strangers that can contribute to the economic interests of the receiving state and are compatible with their religious faith and institutions. Otherwise the state could deny asylum to the supplicant (Price, 2004, p. 39). For Price, Pufendorf's framework under-protected refugees by collapsing asylum with a general duty of hospitality. The duty of hospitality was itself submitted to the expected contribution to the increase of economic power of the receiving state (ibid.). Christian Wolff's asylum approach, on the contrary is a case of overprotection of refugees. His framework overprotected criminal supplicants who otherwise deserved to be punished. This puts Wolff's views on asylum on the antipodes of the Grotius. Furthermore, the exceptions to the duty of hospitality was left to the discretion of the state (ibid., p. 40). Vattel stands for a middle path between Grotius on the one side and Pufendorf and Christian Wolff on the other side, between protection of fugitives and the sovereign's interests in guaranteeing public safety. He required states to protect criminals as well, which brings him close to or further than Wolff went. At the same time, as Price noted, he put practical limits to the principle by allowing major delicts, *delicta majora* – like murder, piracy, and arson be excluded from the right to asylum (ibid., p. 42).

12   This will remind the reader of Mutua's thesis that authors of human rights discourse such as the United Nations, Western INGOs have constructed a three-dimensional prism, with opposes savages (on the one side) against victims and saviors on the other side(s) of the prism. For Mutua, the Savages-Victims-Savior (SVS) prism is uni-dimensional, moral, and pits 'good' against 'evil.' In the SVS metaphor, the state is mainly regarded as the classic savage, the operational instrument of savagery. State become savage when they choke off and oust civil society. The good state controls their demonic proclivities by internalizing human rights. (Mutua, 2001, p. 202).

superiority of its political values vis-à-vis the US by means of soft power. One could further wonder whether the situation would have been different if Snowden were a dissident or a whistleblower who hailed from an undemocratic, dictatorial regime, from any part of the global South. Odds are that he would not only be eligible for asylum but eventually be recommended for a peace prize. Ultimately, it was Russia and Ecuador who capitalized on Snowden's case to rhetorically infringe on US domestic security politics without necessarily exposing themselves to a punitive war.

Welcoming nearly a million asylum seekers in 2015 has enhanced the subjective perception of German soft power worldwide. The effect of soft power through asylum granting is magnified through the democratic political values of the granting states.

Germany is not only protecting numerous Syrians from a sovereign that trod down their human rights and forced them to search for refuge outside their country. It has turned into their major hope for justice, after the UN's failure to thoroughly investigate and sue the war crimes of the Bashaar al-Assad regime. This view is held by journalists, Kampf and Steinke (2018), who argue that Germany shows great prospects in its capability and willingness to find and prosecute perpetrators of torture from Syria in its borders where federal investigators and foreign intelligence service are able to enforce the law. The Federal Republic has vowed its international solidarity in law enforcement and would exert its universal jurisdiction to prosecute war crimes.

If from outside, namely in the international arena, asylum admissions enhance the democratic values of a hegemon, the reality is a little more complex from the inside. The soft power leverage accrued to asylum-admitting countries has its price and the cost is mostly borne domestically. In other words, these benevolent acts of humanitarianism can turn into a curse for the sovereign actor. By opening its borders to asylum seekers, Germany infringed on its own sovereignty. Its approach to asylum granting was not specifically Grotian, nor Pufendorfian, nor Wolffian or even Vattelian. It was arguably all of these approaches at the same time. Germany's generous border opening in 2015 was Grotian as it adhered to the duty of hospitality and granted a right of crossing to Germany to the refugees that called upon it from Hungary. It was also a condemnation of the Syrian regime, its unwillingness to protect its citizens by barring them from human rights. But it failed, in the heat of the action, not only to thoroughly check the identity of those entering its territory or filter out torturers, militant terrorists and people who would cause unrest and fear among the population, as Grotius would have certainly advised.

The asylum largesse of Germany is Pufferdorfian only if one is ready to ascribe to Germany's asylum granting demographic and economic interests. But for such a move, one should take into account the structural changes in the German labor market, which increasingly demand higher-qualified labor force. The low-skilled labor demand of the post-WWII era that led the country to recruit foreign workers has given way to a demand for qualified, technical labor force. After the country stopped the recruitment of foreign workers in the 1970s, it was note a dissuasion approach to asylum seekers, as the number of their application started growing in the 1980s. As such, doubts could be raised on whether the country viewed asylum seekers as agents of economic growth and public welfare.

Moreover, there may be legitimate doubts on whether the refugees from Syria and other countries that came in 2015 held the requisite qualifications to immediately satisfy the present labor demands of the German economy. Indeed internal discussions and the deportation of locally trained refugees and integrated in the workforce suggests that the country's asylum policy is not systematically geared towards the economic contribution of asylum seekers. While politicians from the CDU or CSU argue against a permanent residence permit of asylum seekers/migrants integrated into the workforce, politicians from the SPD for example, call for a permanent residence permit for rejected asylum applicants who have nonetheless taken a vocational training or already joined the workforce. Schuster has argued that it is "beyond dispute that the drafters of the Basic Law, and of Article 16(2)2 in particular, were not motivated solely by narrow national self-interest, economic concerns or political point-scoring. Though there were both material (economic and demographic) and ideal (political) benefits to be derived from welcoming those who came or returned from the East, the drafters intended to use the law to afford protection, both to citizens and to certain foreigners regardless of the costs (2005, p. 184)." Furthermore, a Pufendorfian approach entails the discretion to reject asylum supplicants on the basis of diverging faiths between the supplicant and the receiving state. Pufendorf viewed diverging faiths as a cause of potential unrest. When so-called patriotic Germans against the Islamization of the Occident (Pegida) rage against Merkel's asylum policy, posit a fundamental incommensurability between Islam and Christianity/the West, they are more close to the nineteenth-century asylum policy framework propounded by Pufendorf than to the 1949 Basic Law or the 1951 Convention or even the 1948 Declaration.

Germany's refugee welcoming is *de facto* Wolffian. It offered (over-)protection to potential fugitive torturers and their victims alike. Now it is trying to uncover the identity of potential torturers that fled to Germany, as noted above.

The Vattelian policy may represent the middle path that the country is trying to steer to: the necessity for the country to project and live by its provision for refugee/human rights in its Constitution. It is a dilemma between protecting fugitives and guaranteeing public safety and welfare. Such an approach would require on the one hand, the need for states to protect criminals (one state's criminal is another state's refugee) as well attempting the extradition of rejected asylum seekers and on the other hand, prosecution of potential perpetrators of major delicts, *delicta majora*, not only murder, piracy, and arson as in Vattel's framework by also terrorism, human-trafficking, crimes against humanity.

But what Grotius or Vattel could not have anticipated were the threats emerging from the population rather than from the fugitives. Fugitives, as they argued, can threaten the public safety of the receiving country and reserved to the sovereign the right to deny asylum to such potentially dangerous fugitives. But asylum-related threats to Germany's public safety have not only emerged after 2015 and indeed were not of Islamist terrorist nature. There are two cases where German chancellors came close, as Schuster (2005, p. 179) reminds, to declaring the state of emergency since the creation of the Federal Republic in 1949. The first occurrence was in 1977, when then-chancellor Helmut Schmidt, faced with terrorist attacks by the RAF, nearly declared the state of emergency to confront the homebred left-extremist terrorist attacks by the RAF. Fifteen years later, in the autumn of 1992, Kohl, faced with a number of attacks on asylum seekers in Hoyerswerda and Rostock-Lichtenhagen, spoke of the 'danger of a profound crisis of confidence in our democratic state' as a result of the increase in the numbers of migrants, in particular asylum seekers, that had crossed 'the threshold of our capacity' (*Der Spiegel* 46/1992) (quoted in Schuster, p. 179).

More than 25 years after the pogroms of the 1990s, right-wing riots have dealt a serious blow to German constitutional democracy. Following the stabbing to death of a 35-year-old man named Daniel H. presumably by a 23-year-old Syrian man and a 22-year-old Iraqi man, right-wing mobs took to the streets and "hunted foreigners through the city streets – described as reminiscent of civil war and Nazi pogroms (Connolly, 2018)." The comparison with Nazi pogroms might be far-fetched but there is no denying that the events that enfolded in Chemnitz following the homicide are equally nefarious for the sovereign and its humanitarian soft power. By enshrining the right to asylum in the German Basic Law, as I noted at the beginning of this subsection, the Parliamentary Council hoped to preserve human rights qua refugees' rights on the one hand and the liberal orientation of post-WWII Germany. Ironically, on repeated occasions, the country came close to vilipending this legacy.

Moreover, one should wonder how these cases of xenophobia would impact Germany's plan for an immigration law (*Einwanderungsgesetz*) to attract higher-skilled laborer. There is, despite the specific political programs, a general consensus among the leading political parties in Germany to regulate immigration to Germany, partly to relieve the asylum system and cater to the needs of the economy (See Thym, 2017, pp. 298–299). Whether the political parties ultimately agree on a yearly fixed immigration quota model, or introduce a scoring system, the most decisive question would be the test of attraction. Will a newly minted immigration law reach its objective or will it exacerbate the xenophobic tensions in the country?

4   Hard and Economic Power in Migration Control

In the subsections above, I analyzed German soft power with relation to asylum-seeking qua migration. I argued that one could look at the relation between soft power and migration (regulation) from paradoxical points of view. The first aspect was that a particular (unwanted) form of attraction towards asylum-seekers accrued from the political values enshrined in the Constitution of the country. The provision by article 16(2)2 and the international conventions signed by Germany represented for immigration candidates the ultimate Trojan horse into Germany. This situation revived sporadic xenophobic tensions and could prove a blight on the image of the country on the outside.

The other paradoxical aspect I noted was that a skillful projection of soft power would be necessary if Germany would like to qualitatively redefine immigration into the country to relieve the asylum system altogether.

To complete my analysis of the relation of power to migration regulation, I would now like to turn to an analysis of Germany's hard and economic power and survey how they will play out in the country's efforts to regulate mass immigration. Indeed, the country has already made use of its economic power for example, by signing an agreement with Turkey that should limit the influx of asylum-seekers into Germany. Yielding economic power in international relations means coercing other states through payments, economic sanctions or incentives into a desired behavior. It is as such different from a benevolent soft power that mostly rests on diplomatic power.

The international migration control framework is bound to involve a greater degree of coercion of states of origin for migrants. In the subsections below, I would like to discuss two cases where one could identify hard and economic power coming together among others to prevent migration.

4.1 Germany's Military Involvement in the Sahel Region

The "Sahel," as most geographical concepts, does not represent a neat category. The Sahel is a fluid concept whose geography embraces the semi-arid climate zone south of the Sahara desert. The region has witnessed a renewed interest from the international security community after 9/11. Broadly speaking, the engagement with the Sahel region after 9/11 can be summarized into three main phases.[13] The first phase is the period of preemptive security capacity-building (2002–2011), followed by the Northern Mali crisis and signing of the Algiers Agreement (2011–2015), and the Post- Algiers-Agreement phase which started after the signing of the agreement on 20 June 2015 by the Coordination of Rebel Movements in the Azawad.

I term as pre-emptive security Capacity-Building (2002–2011), the different counter-terroristic initiatives taken in the region mainly by the US in the region prior to 2011 and which were considered by different think tanks as an exaggeration or as bureaucratic imperatives.[14] Explanations offered generally fall under two categories: a genuine concern with terrorism or potential

---

13   To be sure, the Sahel/Sahara region through the Algerian War (1954–1962) has contributed to the emergence of a doctrine of counterinsurgency. This legacy of terrorism and counterterrorism in the Sahara/Sahel has been codified for example in Galula's *1964 Counterinsurgency Warfare: Theory and Practice* and Pacification in Algeria (1956–1958). This legacy that was long neglected has been revived the RAND Corporation which reprinted these classics of counter-insurgency and mostly by General Petraeus's 2007 edited *"Marine Corps Counterinsurgency Field Manual."* In his seminal book, Galula had emphasized the necessity of a holistic approach coupled with classical military operations to pacify Algeria.

14   In its 2005 Report on Africa, the International Crisis Group (ICG, 2005, pp. 1–2) wondered whether the question of Islamic terrorism in the Sahel was a fact or a fiction. It also wondered whether the security threats in the Sahel were not an exaggeration. It should also be recalled that the US military, as the Report stated, had already branded the region bordering the Sahara desert as a new front in the war on terrorism. The Group warned on the contrary that the region was not a hotbed of terrorism and argued for serious, balanced, and long-term engagement with four countries (Mali, Niger, Mauritania, and Chad) to keep the region peaceful. Finnish Institute of International Affairs analysts questioned the choice of the US to focus on the Sahara/Sahel region in 2002 despite the lack of a clear international terrorist link to the region. They reviewed the classical orthodox and critical views of US focus on the region and offered a third kind of explanation, which they called bureaucratic imperative (See Archer and Popovic, 2007). Another example of the ambivalence toward the US-led engagement with the regions was Lianne Kennedy-Boudali's testimony before Senate Foreign Relations Committee in 2009. She emphasized that insecurity in the Sahel is not a new condition, and although terrorist incidents had drawn greater attention to the region, terrorism, to her, was not the primary problem. For her, corruption, civil conflict, smuggling of goods and people, drug and weapons trafficking, and terrorism, she argued, were all contributing to insecurity in the region (Kennedy-Boudali, 2009, p. 4).

terrorism in the region that could threaten US and international security. The Americans particularly fear that if terrorists manage to consolidate bases in the Sahel, the southern fringe of the Sahara desert that extends from Mauritania in the west to Sudan in the east, they may be able to penetrate into the soft underbelly of Europe via Morocco and Algeria. That was the route taken in 2004 by the perpetrators of the train-bombings in Madrid, most of them Moroccan, when nearly 200 people were killed (The Economist, 2007). Some of the early security initiatives were the PSI,[15] the TSTI,[16] and Africom. It is certainly revealing and curious that in 2007 Germany agreed to host U.S. Africa Command headquarters in Stuttgart following protracted negotiations and general unwillingness by African countries, which were first contacted to host the military institution.

The second phase of international engagement with the Sahel is the rebellion in Northern Mali and the ensuing political crisis (2011–2015). Following the fall of Libya, the military coup in Mali in 2012, the conquest of huge swathes of Malian territory by armed rebels and terrorist groups, the worst predictions from the international community seems to have been realized. The French Operation Serval[17] stopped the progression of the rebels. Conversely, whereas the ICG's prediction did not materialize, the Sahel has grown into a new front of terrorism with the regional terrorist groups seeking and pleading allegiance to Al-Qaeda and the Islamic State. The geopolitical crisis has been augmented by the challenges of what sociologist Saskia Sassen calls "governance hotspots."

---

15   The Pan Sahel initiative (PSI) was established in 2002 to combat terrorism and promote peace in the region. Involved countries include: Mali, Niger, Mauritania, and Chad. Ended in 2004. In the case of the PSI this meant Chad, Niger, Mauritania and Mali. The reason why the initiative was limited to these countries, and did not include the countries of the Eastern Sahel, was not a strategic decision but rather the result of bureaucratic rules. In the summer of 2005, the program evolved into the much larger Trans-Saharan counterterrorism initiative (TSCTI) taking in not only states north of the Sahara: Morocco, Algeria, Tunisia and even potentially Libya; but also two to the south of the original Sahel states: Senegal and Nigeria.

16   The Trans-Saharan Counterterrorism Initiative (TSCTI) 2004–2008 is an interagency plan by the United States government he first partner nations in the program included Algeria, Chad, Mali, Mauritania, Morocco, Niger, Senegal, Nigeria and Tunisia. Current membership includes eleven African countries: Algeria, Burkina Faso, Libya, Morocco, Tunisia, Chad, Mali, Mauritania, Niger, Nigeria, and Senegal. The goal of the alliance is not to fight in hot spots, but to provide preventative training and engagement with governments to help prevent the growth of terrorist organizations in the partner countries. The Exercise Flintlock 2005, a joint military exercise first held in June 2005, was the first result of the new program.

17   The French operation Barkhane (Northern Mali) overtook the mandate of Operation Serval on 1 August 2014 and its main mission to repel the assaults of the terrorists.

Unaddressed governance hotspots feed and legitimize resentment against the Sahelian countries.

The third era (2015 and beyond) roughly starts with the signing of the peace agreement, brokered by Algeria, on 20 June 2015 between Mali and secessionist rebel groups. Under it, the Central Government wants to devolve more power to the region. The Post-Algiers challenges are security and territorial administrative. Implementing any peace agreement will also be complicated with various competing factions and splinters among the fighters on the ground and Islamist militants also trying to regain ground in the remote northern region. Multiple security-building initiatives were launched by the international community. They include the MINUSMA, the UN Mission in Mali, which started in July 2013 with the missions of civilian protection, re-establishing the authority of the state and enhancing political dialogue, the EUTM (European Union Training Mission) under the Common Foreign and Security Policy (CFSP), as well as the EUCAP Sahel Mali (2015–2017). Such programs aim to provide assistance for the Malian internal security forces (ISF) police, gendarmerie, National Guard.

Remarkably and in stark contrast to its post-1949 military-averse posture, Germany has increasingly, albeit grudgingly, illustrated a willingness to deploy boots on the ground especially in the Sahel. Its 1955 refounded Bundeswehr, after a Constitutional clarification of Art. 24(2) of the Basic Law by the Federal Constitutional Court, could be henceforth deploy troups within NATO or UN mandates. The Federal Court ruling further tied foreign deployment to parliamentary approval. In 2013, Germany went to Mali upon French request. On the 26 April 2018, a parliamentary mandate extended the deployment of German soldiers in Mali. Accordingly, it allowed the deployment of nearly 1100 German soldiers within the MINUSMA framework. The current mandate is valid until May 31, 2019.

Germany's participation in the ongoing 'pacification' of the Sahel/Sahara region followed the stated stabilization mission and the necessity to secure peace.[18] But there is more to the German intervention in the region; the

---

18 According to the Bundeswehr (2018), its core tasks are to support the ceasefire agreements and confidence-building measures between the parties to the conflict as well as the implementation of the 2015 Peace and Reconciliation Agreement in Mali. In addition to that, the MINUSMA supports national political dialogue, security, stabilization and protection of civilians, without prejudice to the primary responsibility of the Malian authorities for impending physical violence. It also supports the establishment of state authority throughout the country and the reconstruction of the Malian security sector, as well as the protection of human rights and humanitarian aid. MINUSMA also ensures the protection of United Nations personnel and supports the preservation of Malian cultural assets.

stabilization of Mali is central to the territorial unity of the state. After the massive influx of refugees into Germany in 2015, the country understood that terror and instability in Mali would mean sooner or later that refugees from the Sahel will be heading north and this could prove a further instability factor in Europe. Both Mali and Niger are epicenters in the flight route to Europe of asylum seekers and illegal migrants towards the West. It lies on the route from Algeria to Spain. Germany and the EU are committing considerable sums of money to stop the migration from the Sahel to the Mediterranean and part of that strategy is to restore regional stability in the Sahel through direct engagement with the Islamist and irredentist militants.

This latest development which involves a seismic shift in militarily meddling overseas is yet another arena in which the drive to stem the migration tide has forced it to backtrack on its post-World War II military-averse approach. Yet, even where Germany's overseas deployment of troops signals a reassertion of its hard power, it also represents a military charm offensive to regain the respectability among its western peers. By committing personnel and materiel to the Sahel, Germany not only shares the burden already borne by France in the Sahel, but is also chipping away its image as the sleeping giant is descending on the battle field alongside France, its European ally.

CHAPTER 4

On Language, Integration, and Pedagogy

When the Süssmuth Commission formulated and submitted its policy recommendations for an improved migration regulation in Germany, most of its suggestions were, as I mentioned in Chapter 2, either watered or turned down amidst party politics, procedural mistakes, and/or died in the ambient tacit migration denial that arguably characterized the country's migration policies hitherto. But Süssmuth and the Commission she led might have succeeded to draw attention to the pending integration task of inserting the migrants that were living in the country and migrants that would likely want to settle in the country in the future. It called for a unified integration approach to foreigners' integration, in which language acquisition and knowledge of the German society were to play an important role. With the coming into force in 2005 of a new Residence Act (*Aufenthaltsgesetz*), as well as the Regulation Act on Integration Courses (*Integrationskursverordnung*) and the Regulation Act on Integration Class Tests (*Integrationskurstestverordnung*), the country laid the foundation for a unified, Germany-wide and centralized integration testing system, placed under the supervision of the Federal Office for Migration and Refugees (BAMF).

An integration class consists of a German language course followed by an orientation course. The duration of the combined two classes (language and integration classes) can vary between 430 to 1,000 teaching hours, depending on the ability of the individual learners, the specifics of the enrolled course (courses that start with a previous alphabetization class, or special classes for women or youth). The common, frequently enrolled class, the so-called general integration classes (*Allgemeiner Integrationskurs*) lasts 700 teaching hours while intensive classes last 430 such teaching hours. Participants have their language proficiency tested before their enrollment in a language class and they are orientated towards the appropriate class or module for their needs and according to their prior knowledge of the language. Learners showing the lowest level of German proficiency (but not with no lacunae in the knowledge of the Latin alphabet – in which case they would be directed to a alphabetization language class) must start from level A1.1 and work their way to level B1.2. At the end of module B1.2, learners take the exam "Deutsch-Test für Zuwanderer" (DTZ) "German Test for Immigrants." The language class is followed by an orientation class (varying between 30 teaching hours in intensive classes to 100 teaching hours in general integration classes). The orientation class touches on such issues such as the German legal system (basically the Basic Rights enshrined in the first section of the *Grundgesetz*, the German Constitution), history (mainly the post-World-War II GDR and FRG) and culture. With the completion of the orientation course, migrants take the final test "*Leben in Deutschland,*" "Living in Germany". Learners who exhaust the prescribed teaching hours and nonetheless fail to pass the language test are granted 300 additional hours to repeat part of the class and ultimately take the language test a second time.

Since 1 July 2016, public or private integration class organizers are paid 3. 90 € per language student and per teaching hour (45 minutes). The language student is expected to pay 1. 95€ as a contribution to costs (so-called *Kostenbeitrag*). Generally, the costs are fully covered for participants on welfare either by the Migration and Refugee Office, the Foreigner Office, or the Employment Office. Moreover, migrants that live more than 3.5 km away from the course location are refunded their transportation costs during the duration of their integration or state-financed language classes.

Until the massive arrival of refugees in 2015, integration courses were mostly discussed in the specialized spheres of linguists, and migration journalists. Indeed, the 'liberalization' of integration classes (opened to refugees with good prospects of staying in Germany following the massive arrival of asylum seekers in 2015) and the increased budget for integration classes has drawn the public's attention on the integration class. As a case in point, on 29 April 2018 the German newspapers *Frankfurter Allgemeine Zeitung* published in its Sunday edition, figures on refugees' success rate in the German language test for the year 2017. The news item, also published on the Facebook page of the outlet, citing numbers from the Federal Office for Migration and Refugees for the year 2017, recorded that 339,578 people attended an integration course for the first time in 2017. Another 289,751 later took the language test at the end of the course. Out of that number, 48.7 percent of test-takers achieved the set target of "B1". 40.8 percent reached the "A2" level while the rest performed below that proficiency level.

Integration class organizers, language teachers, the BAMF, and the Federal Office hastened to provide explanation for the poor performance of the newly arrived migrants in the language test. According to the course organizers, many of the students came from other language families with no prior contact with an Indo-European language or the Latin alphabet and are in their adulthood – where language acquisition arguably seems to be more challenging than at a younger age. BAMF pointed to illness, work or relocation to explain the poor performance of the refugees in the tests. Adult education centers blamed poor performance on trauma, high expectations, and impatience from the host society. The Federal Audit Office attributes the poor performance to absenteeism from classes (auditors encountered only 43.3% of the 10.000 registered attendants in 528 audited classes), and fraud (cases of infants being registered as course attendants). However, the news item author Christoph Schäfer ultimately points to a flawed system of competing incentives for the poor results of the language students. In this almost-Rashomon perspective, the voice and perspectives of the refugees are sorely missing. These voices are generally the most critical and auto-critical. Some would denounce what they perceive to be incompetent teachers or blame the disinterest, absenteeism of their fellow classmates for the bad results.

To be sure, language has always served as an operator of societal inclusion or exclusion, a Shibboleth that has now mutated into an extensive testing system to assess and certify a foreigner's progress and integration in the host society. The year 2015 nonetheless highlighted a particular Foucauldian aspect of this integration management system. The integration classes were henceforth construed in the political discourse as a measure for crime and violence prevention, ruling the (unruly) bodies of the refugees before frustration, boredom turns them to criminals and religious extremists. A 2015 quote by Joachim Gauck, the then-Federal President, addressing the aforementioned point is instructive. In the words of the then-President, "the sooner people who will likely stay, learn German and work, the better for us all. Otherwise we risk frustration and boredom becoming violence and crime, or political and religious extremism thriving (quoted in Schäfer, 29 April 2018, my translation)." Integration classes and subsequent work should keep the refugees from the streets, busy them with language classes and thus guarantee social peace.[1] The events of the so-called *Kölner Silvesternacht*,[2] where women were assaulted on New Year's Eve in Cologne mostly by North-African and Arab young men, has led to a stronger focus on orientation classes, where German political values are to be imparted to the refugees. But these events do not solely determine the new philosophy of integration. Germany's philosophy and praxis of integration also takes place against the background of what Favell has characterized as "the emergence or re-emergence of ethnic, cultural or religious movements among minority groups; the reappearance of overtly racist and xenophobic attitudes

---

[1] Such statements call for Foucauldian analysis of the management of refugees. Foucault's ideas of governmentality as a set of subtle power and control techniques to the management of migrants/refugees through integration classes. The governmentality regime as a *dispositif, an apparatus* of disparate elements aimed to structure the refugee's every day. In such an approach, welfare transfers, language classes would take a central in the biopolitics of migration control. On Foucault and biopolitics, see Foucault 2011.

[2] On the *Kölner Silversternacht*, See in German, Dürr et al. 2016, Wiermer, 2017.

among majority populations; the continuing difficulties of race relations, and the appearance of the so-called multicultural society; and, at the strongest extreme [...]. In the countries of Western Europe, many of these problems have been brought on by post-war immigration, and the integration of new ethnic groups who came and stayed (Favell, 2001, p.1)." The events in Cologne, the new role of language and orientation classes take place against the background of the perceived (failed) integration of the Muslim migrants, 'imported' to the country in the years of accelerated post-War economic development. 'General' language classes coupled with orientation classes should help exorcise the demons of the past.

The concept of integration as applied to migration is a travelling concept par excellence. Before it came to occupy a central role in migration control mechanisms and fit with other core concepts such equality, public order and tolerance into a normative framework, the concept had already been in circulation (ibid., p. 2).[3] Favell traces a genealogy of integration that runs from American sociological functionalism to the Hobbesian problem of value pluralism, societal need for order and inclusion, to the Chicago School's use of the term to study race and ethnicity (ibid., p. 3). Mastering social integration is not only a question of integrating migrant minorities into the majority social group but a crucial task in preserving the "unity and order of the nation, and the public myths and traditions that hold it together (ibid.)." Bauder has pointed to the ambivalence of integration as used in debates about migration. In a comparative study of migration policies in Canada and Germany, he observed that 'integration' sometimes "stands for the recognition of diversity and difference. More often, the term implies conformity and assimilation to the resident population [...]. Similarly, among both conservative and progressive political circles in Germany, [...], the term integration embodies an 'authoritarian ideology' that requires immigrants to assume the identity and behavior of an imagined German culture (Treibel 1999: 57–58) (Bauder, 2001, p. 9)."

In this chapter, I want to make sense of the role of language as a central instrument in the integration policy. I argue that the development of structural

---

3 Drawing from Berry (1997), Rubin, Watt, and Ramelli (2012, p. 498) have defined integration in the context of immigration as form of acculturation marked by regular contact between immigrants and host national combined with a maintenance of original culture. Alternative strategies involve assimilation, separation, marginalization and rest on limited social contact with locals in the host society. For Rubin, Watt, and Ramelli, social integration facilitates and improves intergroup relations between immigrants and locals, enables access to the social capital of host nationals which translate into better employment and lifestyle opportunities, and the reduction of health risks (2012, p. 499).

linguistics, which run parallel to the constitution of European nations, and language construed as a marker of cultural and national identity, have laid the foundation to demand from the migrant that they master the language of their host society. I introduce the 'foreigner' into the Bourdieusian reading of Sausurrian linguistics. In structural linguistics, language is a learnable and transmittable code and modern integration regimes expect the migrant to master these linguistic codes. Structural linguistics provide the rational, 'scientific' ground that foreign languages are systematically learnable codes while the national imaginary elevates language as the marker of identity, belonging, or 'will to belong' par excellence. Willingness to adhere to the nation is thus tested through the proved competence in the national language of the host society. Therefore, this exigence and indeed the promotion of German foreign language classes, and their relevance for residence permit and citizenship application, appear to be a common-sense policy.

I then move to the second part of the chapter where I discuss the significance and effects of refugees'/foreigners' performances in the language integration exams. I draw from my direct experience as a lecturer in German integration classes as I attempt to understand the poor performance (language test results) by students by assessing them against the theories of second language acquisition.

In the third part of the chapter, I introduce radical pedagogy into thinking about language teaching and integration. Applying Ivan Illich's *Deschooling Society*, I analyse how integration in a society does not simply emanate from language textbooks. Integrating foreigners need not only be delegated to adult education centers or language schools. The grammar of a society – its values, culture, and history – should not only be learned in a classroom, except the classroom is transformed to better reflect the social and political complexity of the host society. Undoubtedly, "educational hardware and software", to borrow a phrase by Illich (Illich 1970, Introduction, p. vii), increased as new textbooks were printed and released as a response to accrued needs of German integration classes after 2015. Nonetheless Ivan Illich's proposition for new "educational webs which heighten the opportunity for each one to transform each moment of his living into one of learning, sharing, caring" needs to be heeded (Illich 1970, Introduction, p. vii). At the heart of Illich's argument is what he perceives to be a confusion between "process and substance" where health, learning, dignity, independence, and creative endeavor are defined by little more than the performance of the institutions which claim to serve these ends, and their improvement is made to depend on allocating more resources to the management of hospitals, schools, and the agencies in question. Integration needs to be more than acquiring a B1-certificate. Instead, it needs to grow into a full-fledged social and political emancipatory opportunity for the migrant/refugee.

Other pedagogues whose works provide critical lenses relevant to analyze the integration issue include Rancière's Jacotot and Paulo Freire. I examine the claim of the universal intelligence of Jacotot in foreign language acquisition as well his conception of auto-didactical learning. Jacotot's language pedagogy contrasts with current methods in language teaching. In Jacotot's pedagogy, language learning and teaching take the dimensions of intellectual emancipation. I also review Freire and find that his *Pedagogy of the Oppressed* is not only a piece of critical pedagogical methodology or the storehouse of key concepts such as the banking concept of education, cultural invasion. I argue that there is more to Freire's book. I re-interpret it as a personal missive to the (mostly) Syrian refugee who fled oppression to find refuge in Germany. Freire seems to have much to say about their struggle, their present condition and the prospect of their integration in the German society.

1   Language, Structuralist Linguistics, and Integration

Hogan-Brun, Mar-Molinero, Stevenson (2009, p. 1) have noted that linguistic and cultural requirements are being increasingly used as instruments of European gate-keeping, for the achievement of citizenship in many EU member states. They thus urged for a 'fuller conceptual and theoretical basic' to come to terms with the new role of language in migration regulation and the societal integration of migrants by drawing on influential works on the centrality of language in identity marking, exclusion, and nationalism including Barbour and Carmichael's (2000), Wright's (2000), and May's (2003). As they respectively remarked, the role of language as an operator of exclusion in nationalist projects, has been widely documented. They explain the rise of language as an instrument of migration control rooted in the geographical expansion that is linked to the 'trials and tribulations'[4] of the state in Europe. In their version of language post-war territory incorporation (as the incorporation of South Tyrol by Italy), or state failure (as the dismembering of the former Yugoslavia), increased mobility of people following the eastward enlargement of the EU which brought together different ways of living and cultures and the ensuing disruption of bureaucratic patterns. These processes have created new perceptions on pressures and needs that ultimately led to the re-adjustment of institutional frameworks (Hogan-Brun, Mar-Molinero, and Stevenson, 2009, p. 2).

---

4 I borrow the term 'trials and tribulations' from Hoffmann (2008).

More concretely, they locate the application of language tests and the tightening of residence rights in many European countries to the eastward enlargement of the EU. When the language and cultural tests were first administered, they relied on a relatively informal and arbitrary basis, but would soon evolve into clear pre-requisites for residence and citizenship applications (ibid., p. 3). Even though their descriptive analysis of the evolution of language into an inner and outer migration control tool is cogent, it does not theoretically help to inform how precisely language was drawn in the gate-keeping scheme. Instead, discussions on language and nation tend to move quickly to what I would term the post-structuralist view on language and integration, with its over-emphasis on the political, ethical implications of language as a criterion for granting residence and citizenship rights. I argue instead that to make sense of this new situation, one can turn to structural linguistics (especially Saussure) to understand the development of the language testing regime. The formalization of the testing procedures, the quasi-scientific approach to measuring proficiency levels outgrow from the structuralist view on language.

Bourdieu reckoned that Saussurian structural linguistics had demarcated the discipline of linguistics from anthropology, sociology or any cognate discipline to consider language as a thing in itself. It is a conception of language removed from social relations (Bourdieu, 1991, p. 33). The critique of this original theoretical gesture by Saussure will constitute the basis for Bourdieu's own post-structuralist attack on linguistics. Bourdieu's charges on linguistics, its blindness from social power relations and its appearance of scientificity (ibid., p. 33), its romanticization of language, i.e. treating language an object of contemplation rather than as an instrument of action and power (ibid., p. 37), or its reductionism of the social world to symbolic exchanges decipherable by means of a code which language itself represents (ibid., p. 37) are ironically the ingredients that promoted language to the main migration and integration policy tool. Parallel to the constitution of structural linguistics is the emergence of standardized language that divested language from external, sociological elements, repressed the heterogeneity of linguistic practices (i.e. dialects), codified the rules of the language and thus enabled the possibility to decide between a right use and a wrong use of the language. Language, indeed 'the social world as a universe of symbolic exchanges [...] destined to be deciphered by means of a cipher or a code, language or culture (ibid., p. 37).' Since language is a (learnable) code (grammar), predicated on the universal linguistic ability of speech (materialized in the individual) to generate an infinite number of grammatically correct discourses and thus participate in the transaction on the 'linguistic market' with inherent 'system of specific sanctions and censorships (ibid.),' the knowledge of grammar ensures the insertion of the individual in society and define its ability to interact in the linguistic marketplace. It is thus assumed that a better command of grammar guarantees the insertion of the individual in the host society.

Such a development would have not been possible if the nation-state had not chosen its official language, constituted a standardized language, and indeed codified its rules. The constitution of a standardized language with a learnable code that guarantees the possibility to interact on the social market lay a perceived rationale not only to expect that migrants acquire the linguistic code of their host society, but indeed to demand and assess their proficiency in the national language. The learnable code is the official language, conscribed within the geographical boundaries of the nation-state, later exported to yonder territories in the imperialistic expansion. The official language displaced the multiplicity of dialects, formalized itself through the labor of grammarians who codifies its rules, lexicographers who performs the inventory of the vocabulary treasure of the language or ultimately teachers that impart knowledge of the language and censor non-grammatical forms of speech. The extension of the official language mobilizes similar agents to ensure that the official language now taught as foreign language within the boundaries of the state. Linguists are called to determine the curriculum of the contents to be imparted to migrants within the framework of integration classes.[5]

Popular wisdom prefers to liken language to a wealth, a *common good* available to all and preserved through practice.[6] It is a treasure that is not only available to the particular linguistic community that shared a standardized language. Learning the new linguistic code of their host society, the migrant is enjoying an inexhaustible source of wealth, equally available to all. For Bourdieu, partaking in the production and consumption of language-treasure is a 'symbolic appropriation,' a 'mystical participation,' the 'illusion of linguistic communism which haunts all linguistic theory (Bourdieu, 1991, p.43).' Bourdieu believes to have identified in the structural linguistics of Saussure remnants of this mystical metaphoric conception of language and the sense of belonging. Bourdieu's impatience with this conception is that he finds fault

---

5 Following the recommendation of the Süssmuth-Commission, experts on migration as well as from the practice of migration and integration were tasked to outline the guideline for integration courses. Linguists Maas and Mehlem have reviewed different integration class policies and formulated their recommendation for the design of the orientation classes (See Maas and Mehlem 2003, p. 4).

6 For Auguste Comte, for example, '[l]anguage forms a kind of wealth, which all can make use of at once without causing any diminution of the store, and which thus admits a complete community of enjoyment; for all, freely participating in the general treasure, unconsciously aid in its preservation (quoted in Bourdieu, 1991, p. 43).'

with the universality of uniform accessibility of language to the individual of the community (ibid., p. 43). In line with the metaphor of language as treasure, migrants could be expected to acquire the language of their host country as a personal, symbolic, mystical investment, an increase of their own linguistic capital.

From the point of view of language policy making, emphasizing the treasure aspect of language (as also open to newcomers), would mean the celebration of multilingual 'treasures' and migrants' contribution to the enrichment of the local language. But migration policy has been slow to let migrants partake in this renewable linguistic treasure, preferring instead to exploit the bodies for economic growth in the early nineteenth century. Migrants were also most likely to occupy the lower segments of the labor market (with limited oral and written language production demands) so that the promotion of linguistic competence did not seem to be the priority of the migration policy makers in the nineteenth century.[7]

Since then, the situation has not radically changed considering the policy of language promotion for migrants in the post-World War II era. Migrants acquired a functional knowledge of the host language that proved relevant for everyday use and communicating with the state's institutions. Functional oral knowledge was what the low-skilled laborer thought they needed to cope while navigating the extensive bureaucratic communication which required linguistic abilities that were not readily teachable to foreigners. As such, when the general and extended integration classes were being planned, Maas and Mehlem, two linguists, were tasked with outlining the strategic aspects of an integration curriculum for Germany. The reviewers suggested that the integration classes should be oriented towards the conditions of the present German society in order to guarantee the optimal participation of the migrants. This meant for the reviewers, that since Germany's linguistic practice is an intensively written one, language acquisition classes for the migrants should focus on the transmission of written language (2003, p. 13). Their proposal did not reflect in the later design of integration language class curricula. Nonetheless, it did reflect an important historical modality of the function of official language in the administrative and regulative apparatus of the state. As Bourdieu knew, codified language is primarily a written official language in the form of grammar textbooks that disseminate theoretical norms of the language (Bourdieu, 1991, p. 45).

---

7   See Chapter 2 on the brief history of migration policies in Germany.

2 The Language Testing Regime and Its Discontent

The critical approach to understanding language proficiency testing program weaves together the strand of critical appraising on language and the nation on the one hand, and a post-structuralist critique on the symbolic power of the testing and examination regime on the other hand. On the count of a critical reading of the testing regime, Shohamy has suggested a critical appraisal of testing. Drawing on Bourdieu, Foucault, and Spolsky, Shohamy expounded the unquestioned ideologies surrounding the symbolic of the testing regime. Drawing from Bourdieu, she takes the idea that tests operate on the level of symbolic power, a kind of unwritten contract meant to perpetuate a dominant social order. They are the token for social order, an indication of control, and ultimately a means of perpetuating rapports of dominance. Governments use the acceptance for tests as an instrument of migration control. From Foucault, Shohamy derives the ideas that tests have an unchallenged authority, a province of expert knowledge, clad in the belief in the ability of test to improve educational systems. From Spolsky, she draws the idea that the general public has been brainwashed into believing in the infallibility, fairness, and meaningfulness of tests and examination (Shohamy, 2009, p. 50).

Horner provides a similar critique on language in the wider migration and integration policies of some European countries. Drawing from Piller, Blommaert, Verschueren, Blackledge, Milani, and Anderson, Horner argues that the recourse of language follows ideological motives and is inscribed within a dogma of linguistic and cultural homogeneism that aim to guarantee the illusion of nation-state (2009, p. 113). Likewise, Billig's early take on language and the nation locates the relationship between language, ethnic identity in a longer geneaology made of eighteenth century romanticism and late modern anxieties on the frailty of the imagined communities. As Billig reminds, Herder and Fichte located the genius of a nation in its language (1995, p. 14). Billig does not however explain the emergence of language with romanticism and anxiety. His comprehensive review of the literature on language and the nation-state reveals more a mosaic of industrialist (Gellner), military (Kennedy), and (commercial) capitalist (Anderson, Mann, Nair, Hroch) reasons that account for the emergence of the official language and the nation-state (ibid., p. 22). Billig's contribution to the debate on the language and the nation-state and nationalism was to suggest that it was nationalism that "creates 'our' common-sense, unquestioned view that there are, 'naturally' and unproblematically, things called different 'languages,' which we speak (ibid., p. 30)."

The confluence of these two streams is best materialized in the regime centralizing and formalizing the teaching of language. A research program emerged to critically appraise the language testing regime from within and reveals the practical shortcomings of the regime. They argue that using language proficiency as a criterion to grant residence and citizenship rights raises ethical and political questions. They wonder if it is appropriate to use linguistic proficiency to this end (Hogan-Brun, Mar-Molinero, and Stevenson, 2009, p. 3). They note that the extension of language to the testing regime is a rekindling of the long-contested relationship between language and nation.[8] They ultimately assert that "the underlying purpose of this discourse is to re-assert an idea of the integrity of the nation rooted in stable monolingualism rather than addressing the perceived challenges of a supposedly divisive multilingualism (ibid., p. 11)."

Indeed, the design of the language integration classes reflects the troubled relationship to multilingualism. Van Avermaet notes that while multilingualism is promoted within the EU, as exemplified by the European Union's policy of mother tongue plus two foreign languages ('M+2') (2009, p. 19), the plurilingualism of migrants is often presented as a barrier in the process of learning the language of the host country, thus hindering the process of participation and integration. Van Avermaet concludes that, "migrants have to adapt to a monolingual policy and discourse that promotes monolingualism as the norm (2009, p. 20)."

It has further been noted that language tests that assess the linguistic proficiency of a speaker can be counter-productive. Language acquisition curricula take the shape of a one-size-fit-all measure to the different types of learners who exhibit different levels of competency in specific language areas. As such, Van Avermaet has pleaded for language teaching and testing programs that consider the specific needs, and possibilities of the individual learners. In Van Avermaet's words, "language teaching programmes or tests developed for measuring the proficiency of the 'official' language(s) should meet those 'parts' of a plurilingual repertoire of task-specific competencies that are absent or are needed by a particular person. This is the case for newly arrived migrant children at school, for people looking for a job, for parents that want to communicate with the school, for integration, for citizenship, and so on (ibid., p. 21)."

---

8 The tension persists even if "it is now formulated in apparently less jingoistic and more inclusive terms of a common language within the state in order to achieve the moral purpose of social justice and cohesion and the political purpose of active citizenship. The language of the national majority is couched in official discourses as both the willingness on the part of the newcomers to accept and learn this majority language as the legitimate national language, and as the appropriate democratic way to include the new arrivals in public life [...]" (Hogan-Brun, Mar-Molinero, and Stevenson, 2009, p. 11)."

Consequently, Van Avermaet has taken aim at the Common European Framework of Reference (CEFR) which serves as a benchmark for language proficiency assessment in several European countries, including the German language teaching assessment framework for migrants committed to attend integration classes. Van Avermaet notices that the framework, originally meant to promote multilingualism in Europe, fails to do justice to learner groups with low level of literacy or functional illiterates (ibid., p. 34). Indeed, the CERF regime is not only predicated on a high degree of literacy, as Van Avermaet argues, but ideally on a high degree of literacy in an Indo-European language. To provide an example, a Syrian engineer, who would have had their entire education in Arabic language, might experience considerable difficulties in coming to terms with the German language or reaching the set target of B1 despite their obvious advanced literacy.

Van Avermaet's biggest challenge is the statement that "knowledge of the standard language does not by definition solve the 'problems' faced by immigrants since they are structurally discriminated against. Their language use is an effect of that rather than a cause. As long as socio-economic marginalization continues, access to the standard language will remain restricted; and as long as the poor performances of immigrant children at school can be explained as systematic and structural, upward social mobility and access to the standard language (which often go hand in hand) will also remain limited (ibid., p. 35)."

To some extent, there is empirical evidence to make sense of Van Avermaet's skepticism. Some migrants would have certainly filled several forms, registered their newborns, rented apartments, and visited several historical places in their city of residence before being exposed to textbook lessons with didactic content related to these issues within the context of their language and political orientation class. Likewise, others who have attended the language class and reached the required B1 will still need assistance to make sense of the official correspondence they receive and most importantly will need to attend additional higher language classes to meet the requirements to start specific vocational training. In other words, except from meeting requirements for residence and eventually for citizenship applications, the practical use of the B1-language certificate appears to be limited. Shohamy's question as to what "extent knowledge of a new language is always *essential* for *all* newcomers in order to function 'properly' in the new society they move to (2009, p. 48, emphasis in the original)" will remain unanswered.

Maybe these dissatisfactions have left some scholars skeptical of language as a criterion of integration. Van Avermaet ends up seeing the immigrant policies "as a token of the revival of the nation-state, with one language, one identity, and one uniform set of shared norms and values. This is supposed to instill in people a feeling of security and confidence (ibid., p. 36)." For Shohamy, language proficiency tests are "biased, discriminating and unattainable requirements that can lead to invalid decisions about the rights of people in societies (2009, p. 45)." However, Shohamy's most worrisome insight is that failure to learn the official language "is often associated with lack of willingness to assimilate and to belong, or as having negative attitudes towards the state [or the host society]. Immigrants are often viewed in stereotypical terms as taking advantage of the economy of the new country with no willingness to be part of the new society and to contribute to its welfare (ibid., p. 47, squared bracket added)." These are the stakes for the migrant.

3   Challenges in Acquiring German as a Second Language, and Integration

Failing to reach the set level of B1 is often considered in public discussion as an integration denial from the migrant, feeding the prejudice of the lazy migrant who enjoys the welfare of their host society but are unwilling to integrate. Success in a language test has turned into the ultimate benchmark to gauge the ability or – better put – the willingness of the individual to integrate into the host society. A response to the negative image of refugees that ensue from perceived poor results cannot simply be limited to hammering arguments on the imagined community and culture, or on nationalism and the 'manufacturing' of the official language that I have reviewed above. There is a need to complement the necessary critical perspective on the age-old relationship between the nation-state and language with a linguistic discussion on second (or third or fourth) language acquisition. Indeed, such an approach will throw some light on the non-linguistic parameters that determine and influence language acquisition. The universal faculty of speech and the a priori 'learnability' of nearly any language has created legitimate expectations that are only tempered by considering the environmental conditions in the acquisition of a second language. Stating that some migrants perform poorly at language tests because they are too old to optimally learn a second language does not do justice to the complexity of the issue on second language acquisition. Having taught German language courses in the so-called integration classes with prior alphabetization classes, as well as regular A1 to B1-integration and orientation classes, and subsequently in B2-level classes, I have had a participant observer's perspective on second language acquisition. I accompanied adults of both sexes, with different learning biographies, from varied cultural backgrounds on parts of their journey to acquiring the German language as a second or foreign language. I offer here a distilled insight on migrants' experience in language learning in the classroom to make sense of the challenges that migrants encounter. I rely on Lightbown and Spada's primer *How Languages are Learnt* to arrange my observations on the migrants' acquisition of the German language and reflect on them through some of the theories presented in their primer. Where their primer does not provide the appropriate framework for my purposes, I return to the original research to deepen my insights and discuss the literature. My hope is to transcend or throw more light on the condescending judgments on some migrants' poor performances in language test and restore the complexity of second language acquisition within the wider debate.

3.1   *Linguistic Interferences and Second Language Acquisition*

Integration class attendants are acquiring the German language mostly as their second, third (or any other fitting ordinal number) language, but mostly, as a foreign language. Between 2016 and now most integration class learners I have accompanied were Arabic speakers. Advanced literates in Arabic understood and used Modern Standard Arabic (MSA), the official language taught in school and used in the administration, the media and most generally in formal situations. But most of the German language learners from Syria or Iraq were more conversant in their native Levantine dialect, which they used for their daily communication with peers or family members both in Syria and now in exile. To some extent, it could be posited that there is a correlation between the degree of mastery of MSA by an Arabic speaker and the time they spent in formal education setting. Nonetheless, speakers with lower levels of formal literacy are auditory competent in MSA. Their learning style, when they have approached other foreign languages, was mainly spoken, a speaking-by-hearing approach. As such, I encountered some Syrians who felt themselves confident enough to have German instructions translated to them in Turkish when no Arabic translator was available. They explained to me that they managed to gather functional oral knowledge during their transit period to Germany. This period varies immensely. The functional competence, however, I would postulate developed in those learners who stayed and worked in Turkey for example for a minimal duration of six months.

A common feature, independent of whether Syrian learners mastered oral and written MSA was that their native language interfered with the acquisition of German, as all second language learners experience at one point or another. For those Arabic learners who (formally) learned an Indo-European language (say English) before taking on German, linguistic interference tended to frequently occur in higher language learning levels such as B2. For other learners, the phonetical, morphological, syntactical, and pragmatic rules interfered with the new language. Linguists have noted that for second language learners, knowledge of the mother tongue or other foreign language can cause "incorrect guesses about how the second language works, and this may result in errors that first language learners would not make (Lightbow and Spada, 2006, p. 30)."

Here is an example to illustrate this point: in MSA, it is possible to omit the copula (to be) in sentences such as I (am) at home, I (am) Ernesto. Instead Arabic allows one to directly say *'I at home'* or *'I Ernesto'*. I have observed Arabic-speaking learners omit the present tense forms (*bin, bist, ist, sind, seid*) of the German copula 'sein.' They thus produced sentences such as *'Ich Ammar,'* *'Ich zu Hause,'* an interference that in some cases was not corrected after 600 hours of German language learning. The situation is of course different when the learner had a previous contact with a Germanic or Roman language where the copula is systematically employed. Another instance: the phonetics of the first language has sometimes played tricks on German learners from the Levant. MSA's vowel system comprises three vowels, *damma, wāw, fatha, alif, kasra,* respectively pronounced as [ū], [a], [ā], [i]. Damma [u], and kasra [i] can be realized as long vowels too. On the other side, the German vowel system comprises eight vowel letters: a, e, i, o, u, ä, ö and ü, and in loan words, the vowels y and é. In total, these monothongs are realized in nearly 16 different phonological pronunciations. Added to these are the diphthongs (written as ai, eu, ei) and the diacritical umlaut that can prove perplexing when one hails directly from a phonological system with only three basic vowels. The (natural) strategy for learners is thus to assimilate German vowels to the most proximate Arabic vowels and ignore diacritic differences altogether. As such, vowels that are not known in the first language are assimilated to those that are known. Incidentally, [i] is pronounced in a proximity to [e] and [u] realized instead of [o]. The consonant [p] which is absent from the Arabic alphabet is mostly phonologically assimilated and pronounced as a [b]. But when learners have been drawn to pay attention to the phonemic differences, they increased the quality of their pronunciation and with that improved the auditory, written discrimination of words featuring these vowels.

A further illustration of the influence of the first language can be found in the written language. Beginners sometimes omit vowels in writing, a possibility in MSA where the diacritical marks for (short) vowels could be written or left out. In written examinations, such orthographic mistakes could lead to marks being withdrawn if the teacher estimates that the mistakes are frequent and endanger the semantic composition of the sentence.

But the influence of the first language is not only negative. Lightbown and Spada explain that (adult) second language learners have assets such as cognitive maturity and metalinguistic abilities that help them solve linguistic problems and discuss language (Lightbown and Spada, 2006, p. 30). Indeed cognitive maturity and metalinguistic abilities appeal to me as resources that are seldom used in language teaching. I have drawn so-called vowel diagrams for beginners, trying to explain the distance between vowels and their mode of pronunciation and explained to them the basic mechanism of the human speech apparatus and how sounds are made. One could have thought it to advanced German linguistic studies for beginners, but adult learners are constantly interrogating the language, looking to work out the rules of the language for themselves. Where younger learners *just*' learn the language, adult learners tend to constantly interrogate the language and are only 'satisfied' when they can understand the logic behind some rules. Providing basic linguistics principles on how language functions, the relationship between morphology and phonology, or the valence of verbs and their importance in the syntactic flexibility of German sentences, or breaking irregular verbs to the phonemic vowel pattern to far more advanced learners, providing etymological explanations, I have noticed, has helped some remember vocabulary items and grammar units that first proved uninteresting or daunting to them. In fact, tapping into the metalinguistic abilities of adult second language learners and their readiness to discuss aspects of the new language can overcome learners' apprehensions and stimulate the learning process altogether. Textbooks could break down relevant linguistic principles for the target language and incorporate them. Some students had reported to me, they found the German language difficult and lost interest because their teachers replied to their questions about language with a lapidary 'It is so. You have to learn it like this.' Indeed, official language as a code is not always easy to decipher and teachers' exasperation with metalinguistic questions is perfectly understandable. Nonetheless, students' metalinguistic questions are proof enough of their cognitive engagement with the language, a resource that should not be neglected in second language acquisition integration classes.

3.2   *Frustration and Stress Avoidance*

All second language learners or indeed all learners of any new subject (to them), experience frustration in their learning curves, mostly in the earlier stages of the learning process. Students have reported to me their frustration that after numerous hours spent learning grammar, building up their vocabulary, they were unable to make sense of most of the official communication when they run their regular errands, visit the doctor, shop or attend job fairs.

Also, annoyed and less empathic interlocutors have sometimes not proven supportive in helping language students in these very crucial stages of the learning process.

Faced with early stage frustration, language learners can persevere in their learning endeavor or exit the endeavor altogether. This depends on whether pedagogical assistance and re-motivation are provided at the right juncture. An indication of frustration is arbitrary absenteeism in language classes. Students that regularly attend their language courses and mid-way abstain from attending classes without health reasons might be in such a crisis. Cases of absenteeism in integration classes or language classes that are state-financed are subject to sanctions. Accordingly, when learners fail to attend classes, they are reported to the BAMF or the employment office who issue warnings. Failure to cooperate can lead to a curtailing of welfare allocations. Students may yield and continue to come class but might be less receptive, daydream or may eventually project this unresolved frustration in the classroom, impeding other learners' progress or picking on the teacher.

When frustration occurrences are identified, a private session with the learner, explaining to them the psychology of learning and the reasons for the situation they are undergoing can boost morale and get the language student back on track. Otherwise, students move from the frustration phase to what one could term in this context a stress-avoidance strategy. This implies the avoidance of situations where they must make use of their perceived modest language skills. They reduce social integration to interaction with interlocutors that share their first language and rely on acquaintances competent in German to help them negotiate official communication situations.

The causes for frustration are nonetheless also rooted in the obvious inability of language textbooks to perfectly reflect the discourse types to which learners would be confronted with. There are discrepancies between the official language taught in the classroom and the real-life occurrences of the students.[9] Lightbown and Spada have argued that, "classroom learners not only spend less time in contact with the language, they also tend to be exposed to a far smaller range of discourse types. For example, classroom learners are often taught language that is somewhat formal in comparison to the language as it is used in most social settings (ibid., p. 32)." Language teaching is at a best a map that reproduces parts of the immense territory of language. There arguably

---

9 Experienced native speakers would adjust their communication when they face a foreigner, going slowly and speaking in a speed that is understandable for the learner. But others who are less empathetic would either code-switch to a common language, mostly English or reduce the communication to the minimum that a situation may require.

cannot be a language textbook or language class that can extensively prepare the students to adequately master the communication situations they will confront in the outside world. Language learning can also be said to be the development of heuristic tools to confront new situations. As such, the contrastive analysis hypothesis (CAH) in structural linguistics implies a heuristic of language learning and guessing. It predicts that language learners should be able to acquire the structures of a target language with ease and where first and target languages differ, learners should experience greater difficulties. Research nonetheless has shown that many of the actual errors learners make are not predictable based on their first language (ibid., p. 33).

Arabic and German hail from different language families and should according to the CAH approach be mutually difficult for learners from these two respective languages. But dissimilar languages can exhibit surprising resemblance that similar languages don't have. For example, English and German are both Germanic languages but their cardinal number systems differ. From 21 to 99, one needs to reverse the number and pronounce them as (i.e. *one and twenty,* for (*einundzwangig*), 21) in German, a structure that is not used used in English. A native English speaker may thus encounter more difficulty internalizing the cardinal number system of German than an Arabic speaker, since their first language's cardinal system operates in the same fashion. An innateness hypothesis that is relevant to make sense of language learning is the acquisition-learning hypothesis. In this framework, language is 'acquired' in an unconscious way, by being exposed to a sample from the target language that one understands and is 'learned' by paying attention to form and rulemaking (p. 36). This seems however remote from the learning styles I could observe.

3.3   *Affective Filters and Trauma*

Krashen (1982) had suggested the 'affective filter hypothesis' to explain why some learners even though widely exposed to considerable linguistic inputs from the target language, nonetheless fail to learn the language. For Lightbown and Spada, the 'affective filter' "is a metaphorical barrier that prevents learners from acquiring language even when appropriate input is available. Affect refers to feelings, motives, needs, attitudes, and emotional states. A learner who is tense, anxious, or bored may 'filter out' input, making it unavailable for acquisition (ibid., p. 37)." There is something commonsensical about the affective filter hypothesis, that learners acquire language skills when they are mentally predisposed to receive language information and process it. Refugees who left their families behind and arrived in Germany have testified on the difficulties they have in concentrating to learn German when family members were still being bombed in their home country, or somewhere in transit in Greece or

Turkey with uncertain prospects of reuniting the family in the near future. But when the affective filter is not applied to the circumstances of the home country, the need to settle in the new country has produced additional affects. When refugees arrived in 2015, they were gathered in camps where the atmosphere was not conducive to learning. For some, the search for accommodation (mostly in the big urban centers) has not been an easy endeavor. It is nonetheless possible to argue that all affects cannot be suppressed before one starts to study a language, especially when the stakes are high. Affects never stop and mostly do not endure.

More disquieting, I find, is the issue of trauma. Even if research on trauma and education in Germany has in recent years been more concerted, it must still be remembered that educational trauma research has a long history. Before the latest wave of refugees from Syria and Iraq, the research program on trauma and education in Germany engaged with the integration and education of traumatized refugees from the Balkan countries in the context of the Cold War in Eastern Europe. Based on this research, Ognjenović has described refugee existence as a chain of destroyed self-images, a continuity of destruction. For her, being a refugee leads to a destruction of individuality. All people who had to flee are marked by the same fate, she argued. They lose their first and last name, their occupation and age, gender, personal and family characteristics, their personal and family history. Everything that happened suddenly disappeared. All that was taken for granted has been erased and must be recreated, or at least demonstrated (Ognjenović, 2005, p. 14).

There have been pedagogical guidelines to help teachers assist traumatized German language learners. The State Institute for School Quality and Educational Research in Munich (ISB) proposed 12 golden rules to design the handling of refugees in the context of German courses. The golden rules emphasize the need for mistakes and the willingness on the part of the educator to learn from their own mistakes. It tries to take the 'pressure of perfection' from the shoulders of the teacher. Furthermore, the guideline recommended clear rules, respect, intercultural competence, motivation, flexibility, participatory content design, affection and determination. Pallasch and Kölln, on the other hand, believe that the key in dealing with traumatized participants lies in the use of language, the diagnostic competence of the teacher.

Indeed, it takes a great deal for teachers in German classes (who have not undergone a specific training) to recognize cases of traumatized language learners, let alone to offer them specific guidance. Unrecognized traumatized learners may exhibit some forms of anxiety, and absenteeism. When the language teacher manages to detect those cases, they can reach for professional help.

3.4 Learning Styles

It is almost intuitive to assert that people learn second languages in different modes and styles. By putting forward learning style as a challenge to effectively learn the German language, I am not primarily referring to an internal differentiation between auditory, visual learner types. Rather, I intend to draw attention to an informal second language acquisition that could help make sense of the challenges some refugees experience when they must conform to the regulated classroom setting, the didactic embellishment and the mediation of societal integration through the language classroom. Some refugees (arguably with modest learning biographies) have accumulated a great deal of knowledge in foreign languages such as Turkish and conversational modern Greek while they were fleeing to Germany. They argue to have picked up a functional knowledge of the Turkish language for example in their workplace. They picked up the language, its basic rules on the go, without formal instruction on how the language operates. In other words, they learned the (even if basic) grammar of those languages *out and from* the society that hosted them. They see formalized language learning settings as an impediment to their language learning style. Their attempt to mingle with German locals to replicate their 'learning style' has not been met with the support they hoped for. There are two observations one can make about this 'socio-cultural' learning type. It is arguable that such a learning approach has its peculiar didactic advantage when it comes to accounting for how information stored in this manner can be retrieved. As Ligthbown and Spada record, "[a]ccording to 'transfer appropriate processing,' information is best retrieved in situations that are similar to those in which it was acquired (Blaxton 1989). This is because when we learn something our memories also record something about the context in which it was learned and even about the way we learned it, for example, by reading or hearing it [...], the hypothesis seems to offer a plausible way of explaining a widely observed phenomenon in second language learning: knowledge that is acquired mainly in rule learning or drill activities may be easier to access on tests that resemble the learning activities than in communicative situations (Gatbonton and Segalowitz 1988, 2005) (Lightbown and Spada, 2006, p. 40)." Accordingly, language classroom prepares learners to perform (well) in language tests while learning in a direct socio-cultural environment is for the communicative integration of the learners. I have found that students who were socially integrated, i.e. mingled with locals, exhibited a better knowledge of German conversational language (the so-called *Umgangssprache*) than students that were taught standard German in classroom situations. However, their learning style being oriented toward oral production, they showed some lacunae when it came to the written production of texts. But even within the sociocultural perspective, one has to mention that first language speakers in the host society can best and effectively support second language learners if the learners are at their zone of proximal development (ZPD).[10] Vygotsky's ZPD as applied to language learning would mean that the autonomous learner has acquired some knowledge on their own and competent first language interlocutors are now helping them make the next step. As such, the sociocultural support of the environment supplements the individual learning efforts but does not substitute it altogether.

Yet, another aspect where the argument of the different learning styles is relevant for making sense of language is what Lightbown and Spada remind us of: "[t]here are many questions about how learning styles interact with success in language learning. For one thing, it is difficult to determine whether they reflect immutable differences or whether they develop (and thus can be changed) through experience. There is need for considerably more research. Nevertheless, when learners express a preference for seeing something written or spending more time in a language laboratory, we should not assume that their ways of working are wrong, even if they seem to conflict with the pedagogical approach we have adopted. Instead, we should encourage learners to use all means available to them. At a minimum, research on learning styles should make us skeptical of claims that a single teaching method or textbook will suit the needs of all learners (ibid., p. 59)." Language textbooks used in integration classes endeavor to cater to the needs of auditory and visual learners by including audio and visuals and in some cases video-materials. But as Lightbown and Spada argue, no textbook can do full justice. In integration classes, the course lecturer or the language school decide on the textbook to be used, mostly without prior consultation with the students. Some language students ask during the enrolment in the language course about the textbook used in the course. They report on their experience with different textbooks, how they found some textbooks difficult to approach or could not identify with the models pictured within the textbook and the situation depicted. But for practical reasons, language schools (in consultation with the teachers) decide on the textbook that students will use for the duration of the language course.

Textbooks have much to say about German lifestyle and what is expected from the learner but less to say about the migrant – it turns into a one-dimensional structure where German cultural preferences are largely echoed while the imagination of the learner, their horizon of experience is only

---

10   For a recent critical assessment in Vygotsky studies, see Yasnitsky & van der Veer, 2015.

secondarily considered. For sure, there is nothing wrong when a Muslim student learns from a textbook which features food items they don't consume or a lifestyle they don't personally subscribe to are showcased. Tolerance is not a one-way street, and indeed people wishing to settle in Germany should definitely reckon with the plurality of lifestyles in the country. But they do not find in the texts the words that reflect their personal everyday reality, the (laicized) cultural references that form the basis of their intellectual formation. When they are given the opportunity in the classroom to discuss matters close to their interests, their everyday experiences their place and role in society as migrants/refugees, they also called for more inclusive textbooks.

3.5   *Motivation in Language Learning*

According to the prevalent hypotheses on motivation and language learning, refugees that arrived in 2015 and thereafter should have high degree of motivation to engage with the German language. A priori, they seem to have more instrumental and integrative motivations than most second language learners to engage with the language. According to Gardner and Lambert (1972), instrumental motivation refers to language learning to fulfill more immediate and practical goals while integrative motivation is defined as learning for personal growth and cultural enrichment (quoted in Lightbown and Spada, 2006, pp. 63–64). It is intuitive that a migrant in Germany will need German for the immediate and practical goals for integration, work. But as I argued earlier, some students have developed pragmatic strategies to resolve the everyday challenges they may encounter either by relying on language proficient acquaintances, avoiding stress producing situations (in spoken or written communication in the target language), or ultimately relying on online translation tools (for good or bad) to fill official forms or make sense of the correspondence they receive. In terms of integrative motivation, language students are aware that the mastering of an additional language constitutes 'a treasure' in itself. How can one then account for motivation failure in second language learning? I think that successful language learning demands the capacity by the learner to constantly renew their interest in the language, overcome inhibitions and the fear of stressful communication situations, and a certain readiness to take risks to express themselves and use their language resources. Reaching the set proficiency target of B1 in integration or requiring particular language levels runs the danger of reducing German language learning to passing language tests. The design and execution should be geared toward enhancing the integrative motivation of learners, their personal benefits in improving their language proficiency.

4 Toward Radical Perspectives on the Pedagogy of Integration

In the first part of this chapter, I turned to structural linguistics to explain the emergence of language as a pivotal element in gauging the integration of foreigners. I argued that the representation of language as a learnable code, open to anyone endowed with the faculty of speech, seems to yield the rationale for expecting aliens in a host society to endeavor to learn the official language. I proceeded to describe the German language course and reflect on second language acquisition that could help make sense of refugees' test performance at written and oral exams for the integration and orientation classes.

At this point in the discussion, I want to apply critical perspectives to survey ways in which the societal integration of the foreigners could evolve into a full-fledged social and emancipation project.

4.1 Illich, or How to Deschool Integration

Ivan Illich, this eclectic philosopher, theologian has not produced a unified social theory but has produced perspicuous insights through his works on the modern (Western) society and its institutions, modern science and technology. Hoinacki has called him a witness, together with Primo Levi and Paul Celan, who "struggled to bequeath a literary monument testifying to the enigmatic monstrousness of our age (p. 3)." His testimony is not a *priori* the chronicling of the savagery of National Socialism (as in Primo Levi) or the rehabilitation of language after Auschwitz (Paul Ceylan). His is a testimony against "the marvels of modern civilization – the impressive and attractive accomplishments of education, transport, medicine, social services, and communications (ibid.)." He laid out his critique of these modern institution and technology in key texts such as *Deschooling Society* (1971), *Tools for Conviviality* (1973), *Energy and Equity* (1974), and *Medical Nemesis* (1976), *Toward a History of Needs* (1978), *Shadow Work* (1981), and *Gender* (1982). Mitcham has identified five central issues in Illich's anarchist and social-critical output: a sociological, historical, anthropological philosophy, ethical, and theological (2002, pp. 16–18).[11] In the following

---

11   Illich's contribution to sociology of modernity is his challenges to institutions such as schools and modern medicine. His key concepts are radical monopoly and counterproductivity. His contribution to history amounts to his unease with received approaches to history in terms of politics, economics, or culture and his emphasis of breaks and ruptures in history. In philosophical anthropology, Illich emphatically rejects the idea of an ahistorical human being, the institutionalization of human services to fulfill human needs, in order to pursue what Mitcham has termed a "historical archaeology of the senses," that is an exploration of "the concrete experiences of the human sensorium (2002,

sub-point, I will focus on the sociological Illich, especially on his work of the schooled society.¹²

Reading Ivan Illich's *Deschooling Society* and thinking about integration classes, one is tempted to think that integration in a society does not only emanate from language textbooks. Integrating foreigners need not only be delegated to adult education centers or language schools. The grammar of a society – its values, culture, and history – should not only be learned in a classroom, except if the classroom is transformed to better reflect the social and political complexity of the society, as I mentioned in the introduction of this chapter. I had also pointed out that "educational hardware and software" – to borrow another phrase from Illich – has been expended to respond to the accrued need of German integration classes after 2015 as new textbooks were printed and released.¹³ I nonetheless mentioned that Ivan Illich's call for a search for new "educational webs which heighten the opportunity for each one to transform each moment of his living into one of learning, sharing, caring" needs to be heeded (Illich 1970, Introduction, p. vii). Illich's scathing critique of the school system further holds that learning happens outside the school environment, in a casual and spontaneous manner and not as a result of school teaching per se. Within Illich's view, most people acquire a second language "as a result of odd circumstances and not of sequential teaching. They go to live with their grandparents, they travel, or they fall in love with a foreigner. Fluency in reading is also often a result of such extracurricular activities. Most people who read widely, and with pleasure, merely believe that they learned to do so in school; when challenged, they easily discard this illusion (ibid., pp. 12–13)." It follows from this that Illich would have not approved of mandatory integration language classes for acquiring the language of the host society. Obligatory school attendance degenerates into 'schooling for schooling's sake

---

p. 16)." The third thematic cluster ushers in the ethical concern of Illich's theory, his take on values such as autonomy, friendship. The last thematic cluster is of a theological nature. Illich addresses the corruption in Christianity (pp. 16–18). Some argued that the radicality of Illich's (sociological) work is his claim that the danger "stems not just from the obvious sources (say, the military, or the hegemony of multinational corporations) but more fundamentally from those elements of modernity that appear to most people as undeniable benefits: education, health care, transportation, equality of the sexes, communication, self-help, labor-saving machines, economic development, and so on (Falbel, 2002, p. 129)."

12 For a biographical note on Illich, see Mitcham, 2002, pp. 9–10; Fitzpatrick, 2002. Illich was a polymath who studied natural sciences and was fluent in eight languages, as one gathers from Mitcham.

13 For an overview of the approved textbooks for the integration, political orientation class, alphabetization classes, see BAMF, October 2018.

(ibid., p. 17).' Does this suggest Illich seeks to do away with the school as an institution of learning? He seems instead to be keen on transforming it into an instrument of emancipatory learning. In Illich's pedagogy, the (adult) learner's motivation is guaranteed by the political relevance of the imparted knowledge for the everyday. Quoting Paulo Freire, who claimed that, "any adult can begin to read in a matter of forty hours if the first words he deciphers are charged with political meaning," Illich trains his teachers to move into a village and to discover the words which designate current important issues, such as the access to a well or the compound interest on the debts owed to the patron (ibid., p. 18). This pedagogy kindles social awareness, encourages political participation (ibid., p. 18) and ultimately separates learning from social control (ibid., p. 19). The mantra of this pedagogy is that "most learning is not the result of instruction. It is rather the result of unhampered participation in a meaningful setting. Most people learn best by being" with it, "yet school makes them identify their personal, cognitive growth with elaborate planning and manipulation (p. 39)." Illich identified three roles that teachers in the 'classical' school system perform, none of them he positively highlights. Teachers act according to him either as custodians, guiding their students through repetitive ceremonies, without 'producing any profound learning', or as moralists, parents' surrogates or therapists (ibid., p. 30). Illich is skeptical of grades, marks or ranking systems (p. 40) and altogether of schools which he thinks are based "on the assumption that there is a secret to everything in life; that the quality of life depends on knowing that secret; that secrets can be known only in orderly successions; and that only teachers can properly reveal these secrets. An individual with a schooled mind conceives of the world as a pyramid of classified packages accessible only to those who carry the proper tags (p. 76)."

Re-engaging with Illich's *Deschooling Society* stimulates a critical rethinking of the role of schooling in the modern society. There is no denying that his informal, spontaneous conception of skill acquisition is not feasible in the present situation of European countries.[14] On the other hand, reading Illich carefully, one gets the sense of what a school-approach to integration cannot perform or what is missing in the integration teaching model: the bottom-up approach to the curriculum-setting and the wider participatory politics. In Illich and Freire, the student takes an active role in setting up the items of the curriculum. In language teaching regimes, the contents of the language and curricula are set up from above by educators, linguists, political scientists who

---

14   Illich later argued that he wrote 'Deschooling Society' not to argue from the elimination of schools, but for a "disetabishment of school for the sake of improving education (2005, p. iii)."

outlined the curriculum of the resources to be taught to the immigrant. This ensures a host-society centric approach to immigration where the expectations, particularities of the host society are clearly transmitted while little room is given to the immigrant's articulation of their role and contribution to the political life of the host society.

Both the integration or the orientation course framework should offer to the immigrant the possibility, as envisioned above, to participate and "play an active part in public life and to shape in a responsible way their own fate and that of their society; instil a culture of human rights; prepare people to live in a multicultural society and to deal with difference knowledgeably, sensibly, tolerantly and morally, and to strengthen social cohesion, mutual understanding and solidarity (Declaration of Education for Democratic Citizenship of the Committee of Ministers of the Council of Europe (CoE), Quoted in Van Avermaet, 2009, p. 38)." Integration needs to be more than about getting a B1-certificate. It needs to grow into a full-fledged social and political emancipation opportunity for the migrant/refugee.

4.2 Rancière or Thinking Integration Classes as Intellectual Emancipation

Rancière wrote in 1987, *Le Maître Ignorant* [The Ignorant Schoolmaster], to recount the biography and the pedagogy of forgotten, controversial, eighteenth-century French teacher and educational philosopher Joseph Jacotot (1770–1840). Credited to be an exceptional talent (Jacotot arguably went on to acquire three doctorates in the humanities, law, and mathematics), Jacotot saw liberty as involving intellectual and political emancipation. Jacotot has been one of the pioneers of the promotion of experimental natural sciences during the French revolution. Under the *Ancien Régime*, in the pre-revolutionary period, physics was taught in the *collèges* but mostly as part of philosophy, in a series of philosophical lectures in Latin, and more metaphysical and scholastic than experimental. Scientific experiments were carried out in the private sphere. The foundation of the *Écoles centrales* during the Revolution promoted the teaching of experimental natural sciences within the school curriculum. These experimental classes in physics or chemistry attracted lots of unregistered students (*auditeurs libres*) who were artisans, health officers. Jacotot's free experimental lectures were regularly attended by many such amateurs. In some localities, these classes adapted to the needs of the students. As such, there were classes where the teacher taught chemistry because the attendants, some health officers, medicine students, wanted chemistry classes or medicine; in other localities, artisans demanded courses on dyeing and tanning, sewing, and their demands were answered. The pedagogical model of *the Ècoles centrales* reflected to some extent the expectation of the student who was involved or influenced curriculum-making (Balpe, 1999, pp. 242, 248–249).

Jacotot was only a partaker of this novel social and educational project on the natural sciences. Hitherto, he has a rich and diversified career. He additionally taught ideology, old languages and mathematics and was elected deputy in March 1815. The second Restauration or – the relative brief return of the Bourbon dynasty to power in France – forced Jacotot into a Belgian exile where he was granted a teaching position at half pay. Rancière's novel on Jacotot begins with his exile and subsequent appointment as teacher of French literature at half-pay in Louvain. Unfortunately, most of his students did not have a command of the French language and Jacotot, the *maîte ignorant*, did not speak Flemish. What first appeared as a weird situation will turn out to be a rich intellectual adventure for the eccentric pedagogue. In the absence of a lingua franca for instruction, Jacotot was to search for the minimal link through a common thing "lien minimal d' une *chose* commune (Rancière, 2016, p. 8, emphasis in the orginal)." The least 'common thing' Jacotot came out with was the bilingual edition of the *Télémaque*. Jacotot had the students learn the French text with the help of the Flemish translation. When they had read half of the text, they were expected to read through the rest of the text and memorize it. This default solution (*solution de fortune*) may be weird to the present-day reader but was for Rancière a small scale "philosophical experiment in the style of the ones performed during the Age of Enlightenment (1991, p. 2)."

After the students have read and memorized the French text through the translation, Jacotot had them write their opinion in French on the text they have read. He was not sure about what to expect from his 'desperate empiricism.' Logically, he expected 'horrendous barbarisms,' the incapacity of the student to understand and resolve the difficulty of a new language. Surprisingly, the students mastered the exercise and 'as many French could have done (ibid.).' Rancière does explain to the readers the specific cognitive operations and skills that the students deployed to master the exercise. Jacotot took from this experiment what would become the central insight of his pedagogical approach: that 'wanting' was the essential criterion in mastering a new skill that all men (sic) can understand what others have understood (ibid.). What Jacotot discovered was not that rote learning was an approach from a pedagogical stone age. This fact, according to Rancière, was known to all 'conscientious' teachers. Likewise, learners were expected to 'avoid the chance detours where minds still incapable of distinguishing the essential from the accessory, the principle from the consequence, get lost (ibid., p. 3).' Because the supposedly un-experienced mind of the learner is young and ignorant, the role of the teacher was *to explicate*, to break down the subject matters into processable pieces for the learner, to simplify the 'elements of learning' as much as possible. Through "reasoned appropriation and the formation of judgment (p. 3)," the student 'elevated to as high a level as his social destination demanded, and he was in this way prepared to make use of the knowledge appropriate to that destination: to teach, to litigate, or to govern for the lettered elite… or make instruments and machines for the new avant-garde now hopefully to be drawn from the elite of the common people (ibid.).' It is difficult to overlook the Bourdieusan sociology of education, social and cultural reproduction in the quoted text above. But there is also something Latourian and Woolgarian in the same passage, where students engage 'in the scientific careers, for the minds gifted with this particular genius, to make new discoveries. Undoubtedly the procedures of these men of science would diverge noticeably from the reasoned order of the pedagogues. But this was not an argument against that order (ibid.).' The mantra of 'conscientious teachers,' an expression which by now had taken an ironic tone, was that 'one should first acquire a solid and methodical foundation before the singularities of genius could take flight. *Post hoc, ergo propter hoc* (ibid.).' It is also reminiscent of Derrida: "there is nothing outside the text" when Rancière argues that there "is nothing beyond texts except the will to express, that is, to translate (p. 10)."

Jacotot was not performing a sort of 'pedagogical break' from the 'conscientious teachers.' He subverts the order of 'things' since he did not take his students through a careful step-by-step introduction into the grammatical units of the French language. He did not *explicate,* even in a peremptory manner the morphological, syntactic, or semantic rules that govern the French language (ibid., pp. 3–4). Where Barthes declares the death of the author, Rancière declares the death of the 'explicating teacher,' who semiotically mediates between a book and a reader (p. 4).[15] Rancière interrogate the politics of explications, "the singular art of the explicator: the art of the *distance*. The master's secret is

---

15   In Jacotot's experiment, everything was "played out between the intelligence of Fénelon [the author of *Télémaque*] who had wanted to make a particular use of the French language, the intelligence of the translator who had wanted to give a Flemish equivalent, and the intelligence of the apprentices who wanted to learn French. And it had appeared that no other intelligence was necessary (ibid., p. 9)." As Lòpez noted, the choice of the Télémaque as a textbook, was not self-evident. It is weird that Jacotot being an anti-monarchist, a fierce partisan of equality between human beings, chose the Télémaque as his standard textbook to base his teaching on. *Télémaque* by Fénelon was a book for the education of a princes, for whom Fenelon was a preceptor. For Lòpez, Jacotot took the text between it was the only bilingual text (French-Flemish) that was available to him and for its stylistic and literary qualities. Fénelon, a pious Christian has succeeded in secularizing Christian morals and for Jacotot, using his book for important because students could draw on notions of religion, morality, mythology. Stylistically, the book is easier to

to know how to recognize the distance between the taught material and the person being instructed, the distance also between learning and understanding. The explicator sets up and abolishes this distance – deploys it and reabsorbs it in the fullness of his speech (ibid., p. 5)." Succintly put, the function of the explicator, is a position of power, control of semiotic contents, their mediation and retention between the mind of the reader and the teaching material.

Therefore, the ideal of the emancipated learner according to Rancière is the toddler learning their mother tongue without the direct mediation of a 'master explicator.' The 'non-scaffolded' toddler, as Rancière underscores, regardless of their 'gender, social condition, and skin color (p. 5)', learn, make mistakes, repeat and correct themselves while acquiring their mother tongue. How then should a toddler, who learned their mother tongue without direct external guidance, now be subjected to an instruction based on an explicative regime? Rancière is unconvinced about the logic behind explication. To explain something to someone is to posit an incapacity by the person to understand a particular subject by themselves. The explicative act rests upon a pedagogical myth, a parable of a world divided between 'knowing minds and ignorant ones, ripe minds and immature ones, the capable and the incapable, the intelligent and the stupid (p. 6).' The pedagogical myth further differentiates intelligence into two forms: a superior intelligence and an inferior one (p. 7). Inferior intelligence is informal, empirical, and operates within the closed circle of need. The superior intelligence, in the pedagogical myth, is reasoned, methodic, scaled and addressed through the explications of the pedagogue. For Jacotot and Rancière, this is the pathway to 'enforced stultification.' Stultification occurs when one intelligence is subordinated to another in a pedagogical relation (p. 13). The Socratic method is described as a perfected form of stultification since Socrates interrogates as a learned master in order to instruct (p. 29). But in an "act of teaching and learning there are two wills and two intelligences. We will call their coincidence *stultification*. In the experimental situation Jacotot created, the student was linked to a will, Jacotot's, and to an intelligence, the book's. We will call the known and maintained difference of the two relations – the act of an intelligence obeying only itself even while the will obeys another will – *emancipation* (p. 13)." Intellectual emancipation, as Rancière envisions it, is the use by the student of their own intelligence, the awareness of the true power of their mind (p. 15). The radical pedagogy Jacotot proposes, is 'universal teaching' as the oldest form of learning since every human

---

be accessed because its narrated adventures were arguably written in an elegant and simple manner (2003, p. 4).

being is learning something on their own without an explicative master guiding them. Furthermore, Jacotot credits this approach for having formed the 'great men' (sic). But Rancière's plan is not to do away with the scholarly learning and teaching or to make of the 'ignorant one the fount of an innate science' (p. 29). The key tenet of intellectual emancipation is the realization that every speaking human being has notions of grammar, logic, acts on principles of private and social morals (p. 34), that the human subjects, as they are, can think or as Rancière puts it, is Descartes' "cogito, ergo sum" read backwards (p. 35). It is a 'panecastic' philosophy of intellectual emancipation which looks for the totality of human intelligence in each intellectual manifestation (p. 39). Jacotot's disciples can teach what they don't know so that a poor and ignorant father can begin educating their children (p. 101).

Jacotot's method eventually triumphed. His conferences filled rooms. As his pedagogical innovation started to spread, teachers came from different corners to witness Jacotot as a revolutionary pedagogue. Jacotot himself had extended his pedagogy from teaching French to subjects such as law, music, and geography among other. At this point one may ask, why we should still pay attention to Jacotot? Put differently, what can Rancière's concept of the "Ignorant Schoolmaster" teach us? According to López (2003, p. 2), the success of Jacotot's pedagogy owes much to the zeitgeist of revolutionary France and the time after the Napoleonic wars. The period saw a strong desire among the populations to access knowledge and culture. The principles of the Encyclopedia and of the French Revolution such as the belief in the equality of human beings, fraternity, freedom, the overthrow of the feudal system, and the cultural and political emancipation of the individual were becoming important fields. Universal teaching and education were considered the panacea for the needy as it channeled them to a knowledge that was hitherto reserved to the rich.

There are several elements that make Rancière's Jacotot relevant for thinking about integration, and second language acquisition.

5 Jacotot's Method and Second Language Acquisition

López has summarized Jacotot's approach in three steps: mnemonics, analysis, and synthesis. In the first phase, the mnemonic one, the student memorizes the first paragraph of the assigned textbook in both languages. After the oral recitation, the student writes the learned text by heart, sentence after sentence. The student repeats every day his new lesson with that of the day before, so as not to forget it; at the rate of half a page a day, in one or two months he will have learned the first book (López, 2003, p. 6). Then come the two following phases: analysis and synthesis, which are developed in parallel. Once portions of a text are analyzed the teacher begins to ask the student questions about the memorized paragraphs (p. 7). The teacher would ask the student how a specific word is translated in the target language and from words move to full sentences. It could be questions about the grammar but the teacher should refrain from correcting the student, trusting that they will auto-correct themselves in their learning path. At a moment, learning the foreign language is akin to learning the mother tongue (French, in the Jacotot model).

Jacotot's is a radical approach that challenges the present-day teaching that grants to explicative grammatical acquisition the central role. To be sure, Jacotot's method of universal teaching or his *Télémaque*-textbook style may not be the panacea to reforming the mode of teaching the *Integrationskurse* or German as a foreign language in general. Nonetheless, research on second language acquisition has not settled the debate on which language learning method is best suited to acquire a second or foreign language. In this respect, a student who would have been introduced to the Jacotot method and desires to learn German on their own (with minimal teaching guidance) should not be discouraged to do so. In relation to pedagogy in general, Jacotot's method can be viewed as an oversimplification because it assumes too easily that this method is 'universal.' Intuitively, one preempts that the method might resonate more with some learners than with others.

His method nonetheless seems to support strong auto-didactic impulses to learn a foreign language. Where Jacotot is relevant for the present-day foreign language-teaching, is his insights. Both Jacotot and Rancière have noted that the explicative model distorts learner's motivation since everything was broken down to them in a structuralist manner. Their emphasis is rather on will and (universal) intelligence as the key to the intellectual emancipation they propound. It puts the learner and their motivation at the center of the pedagogical act. Motivation releases the kind of informal intelligence that transcend the ordered, at times over-didactized textbook which ultimately cannot reproduce the reality of language use and explicate it at the same time.

A student learning German, say at the beginner's level, might be confronted with a sentence that makes use of modal particles, particles like *ja, eigentlich, denn, schon* among others with elusive meanings, generally absent in the written language. Were the student to ask the explicative teacher what the meaning of '*doch*' in '*Das ist doch nicht richtig*!' was, the explicative teacher might find themselves in a sort of dilemma. Modal particles are generally taught in the higher levels of the grammar curriculum but already feature in sample sentences of lower-level classes. They don't represent a separate linguistic class common in most languages such as verbs, nouns or adjectives. Moreover, their meanings are elusive, at times contradictory that no peremptory explication can help the student come to terms with them. If the explicative teacher asks the student for patience, telling them that this will be covered in a different grammatical unit at a higher level, then the student could get the impression that they are not yet ripe to grasp simple occurrences in the target language. I have mentioned modal particles but that could apply to any occurrences the student encounters in their didacticized textbook (out of necessity) but which are covered in a later chapter for example.

Another example that comes to mind is the use of *the Konjunktiv* 1 (usually translated as Subjunctive in English). It is mostly used in the indirect speech style to report the statements of another speaker. It is taught at B2-level but a student learning on their own is likely to encounter this form before a teacher could eventually break it down to them. The trouble with the classical textbook approach is a map-territory relation, the authentic language as it is used by the native speaker, and the filtered, didacticized material the student has to learn from.

The second aspect of Jacotot's method is the role of the teacher. It has been argued that Jacotot is the prototype of the coach, accompanying customers into solving their problems on their own.[16] On a different note, raising and maintaining motivation is key to succeeding in language learning. Policy makers know how to finance language classes and devise a whole Foucauldian apparatus of sanctions to enforce attendance to the language classes, and find teachers to impart knowledge to the new-coming migrants. But the Jacototan or Rancière's concept of will, intelligence and emancipation are also important resources to tap into the acquisition of German as a second language. Refugees, with lower levels of literacy but who have succeeded to earn a living in their Syrian home country before the war, some owning shops and restaurants, have faced immense challenges coming to terms with the German language. It is not rare to hear the excuse that they are no longer in shape to learn something new. These people possess the informal, practical, universal intelligence Jacotot describes and which is key to intellectual emancipation. It is a practical intelligence that is increasingly alienated in the Rancièran and Jacototan dialectic of the knowing minds teaching un-knowing minds. In an ideal situation, the teacher in the integration classes, can activate the motivation to engage with the new language, to master and inscribe it within a wider project of

---

16   The coach, ultimately does not know what the best solution to a problem is. Only the customers are good at curing themselves by reconnecting with the resources to which they have momentarily lost access due to stress or pressure at work or in society (See Tonnelé, 2009).

personal and intellectual emancipation, not simply to comply with regulations around permanent residence status. It emancipates the migrant whose voice is unheard, or not even sought for in matters that regard them although they arguably lack the command of the language. It is about emancipating oneself from the fear of contact with locals or being unable to negotiate communication situations. It is about the appropriation of a free resource to improve one's own life qualities. Jacotot chose a method and a textbook that transmitted the (political and moral) values that mattered to his contemporaries.

In Germany, where some teachers and pedagogical experts speak (mostly after the arrival of many refugees in 2015) of a decline in values (*Werteverfall*) (Paulsen, 2018), of overwhelmed teachers, forced to mend the 'mistakes' of politicians (Freimuth, 2018) and complaining that the integration of migrants cannot succeed as long as the state negates the different hierarchical structures that negatively influence learning and teaching both in school and in adult education (German as second language teaching), it does not harm to remember Jacotot. As Ross, who translated Rancière's text into English, reckoned, Jacotot's story might have had something to do with the post-1968 debates about education in France. Rancière's book appeared at a time where administrators in France were faced with the challenge of North African children in Paris or intellectuals trying to map the reproduction by the French system of social inequalities (Ross, 1991, p. vii).

Rancière did not take any direct reference to these challenges but the subtleness of his critique will not escape present-day readers.[17] Lòpez has for example argued, at the end of her essay on Jacotot's *Télémaque*, that in view of the multiple challenges the educational system has to overcome in general, and especially in the teaching of French as a second or foreign language [to immigrants], Jacotot's radicality in analyzing problems and challenges might be what the present-day educational system needed (2003, p. 9). With a view to the societal integration of the migrant, I can't but agree that Jacotot's radicality in approaching and analyzing would not be superfluous.

5.1 *Paulo Freire's Banking Concept, and Integration in Germany*

Paulo Freire loved humanity,[18] in individuals and collectivities, as well as metaphors. Humans are born to act and transform their world, or as Freire views it,

---

17 See Rancière 2011, 2012.
18 Progesss in Freire is not the inexorable drive toward economic optimization but the move towards an individual and collective 'fuller and richer life' (Shaull, 1996, p. 14). He is wary of the kind of abstract education that produces conformity and continuity and privileges instead an education that is geared toward the practice of freedom, the critical and creative participation of the individual in the transformation in their world (ibid., p. 16).

take their place and role in the world. He is unapolegitically modernist and will not sacrifice the human as a subject and agent of transformation on the altar of postmodernism. Nor does he make use obscure jargon to communicate to the oppressed and their educators. His simple and straightforward message, packaged in metaphors, have come in handy for all those dissatisfied with education and longing for a revolution in education. Nowhere in his writings does his command of metaphors transpire better than in his diagnosis of the troubles of education. The trouble with education, as Freire saw it practiced, was that, it suffers from narration sickness, or when he speaks of the banking concept of education, of conscientization. The narration sickness Freire diagnosed is characterized by a static, compartmentalized, and predictable teaching. There are similiarities here between Freire and Rancière's Jacotot; the apparent difference is Freire's frequent use of metaphors. In Freire's pathological view of (classical) education, the teacher[19] narrates a lot, holds long disquisitions on subjects that are alien to the students' needs and everyday. It is an alienating and hollow narrative that does not impact the lives of the students (Freire, 1997, p. 52). The narration sickness leads to a banking concept of education. Students are containers, receptacles, banks (Freire lived by metaphors) where the narrating teacher mechanically 'deposits' information until the receptables are filled. The deposited knowledge will be retrieved within a carefully designed testing regime. In this logic, good teachers are the ones that most optimally deposit and retrieve knowledge in their students and the best students are the ones that are able to receive and store the deposits of the narrating teacher (ibid., pp. 52–52). Such an education system based on the banking concept is not suited to break the yoke of pedagogical oppression. Instead it perpetuates and raises in the oppressed a feeling of self-depreciation. Oppressed "hear that they are good for nothing, know nothing and incapable of learning anything – that they are sick, lazy, and unproductive – that in the end they become convinced of their own unfitness (p. 45)." The banking concept of education is supplemented by a "paternalistic social action apparatus, within which the oppressed receive the euphemistic title of 'welfare recipients.' They are treated as individual cases, as marginal persons who deviate from the general configuration of a 'good, organized, and just' society. The oppressed are regarded as the pathology of the healthy society, which must therefore adjust these 'incompetent and lazy' folk to its own patterns by changing their

---

19 bell hooks has argued in a playful dialogue that despite Freire's sexist language, he was still relevant for the liberation pedagogy for marginalized groups (See bell hooks, 1993, pp. 146–154).

mentality. These marginals need to be 'integrated,' 'incorporated' into the healthy society that they have 'forsaken' (ibid., p. 55)."

What can one learn from Freire? Is he still relevant or should we forget Freire? Has not all been said, written, critiqued or interpreted on the polarizing pedagogue? Apparently not. It has been recently argued that there was "no other time in modern history when the ideas of Freire are as important, relevant, and urgently required as they are now. We are a culture in crisis, brought about by the complete oppression of thought and action beyond that consistent with capitalist principles (Dale and Hyslop-Margison, 2010, p. xiii)." Dale and Hyslop-Margison argued that "it was imperative during a period when democratic discussion is threatened by instrumental learning and behaviorist teaching practices that critical pedagogues provide space for open dialogue in classrooms (ibid., p. 4)." One finds in Freire, as well as in Rancière's Jacotot, the impatience with the classical pedagogy. For critical pedagogues, sequential, ordered, scaled learning and teaching do not foster the intellectual emancipation (as in Jacotot) and contribute little to the material liberation of the oppressed (Freire). Where Jacotot dispenses with most scaffolding techniques to instead instill in the student the belief in the equality of intelligence and the auto-didactic potential of the individual, Freire turns the critical pedagogic gaze toward society to harness its problem-solving potentialities. Drawing from the critical theory of the Frankfurt School, Freire re-inscribed issues of justice, democracy, within the capitalist workings (Freire, 1996, p. 146).

Freire subverts the idea of a neutral education[20] and teaching a language is not simply about the transmission of the linguistic categories of grammar, syntax or phonology. It is a space for Freire's critical pedagogue to interrogate society and its inequalities, raise in their students the consciousness of their situation and prepare the revolution. The following excerpt from his *Pedagogy of the Heart* defines the educational pathos of his critical pedagogical commitment. In his words:

> A progressive educator must not experience the task of teaching in mechanical fashion. He or she must not merely transfer the profile of the concept of the object to learners. If I teach Portuguese, I must teach the use of accents, subject-verb agreement, the syntax of verbs, noun case, the use of pronouns, the personal infinitive. However, as I teach the Portuguese language, I must not postpone dealing with issues of language that relate to social class. I must not avoid the issue of class syntax, grammar, semantics, and spelling. Hoping that the teaching of content,

---

20 See Shor 1993.

in and of itself, will generate tomorrow a radical intelligence of reality is to take a controlled position rather than a critical one.

FREIRE, 1997a, p. 75

It is certainly not a pure coincidence that critical pedagogy usually draws from language teaching to make its point. In Rancière's Jacotot, the revolutionary pedagogy was the rejection of the intellectual scaffolding of conscientious teachers. Jacotot follows an unusual method to teach French to his students. His combination of mnemonics, analysis and synthesis in foreign language acquisition subverted the scaled, scaffolded, explicative pedagogy of his day and arguably in ours. Jacotot wanted to address the mind, the intellect, which was being freed from the feudal and absolutist yoke and tap into the will to learn that the French revolution had unleashed. Freire does not teach only the mind, he seeks to reach the heart, to provoke that sense of attachment and recognition that transform the oppressed from being the subalterns of the society to liberated members. The trouble with formalized teaching, for all its importance, is that it succeeds most at reaching part of the intellectual mind of the students. The commitment to the learned content (as for example democracy, equality between human beings, religious tolerance) happens when the pedagogue can induce the student to reflect on their condition as oppressed.

Had he been still alive and had the chance to meet, observe and interact with Syrians (and arguably most refugees) in the heyday of the revolution and afterwards, there is no doubt he would have identified them as oppressed and justified their right to revolt.[21] His *Pedagogy of the Oppressed* would read a

---

21   Millions of Syrians have been driven out of the country to escape the regime's scorched earth strategy. The country had turned into a battlefield for proxy wars, foreign intervention, and of Sunni-Shia (Yassin-Kassab and al Shami, 2018, p. xi). More generally, as Yassin-Kassab and al Shami show, oppression in Syria did not start with the counterrevolution in 2011. They remind that the Baathist army in Syria repressed urban uprisings in 1963, 1964, 1965, 1967, 1973, 1980 and 1982. In Hama, more than 20, 000 people were killed. The state of oppression is sustained by a dynastic regime with Bashaar al-Assad overtaking power from his father, Hafez al-Assad in 2000. Bashaar's first decade was marked by an initial appropriation of the discourse of liberal democracy but meant more a neo-liberal economic policy than political opening. The public sphere and intellectuals established forums (*muntadiyat*) to discuss reform ideas, call for an end to the martial, state of emergency (ibid., pp. 13–14, 16–18). Initially the regime responded positively to the spirit of reforms by releasing political detainees in 2000. But the regime's opening was short-lived; discussions forums were denounced and infiltrated with intelligence agents as early as 2001 (p. 20). Institutional racism, the discrimination of Kurds, social control through an prison apparatus, the 1969 prohibition of prosecution of intelligence generals' crimes committed in official capacity which was extended to all security and police forces in 2008 (2018, pp. 22–23). On the overall, the regime failed, according to Yassin-Kassab and

personal missive to the oppressed Syrians in revolution and in exile. After all, the pedagogue made himself the experience of exile. He would have reminded that "sectarianism, fed by fanaticism, is always castrating" and that [r]adicalization (in Freire's own version), "nourished by a critical spirit, is always creative. Sectarianism mythicizes and thereby alienates" and is ultimately in "any quarter ... an obstacle to the emancipation of mankind (1993, 19)." Before the onset of the fateful revolution, he would have encouraged the oppressed Syrians to "liberate themselves and their oppressors as well." In his adaptation of the Hegelian dialectic of the master and the servant, he would explain his injunction by pointing to the fact that "oppressors who oppress, exploit, and rape by virtue of their power, cannot find in this power the strength to liberate either the oppressed or themselves. Only power that springs from the weakness of the oppressed will be sufficiently strong to free both (ibid., p. 27)."

If Syrians during their revolution would tell him that they felt abandoned by the international community, the UN, EU, and the US or any other state or international organization within the poorly defined international community who failed to protect them against the use of prohibited chemical weapons, Freire would likely have his explanation. He would have explained the failure of the international community to yield meaningful assistance in the face of the harshness of the counter-revolution by pointing that "any attempt to 'soften' the power of the oppressor in deference to the weakness of the oppressed almost always manifests itself in the form of false generosity; indeed, the attempt never goes beyond this (p. 27)."[22] One understands that Freire is more a humanist than a humanitarian, that liberation is more desirable to him than humanitarian aid. He would have told them that "true solidarity with the oppressed means fighting at their side to transform the objective reality (ibid., p. 31)." He would have denounced the logic of the reproduction of oppression, which explains why "during the initial stage of the struggle, the oppressed... tend to become oppressors, or 'sub-oppressors' (ibid., p. 27)." If one were to tell Freire that in the Syrian revolution, both armed forces, the insurgents as well as the counter-revolution made use of violence, he would be emphatic and assert that "[n]ever in history has violence been initiated by the oppressed. How could they be the initiators, if they themselves are the result of violence (ibid., p. 37)." Freire is also Fanonian; he does not condemn the use of violence by the

---

al-Shami, to fulfill a set of economic, political and national bargains, setting the scene for the uprising (p. 34).

22 Yassin-Kassab and al-Shami have explained why the Syrian revolution was sometimes called the 'orphaned' revolution. The Syrian revolution, they argue was "unsupported, ignored, misunderstood and slandered, it had to stand alone against the combined forces of local, regional and international reaction(2018, pp. 247–248)."

oppressed. But unlike Fanon, he does not ascribe to violence liberational virtues. He would have supplemented his apology with a linguistic analysis of the language of the oppressors, for whom the oppressed are not oppressed by the barbaric others (p. 38). Freire would highlight the necrophilic behavior that drives the destruction of life and the oppressed by the oppressor (p. 47).

Let's ultimately imagine that Freire were to re-encounter with the disillusioned Syrians who massively left the country – as the prospects of a victory of the rebellion slowly faded away or when the conflict internationalized and Syria dismantled and turned into a geo-political turf for different vested interests by superpowers and 'amateur' hegemons – for Turkey, Jordan, Lebanon, Sweden or Germany. It is likely that he would have wanted to design mass education programs and train teachers for the millions of Syrian children in exile in the neighboring countries and unable to attend schools. But the universal pedagogue would have something to say about the adults, now sitting, say in German integration classes. He would have gone straight to the language instructors, language textbook authors and asked them to refrain from using a banking concept of education to impart knowledge. He would recommend to them his radical pedagogy arguing that the task at hand is not only neutral language teaching; it was also about processing the disillusions of revolt and eventually the hope for liberation. He would argue to them that a banking concept of education would come across as necrophilic because it alienates agency and creativity (ibid., p. 58). He would enjoin the teachers that if they are true "humanists," they cannot make use of the "banking educational methods in the pursuits of liberation, for they would only negate that very pursuit (p. 59)." Freire would have tried to talk them into a praxis of liberation, a "problem-posing education – which accepts neither a "well-behaved" present nor a pre-determined future – roots itself in the dynamic present and becomes revolutionary (p. 65)." He would try to talk teachers into incorporating in the textbook the everyday of the students, their specific interests and not solely reflect the sociological concerns of the host society. Were the teachers to argue that they are bound to a neutral, non-political and certainly non-religious language teaching (and as such the textbooks would not make direct reference to *halal* or *kosher* food when they talk about food and nutrition; talking about vegetarian, vegan food seems less controversial) or turn into a political liberation class, Freire would most predictably sigh and demonstrate to them that teaching is never neutral. It can only overlook its political implications.

What about the disillusioned (Syrian) revolutionary who wanted to see their country freed? Is there any hope for them? Freire would have turned to his 'oppressed,' re-assured them that liberation was still coming (is not revolution an act of faith?) but that as of now, and in the present condition where they have sought and found asylum in Germany, they should do their best to integrate and become active beings in the host society. Freire talks to the heart. His would not be a hollow hectoring on values, migrants' duties towards the host society, or unending jeremiads about the incommensurability and incompatibility of the cultural values of refugees with the values of their host society. His would be a warm exhortation to meaningful action, participation, dialogical action and an injunction to respect the values of their host society. It is even likely that Freire would be tautologically making a point that is all-too obvious and practiced by most refugees/migrants. To the few refugees/migrants who make the negative headlines of the local press through cases of rape or causing insecurity, Freire as an 'integration coach' would warn them to remember their own experience of oppression and beware of become oppressors themselves or practicing a reverse form of "cultural invasion," another form of anti-dialogical action. In the form of cultural invasion, Freire originally described, "[t]he invaders penetrate the cultural context of another group, in disrespect of the latter's potentialities; they impose their own view of the world upon those they invade and inhibit the creativity of the invaded by curbing their expression. Whether urbane or harsh, cultural invasion is thus always an act of violence against the persons of the invaded culture, who lose their originality or face the threat of losing it (p. 133)."

That would be a firm stand for integration and an interesting thesis; disrespect for the culture of another group is a form of violence. Freire would teach these transcultural values in his integration and political orientation classes.

Before closing the case for Freire and this chapter altogether, it is important to reiterate that Freire does not fully reject the classical form of education. In Freire the classical teaching of language and its different categories are not rejected per se, but are complemented with critical consciousness, the drive to practicality and the constant awareness of oppression and liberation. Not all of Freire's categories can be applied to foreign language teaching in Germany. But integration teaching, which is about the transmission of linguistic knowledge and democratic values of the host society (Germany) should avoid following the banking concept of education. There is nothing much more revolutionary for the lecturer of integration to do than to alert their students to the dangers of knowledge accumulated as a self-end (or to pass a test) or the refusal altogether of learning the language of the host society. Ultimately the students could simply be introduced to Freire! Most likely they would be fascinated by Freire's concept of banking education and know that language learning is not about writing down scores of vocabulary items to be stored and ignored, or for the preparation of a written test, but in the constant use of the learned vocabulary (*Wortschatz*) and the adherence and partaking in the democratic principles of the host society. The transmission of democratic values through the *Orientierungskurs*, and the *Einbürgerungstest* that candidates to naturalization take should not be seen by the students as storing and memorizing the right answers to the multiple-choice questions on democracy, equality between women and men, anti-discrimination. It is about the alertness to identify, to intervene and to defend democracy and its principles in situations where the defense of human dignity in the host society is endangered. The formalization induced by the testing regime where knowledge of democracy and society have been reduced to taking and passing an exam should not substitute for the promotion of lively democratic debates and participation.

CHAPTER 5

Civilization-Culture-Character: the Plateaus of the 'Clash Rhizome'

A rhizome in botany is a subterrean system of a plant that sends out roots. In Deleuze's and Guattari's philosophy, a rhizome is made of plateaus, those "[...] continuous, self-vibrating region[s] of intensities whose development avoids any orientation toward a culmination point or external end (Deleuze and Guattari, 2005, pp. 21–22)." The botanical rhizome is (agri)-cultural while the philosophical rhizome is mainly cultural. But Deleuze and Guattari do not take aim at the botanical rhizome *per se*. They lament that Western reality and thought had been influenced by the tree-model. That is, the forest, field, and seed-planting which is an (agri)-culture based on a chosen lineage containing many variable individuals. They oppose the Western model of agriculture the Eastern model of horticulture, with its special relation to the steppe, the garden, the desert, and the oasis, that is the cultivation of small number of individuals. The implications of both models are also felt in the link to the transcendent where the Western 'God sows and reaps,' the Eastern God(s) replants and unearths. The metaphor of the East provides Deleuze with the 'rhizomatic model' they want to use to challenge the 'Western model of the tree' (See, ibid. p. 18).

Deleuze's and Guattari's representation of Eastern (horti)-culture and philosophy is consistent with Almond's characterization of his so-called *New Orientalists* (See Almond 2007). The main difference being that Deleuze and Guattari did not mean the Muslim world in a sense (see the references to the *oasis* for example). They instead lump together different geographies under the label of the East. Their rhizomatic model draws a dichotomy between the centered, static, ordered on the one hand, and the fluid, non-centered and unhierarchized on the other hand. Deleuze and Guattari exhibit here the spirit of "European self-critique which partly springs from a concerted, selective, at times not wholly convincing sympathy with the Islamic world [read here: Eastern other] (Almond, 2007, p. 1)." As he further noted, the resort to the non-European other as "a means of obtaining some kind of critical distance from one's own society will become a familiar gesture, if expressed in a number of different ways (ibid., p. 2)." This was a common feature of so-called 'postmodern' thought which generally distrusts any kind of center, truth or reality (ibid., p. 2).

This is also the background against which one should make sense of Deleuze's and Guattari's concept of a rhizome. Their idiom of rhizomes does not only apply to plants with actual roots or radicles. It also applies to "some animals in their pack form. Rats are rhizomes (Deleuze and Guattari, 2005, p. 6)." Rhizomes assume diverse forms "from ramified surface extension in all directions to concretion into bulbs and tubers (ibid., p. 7)." Rhizomes function according to principles. Their point can and must be connected to anything outside themselves. They can connect semiotic chains to different biological, political, economic regimes of signs but also states of things of differing status or circumstances relative to the arts, sciences, and social struggles (ibid., p. 7). Further, a rhizome may be ruptured at a given spot, but it will start up again on one of its old lines or on new lines.

I propose that the "rhizome" idiom can be applied to make sense of the discourses of clash of civilizations/cultures on the meta-sense. The clash rhizome is a meta-discourse that appears on different plateaus or levels: the international, national, and indeed personal or individual. The different levels are interconnected and the meta-discourse can be ruptured at any of these points. There is no hierarchy between these plateaus. The 'clash of civilizations' thesis (prominent in the discussion on international relations) percolates down into national forums and cultural policy discussions. In the discourses of clash of civilization, the rhizome is used to connect race to cultures. Later developments have seen this rhizome being ruptured (through inter-civilizational dialogue initiatives, epistemic challenges within academia, or the ermegence of competing discourses) and resurrected following terrorist attacks, mass migration movements (to Western countries), and the rise of the Far Right in various Western countries. The clash rhizome may thus be broken or crushed at a given spot, but it will start up again on one of its old lines, or on new lines. Following the principle of multiplicity, the clash rhizome has "only determinations, magnitudes, and dimensions that cannot increase in number without the multiplicity changing in nature (ibid., p. 8)." The rhizome has no deeper structure or genetic axis, is open, connectable in all its dimensions (ibid., p. 12).

In the first subsection of this chapter, I locate the eruption of the clash rhizome in the demise of Cold-War international order following the Fall of the Berlin Wall, and the collapse of the Soviet Union. The clash rhizome is simultaneously a rupture as well as a continuation of the logic of the bipolar world order of the Cold War. It is a rupture since it replaces the old contesting protagonists. In the clash rhizome, the ideologies of the Cold War are replaced with more intangible, fluid, porous, and rhizomatic concepts such as civilizations/cultures. It is nonetheless a continuation of a worldview that sees the international terrain as fundamentally anarchical, marked by a struggle for the survival of the fittest. Even though it is no more the West against the East, it is still the West against the Rest. Taking Huntington's thesis of the 'clash of civilizations' as the strategic nodal point of the clash rhizome, it analyzes the ramifications that the theory has produced. Huntington's thesis is more than 25 years old, but has undergone different rupures and resurrections following the contingencies of world politics and mainly international terrorism. I dwell on Hungtington's thesis, its relation to Fukuyama's thesis of the end of history or the democratic peace theory. The clash rhizome feeds on the Hobbesian, Schmidtan philosophies of an anarchical international system, a constant state of belligerence. Initiatives of inter-civilizational dialogues to advert a putative clash are a tacit vindication of the existence of the clash rhizome. The clash rhizome touches on multiple disciplines and research programs (Islamology, history, political science/international relations, sociology, etc.) and incorporates aspects of race, power, gender which the critique of the clash rhizome reveals.

In the second subsection, I turn to the German reception of Huntington's thesis. I review critical and sociological takes on Huntington's Clash of Civilizations (as in Kai Hafez), calls for international dialogues (as in Udo Steinbach and Roman Herzog) and the simalarities and differences between Tibi's 'War of Civilizations' thesis and Huntington's.

In the third subsection of the chapter, I consider culture as a further plateau of the clash rhizome. It is contextualized to the German context. I show how the clash rhizome, which started on the international plateau is continued, extended, updated in 'national culture.' I look at the debates on *Leitkultur, Verfassungspatriotismus,* the (mono-) culturalist/ethnopluralist arguments of the (New) German Far Right, cultural integration initiatives and argue that they are best made sense as a plateau where the clash rhizome simultaneously relate to the debates the clash of civilization thesis on the international level and are contextualized to the German situation.

1 Civilization in the Clash Rhizome

The events of 1989–91, the fall of the Berlin Wall, the collapse of Soviet communism and its eastern empire, caught many scholars and their research programs unawares. The bipolar world order seemed stable; only very few eccentric scholars, in Haliday's world, could have foreseen the collapse of the Soviet Union (2005, Introduction, p. 1). For scholars who grounded their theories on a 'perennial' bipolar world order, an epistemological crisis necessarily set in. The new empirical reality will be interpreted to fit the existing theoretical framework in feats of despair, reactionary dogmatism. But empirical/epistemological crises also enable new interpretational approaches to emerge and the lay their prediction for the future of the international order.[1] They can be optimistic, jubilatory, and triumphalist as in Fukuyama's thesis of the end of history which prophesied boon days for capitalism, Western lifestyle, culture, values, and democracy. The triumph of capitalism and democracy would mean the end of conflict. Democracies, as the liberal peace theory goes, do not wage war against each other.[2] Or it can be cautionary, pessimistic as in Huntington's thesis of the clash of civilizations, reassembling broken pieces into a new hypothesis. It has thus been claimed that Huntington's work can be seen "in continuity with the realist tradition in International Relations and as one of the most prominent and strong critical critiques of utopianism in international political thought (Orsi, 2018, p. 6)." According to this reading, Huntington should be identified with the tradition of classical realism, as opposed to structural realism. The two brands of realism in international political thought diverge both chronologically and in their central tenets. Classical realism is more philosophical in its approach to international relations while structural realists adopt a quantitative notion of power and the balance of power. Orsi considers Huntingon's hypothesis as continuing the classical tradition of international thought where human nature is characterized by self-interest, the rejection of universalism, bounded rationality and changing circumstances. This strand draws its philosophy from Hobbes, Schmidt among others and sees countries as engaged in a Schmidtian permanent state of belligerence. Nossal believes that, on the contrary, Huntington's thesis of kin country challenges orthodox realist theories that cannot account for those international relationships that are patently *not* marked by the atomism and selfishness. For him, Huntington, introduces sentiments in the philosophy of realist thought by arguing that economic, commercial, familial, political, diplomatic, strategic, linguistic, and

---

1 See for example, Duerr's assessment of Fukuyama, Mearshheimer and Huntington's prediction of the future of the world order after the collapse of the Soviet Union. Duerr found that each thesis is still salvageable even though their predictions have been undercut in their key tenets, be it in the progress of democracy worldwide for Fukuyama, the absence of great competition for Mearsheimer or the limitation of civilizational identity for Huntington. Fukuyama's thesis, he argued was successful in the 1990s, boosted by a wave of democratization, liberal markets. The attacks on the Twin Towers in 2001, and the subsequent wars in Afghanistan and Iraq have brought Huntington to a pedestal as a prophet of the clash of civilizations. On the economic front, the rise of China, and the resurgence seems to be strengthening Mearsheimer's theory of great power politics (2018, p. 78).

2 On liberal or democratic peace theory (DPT), See Doyle 1997. The theory has two major branches, the monadic and dyadic theories. For a recent assessment of the two theories, see Duerr, 2018, pp. 79–80.

cultural ties brings states (2018, p. 69). Huntington seemed to have been casting for potential new adversaries for the West. They were to be a mixture of geographic, cultural, historical, religious entities which Huntington termed civilizations.[3] He identified eight of such civilizations (the West included), which are presented as 'great cultures' and based on non-consistent criteria (Todorov, 2010, p. 88). Huntington posited that, "the relations between states and groups from different civilizations will not be close and will often be antagonistic. The dangerous clashes of the future are likely to arise from the interaction of Western arrogance, Islamic intolerance, and Sinic assertiveness" (Huntington, 1996, p. 183). A simplistic hypothesis even though the idea of the initial article and later the book was borrowed from Islamologist Bernard Lewis[4] and perhaps ultimately explains the success of Huntington's thesis. The 'success' of an academic work is not simply down to a set of neat analytical categories, original argument or even unassailable data. It resides in the simplicity of the language, the breaking down of complex subjects to common-sense generalizations, emotional appeal, and a clear policy recommendation and not least through its ability to make controversial claims or capture a zeitgeist.[5]

---

3   Todorov has noted that the term 'civilizations' used to separate groups of countries is an unclear demarcation line. Distinction based on the nature of political regime were made obsolete through the collapse of Soviet communism. Geographical categorizations (certainly as markers of development level) are also indeterminate since a developing country like Mongolia is located in the North while Australia is in the Southern hemisphere. The East and West display at times more similarities than differences thus Todorov does not deem it to be a clear demarcation line to group countries in international relations (Todorov, 2010, p. 4). For further reviews of Huntington, see Ajami 2003, Bottici and Challand 2006, Russett et al. 2000.
4   See Lewis 2002. More generally, Bettiza and Petito have labelled 'primordialists,' scholars who have presented "civilizations as concrete, macro-cultural entities with long, continuous and distinct histories and boundaries, which profoundly structure the way societies, economies, polities and states within them function in the international system. Primordialists' views of civilizations are most clearly articulated in the writings of 'clash of civilizations' theorists, like Huntington, Lewis or Dugin (2018, p. 39)." They are opposed to what they label critical perspective on civilizations in IR.
5   Ringmar has argued that Huntington's thesis failed to explain the logic of the world politics in the post-Cold war era, was inherently offensive, and exhibited a black box approach to differences. For him, if Huntington "ever wanted to say was that 'culture' matters, he is not saying anything original or new. Only the most doctrinaire of Neorealists ever believed that ideas play no role in world politics. The Cold War, colonialism, Putin in the Crimea, the European Union, economic development and trade, migration and global warming – it is all a matter of ideas and values; that is, a matter of culture. But the rest of us knew that already and we did not need 9/11 to remind us. (See Ringmar 2018, p. 26)." Hayes has explained the 'success' of Huntington's thesis through its ability to capture the end-of-the-Cold War

Very few works on the international world order have made it to such popularity.[6] Huntington's thesis was a simple prophecy toward a defined crowd (an ill-defined West) and an injunction to prepare for the clashes to come. He offered a conceptual vocabulary to come to terms with the changing world order (Orsi, 2018, p. 5). Moreover, Orsi credits Huntington for introducing a paradigm into realist thought that explains the rise of non-state actors such as regional organizations.[7] To be sure, Huntington defined his clashes of civilizations primarily as interstate confrontations, even if he does mention groups from different civilizations as partakers in these coming conflicts.[8] The outcome of his hypothesis is his distrust of utopian political philosophy, which ultimately leads him to dismiss "all visions of world peace, inter-civilizational dialogue, cosmopolitan society, and universal civilization (Orsi, 2018, p.12)." His model sanctifies a constant state of belligerence and imperialist foreign policies; aggressions are hallowed by the appeal to a putative anarchical order, the maximisation of power and self-interest.

Hall contrasted Huntington's view on 'civilization' in The *Clash of Civilizations* with Toynbee's *The World and the West*. Both texts are sweeping in their scope but take different perspectives on the (monolithically defined) West. Writing in the context of late colonial Britain in the 1950s, Toynbee had identified the West as the 'arch-aggressor of modern times' (quoted in Hall, 2018, p. 16). In Toynbee, as Hall notes, the relations between civilizations are more marked by affiliation, fruitful contacts between "([...] Hellenic thought and art on ancient India, and then later on both medieval Christianity and Islam (as well as the Renaissance); some to the near total collapse of civilizations (such as those in the Americas); and some to retrenchment and resistance (as occurred in parts of the 'Far East' and the Muslim world when they encountered

---

  zeitgeist, globalisation and its discontent as well as his re-casting of 'Islamic fundamentalism' in the 'vacancy' left by the collapse of the Soviet Union (Haynes, 2018, p. 53).
6 Contemporary IR theorists's writings have been accused of irrelevance, overuse of impenetrable jargon, and mathematical models that are indeed important for carrier advancement but rarely into the public sphere. The result is an arcane discipline, caught in an Ivory Tower, with no incidence on extra-disciplinary debate (See Nye, 2009).
7 Realist thought was and is still extremely state-centric and sometimes is at pains to account for the presence and indeed the power of non-state actors in the international arena. Huntington's paradigm-shifting contribution to realist thought was thus his affirmation of culture and the rise of new 'civilizational' non-state actors (Orsi, 2018, p. 10).
8 The groups from different civilizations (Huntington does not specify their composition) are certainly affiliated to bigger political entities that champion their worldview. Moreover, Huntington assumes that the civilization blocs he identified are monolithic, homogeneous entities which in turn confront a monolithic, undifferentiated West. This portrayal fails to appreciate the internal civilizational dynamics that influence the configurations of these conflicts on the international civilizational battlefield. The same applies to the seven civilizations he identified and most importantly to his depiction of Islam.

the modern West) (Toynbee 1954b; Hall, 2018, p. 18)." Huntington has repeatedly acknowledged the difficulty of neatly defining civilization, emphasized their historical development and contacts (See Huntington, 1996, pp. 40–48). Huntington accounts for the rise of the West in terms of military technology. Where Toynbee yearned for an ecumenical community of the West and the rest, Huntington was calling for the assertion and defense of Western values (Hall, 2018, p. 22).

Some critics have taken aim at the underlying idea of a 'clash' of civilizations. Drawing on the etymology of cultures and civilizations, Ringmar has suggested that civilizations cannot clash. 'Civilization,' he argued, "depends on the unencumbered circulation of goods, people, ideas, faiths and ways of life. Thus, while cultures require walls, civilizations require bridges (2018, pp. 26, 28)."[9] Moreover, in historical perspective, "[w]ars in Europe from the early modern period onwards were fought between states that all resembled each other. Culturally European states were all alike and what separated them was nothing but their respective *Staatsräson* and the logic of power politics. They were constantly at war with each other mainly since the anarchical logic of their international system made it impossible for one country to trust its neighbors and since the means devised to assure peace – balances of power and alliance politics – often proved insufficient (p. 32)."

Ringmar's sarcastic and trenchant historical analysis fails to reckon with the contemporary pervasiveness of the rhetoric of civilizational clashes, not only in academia but, most importantly, in foreign policies from both sides of the civilizational clash.

Bettiza and Petito have for example asserted that US president Trump's 'Muslim ban' policy, The Islamic State's actions were instances of how foreign policy has been permeated by the primordialist discourse on frictions and tensions between civilizations in the globalized world (2018, p. 37).[10] Bettiza and Petito oppose primordialist discourses to critical ones. Critical approaches reintroduce questions of race, power, gender into the wider discourses on civilizations. For scholars on the critical side, civilizations are ideologies, discourses

---

9   Civilization, for Ringmar, is not a Huntingtonian superform of culture, but a process which works on the principles of openness and exchange. Ringmar illustrates his point by reflecting on the Muslim influence in al-Andalus in the ninth century. The Arabs civilized the region by connecting its cities to the great centres of Arabic culture in the Middle East (Ringmar, 2018, p. 28).

10 Bin Laden and other Islamists are said to have been disciples of the 'clash of civilizations' thesis who believed that the clash was confirmed by the Quran and the traditions of the prophet (Todorov, 2010, p. 91). For the use of the term 'Islamo-fascism' in an attempt to affiliate Islam to European totalitarian system, see ibid. pp. 10, 104.

of power, revamped colonial discourses and narratives that produce, reify, justify and legitimize Western dominance. They are also wary of dialogues of civilizations (Bettiza and Petito, 2018, p. 41). These critics speak instead of clashes of barbarisms, fundamentalisms, definitions of clash within civilization, of worlds at war.[11] But one of the most recent critiques of the clash of civilizations within the critical approach to civilizations is Adib-Moghaddam's metahistory of the clash of civilizations. Drawing on Foucault's truth regimes, Adib-Moghaddam argued that the clash of civilizations is a cultural artefact comparable to nationalisms, imperialisms, or religious fundamentalisms.[12] Further, the clash regime, in Adib-Moghaddam's conceptualization, produces and contains the binary discourses on the West and the Rest (i.e. Islam) spun by right-wing parties and terrorist organizations (2011, p. 6). Once spun, the discourses

---

11   See Achcar (2006). For Achcar, who admired Huntington's scholarship, the clash is not one of civilizations, but of barbarisms from the Western imperialist and Islamist sides. For Achcar, the clash is one of 'barbarisms.' See Tariq Ali (2003) on the Clash of Fundamentalisms. On Said's clash of definitions, see Said (2000). Zizek's condemnation of the 'clash of civilizations' thesis has been, at best, ambivalent. He noted that "there is a partial truth to the notion of a 'clash of civilizations' attested here – witness the surprise of the average American: 'How is it possible that these people display such disregard for their own lives?' Is the obverse of this surprise not the rather sad fact that we, in First World countries, find it more and more difficult even to imagine a public or universal Cause for which one would be prepared to sacrifice one's own life? (Zizek, 2006, p. 277)" Zizek sees an ideological antagism between Western consumerism and Muslim radicalism which he exemplified within the philosophies of Nietzsche and Hegel. For Zizek, "[w]e in the West are the Nietzschean Last Men, immersed in stupid daily pleasures, while the Muslim radicals are ready to risk everything, engaged in the struggle up to the point of their own self-destruction.[…] Furthermore, if one perceives this opposition through the lens of the Hegelian struggle between Master and Servant, one cannot avoid noting the paradox: although we in the West are perceived as exploiting masters, we are the ones who occupy the position of the Servant who, because he clings to life and its pleasures, is unable to risk his life (recall Colin Powell's notion of a high-tech war with no human casualties), while the poor Muslim radicals are the Master, prepared to risk everything (ibid., p. 277)." But after his Nietzschean and Hegelian disquisitions, Zizek suddenly takes a radical turn to argue that the "notion of the 'clash of civilizations' must be thoroughly rejected: what we are witnessing today is rather clashes *within* each civilization (ibid., p. 278)." The leftist intellectual nonetheless leaves one with the sense that he adheres to the Manichean, indeed primordialist vision of civilzations and when he shifts the clash into a clash within civilizations, he does not provide the reader with means to understand this intra-civilzational clashes.

12   The clash regime is, in Adib-Moghaddam's thesis, a more systemic, animate, productive cultural artefact. It is more powerful than meta-narratives, discursive formation (Adib-Moghaddam, 2011, p. 5). It is engendered through a 'technique of enmeshment' that artificially aggregate disparate conflicts in order to legitimate and prescribe the use of violence (Adib-Moghaddam, 2011, Introduction, p. xv).

of the clash regime penetrate social structures, mental cognitions to sustain a parasitical existence (ibid., p. 10). It is constructed by privileged elites on both side of the clash divide "who have objectified and disseminated it to enforce their political, economic, cultural and social agendas (p. 11)." The privileged that exercise power over the clash regime are among others "[m]ullahs, journalists, scholars, academic disciplines, political and socio-economic institutions, political parties, preachers, marketing managers, etc. (p. 16)."

Bettiza and Petito are irritated by both primordialist views on civilizations (as in Huntington) as well as by critical perspectives on civilizations. Both fail to offer a satisfactory explanation of the increased use of civilizational reference frameworks since the end of the Cold War. Consequently, Bettiza and Petito turn to a sociological approach to account for the resurgence of civilizations. They argue that civilizational imaginaries have become prominent in world politics for three different reasons. First, civilizational imaginaries articulate a politics that prioritise the state, economics, or the individual. Bettiza and Petito emphasize that identity politics take multiple forms (race, gender, sexuality), can be pernicious or emphasize multiculturalism and the politics of recognition. Second, they act as strategic frames of reference in a globalized world marked by uncertainties and the de-territorialization of national identities. Third civilizations act as normative critiques of universalism, modernity (pp. 44–46). To be sure, what Bettiza and Petito present as a third way in the understanding of civilizations in world politics is little more than a synthesis of the primordialist and critical approaches to civilizational imaginaries. Huntington's primordialist theory entailed a critique of universalism. However, the sociological take can help explain how a counter narrative emerged stressing how vitally important it is for harmonious international relations that there is improved dialogue to deter a 'clash of civilizations.'[13]

2 The German Reception of the Clash of Civilizations

The German reception of Huntington's thesis oscillates between sociological and critical approaches on the one hand, and calls for inter-civilizational dialogues on the other. The closest protagonist to Huntington's thesis is Bassam Tibi while the other protagonists' position are concerned with outlining ways

---

13 For an overview of the initiatives to promote inter-civilizational dialogue from the UN, the UNESCO, see Haynes 2018, p. 54. For Muslim initiatives on inter-civilizational dialogue and calls for dialogue, see ibid., p. 58.

of averting the prophesized clash. In the following sub-points, I review some of these positions and the arguments of the main thinkers I identify with them.

2.1   Critical and Sociological: Kai Hafez on Huntington's Clash of Civilizations

Hafez, a media theorist and Islamologist has offered an early critique of the 'Clash of Civilizations' thesis that is simultaneously critical of the central argument in Huntington as well as sociological in its emphasis on the construction of the narrative of clashes in the imaginaries with in the construction and representation of the clash between civilizations. His introductory essay to his edited volume on Islam and the West ends with political recommendations on how to further dialogue with Islam.

Hafez's essay nonetheless opens with a reflection on the success of Huntington's thesis. He explains Huntington's success and the influence on his thesis by the fact that Huntington has discovered the zeitgeist of the immediate post-Cold War era (Hafez, 1997, p.15). But to be sure, if there was a zeitgeist to the early 1990s, this zeitgeist could have also been Fukuyaman as on the expansion of democracy and the end of history, or Mearsheimerian, as on on the tragedy of great power politics and a clear comparative assessment of these three scholars is not easy. It is also possible that to Hafez, as an Islamologue, Huntington provided a direct point of entry to bring in his own expertise so that other relevant publications on the structure of international relations after the collapse of the Soviet Union did not immediately appeal to him.[14]

Interestingly Hafez collapses "cultures" [*Kulturen*] with "civilizations" [*Zivilisationen*] but does not provide a rationale for the interchangeability of both terms. He notes quite rightly that they are only of limited use as working concepts for an analysis of international politics. Huntington's mistake, was to treat the Islamic ('the Orient' is the term Hafez uses) and Western cultures as clearly delineable, oppositional characters (ibid., p. 16). From Hafez's perception of cultural anthropology, Huntington is wrong to treat civilizations as ontological truths. Huntington emphasizes the differences more than the strong parallels that are found in the three monotheistic religions (Judaism, Christianity and Islam) (ibid.).

In the 1990s, as Huntington was formulating his thesis and Hafez his critique, the 'Western' public opinion had seen the rise to power of an Islamic inspired theocratic rule in the post-1979 revolutionary Iran, the fatwa against

---

14   For an extensive review of Huntington, Fukuyama and Mearsheimer in the prediction of the nature of international order, see Duerr, 2018.

Salman Rushdie and certainly the conviction came that political Islam was a force to be reckoned with in international politics. Nothing beforehand really seemed to have prepared the West for this eruption. The theocratic regime in Iran, Hafez argues, which supported by a strong value conservatism that validates hard criminal sanctions such as the death penalty for apostasy or stoning for "fornication" was without precedent in both Sunni and Shiite Islam (ibid., p. 17). But Iran, despise its radical interpretation and application of Islam, has maintained 'Western achievements' (*westliche Errungenschaften* in Hafez's words): constitutionalism, parliamentarism, industry, technology, and much more. Apart from its clerical leadership, Hafez notices, the Iranian revolution shared most of the characteristics of other upheavals in world history: marginalized elites were able to mobilize pauperized masses for their own ends. Islamic fundamentalism can only be explained if it is judged not by what it claims to be, but by what it is: not a religious movement, but a state and the search for a successful modernity through a partly real, partly symbolic return to the traditional Islamic social order (ibid., p. 18). Hafez's demystification of the Iranian regime has something worthwhile in it. The reader would have been extended to reflect on the parallels on violence both in 'secular' and Islamic revolutions.

On a different note, one could question whether Hafez's move to collapse culture with civilization does not add to the confusion of the use of catch-all concepts, and ultimately reduces civilizations to religions. Huntington's view of the civilizations encompasses more than religious or cultural features; it expands and covers geographical, linguistic and of course religious features. Moreover, Hafez's treatment of constitutionalism, parliamentarism, industry, technology as (unproblematic) Western achievements might make postcolonial theorists raise an eyebrow. The question would be whether the interpenetration of civilizations Hafez underlines is merely a cultural, religious one or whether in a certain sense, the 'West's achievements' he mentions were accelerated through the contact between Western powers in the nineteenth century and the civilizational others.

Hafez's essay then turns away from his denial of a clash of cultures to reckon with the ways in which the dichotomy "Islam" and "the West" exists, shapes and influences self-perception and the rapport to the other. If there are civilizations, then certainly as civilizational imaginaries, subjective entities, fed with the multiple skewed encounters between the Islamic and Western World in history and that continued to the present. Huntington's present was to understand how the resulting perceptions of self and the other translate into foreign policies from both and to ultimately set forth possible consequences for world politics (ibid., p. 19).

Hafez noted that the collapse of the Eastern Bloc and Yugoslavia has led from Central Asia via Chechnya to Bosnia-Herzegovina to the strengthening of Islamic-colored nationalism but saw no new Islamic supranationalism emerging to restore the 1924 abolished caliphate with contained multiple ethnic minorities. The reason why the restoration of the caliphate as a supranational theocratic order was out of question was that in part of the Middle East and North Africa, nation-building processes were well under way and leaders were not going to give up their sovereignty to revive the abolished caliphate. This, one could draw from Hafez's reading, meant that the no supranational entity would arise to confront the West so as to deserve the characterization of a clash of civilizations. Beyond the political, Hafez observes that only a minority of Muslims were attached to fundamentalism, while the majority tended towards a revival of religious practices, the display of religiosity (ibid., pp. 19–20).

Parallel to the revival of religious practice, Hafez noted the loss of influence for what he characterizes as "recognized Western virtues," (*anerkannte westliche Tugenden*) such as education, science, aspiration and a spirit of initiative. While these 'Western values' were increasingly falling out, the West was increasingly identified with stereotypes of materialism and selfishness, moral brutality and lack of community spirit (pp. 20–21).

In the West, the 'civilizational imaginary' on Islamic politics and culture has been influenced by the Iranian Revolution of 1978/1979, the fatwa of Ayatollah Khomeni on Salaman Rushdie in 1989 for the *Satanic Verses*. These episodes have updated historical clichés of Islam as violent, fanatical, expansionist and anti-Israeli (pp. 21–22). Hafez was keen to deflate these perceptions, arguing that these episodes did not represent cultural conflict. The Rushdie case was not to be a sign of Islam's incompatibility with human rights since Islam has numerous humanitarian principles, and the fatwa (legal opinion) of Iran's ayatollah has no binding force (ibid.). The West, Hafez argues, because it has turned laic, has difficulties to understand the importance of religious symbols in other cultures. Nonetheless, it should not let its opposition to barbaric Islam turn itself into a fundamentalist Enlightenment or allow it to degenerate into xenophobia against the minorities living in the country (pp. 22, 23).

Hafez went on to suggest ways to bridge the 'cultural' divide between Islam and the West. He draws a parallel between Willy Brandt's *Ostpolitik*[15] to argue that a combination of principledness (*Prinzipfestigkeit*) and willingness to dialogue are key in maintaining successful relations with the Islamic world. Hafez believed that such an approach would put the necessary pressure on

---

15 On the *Ostpolitik*, see Fink and Schaefer, 2009.

authoritarian system while promoting human rights. He further argues that the ideological discourses on disbelieving, egoistic-materialistic West or of an irrational fanatical, expansionist Islam can only be addressed through an offensive peace policy (p. 25). Hafez did not expand on how practical tenants of Willy Brandt's and Egon Bahr's *Ostpolitik* are transferrable to the perceived crisis with the Muslim world. His policy recommendation further assumed a unitary, common foreign policy of a monolithic 'West.' More than two decades after Huntington's thesis, it is difficult to identify a coherent and cohesive foreign policy of the West, or even of the EU members that could apply Hafez's recommendations. One could further ask whether a state-centric approach is the best course of action to further a dialogue between cultures. Will such an approach concentrate on high politics (foreign and security policy and diplomacy) and low politics (economic, cultural and monetary policy)? A sustainable dialogue between civilizations will certainly gain from addressing both levels.

2.2 Udo Steinbach and Roman Herzog: A Plea for Inter-civilizational Dialogue

For Steinbach,[16] the Islamic World in the 1990s was in a process of re-islamisation after imported ideologies, developmental approaches, legitimation paradigms and forms of government from the West have largely lost their validity. Liberalism, socialism or communism have failed the Muslim world and prompted it to return to its religious roots. Such a move, it is hoped, will unleash new sources of legitimacy (1997, p. 215). Writing in the late 1990s, Steinbach identified the roots of the malaise in a capture by elites who chose to cling to power, cling to their privileges rather than allowing for called-for reforms.

Furthermore, relations between the West and the Muslim world have been marked by "double standards" that have strongly undermined the credibility of the West (ibid., p. 217). But there is a mutual dependence of both sides on each other that the deceived Muslim world and the scandalized West will not clash. The resulting disillusion of imported Western political and governance models does not necessarily lead to a crisis of civilizations. Steinbach sees instead an opportunity for the West and Islam to improve their communication. The

---

16   Udo Steinbach completed a military training as a reserve officer in the German military before studying Islamic Studies and classical philology. Since 1991 he has been also been honorary professor at the University of Hamburg and retired in 2008. Steinbach has been a founding director of the Institute of Middle East Studies (IMES), the Middle East department of the GIGA Institute. Steinbach has published on contemporary Islam, Turkey, and Germany's Middle East policy. See among others: Steinbach, 2003, 2004.

communication model he envisages should transcend complexes of inferiority and superiority (ibid., p. 214). Steinbach's optimistic view is based upon his belief that the re-islamization does not per se exclude democracy and human rights. He notes that many Islamists subscribe to the idea of democratic values and human rights. These values should be re-instated within wider cultural contexts of meaning. Despite the difficulties and problems of understanding in the face of new forms of encounter, the signs are not of struggle of civilizations, but the coexistence under altered conditions (ibid., p. 217). For the West, the necessity to engage more productively with the Muslim world has a direct impact on the domestic politics of its countries, considering the strong presence of Muslim minorities in Europe (ibid., p. 218). Steinbach feared that unappeased relations with the Muslim world will impede the integration of Muslim migrants in Western countries, ostracize them in their identity (ibid.). Steinbach's concluding remarks are that not the prophesized cultural clashes, but tensions, irritations and occasionally individual conflicts are plausible in the relations between the West and the Muslim world (ibid., p. 219).

Former Federal President of Germany Roman Herzog has been a vocal critic of the thesis of the clash of civilizations. Indeed, he has been arguably one the most active Western statespersons to take a stand against Huntington's thesis and instead plead for civilizational dialogue. He pursed a diplomacy of intercultural understanding (*Diplomatie der interkulturellen Verständigung*) to counter what he himself saw as a self-fulfilling prophecy, Huntington's thesis of the clash of civilizations. In numerous speeches on international official visits, he has constantly searched for commonalities between the Muslim world and the West, Asia and the West, warning against the danger of propagating ideas on an imminent and unavoidable clash of civilizations. How such a consensus and mutual trust – in the face of the troubled historical encounters between the West and Islam – can be reached, does not clearly transpire in his speeches. The discursive strategy of the former President was to co-opt bridge-building (historical) personalities from his target crowd, expound the commonalities between them and German culture (in the ideal case) or to the wider European civilizations. The edited collection of speeches by President Herzog, published under the title *"Wider den Kampf der Kulturen – Eine Friedenstrategie für das 21. Jahrhundert"*, which also appeared in English as *"Preventing the Clash of Civilizations,"* provides an overview of his rhetorical strategies. In Pakistan, he made references to Muhammad Iqbal, one of the most important poets in the history of Pakistan and who spent some time in his formative years in Germany and also co-opted the founder of Modern Pakistan, Jinah, for whom there was no contradiction between democracy and Islam (ibid., p. 16). In China, Confucius and Aristotle (on law and ethics) provides the cultural references for the speech and helped the President build the bridge he needs between law and ethics, the West and China. Both thinkers, he stated, differentiated between law and ethics. In the Western tradition, law and civil liberties prevailed (*In der westlichen Tradition gewannen dann das Recht und mit ihm die bürgerlichen Freiheiten größeres Gewicht*). In the Confucian tradition, ethics prevailed and with it the civil duties (*... in der konfuzianischen die Ethik und mit ihr die bürgerlichen Pflichten*) (Herzog, 2000a, p. 50). The President refrains from any moral judgement on the dichotomy he has identified or whether Aristotle can triumph in China or Confucius in the West. Indeed, his disquisition on the two traditions does not go much beyond that. One could have hoped for more, since the President has been also a valiant supporter of human rights.[17]

After Herzog has found and worked out cultural commensurability, he could then appeal to uniting against the clash of civilization. In the speech delivered in Pakistan, he saw the task at hand as being the erecting of a common civilization based on consensus and mutual trust (Herzog, 2000, p. 16). His appeals rest mostly on the cultural legitimacy of the references he has selected. When he does not find such personalities that bridge the two cultures, the President simply refers to the Golden rule, that universalistic Kantian imperative.

For him, science, technology of global information, economic interdependence and new emerging security structures are the bulwark against prophecies such as the clash of civilization. But they don't necessarily guarantee a peaceful cohabitation between the West and the Muslim world (ibid., p. 223). The peaceful cohabitation (*friedliches, menschenwürdiges Miteinander*) requires, in his terms, a passionate endeavor to fight global poverty. One should ensure, according to Herzog, that in the long run, the boundaries between cultures don't remain boundaries between poverty and wealth. Free markets, economic cooperation, development aid, he believed, will help curb global poverty and avoid that economic deprivation feeds perceived differences between the West and the Muslim world (ibid., pp. 223–224). In his speeches, one reencounters the principledness of other defenders of a pro-civilizational dialogue: the professed unflinching belief in human rights. Human rights is an instrument to guarantee peace between people and states and ultimately cultures (ibid., p. 224) and should not be sacrificed on the altar of foreign policy interests or a weakish cultural relativism (*schwächlicher Werterelativismus*). He fends off, without quoting names, the relativism that portrays human rights as particular Western values. Human rights, freedom of speech, the prohibition of torture, the dignity of the human being among others, are the non-negotiable

---

17 See for instance, Herzog, 2000b. In his article, he defended relativistic views on human rights, or concepts of Asian values.

essentialist values in the dialogue with the Islamic civilization (pp. 225, 227). Herzog sees in (Islamist) fundamentalism nothing more than the instrumentalization of religious sentiments to grasp totalitarian power (p. 225). But unlike Steinbach who refers to the re-Islamisation as the result of the disillusion with imported political models and frameworks of legitimation, Herzog trusts open markets among others to spare us the trouble of a global cultural struggle (p. 227).

2.3 Bassam Tibi and the War of Civilizations

It is difficult – even within this brief review of the German reception of Huntington's *Clash of Civilizations* – to forgo Bassam Tibi. Arguably, no other scholar in the German-speaking world has been close to Huntington's thesis as Tibi has been. But one should beware of thinking of Tibi as Huntington's student not only because they are better viewed as colleagues than rather student and master, but also because (at least) Tibi has been keen in emphasizing his scholarly divergences to Huntington. However, both scholars have exhibited a certain number of commonalities. As scholars of international relations, they both 'revolt' against the side-lining of cultures and civilizations that has been predominant in the major research programs on international relations. For Tibi, civilizations and culture are reference frameworks that influence and inform states' conduct in international politics are always present.

To be sure, dominant IR theories (i.e. neorealism) have been, in their state-centrism, relatively blind to religion or culture. The search and maximization of power seems to have been considered within these theories as the main drivers of state conduct in international affairs. The end of the Cold War has made it possible for theories of the intangible (civilizations) to lay explanatory (and at time) prophetical claims on the structure of the post-Cold War era and, as Tibi would have it, the coming world disorder. The Gulf War, perceived in the Islamic World as a collective humiliation of Islamic culture and civilization, has added to the historical resentment against the West (2001c, p. 13). Huntington imports Islam studies, and world history to IR theory. Tibi seems to take the reverse route. Tibi had published on Islam, Islamic societies and modernity, before the advent of Huntington's thesis. Arguably, sympathetic readers of Tibi's previous work would have preferred Tibi had not joined the controversial debate on civilizations that Huntington's 1993 and 1996 texts have unleashed. Certainly, Huntington's thesis struck a chord with Tibi so that in 1995, two years after Huntington's article in *Foreign Affairs* and a year before the publication of Huntington's text in a book form, Tibi had reframed his earlier thinking about civilizational conflicts between the West and Islam. Tibi enters the debate on the clash of civilizations in IR by affiliating mainly his key propositions to Raymond Aron, and Hedley Bull. He draws from Aron's 1962 *Paix et Guerre entre les Nations* to argue that there was always an underlying heterogeneity of civilizations in international relations, which was temporarily concealed and displaced by the international structure of bipolarity and the competition of the former superpowers.[18] This competition had only superficially veiled the underlying heterogeneity of cultures and now civilizations were returning to cause disorder. To be sure, Aron's theory of international relations is more extensive than the idea of the heterogeneity of civilizations that Tibi had picked. One finds in Aron the recognition that the international system of state does not rest on the monopoly of violence by the state. States who compete for power, security, and glory may clash. Where Aron differs from realists is that he emphasizes the role of ideology, norms, values within a nation and their influence on foreign policy: an insight which is commonly associated with the so-called English school. In Tibi, cultures determine a nation's perception of foreign policy and kin cultures conglomerate into a civilization that ultimately content and displace the hegemony of the Western cultural model. Tibi envisioned the conflict on the ideological plane, not on a military basis (2001a, p. xi).[19] Only the Western and Islamic civilization are laying claims of universalism (2001c, p. 18).

---

18 Arguably, Tibi's regular chastising of fellow intellectuals, will remind the reader of Aron's *The Opium of the Intellectuals*, where the French scholar criticized Marxist intellectuals for their false tolerance of the atrocities committed in the name of communism and their exaggerated critique of democracy and capitalism. Tibi has frequently accused other scholars of being shallow thinkers, *Flachdenker* (2001a, p. xix). Where Aron criticized the Marxists for their blindness, intellectual dishonesty in the 1960s, Tibi charges against Western Marxists, post-Marxists, and non-Marxists alike. They have, according to him, always seriously underestimated the importance of belief systems in world politics, and their implications in understanding non-Western civilizations for the West (2001c, p. 7). When Tibi laments a kind of censorship that prevents critical thinking about the relation between the West and Islam, he chastises a so-called *political correctness – Denkverbot*, a censorship induced by political correctness, and which collapses critical thinking with cultural racism (ibid., p. 10). Postmodernism is another 'opium' that negatively influences the stand of the West. By preaching relativism, Tibi argues, cultural relativists are weakening the values of Europe, while the civilizational consciousness (*Zivilisationsbewusstsein*) is not being strengthened (ibid., p. 22). Postmodernism and cultural relativism engender a civilizational self-denial (*zivilisatorische Selbstverleugnung*) in the name of a misinterpreted tolerance and ignorance. And the self-appointed cultural mediator (*Kulturvermittler*) Tibi, reminds his German readers (and certainly without hypocrisy) that those who do not respect themselves cannot expect respect from others (2001c, p. 23).
19 After the attacks of September 11, 2001, Tibi argued that he had to reckon with the fact his hitherto value-based war had now taken a military dimension and manifests itself in form of the terrorism of Jihadists. Incidentally, the terrorism of a bin Laden cannot be compared with that of the RAF, the *Rote Armee Fraktion* (Red Army Faction), a German

In addition, Tibi argues that the process of globalization, which was taken by some to be a process of worldwide cultural standardization, has led to the opposite, to the reassertion of singular identities. The collapse of the bipolar world order has given to the (repressed) civilizational identities the opportunity to come to light and challenge the Western-led model. The current situation is a situation of a (second) revolt against the West. Drawing from Hedly Bull, Tibi argues that the first revolt against the West, in the anti-decolonization, was more a process of appropriation of Western political categories (such as sovereignty, the nation-state) to claim national sovereignty. The second, new revolt against the West is the rejection of the Western political ideas, associated with a strong anti-Western current, which he identified in Islamic civilization. Tibi identified the rise of Islamic fundamentalism and its challenge to the secular nation-state, the rejection of popular sovereignty in favor of a *Hakimiyat Allah*, Allah's rule as a backlash. Tibi nonetheless points that this backlash is due to the failed Western project of modernization and the naïve belief in acculturation. The subsequent revolt against the West is taking the form of a re-traditionalization (*Retraditionalisierung*), counter-acculturation (*Gegenakkulturation*) and de-Westernization (*Entwestlichung*). This retaliation can be considered as an expression of the clash of civilizations (Tibi, 2000, pp. 143–144, 147, 150, 154). Tibi further asserts that Muslims pursued the first world conquest project (*Welteroberungsprojekt*), spreading globalization in the 7th century. However, with the emergence of the West roughly in the period 1500–1800 and parallel to the process of industrialization, Muslims were prevented from continuing their conquests. From an Islamic perspective, according to Tibi, the emergence of Western civilization took place at the expense of the Islamic world conquest project. In the uninterrupted historical perception of Muslims, this project is backdated to the time of the Christian Crusades, so that every action of the West is classified as an anti-Islamic conspiracy within this framework (2001a, pp. xii–xiii). To think that globalization will erase cultural differences is wishful thinking because every civilization retains its own worldviews (2001a, p. xix).

Where Tibi differs from Huntington (in his own sight), is that in Tibi differences can be overcome through dialogue whereas in Huntington the clash of civilizations is an unavoidable scenario coupled with policy recommendations

---

terrorist organization that killed more than 30 people in their active years between 1970 and 1998. Both terrorisms are of different nature because Bin Laden had an international network and a larger logistical network than the RAF and could rely on a mass support (See Tibi, 2001a, p. xi–xii).

for foreign policy. Tibi arguably speaks of conflict only as a way to overcome it with friendly dialogic solutions. Tibi laments the demonization (*Dämonisierung*) of Huntington and asserts that it has been extended to his person and his work. Tibi found in this demonization an attempt to forbid critical thinking (Tibi, 2000, pp. 145–146). Where does Tibi diverge from Huntington? Tibi's 1995 *Krieg der Zivilisationen* [war of civilizations] seems to be the German pendant of Huntington's *Clash of Civilizations*. For Tibi, his *War of Civilization* is simply a metaphorical description of the ideological frictions between Islam and the West, not Huntington's sweeping typology of several civilizations, collapsing together cultural, geographical, and religious characteristics alike. Moreover, Tibi's civilizations don't fight wars because they don't have armies. And this is the major difference between Tibi and Huntington. Huntington is Western-centric, Tibi can claim not to be. Huntington wanted to overcome Eurocentrism by drawing attention to other worldviews but ended up being imprisoned in Eurocentrism because all of his historical sources all refer to European history. Moreover, even if Huntington does differentiate between civilizations and their politicization through fundamentalisms, he does not, according to Tibi, differentiate between Islam and fundamentalist Islam (Tibi, 2001c, p. 33). Now that Tibi has drawn the West's attention to the dangers of fundamentalist Islam, one wonders whether fundamentalism is simply a feature of Islamist expansionism. What is the counterpart of Islamist fundamentalism in the West? And Tibi had a proposal on how to escape the Huntingtonian prophecy, which is by adhering to a concept of international morality. This international morality is a consensus, a canon that should be developed between civilizations on fundamental values such as secular democracy and individual human rights (2000, pp. 155, 162). And Tibi seems to re-assert his own loyalty to the enlightenment values of Europe and remind us that he is a spiritual founder and champion of Euro-Islam, a synthesis of open Islam and enlightened Europe. At least, Europe and Germany could be sure that Tibi has been a defender of their constitutions against the introduction of '[o]riental states of non-freedom to Europe in the name of tolerance' (2001a, p. xxiii).

3 Culture in the Clash Rhizome

Nearly a quarter of century after the debates in international relations on civilizations, it seemed at times that the West might be turning into the cultural battlefield for civilizational clashes as in Huntington or the ideological/Islamist fundamentalist battleground Tibi envisioned it. Plainly put, the

German version of Huntington's clashes of civilizations is a cultural war waged by conservative and traditionalist Germans, worried about their national identity, who fear "that they are now being invaded not by armies and tanks but migrants who speak other languages, worship other gods, belong to other cultures, and they fear, will take their jobs, occupy their land, live off the welfare system, and threaten their way of life" (Huntington, 1996, p. 200). It is tempting, reading Huntington through the lens of the German refugee and migration crisis, to conclude that we are witnessing a clash of civilizations as he portrayed it. Culture (language), religion, welfare, and way of life would be in this analogy the open fronts of the civilizational war. And there are the gesticulations, framing offensives, from right-wing movements, parties or intellectuals, for whom Germany is being reversely assimilated by foreigners. The rise of the AfD,[20] a 2013 founded far-right political party, now the third largest political party in the Bundestag in the 2017 federal elections, the surge of the Pegida movement,[21] or the growing intellectual and philosophical influence of the German New Right (*Neue Rechte*),[22] the actionist politics of *die*

---

20   Kastrup has argued, that within the AfD, one could observe a bundling of what he termed as 'autoritärer Kulturkampf,' an authoritarian Kulturkampf which manifests itself in disappointed nationalism, anti-Muslim racism, anti-feminism, or the advocacy of traditional family forms (2016, p. 11). Kastrup interprets the rise of the AfD as the projection of the externalities of neo-liberalism on immigrants from abroad. They are persecuted as competitors, who simply did not belong here because they hail from a foreign 'culture' (*fremder Kulturkreis*) and have different customs and manners (ibid., p. 12). Kellershof analysed the AfD program and found that the ideology of AfD is neo-(nationalist) liberal. At the international level, the party advocates a re-nationalisation of the economic, finance, currency policies (which entails curtaling the influence of the EU, the Euro currency and ultimately free-trade agreement as TTIP). In domestic politics, it commits itself to a neo-liberal economic policy. This translates among others in their programmatic call for a slim but strong State (schlanker, aber starker Staat). The State the AfD envisions should concentrate on four key areas: Security, Justice, Foreign Relations and Financial Administration for. The cultural policy is tainted by anti-Islam and a de facto politics of assimilation. The AfD advocates a German *Leitkultur*. Sanctions against anti-constitutional imams, abolition of Islamic theories, the prohibition of minarets, the muezzin calls, the full veiling or the headscarf for teachers and students in educational institutions (See Kellershohn, 2016, pp. 14–15; 22–23).

21   Pegida stands for *Patriotische Europäer gegen die Islamisierung des Abendlandes* [Patriotic Europeans against the Islamisation of the Occident]. As the acronym suggests, Pegida sympathisers, mostly but not only from the far-right believe that Germany is being islamicized. The movement was founded in October 2014.

22   Die Neue Rechte is the German equivalent to the *Nouvelle Droite* or New Right. This (self-) perception of far-right militants is not only a demarcation attempt from the old conception of the far-right, which was caught in National Socialism. Bruns, Glösel, and Strobl have argued that the movement has introduced a theoretical novelty to the hitherto existing philosophy of the far-right. This novelty resides in the concept of ethnopluralism,

Identitären,[23] a youth organization of the New Right, are actors whose political credo indirectly feeds into the scenario of the clash of civilizations/cultures that Huntington and his kin intellectuals envisioned. Nonetheless, an analysis of culture as part of the clash rhizome should not stop at the neo-racist agendas of the far right. It also has to reckon with the rhizomatic discursive ramifications within the wider society. In the following subsections, I want to revisit key concepts that illustrate the rhizomatic development of culture in Germany since the 1990s.

3.1 Leitkultur and Verfassungspatriotismus

Leitkultur was the leitmotiv in cultural debates in the 1990s. This concept was coined originally by Bassam Tibi. Tibi, an opponent of multiculturalism, which he identifies with cultural relativism, proposed instead the concept of a European *Leitkultur*, which appeared in his 1998 book *Europa ohne Identität? Die Krise der multikulturellen Gesellschaft*. He saw Europe as caught between two extremes in the multi-cultural age, which translated into a commuting between Eurocentric arrogance and a cultural-relativistic self-denial. As the title of his book suggests, Tibi was worried that in a multiculturalist model of society, or *Kulturpluralismus* (1998, p. 49), there were no binding values between the different cultures that lived in it. Moreover, the European nations were

---

which the authors characterized as a form of modernized racism (2016, p. 82). Ethnopluralism recapitulates key tenets of the traditional right-wing movement. As the scholars remind, in ethnopluralism, one re-encounters the belief in the inequality of people, which is presented as an ahistorical and natural event and not as a historical process, determined by power relations, the distribution of resources or imperialism. In addition to this, theorists of the New Right such as Henning Eichberg and Alain de Benoist argue that the Old Right was caught up in biologism and ignored the imprint of the environment, that is, the sociological component. Ethnopluralism, as a concept, ultimately subverts racism. In their perception, it is racist to force people to assimilate and even leave their home countries. It is antiracist to bring them back to their countries of origin, where they could live in their culture (see Bruns, Glösel, and Strobl 2016, pp. 82–83).

23 Bruns, Glösel, and Strobl have provided a historical analysis of the emergence of the movement in Germany, their ideological affiliation to the New Right, as well as its singularity. As such, the movement commonly referred to as *die Identitären*, originated in France in the fall of 2012, when a youth group named *Génération Identitaire (GI)*, occupied the roof of a mosque under construction in Poitiers in October of the same year as an actionist protest. They evolved into the actionist arm of the New Right. Right-wing activism, youth, the use of references from popular culture are the characteristics of this movement. Hitherto, the New Right and its most well-known minds so far have been older, male academics. They relied mostly on think tanks, journalism or networking in their outreach to the public. Actionism, as practised by the youth movement, arguably only evolved into a outreach strategy of the movement (Bruns, Glösel, and Strobl, 2016, p. 82; also see ibid., 2014).

now in an identity crisis while migrants arrived to Europe with their own identities shaped by their cultures of origins. Global migration was not bringing to Europe a "revolt against the West" in a time where the European secular nation was in a crisis. What resulted was the creation of parallel societies, ghettos of multiculturalism made possible and legitimized by the cultural relativistism at the heart of multiculturalism.

There ensues, for Tibi, a loose concept of multiculturalism that will lead to a cultural 'anything-goes,' which the essentialist sociologist is not ready to tolerate. His concept of *Leitkultur* should provide an orientation for a democratic polity (*demokratisches Gemeinwesen*), where its members subscribe to secular norms and values, irrespective of their origins or religious background (ibid., p. 61). Only adherence to the *Leitkultur* can guarantee domestic peace. Tibi appealed to rational-thinking Europeans (*nüchtern denkende Europäer*) to establish a *Leitkultur*. A failure to do so, Tibi warned them, would put Europe in front of incalculable consequences (*unkalkulierbare Folgen*) (ibid., p. 182).

One such 'rational thinking European,' Tibi addresses in his policy recommendation for a *Leitkultur*, who sensed the opportunity[24] of the concept to win votes was then-chairman of the CDU parliamentary group in the Bundestag, Friedrich Merz. In 2000, Merz spoke of rules *of a "freiheitliche deutsche Leitkultur"* [liberal German Leitkultur] (See for example Merz, 25 October 2000). The liberal German *Leitkultur* or the modern *Leitkultur* (2004, p. 146) Merz envisioned was to serve as standard values and a general social consensus. Faced with criticism, he lamented (as if echoing the different charges against multiculturalism) that there was no generally accepted definition of what our (German) culture was and that only law (Merz is a lawyer by training) sets the limits, not a common social consensus based on values. One must say that Merz did not anticipate the negative reactions to his attempt. Nor did Tibi. An embittered Tibi wrote in 2006, eight years after his first publication featuring the concept of *Leitkultur*, and six years after Merz' attempt to establish his 'liberal German Leitkultur' to settle score with cultural Germany. The overall situation had changed since the end of the 1990s and the debates in the 2000s. The wider audience had suddenly woken to the Islamist threats of Tibi, and the

---

24 Pautz has argued that Friedrich Merz anticipated that policy on foreigners, their societal integration, would play an important role in the forthcoming elections. In 1999, the conservatives had won the regional elections in Hesse by partly campaigning against federal government attempts to introduce dual citizenship. It appeared then that the concept of the *Leitkultur*, accusing the ruling party of jeopardising 'German cultural identity' through loose requirements for immigration and citizenship, could win votes (2010, p. 40).

anti-democratic leanings of fundamentalist Islamists. On November 2, 2004, Theo van Gogh, a Dutch filmmaker had been killed by Mohammed Bouyeri. Then followed the terrorist attack on July 7, 2005 in London and the riots in France in 2005. There was the feeling that the multicultural model Tibi hated had failed and that the integration of mostly Muslim foreigners was an urgent matter. Nonetheless, Tibi, as he affirms, did not expect much from the re-run of the debate. He laments that his concept had reduced to what Mohr had called *"Operation Sauerbraten"* (06 November 2000). Mohr did not see more to the *Leitkultur* debate than the latest act in a German self-discovery theater.[25] As for Tibi, he had suddenly realized that not only the leftist intellectuals were misunderstanding his concept. Now he had to distance himself also from the conservative monoculturalists (*Konservative Monokulturalisten*) who are the proponents of the German Leitkultur.

From 2016 to the present, there have been a number of contributions made in journals that point to a revival of the Leitkultur debate. The background to this revival is the arrival in Germany in 2015 of refugees. Petra Bahr has for example, identified refugees as not the only but the main addressees of a *Leitkultur*. Germany has turned into an immigration country, and newcomers needed an orientation that helps them to understand the expectations, rules and ways of life of their host society (Bahr, 2018, p. 66).

The three rounds (in the 1990s, the 2000, and post-2015) of the debate on *Leitkultur* exhibit commonalities. Only the background has been changing.

Proponents of the *Leitkultur*, on the one hand, argue that the concept is not about conservative cultural folklore. What was at stake were common obligations (*Verbindlichkeiten*), convictions and orientation that a modern society needed. Constitutions alone cannot fulfill these tasks since they 'don't all fall from heaven or are stored there' but, so one understands, are embedded in a cultural context that guarantees the sustainability of the basic rights provided by constitutions (Lammert, 2018, pp. 39). In the 2006 debate, *Leitkultur* had been recognized as legitimate and the *Leitkulturstandards* (human dignity, freedom and equality) were to be rightfully defended by Germans.

---

25   Following Nietzsche, Mohr argues that the question *What is German?* never dies out. Germans are trapped in a perpetual self-discovery process. Mohr is impatient with the re-run of this old debate which has not disappeared despite the numerous contribution of foreigners to German culture. He reminds among others that a Brit rebuilt the Reichstag, a native Pole designed the Jewish Museum in Berlin, and an American shaped the Berlin Holocaust Memorial. (See Mohr, 6 November 2000).

Zimmermann finds that the concept of constitutional patriotism[26] (*Verfassungspatriotismus*) which was put forward accordingly falls short, since the above-mentioned cultural standards are not only provisions guaranteed by the Basic Law but needed to be proven and lived in cultural contexts within society (Zimmermann, 2018 [2006], p. 37).

Critics, on the other hand, remind that the concept of *Leitkultur* is elusive as 'a pudding that one wants to nail to a wall' (Lösche, quoted in Lammert, 2018, p. 39), that it was more the culture of the dominant group, of the elites by evoking Bourdieu's concept of habitus, an habitus engrained in the elite of the majority group. Fuchs had argued there was the conviction among Leitkultur experts that they knew what the German *Leitkultur* is and only when the immigrants know Bach and Schiller, only when they all go to theaters and concert halls to listen to Bach's music or theater performance of Schiller's plays, only then can one conclude that their integration is complete. Such a position, as Fuchs argued ignores that at least 70 to 80 percent German-born do not know much about Schiller and Bach, or visit theaters and concert halls. It follows that, as good as the idea of a general cultural canon was, its practical operationalization would prove problematic. Equally problematic is a definition of a Leitkultur in terms of European values of freedom, justice without remembering the double standards and hypocrisy that sometimes taints European foreign relations (See Fuchs, 2018, pp. 46–47).

It has even been argued that the concept of *Leitkultur* was forged to replace and perform "the same exclusionary function as race," bringing it close to the ideology and the agenda of the New Right (Pautz, 2010, p. 41). I would not go that far. It is possible that the proponents of the *Leitkultur* work with unquestioned assumptions about the nature of a basic culture, how it develops and whether a canon, whatever form it might take, can stimulate the desired emotional bonds. The *Leitkultur* debate is part of the clash rhizome, which encompasses the politicization of culture. On the international level, it is the clash of civilizations; in the domestic arena, the discourse of *Leitkultur* feeds on the narratives of the fundamental, essentialist, incommensurable and ultimately incompatible cultures.

3.2 *Cultural Integration Initiative*

In December 2016, the Federal Government Commissioner for Culture and the Media, the Federal Government Commissioner for Migration, Refugees and

---

26   Proponents of constitutional patriotism include Claudia Roth. She argues that what was needed was not a German *Leitkultur*, but a culture of mutual recognition, a culture that was sensitive to human and civil rights, based on the Basic Law (See Roth, 2006, p. 58).

Integration, the Federal Ministry of Labor and Social Affairs, the Federal Ministry of the Interior and the German Cultural Council launched The *Initiative Kulturelle Integration* (Cultural Integration Iniatiative). The platform brought together different stakeholders from the media, cultural and educational institutions, churches and other religious communities among others to discuss the role culture can play in furthering social cohesion. The inaugural meeting took place on 15 December 2016 at the Federal Chancellery.

On 16 May 2017 the members of the Cultural Integration Initiative submitted fifteen theses to promote social cohesion and cultural integration in Germany.

The preamble of the document praised the hospitality tradition of Germany, which has become home to the people of many different countries who came, eventually acquiring the German citizenship. It reminds us of the societal and political solidarity which the country displayed in face of the arrival of large numbers of refugees (Initiative Kulturelle Integration, 16 May 2017, p. 1). The reader understands that cultural integration completes a triadic integration regime that encompasses social integration and labour market integration, and contributes substantially to social cohesion. The theses were based on the concept of culture that was defined by the international UNESCO community at the 1982 UNESCO World Conference on Cultural Policies in Mexico. In said conference, it was agreed that, "in its widest sense, culture may now be said to be the whole complex of distinctive spiritual, material, intellectual and emotional features that characterize a society or social group. It includes not only the arts and letters, but also modes of life, the fundamental rights of the human being, value systems, traditions and beliefs (UNESCO, 6 August 1982, p. 1; Initiative Kulturelle Integration, 16 May 2017, p. 2, footnote 1)."

The authors of the 15 theses do not provide a rationale why this definition of culture had been chosen. Max Fuchs has reminded that the UNESCO was a political organization, whose cultural-political statements, however, are always up to date with the theory debates on cultural policy. For instance, former deputy director, the acknowledged social anthropologist Lourdes Arizpe, in the preface to the Second World Culture Report entitled "Cultural Diversity, Conflict and Pluralism" states that cultures were no longer the solid, limited, crystallized containers of the past. In this vein, Arizpe[27] even rejects the image

---

27   In her words, "At present, globalization, telecommunications and informatics are changing the way in which people identify and perceive cultural diversity. In particular, the outworn metaphor of the 'mosaic of cultures' or the 'global cultural mosaic' no longer describes different peoples' cultural preferences as they enter the world of the twenty-first century. Cultures are no longer the fixed, bounded, crystallized containers they were formerly reputed to be. Instead they are transboundary creations exchanged throughout

of cultures as a mosaic because it is too static. She uses the picture instead from a river to describe culture (See Fuchs, 2018, p. 46). Why then does the author settle for the 1982 definition instead of a most recent definition that emphasizes the fluidity of culture? Is the initiative on cultural integration a conceptualization of culture as a crystalized container? A reification of Leitkultur? Not necessarily. The theses appear as a mix of *Verfassungspatriotismus* (constitutional patriotism) and Leitkultur ideas.

Thesis 1 on the centrality of the Basic Law, thesis 3 on gender equality as guaranteed in the Basic Law, thesis 5 on artistic freedom, thesis 6 on democratic culture through freedom of speech and press, thesis 8 on Liberal democracy, thesis 9 on parliamentary democracy, and thesis 10 on civic engagement recapitulate the central propositions of the *Verfassungspatriotismus* side. Thesis 2 on cultural habits, thesis 4 on religions in the public sphere, thesis 11 on education, thesis 12 on the German language, and thesis 13 on the critical examination of Germany's history touch upon key aspects in the debate on the Leitkultur. Thesis 14 on employment for participation, identification and social cohesion transcends cultural dimensions of employment. Thesis 15 reasserts cultural diversity against the phantasies of *Leitkultur* monoculturalists.

4 Character between Affects and Late Modernity and Capitalism

In this chapter, I have suggested the metaphor of a 'clash rhizome' to make sense of the ramifications of the discourses on clash of civilizations and cultures. I have suggested three different units where the clash rhizome operates. In the first part of the chapter, I look at the first level of the clash rhizome, i.e. civilizations. I argued that the clash of the civilizations operates mostly at the international relations level. It is a discourse constructed and nourished by state and non-state actors alike, who seek to redefine the world order or claim their own hegemony. It does not particularly matter that the clash is a construct, where state and non-state actors who regularly evoke the incommensurability and incompatibility of civilizational blocs enact the very clash they want to see. International terrorism, the rise (and fall) of transnational terrorist organizations, such as Al-Qaida and the Islamic State (IS), rhythm the life and development of this rhizome unit. I revisited the debate in international relations on Huntington's clash of civilization, which was influential in

---

the world via the media and the Internet. We must now regard culture as a process rather than as a finished product (Arizpe, 2000, p. 15)."

re-centering culture at the study of international relations theory. He might have caught a zeitgeist when he proposed the 'clash of civilizations' thesis to define the new international (dis)order after the collapse of the Berlin Wall and the Soviet Union. But ultimately, it was international terrorism (mostly the attacks directed toward the USA) that brought him the reputation of a prophet. From thence, the thesis could be appropriated by anyone who wanted to reify the other, dispense of human rights and make use of disproportionate preventive and retaliatory violence in settings of asymmetrical warfare. However, when the enemy is construed as a crystalized civilization, then all sense of proportion also seems to be distorted. The international arena remains the battlefield where one's civilization battles other civilizations in an almost Darwinian survival of the fittest. I have presented cases of the German reception of Huntington's thesis and reviewed Tibi's take on the subject. I showed the commonalities between him and Huntington.

The second level of the clash rhizome is located in the domestic arena, the geographical place of the nation-state. It is culture tacitly portrayed as a crystalized, unchanging container that determines the individual's values, moral codes, actions. It is immutable, unchanging, static, a 'web of meaning' that imprisons the individual. Looking at Germany, I have suggested that there were different plateaus to the battle for 'culture.' Starting from the 1990s, there were three rounds of the so-called *Leitkultur* debate. *Leitkultur*, as an attempt, by cultivated, conservative elite to define a guiding culture, a reference culture that will take preponderance over migrants' cultural frameworks. Tibi had sown the seed of the *Leitkultur*. He had spent nearly a decade analyzing Islam before Huntington came to speak of the clash of civilizations. He saw threats in the Muslim migration to Europe and wanted to shake Europe from its identity crisis. Some politicians in Germany have seen the electoral opportunity of Tibi's thesis. Terrorist attacks in the 2000s and the arrival of refugees in 2015 are convincing some elites that a debate on *Leitkultur* was not only needed, but Leitkultur needed to be codified. The clash rhizome can be ruptured and reunited at any point of its discursive continuum. It emcompasses disparate, at times contradictory semiotic, political, cultural, and economic 'regimes of signs' but also states of things of differing status or circumstances relative to the arts, sciences, and social struggles (Deleuze and Guattari, 2005, p. 7).' By *Leitkultur*, elites meant cultural gems of literature, music, theater, or simply put *Hochkultur*. Conservative politicians spoke of the unveiled (females) faces, handshaking and other (non-binding) social conventions as the *essence* of the concept of *Leitkultur*. They might also mean emotional attachment to a country (such as singing the national anthem for binationals) that they feel migrant communities lack. *Verfassungspatrioten* (constitutional patritots) rely on the Basic Law to guide and regulate not only interaction between the State and the individual but also between the individuals within the state. In 2017, the *Initiative Kulturelle Integration*, a platform that re-united different cultural stakeholders, proposed its 15 points for cultural integration. It aggregates to some extent the concerns of both conservative Leitkultur proponents as well as liberal constitutional patriots.

In this part of the chapter, I want to point out to another level where the clash rhizome strongly plays out: the individual plateau. I chose the term 'character.' Both civilizational and culturalist essentialists neglect individual agency in the clash debates. Culture (if properly defined at all) is presented as an iron-cage, in which the individual is imprisoned and unable to escape. Here I want to suggest some avenues, where 'character' can be integrated in our thinking about the clash rhizome.

On the first level, it enables us to re-integrate the individual migrant into the late modern society they arrived in. Observing Germany in the aftermath of 2015, one does not get the sense, despite the gesticulations of politicians from the right and the extreme right and their framing offensives, that Germany is being reversely assimilated by foreigners or that German culture or language are in peril. There have possibly never been so many people learning German in Germany at a given time as it has been since 2015. Most refugees/migrants are certainly not avid proselytizers who want to change the religious identity of Germany (if highlighting a single religious identity is possible at all). To portray the migrants/refugees as 'jobs thieves' for Germany is factually wrong since most of the refugees/migrants that arrived in 2015 are on welfare. In contrast, the clash rhizomes one observes are what I would term "clashes of modernities," that are felt on the individual level. In other words, migrants/refugees arrived in 2015 to a late modern society, characterized by its advanced secularization, acceleration, total optimization drive and paradoxically also by its saturation, societal fatigue, and disenchantment about modernity. Late modern Germany is clashing with a kind of syncretic, hybrid modern universe(s) of the new migrants. Importantly, the idiom of the clash of modernity can yield important insights on integration. German sociologist Hartmut Rosa has gone to substantial lengths to map the late modern condition of Germany under capitalism (See Rosa, 2013). His sociological diagnosis combined with the discussions on disenchantment of (arguably middle-class) Germany provide an important point of departure to re-construct the modernity in which the refugee as a subject interacts and their daily collisions with late modern Germany.

The second aspect where 'character' as a plateau is relevant in the clash rhizome is in making sense of the individual affects and emotions of both migrants and host society and how they eventually clash. There is here need to adapt Moïsi's and Todorov's geopolitics of emotions (See Todorov, 2010, pp. 4–5; Moïsi, 2010). Drawing from Moïsi, Todorov had suggested a topology of countries based on their emotions. According to his typology, the first group of countries' predominant passion is appetite. These countries want to benefit "from globalization, consumption and leisure – and they will not skimp on the means needed to achieve this (Todorov, 2010, p. 4)." The second group's dominant passion is resentment, which resulted from real or imaginary humiliation. And as one could have anticipated, the countries are mostly Muslim countries (ibid., p. 5). Then there are Western countries, marked by fear. These Western countries fear "[...] the economic power of the 'countries of appetite,' their ability to produce goods more cheaply and thus make a clean sweep of the markets ... [a]nd they fear the physical threats that might come from the 'countries of resentment,' the terrorist attacks and explosions of violence – and, in addition, the measures of retaliation these countries might be capable of when it comes to energy supplies, since the biggest oil reserves are found in these countries (Todorov, 2010, p. 5)." And then there is the fourth group of countries marked by indecision, as not belonging yet to any of the groups he identified in his typology, but susceptible to tilting to any of these categories (ibid., p. 5).

If one reads Todorov's typology under the new condition of increased migration and globalization, then we might have to witness more clashes not between civilizations and cultures per se, but between passions and emotions, transported by the immigrating subject on the one hand, and the host populations' effects on the other hand. Migration from 'the countries of resentment' to 'those of fear' could create the spaces for the clashes Huntington or Tibi envisioned. But the reality of the immigrant is far less static as Todorov's (geo) politics of emotions. Fear, resentment, appetite, or even indecision are not characteristics that can be simply ascribed to particular individuals or group of countries. And migrants/refugees from the Muslim world who sought refuge in the West certainly do not – in their overwheliming majority – reproduce historical resentment on the West. It is even more likely that *appetite* drove migrants to seek refuge in Western Europe. In fleeing from civil wars and terror attacks, refugees looked to restore or rebuild for themselves an economic stability. The (safe) countries located on their flight route from Syria throughout the Balkans did not offer much of a chance to start a new life. The only viable option was to press further towards the arguably greener pastures in the heart of Europe. The driving *appetite* of individuals to partake in globalization has led some potential migrants to make strategic choices in the face of restrictive migration policies. Potential migrants had to opportunistically rebrand themselves as refugees to access Europe. Refugees are (economic) migrants to a certain degree not least because they chose the path to economically prosperous countries and wish no more than a chance to earn their living. Their dream is not to be cajoled into a golden cage of social welfare but the possibility to reconstruct a living through a prompt integration in the workforce.

CHAPTER 6

The "Deep Story" of the Elder Son

The religious and the 'sacred' have returned to philosophy. Or maybe they have never been absent from theory, or were superficially covered only to re-emerge in the late twentieth century. References to religious phenomena or doctrines and figures from Christianity, as Keucheyan (2014, p. 28) has noted, have figured in the writings of theorists of the revolutionary Left in the twentieth century and even long before. He mentions the influence of Pascal on Lucien Goldmann, or Ernst Bloch's study of Thomas Münzer, the sixteenth-century revolutionary theologian, or the role of revolutionary millenarianism in sixteenth century peasant revolts. These influences show that the religious was never totally absent from the philosophy or the praxis of revolution. Indeed the religious played an important role in twentieth-century philosophy of revolution in Western Europe as well as liberation movements in the global South.[1] In Western Marxism, scholars had recurred to the religious, the 'sacred' or the theological in their theories. The outworn cliché of religion as the opium of the people does not capture the complexity of the relationship between Marxism and theology.[2]

For contemporary prominent thinkers of the Left, theology has turned into a rich source for theoretical renewal. Contemporary critical theory has drawn on the (Western) Christian tradition and religious figures to make sense of the failure of the revolutionary socialist project, re-conjure utopia, or reconstruct the project of political and social emancipation. Past are the days where religion was considered quite schematically as the 'opium of the people.' Contemporary critical theorists are rediscovering Christian religion as a subversive force and a politics of universal emancipation (Slavoj Žižek) or rehabilitating

---

1 Simon Kimbangu's influence in colonial Congo, under the rule of Belgium testifies to the potential of a religion to stand to power. Simon Kimbangu (1887–1951), a Congolese religious leader, founded Kimbanguism, a local religious movement. In colonial Congo, he arguably cured by hand impositions and attracted many followers. Colonial authorities eventually got insecure and feared mass revolts. They tried to apprehend him and failed. Simon Kimbangu surrendered himself and was placed before a military court that sentenced him to death. King Albert later reduced his life sentence to life imprisonment. On Kimbangu, its religious movement, place and role in colonial Congo as well as his present-day influence, see M'Bokolo and Sabakinu, 2014.
2 On major Marxists' engagement with theology and its reflections on their theories, see Boer, 2007.

figures of the Holy Scriptures as radical revolutionaries (Terry Eagleton on Jesus or Badiou on St. Paul).

The reason for the rediscovery of theology in contemporary critical theory is, according to Keucheyan, twofold: belief and sociology (ibid.). (Christian) theology is essentially about belief, the unseen, the hoped-for, and promises. Revolution as well. The interest of the critical theorist in the transcendental goes as far as it can to offer new perspectives on the theoretical concerns of the current age. As such, religion has not only returned to critical theory. It returns to (Western) societies through the arrival of migrants on the one hand, and the discontent with the hollow, non/a-theism of late modernity.[3] More globally, it is the rise of fundamentalisms, the self-fulfilling prophecy of the 'clash of civilizations' thesis – regularly kindled by terrorist attacks – that brought the realization that religion was a force to be reckoned with both in domestic and international politics. More recently, it is the wave of revolts in Muslim countries since 2011, commonly known as the Arab Spring, and the roles played by moderate and fundamentalist state and non-state actors that testify to the relevance of the religious in political theory. But there is another reason why one should pay attention to (Christian) theology: its hermeneutic productivity. Each reader can bring into the religious text their own hermeneutic horizon, depending on the historical context and time from which they approach the texts. Canonical religious texts are thousands of years old and have catered to the needs of different generations, to orthodox, critical, heretical believers, and non-believers alike. As such, readers have returned to them time and again for orientation, reform impulses. Let me try to explain my point by referring to St. Paul and Pasolini. Saint Paul is arguably one of the most commented figures of Christianity in contemporary critical theory. Pasolini believed in the Communist revolution, became a member of the Italian Communist Party at a time where Leftist intellectuals were active in political parties and theory had not yet distanced itself from praxis. And Pasolini's biography has also been marked

---

3   But not everyone has been jubilatory about the so-called return to religion. Simon Critchley's *The Faith of the Faithless: Experiments in Political Theology* reassessed the role of faith. Critchley defines faith as "the lived subjective commitment to an infinite demand, [...] a declarative act, as an enactment of the self, as a performative that proclaims itself into existence in a situation of crisis where what is called for is a decisive political intervention (p. 13)." His faith of the faithless is a non-triumphalist atheistic conception of faith, opposed to what he has termed "the evangelic atheism of Richard Dawkins or Christopher Hitchens." Their atheist triumphalism sees God and religion as historical errors that scientific progress can refute and correct (2014, pp. 18–19). Critchley further warned of seeing the new interest in Paul as a return to conservative gestures. It is instead a "demand for reformation [...] for a new figure of activism, [...] a new militancy for the universal in an age defined by moral relativism, a communitarian politics of identity, and global capitalism (ibid., p. 157)."

by Catholicism. Pier Paolo Pasolini's screenplay St. Paul is an account of the history of the Early Church and Paul the Apostle, set temporarily not in the original first century of the church history, and not topologically in Damascus or Rome, but post-WWII cities such as New York, Barcelona. Pasolini thus manages to contrast Saint Paul's teachings with the great upheavals of the twentieth century, fascism and the resistance to it, capitalism and the rights of ethnic minorities. Pasolini's Saint Paul is a figure caught in the tension between the institutionalized religion and its radical and revolutionary potential. In Pasolini's words:

> I make a double Saint Paul, I mean, schizophrenic, completely dissociated in two: one is he saint (obviously Saint Paul had a mystical experience – that's clear from the letter – that was also authentic), the other instead is the priest, ex-Pharisee, who recuperates his prior cultural situations and who will be the founder of the Church. For this I condemn him: insofar as he is a mystic, that's all right, it is a mystical experience like others, respectable, and I don't judge it, but rather I violently condemn him as the founder of the Church, with all the negative elements of the Church already: the sexphobia, the anti-feminism, the organization, the collards, the triumphalism, the moralism. In sum, all the things that have created the evil of the Church are all already in him.
> quoted in CASTELLI, 2014, p. xxxix

Pasolini's St. Paul is more than simply about Church and religion. In his foreword to the publication of Pasolini's *Saint Paul*, Badiou has read Pasolini's St. Paul in the light of the sclerosis of the Italian Communist Party (PCI) (Badiou, 2014, p. viii). In his reading, St. Paul is a Lenin, respectively inventors of the (catholic) Church and the (communist) Party, preachers of religious salvation and communist emancipation (p. ix), both historical figures are caught in a nostalgic longing for a 'new cycle of the True,' the metaphorical resurrection of Christ and the Communist revolution, fidelity and exhaustion, holiness and disinterested militancy (p. x). Badiou further sees St. Paul as a critic of imperialism within the topological substitution of St Paul's Rome with the United States and a fierce opponent of the intellectual elites (p. xi).

Reading Pasolini's St. Paul does not bring me to think directly of the nostalgia for a communist revolution. Maybe because each interpretation of St. Paul tells a lot about the concerns and context of the reader more than the historical conditions of St. Paul. Indeed, Pasolini had vowed an essentialist fidelity to the words of St. Paul, but altered the topography to contextualize his critic in the twentieth century. Reading his St. Paul, I am brought to think about terrorism, religious fundamentalism, as it violently re-surfaced following the rise of the Islamic State. I see parallels between Saul of Tarsus (as St. Paul was called, before going on to become Paul, or St. Paul after his 'mystic' encounter with the Thunderbolt that radically changed his life) and the radical fundamentalists that persecuted non-believers in their view of the world. Saul of Tarsus, prior to his conversion, his Universalist preaching, and multiple missionary journeys, was characterized by his great wickedness towards Christian Jews, considered as members of a sect in that period. He also resents the colonial domination of Rome on Jewish territories. Pasolini views Paul as "a Pharisee, a bourgeois profoundly interpolated in his society, by means of a long familial tradition: he [St. Paul] is opposed to foreign domination solely in the name of a dogmatic and fanatical religion (Pasolini, 2014, p. 6)." Here one sees how fanatical religious convictions combined with violence and colonial resentment are directed towards one's own brethren. ISIS has been portrayed as a child of the wars waged by Western powers in the Middle East. The more recent trigger is the 2003 US invasion of Iraq and the war in Syria (Cockburn, 2014, p. 8). The resentment on the part of ultra-orthodox Sunnis has translated into a violent attempt to reshape the world. Like Saul/St. Paul and his fellow hard-core Pharisees, the persecution of other sects, religious communities by Sunni religious extremists was an integral part of an ultra-conservative Cultural Revolution. Saul of Tarsus had taken persecution to a trans-national level. He had requested to extend the persecution of Christians to Damascus. In Pasolini, the Biblical Damascus is a city outside the domination of the Nazis where Peter and other disciples are seeking refuge (Pasolini, 2014, p. 6). ISIS has tried to stretch its attacks to Western countries where refugees have found asylum. Or let's consider the passage where St. Paul arrives in Rome (ibid., p. 9), the prototype of a modern city at its time, its saturated life, his multi-culturalism. Paul, the converted ultra-conservative, had to spread the Gospel of Christ, with non-violent means. My point in this short disquisition was to show that Saint Paul and by extension the religion is a self-renewing source of re-interpretation, depending on how and from where one approaches it.

Here however, I do not intend to further expand on St. Paul. Indeed, I do not want to conjure a spirit of new militantism, a new hope in the ultimate triumph of a Communist revolution. I also don't take aim at universalism. My focus here is more on migration. Arguably, the Bible is a book on migrants, exiled, ethnic nationalism, and the globalizing universalism of Christ's Gospel.[4] Here

---

4 A panoramic overview of the themes in the books of the Bible can drive this point home. Genesis, the first book in the Bible is not only about creation, the fall of 'man,' the Great Flood. It almost opens with the expulsion of Adam and Eve from Eden (Genesis 3: 23–24),

I want to focus on a passage in the New Testament (Luke 15: 11–32) that even non-practicing Christians are familiar with, not least because it provided inspiration to visual artists or simply because of its nearly universal moral appeal: the story of the prodigal son. The main characters of the parable are two brothers (a younger and an elder one) and their father. I redirect the spotlight to the third character of the story: the elder son, the faithful one that has to cope with a new situation his father singlehandedly designed. I survey his reaction and suggest that the elder son was confronted with three options – to adapt Hirschman's typology – in his situation of dissatisfaction: exit, voice or loyalty. I examine the perceived deprivation of the elder son, and try to inscribe the rise of right-wing populism in the framework of a third-way reaction between exiting (the homeland) and uncritical submission to patriarchal decisions.

1 The Prodigal Son in the Biblical Narrative

Jesus, like Socrates, has probably never personally authored a book. The written records on his life and teachings are mostly found in the gospels of Matthew, Mark, Luke, and John. The gospels of the first three authors are synoptic, because they exhibit similarities in their chronology, the recounted episodes and literary style. The parable of the prodigal son figures however only in the Synoptic gospel of Luke. I reproduce below the passage on the prodigal son in the gospel of Luke:

> [11] And he said, A certain man had two sons: [12] And the younger of them said to his father, Father, give me the portion of goods that falleth to me. And he divided unto them his living. [13] And not many days after the younger son gathered all together, and took his journey into a far country, and there wasted his substance with riotous living. [14] And when he had spent all, there arose a mighty famine in that land; and he began to be in want. [15] And he went and joined himself to a citizen of that country; and

---

arguably the first refugees in the Bible. After the Great Flood that ravaged the humanity of this time, follows an eastward migration and ultimately the attempt to erect a Tower which reaches to heaven (Genesis 11: 1–9). Historic catastrophes have always brought humanity to feats of solidarity or the creation of international institutions to exorcise the demons of the past, as in the Biblical account mentioned earlier. Then follows a divine intervention and the introduction of multiple languages. This is certainly not the modern linguistic account for the more than 6000 languages spoken in the world. But it remains that migration is a linguistic experience. Another example is the migrational movements of Abram from Haran, Canaan, Egypt and back to Egypt (Genesis 12; 13).

he sent him into his fields to feed swine. [16] And he would fain have filled his belly with the husks that the swine did eat: and no man gave unto him. [17] And when he came to himself, he said, How many hired servants of my father's have bread enough and to spare, and I perish with hunger! [18] I will arise and go to my father, and will say unto him, Father, I have sinned against heaven, and before thee, [19] And am no more worthy to be called thy son: make me as one of thy hired servants. [20] And he arose, and came to his father. But when he was yet a great way off, his father saw him, and had compassion, and ran, and fell on his neck, and kissed him. [21] And the son said unto him, Father, I have sinned against heaven, and in thy sight, and am no more worthy to be called thy son. [22] But the father said to his servants, Bring forth the best robe, and put it on him; and put a ring on his hand, and shoes on his feet: [23] And bring hither the fatted calf, and kill it; and let us eat, and be merry: [24] For this my son was dead, and is alive again; he was lost, and is found. And they began to be merry. [25] Now his elder son was in the field: and as he came and drew nigh to the house, he heard musick and dancing. [26] And he called one of the servants, and asked what these things meant. [27] And he said unto him, Thy brother is come; and thy father hath killed the fatted calf, because he hath received him safe and sound. [28] And he was angry, and would not go in: therefore came his father out, and intreated him. [29] And he answering said to his father, Lo, these many years do I serve thee, neither transgressed I at any time thy commandment: and yet thou never gavest me a kid, that I might make merry with my friends: [30] But as soon as this thy son was come, which hath devoured thy living with harlots, thou hast killed for him the fatted calf. [31] And he said unto him, Son, thou art ever with me, and all that I have is thine. [32] It was meet that we should make merry, and be glad: for this thy brother was dead, and is alive again; and was lost, and is found.

    LUKE 15: 11–32, King James Version (KJV)

The story of the prodigal son can be summarized as follows. A son claims his part of the inheritance while the father is still alive, squanders it and after some time of introspection and repentance finds courage and returns to the father's home. Acknowledging that he does not deserve any mercy and cannot claim anything from the remaining *res patria*, he offered to be a simple wage worker, to ensure his own survival. Unexpectedly, the forgiving loving father rushes to the contrite son, embraces and orders a feast to celebrate the return of his lost, once ungrateful child: a parable of mercy and compassion.

    Told from a secular perspective and without the moral framing, the parable would fit appropriately as a humanitarian tale. A distraught people calling for help after losing their landed inheritance and with no shelter and a 'good Samaritan' rescues them without first trying to inflict additional humiliation on them or lecturing them on the perils of hazardous revolutions. But to catch the dramatic sense of the parable, one needs, I think, to redirect the spotlight to the third character of the story: the elder son, the faithful one that has to cope with a new situation his father singlehandedly designed. Did the father anticipate the reaction of the elder son when he was organizing the welcome feast? As I will try to explain later, the reaction of the elder son should not only be seen as a manifestation of hubris or heartlessness. It plays much deeper into the politics of recognition, loyalty, voicing dissatisfaction, and the costs of radical courses of action.

2 The Younger Son's Revolutionary Wager

Starting a revolution is an act of faith, a wager, a Pascalian wager, as Lucien Goldmann would have it, a revolutionary action. His Pascalian wager is the synthesis of elements including risk, the possibility or danger of failure and the hope of success. These elements ultimately define the human condition (Goldmann, 1964, p. 301; also see Cohen, 1994, p. 4). The outcome of a revolutionary action can never be fully anticipated in advance. Only in hindsight is it possible to work out the determinant of a successful or failed revolution. Until then the revolutionary act is a singular wager. Having faith alone does not guarantee a happy end. Not even in the Bible. In its 'hall of faith,' as Hebrews 11 is sometimes referred to, the first three heroes of faith mentioned there encounter different fates. Abel, Cain's brother, a shepherd, had faith and died, murdered by his brother (Genesis 4: 1–18). The second hero Enoch had faith and did not die. Noah, the hero in the Great Flood was also a man of faith but nonetheless nearly everyone else perished (DeYoung, 2009, p. 28; See also Waltke, 1995, p. 15).

The Younger Son enters this revolutionary wager the moment he decides to give up his bourgeois life and emancipate himself from the figure of the father. It is a personal revolution. But revolutions that are also a collective struggle for emancipation are no less gambles. Revolutions can succeed or fail. To start a revolution, one must have faith in, the "[…] substance of things hoped for, the evidence of things not seen (Hebrews 11:1, KJV)." The Arab Spring revolutions are acts of revolutionary faith. And here one observes different outcomes to the revolutionary faith that took people to the streets. Let's schematically consider the Tunisian, the Egyptian, and Syrian revolutions since 2011. The Tunisians had faith in the triumph of their revolution, ousted Ben Ali and might be on the track to rebuild their democracy. The Egyptians also had faith in their revolution, ousted Mubarak, voted for Morsi only to see him toppled and the revolution captured by an army general. The Syrians also had faith when they started their revolution even in the early violent counter-revolutionary repressions. Theirs was a shaken faith as sectarian fault lines, regional hegemonic interests and international geo-political stakes collided to leave them with an 'impossible revolution.' Counterrevolution does determine the outcome of a revolution but it does not determine its meaning in history. If it weren't so, then as Yassin-Kassab and al-Shami argued toward the end of their monograph on the Syrian revolution, "there's been no revolution in modern times. The French Revolution ended crowning Bonaparte. The Russian revolution called for all power to the soviets (sic) but ended with all power in the Kremlin. The Chinese revolution ended in authoritarian capitalism. The Spanish Revolution was defeated first by Stalin, then by Franco (2018, p. 220)." Yassin-Kassab and al-Shami instead stress the different ways people learned to live and organize under revolution, the collapse of a system. And the rest of the world, as they further argued "could learn from those *cursed* enough, or sufficiently *blessed*, to have experienced the collapse of a system, those who have been thrown by necessity into the business of building something new (ibid., p. 221, emphasis added)." A revolution can turn into a blessing or a curse. The latter one has more to teach than the former one.

3   The Father and the Cost of Humanitarian Largesse

The parable of the prodigal son is about love, compassion in the face of contrition, and redemption in the primary religious sense. If we focus on the distraught condition of the son needing shelter and food, and bracket out the direct familial ties between the sons and the father, the younger son's moral choices and conduct, then we are in the presence of a case of refugee protection. The two main characters of the parable (the younger son and the father) represent any refugee and their host society. The father provided hospitality to the distraught. What the parable does not directly approach is the cost of this gesture in terms of domestic legitimacy. Within the Biblical narrative, God's love for sinful humanity cost him his only beloved son (John 3:16), whom he gave for the salvation of humanity. The parable in Luke however does not specify to us the cost of the father's largesse for the domestic politics of the family. The father does not only restore his dignity to the younger son. He also restores him to (his) old privileges when he ordered his servant to "[b]ring forth the best robe, and put it on him [the younger son]; and put a ring on his hand, and shoes on his feet (Luke 15: 22)" He then organized a party to celebrate the return of his son.

I want to argue that there are parallels between the Biblical largesse and hospitality of the father and the welcoming of refugees in Germany in 2015. I don't necessarily mean a priori the commendable efforts of the country to grant welfare to the refugees it welcomed. This gesture has to be commended in all its dimensions. In the first chapter of this book, I referred to Germany's welcoming refugees in 2015 as an event in Badiou's sense. I outlined the dimensions of this humanitarian largesse and hospitality. Angela Merkel and her Austrian counterpart had waved entry restrictions and decided that the refugees should be allowed to pass the German border basically without prior security clearances. If one keeps in mind that Merkel is a member of the Christian Democratic Party, then it might sound logical that she welcomed the refugees without discrimination. In Germany, refugees were welcomed in 2015 in train stations and in different localities welcome parties were organized for them.

Still in this chapter, I also showed that there was more to Merkel's decision than a punctual humanitarian gesture. Her border opening took the dimension of an unparelled historical event whose repercussions could be read on two main axes: On an international level, the refugee crisis has revealed once again the structural weakness of the EU, its internal dissensions as well as the failure of international organizations and community to respond to conflicts. But it is in Germany, the country that welcomed approximately nearly 1 million refugees since the summer of 2015, that the coordinates of the political and social have been fundamentally shifting. The enthusiasm of the early days, the euphoric welcome by Germans of the refugees, the optimism – maybe best encapsulated in Merkel's *"Wir schaffen das"* (we can do it) – has given way to a growing antisemitism, xenophobia, and a reinvigorated right-wing populism that stirred up Germany's 2017 federal parliamentary elections. Merkel survived her humanitarian feat in the federal elections but has since nuanced her original stance, seeming at times to concede that those September days were an exception to her political operational code. But repeated bad performances in regional elections have forced her to resign as a leader of the Christian Democratic Union (CDU), a position in which she served from 2000 to 2018. A humanitarian largesse has its cost.

4 Exit, Voice, Loyalty, and the 'Anger and Mourning' of the Elder Son

The decision of the father to welcome back, celebrate and organize a party for the return of his prodigal son did not please the elder brother. The parable ends with the hubris of the elder son and the story does not tell us how the new cohabitation between the repentant son and his faithful brother evolved after the father's controversial decision. But relationships between siblings in the Bible, especially when generally (older) siblings perceive differences in treatment between them and a younger one can help us carefully extrapolate on the shape of the re-united family and the relationship between the two siblings. As such, the story of the first two siblings in the Bible, Cain and Abel ends in the murder of the latter by the former after God (the Father) found favor with the offering of Abel, the shepherd, and despising Cain's offer. Bible commentators blame Cain for his "all-consuming jealousy against his brother" (See Mahoney, 14 September 2018) and urge believers to accept sovereign decisions by the Father. Jacob, another Biblical figure involved in a siblings' dispute, had a different fate. After usurping the birthright from his elder brother Esau, – a birthright meant for the firstborn and which entitled them to a double portion of the paternal inheritance – he saw his relationship with his brother undergo a 20-year 'cold war.' When Esau, the deceived brother was ready to take military action against his brother, Jacob appeases him through diplomacy (See Genesis 32, 33). In another story of sibling rivalry, the offsprings of Jacob (now named Israel), displeased with the hubris and hegemonic dreams of their brother Joseph, plot to kill him before ultimately selling him as slave to Egypt (Genesis 37). A late reconciliation ensued when Joseph, who rose to the position of a minister in Egypt, reencountered his famine-ridden brothers.

In the face of these early examples, there are reasons to wonder how the reality of the relationship after the return of the prodigal son in the family and the father's estate would be. I have argued in the introduction that one should also pay attention to the elder son, his desire for fatherly recognition. Through the elder son, I argue, it is possible to introduce political science and sociology into the parable. The elder brother, dissatisfied with the father's decision has three options: exit, voice, or loyalty. Hirschman outlined this typology of how customers react to a perceived deterioration in the quality of a product (or a service). He believed that his framework would appeal both to economists and political scientists. In the *exit* option, the dissatisfied customer stops buying a product or in the case of an organization, withdraws their membership. The resulting drop in revenues or membership declines prompts the management to search for the causes of their poor performance. In the *voice* option, the dissatisfied *voices* their discontent to the management or to whom it concerns (Hirschman, 1970, p. 4). *Exit,* Hirschman believes, was a strategy that applied in economics while *voice* was employed in politics. In the market economy, customers could easily exit one product or substitute the product of one firm for another (ibid., p. 15). Hirschman pleads for *voice* as a strategy that "should complement and occasionally supersede exit as a recuperation mechanism when business firms, public services, and other organizations deteriorate (ibid., 1980, p. 431)."

Loyalty appears in Hirschman's thesis as a synthesis of exit and voice. It is a set of institutional barriers that compensates for ineffective conditions for the use of voice strategies and the sheer ineffectiveness of exit strategies (ibid., 1970, pp. 77, 80).

The elder son is dissatisfied with the privileged treatment his younger brother receives. But instead of exiting the father's estate, he stays instead on the father's estate and does not activate the exit option, maybe out of loyalty to the father. However, leaving the estate or a country, in Hirschman's framework, is an option to contemplate. Hirschman argued, "[l]oyalty to one's country [...] is something we could do without, since countries can ordinarily be considered to be well-differentiated products. Only as countries start to resemble each other because of the advances in communication and all-round modernization will the danger of premature and excessive exits arise, the "brain drain" being a current example. At that point, a measure of loyalty will stand us in good stead (ibid., p. 81)." But the elder son does not stay on the father's estate only out of loyalty. It can also be argued that exit is simply not a feasible option. Exit is a radical cut, a break from the structures that sustained and gave meaning to one's world. Similarly, the dissatisfaction with the migration and asylum policy did not lead the most radical critics of Merkel to systematically exit the country. Emigration is not an option that can be spontaneously pursued. The elder son ultimately returns to the voice strategy. What will the elder son voice then? No better concept comes to mind than Arlie Russel Hochschild's "deep story" to make sense of the anger, resentment, and feeling of the elder son. Its 'American' version, which has been conceptualized by Hochschild, has also now gone global. What is a deep story? Hochschild defines "a deep story" as "a *feel-as-if* story – it's the story feelings tell, in the language of symbols. It removes judgment. It removes fact. It tells us how things feel. Such a story permits those on both sides of the political spectrum to stand back and explore the *subjective prism* through which the party on the other side sees the world. And I don't believe we understand anyone's politics, right or left, without it. For we all have a deep story (Hochschild, 2018, p. 135, emphasis in the original)." The deep story represents in metaphorical terms "the hopes, fears, pride, shame, resentment, and anxiety (ibid.)." Many are quick to condemn and dismiss the anger of the Far Right as non-rational, a factless posturing. Hochschild opposes to this kind of intellectualist arrogance a humble sociology that immerses in the deep story of these individuals. Her work with sympathizers of the Tea Party is an illustration of this humble sociology. The American right's 'deep story' involves a self-perception as law-abiding, faithful, the belief in the American dream, the revolt against liberal values and political correctness (ibid., p. 136).[5] The right resents the 'liberals' for condemning their ultra-conservative views on gender, sexual orientation as outmoded, and immigrants, refugees, women (ibid., p. 137). As 'line-cutters,' they usurp with the 'complicity' of the federal government's affirmative action "apprenticeships, jobs, welfare payments, and free lunches (ibid.)." Hochschild has argued that the 'deep story' has gone global and can be found in India, France, the UK, and Germany.

There is no doubt that there are similarities in the far right's 'deep stories' in what one could the 'global Right' in general. The themes in the German right's deep story involve *Überfremdung*,[6] the distrust of the mainstream press (called *Lügenpresse* in the Far Right language), anti-Islam, homophobia, historical revisionism, linguistic revolt against political correctness.

Hochschild has warned that the 'deep story' translates feelings not facts. As such, it is not guaranteed that reminding the Far Right that most Africans – even when they are refugees – do not try to cross the Mediterranean Sea for Europe, or that the refugees that arrived in Europe in September 2015 were not Africans or that the continent is too diverse to allow for peremptory statements

---

5   In Hochschild's metaphorical language, the American right perceives itself as patient and waiting in line. In her words, "You [the American right] are patiently standing in a long line leading up a hill, as in pilgrimage... Just over the brow of the hill is the American dream.... Many in the back of the line are people of color – poor, young and old, mainly without college degree (2018, p. 136).''

6   *Überfremdung* encapsulates the fear that one's country is being controlled by foreigners within its geographical borders. The concept is not new and has outlived National Socialism to become one central demographic concept of the Far Right in Germany. It is a concept with a long pedigree that arguably runs parallel to German history. Following Germany's welcoming of nearly a million of refugees, far-right politician Björn Höcke's has referred to elements of the *Überfremdung* thesis in a speech during a congress of the intellectual German Far-Right in Schnellroda, a locality in Saxony-Anhalt at the end of November 2015. The congress was organized by the *Institut für Staatspolitik* (IfS), and the speech was uploaded by the IfS before being taken down. In his speech Höcke puts forward the thesis that evolution has given Africa and Europe "two different reproduction strategies". In Africa, the "r-strategy" predominates, aiming for the highest possible growth rate, which translates into a demographic surplus. In Europe however, according to Höcke, the K-strategy predominates. It is a strategy that aims at maximizing the *Lebensraum,* the living space. Africa's demographic strategy arguably effects that Africa's population surplus is about 30 million people per year. Höcke's policy recommendation is a European border, a German border to incentivize Africans to adopt "an ecologically sustainable population policy" (See Hurtz, 12 December 2015). For Jobst Paul who analyzed the speech, it is an act of 'racial demagogy' *"rassistische Demagogie,"* and he sees in the de-humanizing strategy (r- and K-reproduction strategies) a hazardous import of biology concepts to racism (Paul, 2016, p. 122).

on reproduction rate. However the 'deep story' also has its internal diverging currents.[7] To be sure, these different streams do reflect the key elements of the 'deep story' highlighted above. The Far Right has imagined a 'deep story' with all its internal contradictions and will go as far as these contradictions to not discredit their deep story.

---

7 In the AfD, three main currents coexist within a party: a neoliberal or national-libertarian stream, a Christian or anti-secular stream and a neo-national-socialistic stream (See Kemper, 2016, p. 147).

CHAPTER 7

'Muslim Girls' and *'Muslim Men'*: Cursory Notes on Entangled Subalternities

Postcolonial or subaltern studies seem to be the 'natural' research program to turn to in order to make sense of the category of the 'subaltern.' However, these research programs have exasperated many readers. Within postcolonial/subaltern studies, it is sometimes difficult to tell whether they are a chronological category, a discourse on the aftermath of colonialism, a denunciation of neocolonialism, a kind of post-imperialism, or a random combination of the afore-mentioned elements. On the outside, delineating and demarcating the postcolonial is neither straightforward since the field continually expands.[1] Even its origins are equally disputed.[2]

It is considered that the writings of Edward Said, aguably wrongly assumed as the originator of postcolonialism,[3] Homi Bhabha, and Gayatri Spivak have

---

1   Amardeep Singh warned against a bad over-extension of postcolonial theory. Applying for instance postcolonial theory to medieval studies or early modern studies is from his point of view a questionable overextension since the British Empire dates from the 19th century (Singh 2005). Erin O' Connor (2003), a Victorian scholar, has emphasized the colonizing gestures and condescension of postcolonial scholars in other fields. Her attack is particular directed at Spivak's 1985 *Three Women's Texts and a Critique of Imperialism*. These are examples of how the postcolonial theory is exporting itself to other fields of theory.
2   Robert Young, a sympathetic critic of post-colonialism emphasizes that the rise of postcolonial theory should not be separated from the debates between intellectuals and politicians in the 'Third World' during the 1960s and 1970s about the limitations of nationalism and Marxism as effective models of political emancipation (Young 2003). Despite the richness of the debate, it is still difficult to delineate the agenda of postcolonial theory. This is partly due to the diversity and ambivalence of post-colonialism. Achille Mbembe noted that 'to be sure, the postcolony is chaotical, pluralistic, yet it has nonetheless an internal coherence (Mbembe 1992, p. 3).' Central to the project of post-colonialism is the colonial encounter. The colonial encounter has widely been left out in many contemporary disciplines which at times concealed their colonial legacy (Jones 2013, p. 49).
3   Ashcroft has spoken of the 'myth of Said's originary status' (Ashcroft 2001, p. 73). For him it is clear that Said has neither 'a close acquaintance with postcolonial theory, nor, in many of his statements (because he hates all 'isms'), a clear understanding of its aims' (Ashcroft 2001, p. 73). Ashcroft, as it was reported, claimed to have been among the first to use the word 'postcolonial' to characterize the literatures from former colonies. His criticism of Said and the relation of the latter to postcolonialism should be viewed in the light of literature. Said has on occasions said that he is not interested in traditional literature theory but in world issues. The concept of 'worldliness', Bill Ashcroft argues, is Said's most important contribution

influenced the subfield of postcolonial studies. Edward Said's 1978 *Orientalism* is a seminal work in postcolonial theory. The book drew from Foucault's theorizing of power and knowledge to critique the field of orientalism and its complicity with European imperialism. For Said, the study of the 'Orient' has been contaminated with the imperial agendas of the colonizing powers so that anthropological, literary productions were geared towards providing rationales for the colonization and the occupation of a constructed 'Oriental.' From Said's work, it could be deduced that postcolonial theory is concerned with unraveling the intellectual complicities of (Western) academia that rationalized colonialism and oppression. Said's work nonetheless reflects the ambiguities that are typical of postcolonialism and subaltern studies. His critique of Orientialism lumped together different regions, ranging from the Middle East to the Far East in the single category of the 'Oriental.' It assumed a unity and homogeneity in the categories of the colonized and the colonizer and did not expand on the resistance strategies by the oppressed.[4] In its iconoclastic frenzy, the book

---

to postcolonial theory, because it is the commitment which underlies Said's treatment of Orientalism, rather than Orientalism itself (Ashcroft 2001, p. 76). In Ashcroft's words, 'it is the approach to the text's worldliness, and the desire for criticism to actually speak to an intellectual's public audience, that drives Said. All approaches to literary criticism, he claims, have fallen into the trap of specialization, a 'cult of professionalism expertise' which has rendered them marginal to the pressing political concerns of contemporary society (Said 1983:1, as quoted in Ashcroft 2001, p. 76).'

For Said, 'criticism goes beyond specific positions. Criticism that is "modified in advance by labels like "Marxism" or "liberalism" (1983: 28)" (or "feminism" or, paradoxically, "postcolonialism" as well, we may assume), is to him an oxymoron' (Ashcroft 2001, p. 82). Said's own life, with its paradoxes and contradictions, ultimately reflects the concept of worldliness. 'The celebrated American academic who passionately and paradoxically claims his status as a marginalized and besieged Palestinian, reveals contradictions at many other levels. The cultural critic reveals himself to be a cultural elitist in his tastes, preferring Western music and canonical literature; the cultural critic who repeatedly constructs himself as an exile has a home in Columbia University, indeed, could not live anywhere but New York. Lionized and famous yet victim of a "uniquely punishing destiny," the destiny of an exile, Edward Said demonstrates above all the paradox of the *textual* nature of identity, the wordliness he espouses so forcefully, being one which in his case is 'written' constantly, inscribed in all criticism. Paradox and contradiction are the very essence of Said's own worldliness, because this 'world' is the world of the exile (Ashcroft 2001, p. 85, emphasis in the original).'

4   Ashcroft and Kadhim have reviewed Said's relation to the postcolonial and reflected on the methodological shortcoming mentioned earlier. They nonetheless blame these contradictory aspects in the writings of Said not on the postcolonial agenda but on Said's understanding or misunderstanding of postcolonial theory. They noted that the most contradictory aspect of his place in contemporary theory is his relationship with the 'post-colonial.' For them, it is clear that Said did not have a close acquaintance with the contemporary post-colonial theory nor a clear understanding of its goals. They nonetheless agreed that the ambivalence and contradictions are not unusual in postcolonial theory (See Ashcroft and Kadhim, 2001: p. ix).

has not hesitated to take aim at Marx and his rapport to the 'Oriental.' Neo-Marxist scholars have also not been tender with Said and his treatment of Marx.[5]

A little bit like Said's critique of orientalism, postcolonial theory also seems to embrace vast chunks of geographies and cultures, appearing at times to be like a multivalent field of study, resisting categorization and constantly generating controversies. In Ashcroft and Kadhim's words, '[t]here is possibly no other contemporary movement beset by such a range of definitions and interpretations, and, consequently such a multi-facetted collection of objection and controversies. In what other field of study do we see greater confusion and anxiety about its very name; what other theory experiences such complaint and condemnation from the very people whose name have come to be associated with it?' (2001, p. x).

The second name generally associated with postcolonial theory is Homi Bhabha. Bhabha arguably shows more sensibility to the diversity and contradictions inherent in colonial discourse. His work sought to reveal the ambivalences in the identities of both the colonizer and the colonized. 'Mimicry' and 'hybridity' are some of the conceptual tools he came up with to make sense of these ambivalences. His 1990 *Nation and Narration* draws on the ideas of the Lacanian conceptualization of mimicry and ambivalence. Bhabha sought to show that imperial power was never as secure and stable as it was thought to be by figures such as Said. Moreover, Bhabha is interested in the agency of the colonized in the process of colonization. He also draws attention to the inherent difficulties between the concepts of colonizer and colonized. Like many other postcolonial theorists, Bhabha is influenced by poststructuralist thinkers, such as Deleuze, Foucault and Derrida. His colonial discourse analysis is interested in a psychoanalytic approach of colonial power. Colonial power, it claims, is anxious to find a final, stable distinction between its 'civilized self' and its supposedly 'barbaric other.' So far, one can see the similarities between Said's project and Bhabha's take on colonialism. But unlike Said, Bhabha does not only focus on colonial power but tries to investigate the spaces of resistance even in the presence of colonial violence and oppression. These 'liminal'

---

5 Ahmad reacted to what he called Said's 'breezy dismissal' of Marx by pointing out the historical role of Marxism in resisting imperialism and considers that Marxism cannot be dismissed as a child of orientalism and an accomplice of British colonialism (Aijaz 1992, p. 19). Dirlik's (2001) greatest fear however, is that postcolonialism's strong cultural orientation and overemphasis of identity on politics, culture, sells issues of political economy very short, which basically amounts to complicity in the structures of domination. Dirlik's criticism of Said is premised on his own allegiance to neo-Marxism and its frame of analysis. For him, failing to denounce global capitalism in a Marxist way makes one an accomplice of the system.

spaces transcend the established identities of a colonized self and decolonized other. Liminality also brings modernity to confront its concealed and repressed colonial origins. If Bhabha thinks that Said has overlooked the liminal spaces between the colonizer and the colonized, Bhabha's texts are not directly inscribed in contemporary world politics as Said's texts. The low 'worldliness' of his production and the difficulty of his text prevent a greater reception of his ideas in the sphere of other academic disciplines. Furthermore he makes no systematic attempt to delineate the theoretical scope and agenda of postcolonialism – maybe in accordance with his preference for liminal spaces – and his ambiguous relations to both Marxist theory and critical theory. This is not to deny the importance that concepts such as hybridity, mimicry, ambivalence have gained in critical analysis. These concepts are nonetheless still stained with their original context of emergence.

But let me now turn to the third figure in the so-called 'trinity of postcolonial theory' to see how the postcolonial agenda touches on subaltern studies. Although Gayatri Spivak is considered as a prominent postcolonial scholar, it would be more rightly to see her as a cutting-edge scholar whose work does span from postcolonial theory to Third-World feminism to Marxism, deconstruction, literary criticism and even globalization. Spivak's academic production focuses on the voices of those marginalized by the dominant (western) culture. Postcolonialism's role is then to champion and represent the voices of these marginalized groups. Her texts challenge the dominant discourses on the civilization, development and democratic superiority of the West. She argues that past colonial structures still influence the postcolonial condition of former European colonial powers. She also emphasizes the bourgeois character of anti-colonial nationalism, which ultimately reproduced the dominant condition of the former colonial powers. Like Said, Spivak's theory is marked by the experience of colonialism. Growing up in colonized India and influenced by the legacies of the British educational policies, Spivak has a firsthand colonial experience to draw from for her critical purposes. Added to this is Spivak's commitment to deconstruction. Writing her doctoral thesis on W.B. Yeats under the supervision of Paul de Man and her translation of Derrida's massive *De la Grammatologie* are signs of Spivak's commitment and deep familiarity with deconstruction and to French theory in general. Spivak's emphasis on deconstruction and simultaneous advocacy of marginalized groups may sound like a little bit of a contradiction as deconstruction is generally thought of as anti-essentialist and flowing. For Spivak, deconstruction is a political gesture (Morton 2003, p. 5). Additionaly, Spivak is further associated with subaltern studies. Subaltern studies originated as a critical historiography of India. Subaltern studies started in the 1970s when Ranajit

Guha gathered a group of younger scholars[6] who sought to articulate alternative critical reading of India's history by drawing from critical theorists such as Gramsci, Hobsbawn to offer a history from below. They were equally dissatisfied with colonial historiography as well as the historiography of Indian nationalism as spearheaded by the domestic elites. Theirs is an attempt to recover the agency of the peasant, as subaltern, and offer a history of their consciousness. Spivak's contribution to this specific sub-field has been, as Morton argued, to 'correct the class and gender blindness of elite bourgeois national independence in India by re-writing history from below' (2003, p. 6). More generally, she questioned the relations between First World Feminism and Third World Feminism, pointing to the complicity between Western Feminism and imperialism. 'Globalized' subaltern studies is not only about the 'Indian peasant' but has diversified their subjects of emancipatory politics. Further, they are not simply about historiography but also the sociology of majority and minority groups. There have been attempts to anchor postcolonial/subaltern studies in the academic landscape in Germany. Nikita Dhawan wonders, in an article she published online in 2007, whether the Subaltern can speak German. But, the pioneers of subaltern studies in Germany have identified the subjects of their militant scholarship: migrants, refugees, and, of course, the migrant intellectual, as their spokesperson. Dhawan herself urged to scandalize the experiences of racism that migrants are regularly confronted with and stressed the productive ground for research between postcolonial critique and migration studies. Subaltern/postcolonial studies has always been a contested field. It purported to critique the social and economic policies that account for the poverty of the Global South and re-establish, maintain quasi-colonial conditions in the relations between the third world and the first world. The advocacy of the subaltern and the call for reforming unfair economic policies could be said to be the cornerstones of the political and intellectual praxis of subaltern studies. Dhawan thought that the German academic discourse had succeeded for years to deny the necessity of anchoring postcolonial studies in the curriculum on the account that German-speaking countries were not major colonial powers to justify an in-depth engagement with this

---

6 Among the young scholars gathered around Ranajit Guha were Sumit Sarkar, Partha Chatterjee, David Hardiman, Gyanendra Pandey, and Dipesh Chakrabarty who authored some of the seminal books in the field of subaltern studies/ colonial studies. On the initial series on subaltern studies, see Guha (1982, 1983, 1985, 1987,1989), Chatterjee and Pandey (1992), Arnold and Hardiman (1994), Armin and Chakrabarty (1996), Bhadra, Prakash and Tharu (1999). For an overview of key texts in Subaltern Studies, see Chaturvedi (2012[2000]) (Eds.). For more writings in this research program see Chatterjee (1994), Chakrabarty (2008), Guha (1997).

strand of research.[7] Nearly a decade after Dhawan's diagnosis and call, German academia and the public are increasingly engaging the colonial legacy of the country, colonial art theft, albeit not through the lens of subaltern studies. The resistance to postcolonial studies (including the German context) has also epistemological and methodological grounds. Chibber's critique is perhaps the most exhaustive critique directed toward the research program. In assessing the key tenets of subaltern studies, Chibber (2013) argues that the project is a failure. He contends that the claims of subaltern studies for a radical difference between the East and the West, the working of power in a colonial setting as well as the motivations of the political actors are irremediably flawed. He asserts that Subaltern studies systematically fail as an explanatory framework because it misrepresents the fundamental categories of its critique. Critics, like Chibber, don't perceive any novel ontological or epistemological contribution to the existing body of critical knowledge. However, novelty is a problematic category to assess the relevance of a research program or its right to exist. To be sure, most working concepts of postcolonial/subaltern studies are derived from other fields or borrowed from French philosophers. Academic research, it could be argued, relies to a certain extent on borrowing, transforming, and recombining existing concepts. Furthermore, post WWII-philosophy of (natural) sciences did not succeed to come up with a definitive framework to assess the novelty or progressive nature of research programs. As such, it would be unfair to discard subaltern studies on these grounds.

Looking at the subjects of subaltern studies in Germany, one can identify different fault lines. Subaltern studies are caught in a dichotomy they can hardly transcend: the migrant versus the oppressive institutions of the host country. As a research program, subaltern studies differentiates poorly, demonizes and sanctifies quickly, demystifies little, surprises less, scandalizes much but examines less the multitudes contained in the "subaltern." It fails to provide richer accounts of the entangled subalternities and the recuperation of the subaltern discourse. In this chapter, I try to illustrate how different discourses on subalternity have emerged in order to invert or subvert the vertical oppression line posited by subaltern studies. For example, the male (mostly) migrants/refugees are depicted as "subalternizers" who deprive women of their autonomy. The discourse views interaction between Muslim men and their wives as being fundamentally a relation of oppression. Procreation, child-rearing, religious symbols, or household dynamics are systematically viewed through the lens of an 'oppressive Muslim macho.' In addition to the label of

---

7   On research on subaltern studies in Germany, see Steyerl (2002), Steyerl, Gutiérrez Rodríguez (2003), Castro Varela and Dhawan (2005), Chow (1993), and Dhawan (2005).

the domestic macho, the male migrant is himself subalternized as a criminal or terrorist threat and a (burden) to the state whose institutions are portrayed as oppressive toward migrants.

1   'Muslim Women' and Epistemic Violence

Sineb el Masrar is not a postcolonial/subaltern scholar, maybe not a scholar in the classical sense. She does not use the vocabulary of postcolonial studies or write in an academic jargon. As a public intellectual, her 2008 *'Muslim Girls'* and her 2018 *'Muslim Men'* have offered an insider's perspective on the diversity and challenges of Muslim living in Germany from the 1960s onward. El Masrar is herself the offspring of migrants. She founded a women's magazine, which addresses issues relevant to female migrants' lives. She writes her books in a journalistic style: she interviews Muslim men or girls, browses through their chatrooms, reads the academic research on migrants' lives, follows, participates to public debates, and writes in newspapers. She offers the product of her reflections in a reader-friendly, humoristic text (See El Masrar, 2018, p. 11). There is nothing of a laborious poststructuralist jargon in El Masrar's books. She works with relatively straightforward and catchy typologies.[8] However, she does not fall prey to an easy deflation of the subjects she writes on. Reading El Masrar, I get the sense that her engagement contributes to the wider concerns of postcolonial/subaltern studies.

The epistemic violence she denounces is among other things the permanent discussions and scandals on headscarves, forced or arranged marriages, genital mutilations that are conducted *about* the Muslim women *without* their voice or opinion being asked on the subject. Muslim women are mostly talked about, not talked to (El Masrar, 2010, p. 16). The epistemic violence is fed with half-knowledges about Islam and its female adepts (how could well-educated, attractive, humorous and even native German women opt for Islam, arguably

---

8 See for example, her typology of Muslim women. Her typology is aimed to argue that 'Muslim Girls' are not a homogeneous group and do not necessarily serve for an advanced academic discussion. Her typology includes high-potential Muslim girls, Black-Beauty-Muslim-Girls, Muslim version of the IT-Girls, the frustrated Muslim Girls, and the converted Muslim girls, among others. She describes these various sub-groups in their relation to religious practices and symbols, their self-perception as women and their rapport to family. She also refers to what one could term the 'subalternized' Muslim girls. In El Masrar, these Muslim 'Girls' have been exposed to numerous prohibitions since childhood. Their behavior and outer appearance are subservient of an 'archaic concept of honor' and they learn to pay respect to little boys (El Masrar, 2010, pp. 11–13).

a religion with a 'known' misogynist record), fleeting and one-sided contact with the Muslim women (ibid., p. 17). Knowledge about the Muslim women has been mediated by popular culture and singular negative experiences are generalized. El Masrar reflects on the release of the filming of Betty Mahmoody's *Not without my Daughter* in the 1990s. The movie did not only upset Iranians but, as El Masrar argued, but has also exacerbated the fears and prejudices on the Muslims in general (ibid., p. 18). El Masrar does not deny that there are cases where 'Muslim girls' are treated by their relatives as 'dogs,' forbidden to have contact with anyone from outside or forced to silence (ibid., p. 19). These instances are however few to justify the depiction of all Muslims as backward, violent, or pedophilic (pp. 22–23).

El Masrar reminds that the niqab and burka are portrayed as the ultimate symbols of the subalternization of the Muslim women. However she is critical of attempts to 'liberate' the Muslim women through a niqab ban. Her reasons to resist a ban are pragmatic. She believes that if a woman were actually forced to wear the burqa or niqab, a ban would probably only worsen her case, leading to her being prevented from leaving the house (ibid., pp. 26–27). And for those women who wear them without direct external coercion, the ban means a senseless dress code and only likely to increase aggression and intolerance toward Muslims and their religion (ibid., pp. 22–23).

In El Masrar's view on gender violence, one does not need to refer to religion to address it. Labelling Islam a 'misogynic religion' is wrong because gender violence on Muslim women from their Muslim relatives does not proceed from Islam but from what she calls 'a false sense of honor' and wrong family priorities by the perpetrators. Perpetrators regularly justify acid attacks or female homicide by referring to their need to protect their social reputation. The fear of losing one's social reputation or its protection, as El Masrar argues, is not a written Quranic commandment. It flows instead from a lack of social 'self-confidence' (*Selbstbewusstsein*). Social self confidence, as she depicts it, needs a sense of achievement (*Erfolgerlebnisse*), opportunities (*Chancen*) and the courage to take advantage of opportunities. El Masrar performs here a double critique where she simultaneously takes the (German) society and the (self-alienating Muslim) individual to task. The sense of 'self-confidence' she believes some gender-violent, misogynic Muslims are lacking should be confronted by the individual and society. Society should provide opportunities but ultimately the individual is called to take action and seize the opportunities. Her critique makes sense but violence against women is not the province of the uneducated, socially frustrated or the 'loser'; it affects different 'classes' of the society. Here, El Masrar realizes that her argument needs to be strengthened. She strengthens her argument by pointing out that not long ago, European men and women also depended on a 'false sense of honor' (she sees in the Macho Muslim) and had a patriarchal mindset. She mentions as an example the "wreath money" (*Kranzgeld*), which was until 1998 in the Civil Code (*Bürgerliches Gesetzebuch*) of Germany. Under this law, a woman could sue for damages if her fiancé did not marry her after previously having intercourse with her (ibid., p. 28). After this comparison, the reader would have by then agreed with her that a false sense of 'honor' and a patriarchal mindset are not only specific to people with a Muslim cultural background – even before they read her take on the belated women's suffrage in Europe (ibid., p. 29). The reduction of gender-violence, in El Masrar's eyes, will not proceed from grand-theoretical hectoring on the need to reform Islam or through a sexual revolution. El Masrar again draws on parallels between Christianity to explain why the sexual revolution of the late 1960s is unlikely to happen in Islam. Sexual revolutions don't happen within religion (through a reformation of the religious moral codes), but within the societies in which the religion is practiced.

Since Islam is not a country or a society, one should not hope to see a sexual revolution happening in Islam. It is up to Muslim societies and Muslims to redefine their rapport to sexuality. Comparing again the condition of Islam to Christianity, she argues that the sexual revolution in Europe did not refrain Christian priests from preaching sexual abstinence, ranting about contraception or homosexuality (ibid., pp. 30–31). In other words, she sees no need to call for a reform of the religion to redefine the believer's rapport to sexuality.

2   Migration and (Post) Colonial Path Dependency

At first glance, one would not systematically think of Germany's post-WWII migration policies and its colonial past. One would remember Germany's role in the scramble for Africa through the organization of the Berlin conference 1884–1885 and its fateful consequences for Africa. As such it is difficult to make sense of the trials and tribulations of statehood in Africa, ethnic conflict long after the major wave of independence in the second half of the 20th century without going back to European colonial history. British and French empires as the major colonial powers have had the lion's share in the colonial race. Germany acquired some colonies by settling in South West Africa (present-day Namibia) in 1883, before colonizing Cameroon and Togo in 1884, German East Africa (Tanganyika and now part of mainland of Tanzania), and Ruanda-Urundi in 1885. Its colonial experience lasted approximately three decades and when the country lost the First World War, its colonial empire was dismantled and placed under different protectorates. The German empire had nonetheless managed in its short rule to exterminate nearly 85,000 Herero and Nama in the South West Africa colony (Namibia) and repressed an armed rebellion in German East Africa, claiming around 250,000–300,000 casualties through the counter-insurgency war and the resulting famines (See Zimmerer and Zeller 2003, Becker and Beez 2005). The attempted genocide on the Herero and Nama appears to be a forerunner to the horror of the holocaust and the techniques used in concentration camps during World War II.

The necessary processing of the crime of National Socialism has predominantly busied historians since the end of WWII. It has been suggested that German colonialism experience is not defining for the current political-historical consciousness. Gründer spoke in the introduction to his seminal *Geschichte der deutschen Kolonien* [History of German Colonies] of a relative lack of consequences of the colonial experience (*relative Folgenlosigkeit*) for the contemporary historical-political consciousness (*das gegenwärtige historisch-politisches Bewußtsein*) in Germany (Gründer, 2000, p. 9). To be sure, Germany's rapport to its colonial legacy is evolving even though slowly. The increased debate on colonial stolen art, colonial reparations, and restitution are signs that the colonial is striking back.

The engagement with the colonial past has been slow to come by, partly because German's short colonial history did not produce intellectuals from the colonies to challenge the Empire from the center of its universities, unlike France or Great Britain. The short colonial history, I also thought, also explained why Germany did not have large diaspora from its former colonies.

El Masrar brought colonialism and imperialism to bear on Germany's post-WWII immigration policies. German colonialism and imperialism in WWII have created a path that Germany's post-WWII *Anwerbeabkommen*, its worker recruitments agreements with third-countries between 1955 and 1973, followed. Recruitment agreements were signed with former war allies (Ottoman-ruled Turkey in WWI, Spain and Italy in WWII), colonies that imperial Germany desired but could not get (Morocco) (El Masrar, 2010, p. 37). But El Masrar omits that Greece, with whom Germany concluded one such agreement in 1960, was neither an ally of Germany in WWI or WWII. Moreover, Germany's imperialist immigration policies reach as far back as the foundation of the German Reich in 1871, the recruiting of Polish workers that was common both under Wilhelmine Germany and the Weimar Republic. What has changed is the country's treatment of its immigrants. In Chapter 2, I had characterized as command-and-control the policies that were predominant in Wilhelmine Germany. A competing model of migration management was a partnership between state power and economic interests. It loosens the grip of securitized migration and granted comparatively more rights to the immigrants. But after the foundation of the West Germany in 1949, under the sign of democracy, the acquisition of foreign workers, happened under relatively more humane conditions than in the previous decades.

3 *Muslim Men* and a Critique of Patriarchal Reason

El Masrar's 2018 *Muslim Men* takes the patriarchal structures in (Muslim) migrant circles to task. Her journalistic methodological approach had not changed. She conducts interviews with male Muslims, blends these interviews with sociological research, reflects on the 'blend' and renders the whole in a reader-friendly prose. She makes clear at the onset that *Muslim Men* mirrors some repressed aspects of the male immigrant's condition of many first-generation immigrants, as well as second and third generations experience. She believes that failing to address the migrants' issues adds to already exiting conflicts. By turning a blind eye to the patriarchal trap, one will not deter right-wing groups from continuing their misanthropic wrenching. Silence, on the contrary, paradoxically supports and maintains an oppressive system (2018, pp. 11–12).

Her aim is instead to shed some light on the tensions, in which they find themselves with their female counterparts, and their ethnic and religious faith group on the one hand. On the other hand, El Masrar wants to highlight the contribution Muslim men can make to fighting Islamism and furthering emancipation (ibid., p. 13).

Muslim men are a heterogeneous group, engaged in different walks of life. The first generations of Muslims that arrived in Germany were not firstly referred to as 'Muslims' but according to their country of origin. They were called Turks, Iraqis, Moroccans or Tunisians. Religion did not seem to play an important role in the (self-)perception of the foreign workers. El Masrar explains that the attacks on the Twin Towers in September 2001 have been the tipping point of a deeper process that brought religion, not nationality, to the forefront of international relations, and indeed of the perception of migrants in Germany. The offspring of the migrants of the first generation who characterized themselves as belonging to two places, 'German-Turks' for instance, started perceiving themselves as Muslims in order to free themselves from the territoriality of the national identities and embracing a more universal identity marker (pp. 18–19). El Masrar documents the major post-WWII arrival in Germany of successive generations of Muslim migrants. The first Muslim migrants (Turks, Moroccans, Tunisians, former Yugoslavians) came in the 1960s, followed by asylum seekers from the Gulf War between Iran and Iraq (1980–1988), Iran political asylum seekers (1990–1995), refugees from the Bosnian war between 1992–1995, and most recently the massive arrival of refugees from the Syrian revolution turned Civil War, Iraqis, Afghans, Kossovars, Albanians, or asylum-seekers from the Maghreb who also found refuge in Germany in autumn 2015 (pp. 24–34). El Masrar's demographic overview does not deal with the set-up of the Muslim, whether there are Sunnis or Shiites, or to which particular Islamic sub-groups they belong and indeed whether these categories are relevant to make sense of emancipation and Islamic terrorism.

The early generations of Muslims have established a system of patriarchy through which they coerce younger generations into obedience. Fathers within this system are not primary educators but an instance of control and punishment (ibid., p. 155). This patriarchal coercion expresses itself in arranged-marriage, a *'raison de famille'* through which the individual preferences of the youth can be sacrificed to the wider interests of the group. El Masrar's own emancipatory call to the younger generation is to free itself from the shackles of patriarchy and develop their own emancipatory concepts (ibid., p. 63).

The migrant patriarchal system is reproduced in the understanding of masculinity as repressing and inhibiting sexuality through moralization. In youth culture, the patriarchal system manifests itself as an 'Adonis complex,' which El Masrar portrays as the veneration of the muscled body, the need to impress other people (mostly men) and earn admiration from them. It is not free from homoeroticism. The veneration of the worked-out male body conceals, in El Masrar's eyes, a deep insecurity and fear of social rejection (p. 168). She further thinks that German gangster rap has turned into the province of musicians with dominant Arab, Maghreb, Kurdish or Turkish roots. The music genre uses anti-Semitic clichés (p. 159), misogynistic and violent language to celebrate primitive ideals of masculinity (p. 164).

It leads in turn to double standards, where victims of sexual abuses within mosques or their communities are mocked and abandoned while the perpetrators are protected and covered (ibid., p. 105). El Masrar is aware that uncovering sex and crimes stories in organized religious settings can be risky for the 'whistleblower.' Muslims that loudly resist and publicly criticize, as she states, could be denied their religious affiliation, called and treated as traitors or opportunists (ibid., p. 110). But the weight of patriarchy rests more heavily on the shoulders of girls as the bearers of so-called *Namus*, virtue (ibid., p. 156). While many European societies have been discussing traditional masculinity publicly for decades and have achieved breakthroughs in their struggle against them, this engagement is missing in both right-wing extremist groups and so-called honor cultures, where a rigid and sometimes archaic patriarchy predominates (ibid., pp. 173–174).

El Masrar draws on Simone de Beauvoir, and Olivia Gazalé among others to highlight the destructive consequences of masculinity. From Simone de Beauvoir she arguably takes the sentence "the private is political." El Masrar does not provide bibliographical or page references when she quotes the thoughts of other writers. As such, it is not possible to locate where or in which de Beauvoir's book El Masrar drew the sentence that the private is political. The sentence could also be more aptly associated with the sudents' movement the 1968 or the second wave of feminism in general. Maybe one has to keep in mind that El Masrar is not conducting a scholarly discussion but a militant activism on the misfits of partriarchy.

From Olivia Gazalé, she borrows the idea of masculinity as a harmful, constructed myth. The codes of virility are enforced in childhood when boys are brought up to associate weakness with femininity, and courage, success, physical power as specific male qualities (ibid., p. 174). 'Le mythe de la virilité' (and Gazalé uses the French word 'virilité,' which not only translates as masculinity, but also as manhood, virility, potency) leads, according to El Masrar, to the rejection of non–heterosexuals, to brutality towards homosexuals, hatred of the purportedly deviant, misogynic gangsta rap, violence at work or in the household (p. 178). In the most extreme cases, the myth of manhood is an anxiety of potency that besets patriarchal societies, ideologies and religions alike. El Masrar contextualizes Gazalé's critique to the conditioning of non-progressive Muslim men and reminds us that in traditional interpretations of Islam, the female body is a reputation to be protected, submitted to a dress code. Furthermore, the female Muslim is not allowed to choose a partner outside of her faith group, let alone to be a lesbian, live promiscuously (without being vilified) as many men do (ibid., p. 175). Gazalé believes that this constructed myth is damaging for both sexes. El Masrar points to female complicity in perpetuating the patriarchal system and the myth of the macho man. She follows Lebanese journalist and women's activist Joumana Haddad to indict the education methods of Arab mothers. Male abuse is not the product of society or culture but of a faulty education of young men (ibid., p. 186). One would like to ask whether it is possible to make sense of this 'complicity' of mothers through the lens of the dichotomization of women in two categories: saints or whores, El Masrar later conceptualizes (ibid., p. 189). In patriarchal systems, she had argued, women are valued as mothers, married women. More difficult is the condition of the young girl, the unmarried, the divorced, and the single-mom. The merit of El Masrar's critique, however, is to break up the wholesale perception of women as a single category, be it the woman in the first or the third world.

By pointing to motherly complicity in reproducing and perpetuating patriarchal system, El Masrar is simultaneously indicting a brand of feminism which she seems to characterize as naïve and beset by what one could name as the 'scepter of irrelevance.' According to her, it lacks the knowledge of ethnic, religious, multicultural realities, is undifferentiated, produces superficial platitudes or phrases such as "intersectionality" which do not advance anyone except a few (ibid., p. 189). This brand of feminism is not helpful for the emancipation from patriarchy and must learn to develop meaningful and helpful concepts (ibid., p. 188). It needs to uncover and rethink the multiple entangled subalternities. El Masrar, without being an avowed feminist or a scholar, has made a meaningful contribution in this direction.

Bibliography

Abraham, G.A. (1991). Max Weber: Modernist anti-pluralism and the polish question. *New German Critique*, 53, 33–66.

Achcar, G. (2006). *The Clash of Barbarisms: The Making of the New World Disorder.* London: Paradigm Publishers.

Ackermann, V. (1990). Integration: Begriff, Leitbilder, Probleme. in K.J. Bade (Ed.), *Neue Heimat im Westen: Vertriebene, Flüchtlinge, Aussiedler* (pp. 14–36). Münster: Westfälischer Heimatverbund.

Adib-Moghaddam, A. (2011). *A Metahistory of the Clash of Civilisations: Us and Them Beyond Orientalism.* London: Hurst & Company.

Agamben, G. (1998). *Homo Sacer: Sovereign Power and Bare Life* (D. Heller-Roazen, Trans.). Stanford, CA: Stanford University Press.

Ahluwalia, P. (2010). *Out of Africa: Post-structuralism's Colonial Roots* London: Routledge.

Ahmad, A. (1992). *In Theory: Classes, Nations, Literatures.* London: Verso Books.

Ajami, F. (1993). The Summoning. *Foreign Affairs* 72(4), 2–9.

Al-Shami, L. & Yassin-Kassab, R. (2018). *Burning Country: Syrians in Revolution and War* (new edition). London: Pluto Press.

Alba, R., & Nee, V. (1997). Rethinking Assimilation Theory for a New Era of Immigration. *The International Migration Review, 31*(4), 826–874.

Ali, T. (2003). *The Clash of Fundamentalisms: Crusades, Jihads and Modernity.* London: Verso.

Ali, T. (2015). *Shadows of the Pomegranate Tree.* London: Verso.

Aljazeera (2018, April 14). Syria's civil war explained from the beginning. Retrieved from: https://www.aljazeera.com/news/2016/05/syria-civil-war-explained-160505084119966.html.Last accessed: 21 August 2018.

Almond, I. (2007). Introduction. In *The New Orientalists: Postmodern representations of Islam from Foucault to Baudrillard* (pp. 1–4). London, New York: IB.Tauris.

Almond, I. (2007). *The New Orientalists: Postmodern representations of Islam from Foucault to Baudrillard.* London, New York: IB.Tauris.

Alt, J. (2003). *Leben in der Schattenwelt. Problemkomplex illegale Migration.* Karlsruhe: Von-Loeper-Literaturverlag.

Althusser, L. (1969). *For Marx* (B. Brewster, Trans.). London: Allen Lane.

An-Na'im, A.A. (2002). Upholding International Legality against Islamic and American Jihad. In K. Booth, & T. Dunne (Eds.), *Worlds in Collision: Terror and the Future of Global Order* (pp. 162–72). London: Palgrave.

Anderson, B. (2006). *Imagined Communities.* London: Verso.

Ang, I. (1996). *Living Room Wars: Rethinking Media Audiences for a Postmodern World.* London: Routledge.

Arizpe, L. (2000). General Introduction. In UNESCO World culture report: *cultural diversity, conflict and pluralism* (pp. 14–19). Paris: UNESCO Publishing. Available online: https://unesdoc.unesco.org/ark:/48223/pf0000121058. Last Accessed: 28 December 2018.

Armin, S., & Chakrabarty, D. (Eds.) (1996). *Subaltern Studies* IX: *Writings on South Asian History and Society.* Delhi: Oxford University Press.

Arnason, J.P. (2003). *Civilizations in Dispute: Historical Questions and Theoretical Traditions.* Leiden: Brill.

Arnold, D. & Hardiman, D. (Eds.) (1994). *Subaltern Studies* VIII: *Essays in Honour of Ranajit Guha.* Delhi: Oxford University Press.

Arnswald, U. (1997). *Hirschman's theory of exit, voice, and loyalty reconsidered.* Heidelberg: Europ. Inst. for International Affairs.

Aron, R. (1957). *The Opium of the Intellectuals* (L.H. Brockway, Trans.). London: Norton Library.

Aron, R. (1962). *Paix et guerre entre les nations.* Paris: Calmann-Lévy.

Arts, B., Noortmann, M. & Reinalda, B. (Eds.) (2001). *Non State Actors in International Relations.* Aldershot: Ashgate.

Ashcroft, B. (2001). Worldliness. In B. Ashcroft & H. Kadhin (Eds.). *Edward Said and the Postcolonial* (pp. 73–89). New York: Nova Science.

Ashcroft, B. & Kadhin, H. (Eds.) (2001). *Edward Said and the Postcolonial.* New York: Nova Science.

Assiter, A. (1984). Althusser and Structuralism. *The British Journal of Sociology* 35(2), 272–296.

Auswärtiges Amt (2018). Wie viele Botschaften und Konsulate hat Deutschland im Ausland? Retrieved from: https://www.auswaertiges-amt.de/de/newsroom/buergerservice-faq-kontakt/faq/10-wievieleaven/606464. Last accessed: 07 October 2018.

Bachrach, P. & Baratz, M. (1970). *Power and Poverty: Theory and Practice.* New York: Oxford University Press.

Bade, K.J. & Bommes, M. (2000) 'Politische Kultur im "Nicht-Einwanderungsland": Appellative Verweigerung und pragmatische Integration', in K.J. Bade & R. Munz (Eds.) *Migrationsreport 2000: Fakten — Analysen — Perspektiven* (pp. 163–204). Frankfurt am Main, New York: Campus.

Badiou, A. (1982). *Théorie du Sujet.* Paris: Séuil.

Badiou, A. (2003). *Saint Paul: The Foundation of Universalism* (R. Brassier, Trans.). Standford: Standford University Press.

Badiou, A. (2005). *Being and Event.* (O. Feltham, Trans). London: Continuum.

Badiou, A. (2007). The Event in Deleuze (J. Roffe, Trans.). *Parrhesia* 2, 37–44. Retrieved from: http://parrhesiajournal.org/parrhesia02/parrhesia02_badiou02.pdf. Last accessed: 18. 08. 2018.

Badiou, A. (2009). *Logics of Worlds: Being and Event* (Vol 2, A. Toscano, Trans.). New York: Continuum.

Badiou, A. (2014). Foreword. In Pasolini, P.P. (2014). *St. Paul: A Screenplay* (E.A.Castelli, Trans.) (pp. vii–xi). London: Verso.

Bahr, P. (2018). Bewegung im Werden: Zehn Thesen zur Leitkultur in der Einwanderungsgesellschaft? In O. Zimmermann & T. Geißler (Eds.) *Wertedebatte: Von Leitkultur bis kulturelle Integration* (pp. 66–69). Berlin: Deutscher Kulturrat. (Reprinted from *Bewegung im Werden: Zehn Thesen zur Leitkultur in der Einwanderungsgesellschaft*, 2006, Aus Politik &Kultur 2).

Baldwin, R., Cave, M., & Lodge, M. (2011). *Understanding Regulation: Theory, Strategy and Practice* (2nd ed.). Oxford: Oxford University Press.

Balpe, C. (1999). Constitution d'un enseignement expérimental : La physique et chimie dans les écoles centrales. *Revue d'histoire des sciences* 52(2), 241–284.

Balzacq, T. (Ed.) (2011a). *Securitization Theory: How Security Problems Emerge and Dissolve*. London and New York: Routledge.

Balzacq, T. (2011b). A Theory of Securitization: Origins, Core Assumptions, and Variants. In T. Balzacq (Ed.), *Securitization Theory: How Security Problems Emerge and Dissolve* (pp. 1–30). London and New York: Routledge.

Balzacq, T. (2011c). Enquiries into methods: A New Framework for Securitization Analysis. In T. Balzacq (Ed.), *Securitization Theory: How Security Problems Emerge and Dissolve* (pp. 31–53). London and New York: Routledge.

BAMF (2017, July 12) *Integrationskurse*. Retrieved from: http://www.bamf.de/DE/Willkommen/DeutschLernen/Integrationskurse/integrationskurse-node.html. Last Accessed: 04 November 2018.

BAMF (2018, April 04). *Bericht zur Integrationskursgeschäftsstatistik für das Jahr 2017*. Retrieved from: https://www.bamf.de/SharedDocs/Anlagen/DE/Downloads/Infothek/Statistik/Integration/2017/2017-integrationskursgeschaeftsstatistik-gesamt_bund.pdf?__blob=publicationFile. Last accessed: 05 November 2018.

BAMF (2018, October). *Liste der zugelassenen Lehrwerke in Integrationskursen* [List of approved textbooks in integration courses. Retrieved from: https://www.bamf.de/SharedDocs/Anlagen/DE/Downloads/Infothek/Integrationskurse/Lehrkraefte/liste-zugelassener-lehrwerke.pdf?__blob=publicationFile. Last accessed: 16 December 2018.

Barnett, M. & Duvall, R. (2005). Power in International Politics. *International Organization* (59)1, 39–75.

Bartmann, D. (2014). Ausgestellte Werke. In Nentwig, F. & Bartmann, D. (Eds.). *Matthias Koeppel: Himmel, Berlin!* (pp. 44–166). Berlin: nicolai.

Baubock, R., Heller, A., & Zolberg, A. (Eds.) (1996). *The Challenge of Diversity: Integration and Pluralism in Societies of Immigration*. Aldershot: Avebury.

Bauder, H. (2006). *Labor Movement: How Migration Regulate Labor Market*. Oxford: Oxford University Press.

Baudrillard, J. (1983). *In the Shadow of the Silent Majorities, or, the End of the Social, and other Essays*. (P. Foss, P. Patton, & J. Johnston, Trans.). New York: Semiotext(e).
Baudrillard, J. (1992). *La grève des événements*. Paris: Galilée.
Baudrillard, J. (2007). *Event and Non-Event* (S. Kendall, Trans.). Retrieved from http://insomnia.ac/essays/event_and_non-event/. Last accessed: 10 August 2018.
Baudrillard, J. (2012). *The Spirit of Terrorism* (C. Turner, Trans.). London: Verso.
Baudrillard, J. (1995). *The Gulf War Did Not Take Place* (P. Patton, Trans). Bloomington: Indiana University Press.
Bauer, T., Lofström, M. & Zimmermann, K.F. (2000) Immigration Policy, Assimilation of Immigrants and Native Sentiments towards Immigrants. Evidence from Twelve OECD Countries. *Swedish Economic Policy Review* 7(2), 11–53.
Bauman, Z. (1998). *Globalization: The Human Consequences*. Cambridge: Polity Press.
Bechhaus-Gerst, M. & Gieseke, S. (Eds.) (2007). *Koloniale und postkoloniale Konstruktionen von Afrika und Menschen afrikanischer Herkunft in der deutschen Alltagskultur*. Frankfurt am Main: Peter Lang.
Beck, C. & Gleyzon, F.-X. (2016) Deleuze and the Event(s). *Journal for Cultural Research* 20(4), 329–333.
Beck, U. (1992). *Risk Society: Towards a New Modernity*. London: Sage.
Beck, U. (2006). Risk Society Revisited: Theory, Politics and Research Programmes. In J.F. Cosgrave (Ed.), *The Sociology of Risk and Gambling Reader* (pp. 61–82). London, New York: Routledge.
Becker, F. & Beez, J. (Eds.) (2005). *Der Maji-Maji-Krieg in Deutsch-Ostafrika.1905–1907*. Berlin: Ch Links.
Benoist, A. de (2017). *Kulturrevolution von rechts. Gramsci und die Nouvelle Droite*. Dresden: Jungeuropa Verlag.
Berger, H. (1990). Vom Klassenkampf zum Kulturkonflikt — Wandlungen und Wendungen der westdeutschen Migrationsforschung. In E.J. Dittrich & F.-O. Radke (Eds.), *Ethnizität, Wissenschaft und Minderheiten* (pp. 119–38). Wiesbaden: Springer VS.
Berger, J. et al. (1972). *Ways of Seeing*. London: Penguin Books.
Berkowitz, D.A. (Ed.) (1997). *Social Meanings of News: A Text-Reader*.California: Sage.
Berlinghoff, M. (2012). *Das Ende der „Gastarbeit". Europäische Anwerbestopps 1970–1974*. Paderborn: Verlag Ferdinand Schöningh.
Berressem, H. & Haferkamp, L. (2009). Deleuzian Events: Writing History. In H. Berressem & L. Haferkamp (Eds.) *Deleuzian Events: Writing History, Vol. 3*. Paper presented at n-1| work-science-medium, Cologne (pp. 2–30). Berlin: Lit-Verlag.
Berry, J.W. (1997). Immigration, acculturation, and adaptation. *Applied Psychology: An International Review* 46, 5–68.
Bettiza, G. and Petito, F. (2018). Why (Clash of) Civilizations Discourses Just Won't Go Away? Understanding the Civilizational Politics of Our Times. In Orsi, D. (Ed.).

The 'Clash of Civilizations' 25 Years On: A Multidisciplinary Appraisal. Bristol: E-international Relation Publishing (pp. 37–51). Retrieved from: https://www.e-ir.info/publication/the-clash-of-civilizations-25-years-on-a-multidisciplinary-appraisal/. Last accessed: 01 December 2018.

Bewarder, M. (2018, September 28). *Jetzt macht auch das Saarland bei Seehofers Ankerzentren mit.* Retrieved from: https://www.welt.de/politik/deutschland/article 181700826/Migrationspolitik-Jetzt-macht-auch-das-Saarland-bei-Seehofers-Ankerzentren-mit.html. Last accessed: 30 September 2018.

Bhadra, G., Prakash, G. & Tharu, S. (Eds.) (1999). *Subaltern Studies X: Writings on South Asian History and Society.* New Dehli: Oxford University Press.

Billig, M. (1995). *Banal Nationalism.* London: Sage Publications.

Biskamp, F. (2016). Antimuslimischer Rassismus als systematisch verzerrtes Kommunikationsverhältnis. Das Sprechen über den Islam zwischen Befreiung und Festschreibung. In H. Kellershohn, & W. Kastrup (Eds.) *Kulturkampf von rechts: AFD, Pegida und die Neue Rechte* (pp. 180–193). Münster: UNRAST Verlag.

Blackledge, A. (2009). Being English, speaking English: Extension to English language testing legislation and the future of multicultural Britain. In C. Hogan-Brun, C. Mar-Molinero, & P. Stevenson (Eds). *Discourses on Language and Integration: Critical perspectives on language testing regimes in Europe* (pp. 83–107). Amsterdam, Philadelphia: John Benjamins Publishing Company.

Blaut, J.M. (1993). *The Colonizer's Model of the World: Geographic Diffusionism and Eurocentric History.* New York and London: The Guilford Press.

Block, D. (2003). *The Social Turn in Second Language Acquisition.* Edinburgh: Edinburgh Universiry Press.

Blommaert, Jan (Ed.) (1999). *Language Ideological Debates.* Berlin: de Gruyter.

Bloom, H. (1973). *The Anxiety of Influence: A Theory of Poetry.* New York: Oxford University Press.

Blume, G. et al. (2016, August 30). *The Night Germany Lost Control.* Retrieved from: https://www.zeit.de/gesellschaft/2016-08/refugees-open-border-policy-september-2015-angela-merkel/komplettansicht. Last Accessed: 27 August 2018.

BMZ [Bundesministerium für wirtschaftliche Entwicklung und Zusammenarbeit] (2017, April 11) Deutsche ODA-Quote steigt bedingt durch die Flüchtlingsausgaben im Inland erstmals auf 0,7 Prozent. Retrieved from: http://www.bmz.de/de/presse/aktuelleMeldungen/2017/april/170411_pm_040_Deutsche-ODA-Quote-steigt-erstmals-auf-0-7-Prozent/index.jsp. Last accessed: 07 October 2018.

Boal, A. (1979). *Theatre of the Oppressed.* London: Pluto Press.

Boatcă, M. (2013). From the Standpoint of Germanism. A Postcolonial Critique of Weber's Theory of Race and Ethnicity. *Political Power and Social Theory* 24, 55–80.

Boer, R. (2007). *Criticism of Heaven: On Marxism and Theology.* Leiden and Boston: Brill.

Bommes, M. (2006). Migration and Migration Research in Germany. In E. Vastia, & V. Vuddamalay, (Eds). *International Migration and the Social Sciences: Confroting National Experiences in Australia, France and Germany* (pp. 143–221). New York: Palgrave MacMillan.

Bottici, C. &Challand, B. (2006). Rethinking Political Myth: The Clash of Civilizations as a Self-Fulfilling Prophecy. *European Journal of Social Theory* 9(3), 315–336.

Bourbeau, P. (2011). *A Securitization of Migration: A Study of Movement and Order.* Security and Governance Series. London and New York: Routledge.

Bourdieu, P. (1990). *The Logic of Practice* (R. Nice, Trans). Cambridge: Polity Press.

Bourdieu, P. (1991). *Language and symbolic power.* Cambridge, MA: Harvard University Press.

Bourdieu, P. (2002). Against the policy of depoliticization. *Studies in Political Economy* 69, 31–41.

Boyer, R. (1990). *The regulation school: A critical introduction.* (C. Charney, Trans.). New York: Columbia University Press.

Bruns, J., Glösel, K., & Strobl, N. (2014). *Die Identitären: Handbuch der Jugendbewegung. der Neuen Rechte in Europa. Münster* Münster: UNRAST Verlag.

Bruns, J., Glösel, K., & Strobl, N. (2016). Die Identitären: Der modernisierte Rassismus einer Jugendbewegung der Neuen Rechten. In H. Kellershohn,& W. Kastrup (Eds.) *Kulturkampf von rechts: AFD, Pegida und die Neue Rechte* (pp. 82–91). Münster: UNRAST Verlag.

Builder, C.H., Bankes, S.C., & Nordin, R. (1999). *Command Concepts: A Theory Derived from the Practice of Command and Control.* Santa Monica, CA: RAND Corporation. Retrieed from: https://www.rand.org/pubs/monograph_reports/MR775.html. Also available in print form. Last accessed: 14 September 2018.

Bull, H. (1990). The Importance of Grotius in the Study of International Relations. In H. Bull, et al. (Eds.), *Hugo Grotius and International Relations* (pp. 65–93). New York: Oxford University Press.

Bull, H. ([1977] 2000). *The Anarchical Society: A Study of Order in World Politics* (3rd ed.). London: Macmillan.

Bundeswehr (2018, May 7). *Die Stabilisierungsmission in Mali (MINUSMA).* Retrieved from: http://www.einsatz.bundeswehr.de/portal/a/einsatzbw/start/aktuelle_einsaetze/mali/info/. Last accessed: 14 October 2018.

Busch, B. (2009), Local actors in promoting multilingualism. In G. Hogan-Brun, C. Mar-Molinero, & P. Stevenson, (Eds). *Discourses on Language and Integration: Critical perspectives on language testing regimes in Europe* (pp. 129–151). Amsterdam, Philadelphia: John Benjamins Publishing Company.

Butler, J. (2004). *Precarious Life: the Power of Mourning and Violence.* New York, NY: Verso Books.

Butterwegge, C. (2005, March 15) Von der "Gastarbeiter"-Anwerbung zum Zuwanderungsgesetz: Migrationsgeschehen und Zuwanderungspolitik in der Bundesrepublik. Retrieved from: http://www.bpb.de/gesellschaft/migration/dossier-migration-ALT/56377/migrationspolitik-in-der-brd?p=all. Last accessed: 25 September 2018.

Caldwell, C. (2017, July 8). Germany's Newest Intellectual Antihero. Retrieved from: https://www.nytimes.com/2017/07/08/opinion/sunday/germanys-newest-intellectual-antihero.html. Last accessed: 26 December 2018.

Casati, R. & Varzi, A.C. (1996). *Events*. Dartmouth: Aldershot.

Castelli, E.A. (2014). Introduction: Translating Pasolini Translating Paul. In Pasolini, P.P. (2014). *St. Paul: A Screenplay* (Castelli, E.A., Trans., pp. xv–xlii). London: Verso.

Castro Varela, M. & Dhawan, N. (2005): *Postkoloniale Theorie. Eine kritische Einführung.* Bielefeld: transcript.

Cerletti, A. (2005). La Politique Du Maître Ignorant : La Leçon De Rancière. *Le Télémaque* (1)27, 81–88. Reteieved from: https://www.cairn.info/revue-le-telemaque-2005-1-page-81.htm. Last accessed: 09 December 2018.

Chakrabarty D. (2008) *Provincializing Europe. Postcolonial Perspectives and Historial Difference.* Princeton, New Jersey: University of Princeton Press.

Chatterjee, P. (1994). *The Nation and its Fragments: Colonial and Postcolonial Histories.* Dehli: OUP.

Chatterjee, P. & Pandey, G. (1992) (Eds.) *Subaltern Studies VII: Writings on South Asian History and Society.* Delhi: Oxford University Press.

Chaturvedi, V. (Eds.) (2012 [2000]). *Mapping Subaltern Studies and the Postcolonial.* London, New York: Verso.

Chibber, V. (2013). *Postcolonial Theory and the Specter of Capital.* London: Verso.

Chisholm, R.M., (1990). Events without Times. An Essay on Ontology. *Nous* 24, 413–428.

Chow, R. (1993): *Writing Diaspora. Tactics of Intervention in Contemporary Cultural Studies.* Bloomington, Indianapolis: Indiana University Press.

Chowdhry, G & Nair, S. (Eds.) (2002). *Power, Postcolonialism, and International Relations: Reading Race, Gender, and Class.* London: Routledge.

Christoffel, U. (1997) (Ed.). *Matthias Koeppel: Neue Bilder von 1987 bis 1997.* Berlin: Kunstamt Wilmersdorf.

Cockburn, P. (2014). *The Rise of the Islamic State: ISIS and the New Sunni Revolution.* London: Verso.

Cohen, M. (1994). *The Wager of Lucien Goldmann: Tragedy, Dialectics, and a Hidden God*, New Jersey: Princeton University Press.

Cohen, R. (1987). *The new helots: Migrants in the international division of labour.* Aldershot, UK: Avebury.

Cole, P. (2000). *Philosophies of exclusion: Liberal political theory and immigration*. Edinburgh, Scotland: Edinburgh University Press.

Connolly, K. (2018, August 28). German police criticised as country reels from far-right violence. Retrieved from https://www.theguardian.com/world/2018/aug/28/german-police-criticised-as-country-reels-from-far-right-violence. Last accessed: 13 October 2018.

Convention Relating to the Status of Refugees, July 28, 1951, 189 U.N.T.S., 137. Retrieved from: https://treaties.un.org/doc/Publication/UNTS/Volume%20189/volume-189-I-2545-English.pdf. Last accessed: 08. October 2018.

Council of Europe (2000). *Recommendation Rec. (2000) 24 of the Committee of Ministers to member states on the Development of European Studies for Democratic Citizenship*. Retrieved from: https://rm.coe.int/16804e0a9c. Last accessed: 09 February 2019.

Council of Europe (2001). *Common European Framework of Reference for Languages: Learning, Teaching, Assessment*. Cambridge: Cambridge University Press.

Critchley, S. (2014). *The Faith of the Faithless: Experiments in Political Theology*. London: Verso.

Dale, J. & Hyslop-Margison, E. (2010). *Paulo Freire: Teaching for Freedom and Transformation. The Philosophical Influences on the Work of Paulo Freire*. (Explorations of Educational Purpose, Vol. 12). Dordrecht, Heidelberg, London, New York: Springer.

Davidson, D. (1991). *Inquiries into Truth and Interpretation*. Oxford: Clarendon Press.

Davidson, D. (2002). *Essays on Actions and Events*. Second Edition. Oxford: Clarendon Press.

Decker, O. & Brähler, E. (2005). Rechtsextreme Einstellungen in Deutschland. *Aus Politik und Zeitgeschichte* 42, 8–17.

Deleuze, G. (1973). À quoi reconnaît-on le structuralisme? In F. Châtelet (Ed.) *Histoire de la philosophie, Idées, Doctrines. Vol. 8: Le XXe siècle* (pp. 299–335). Paris: Hachette.

Deleuze, G. (1990). *The Logic of Sense* (C.V. Boundas, M. Lester, & C. Stivale, Trans.). (European Perspectives: A Series in Social Thought and Cultural Criticism). New York: Columbia University Press.

Deleuze, G. (1994). *Difference and Repetition* (P. Patton, Trans). New York: Columbia University Press.

Deleuze, G. & Guattari, F. (1994). *What is Philosophy* (H. Tomlinson & G. Burchell, Trans.). (European Perspectives: A Series in Social Thought and Cultural Criticism). New York: Columbia University Press.

Deleuze, G., F. Guattari (2005). *A Thousand Plateaus: Capitalism and Schizophrenia*. (B. Massumi, Trans.). London, Minneapolis: University of Minnesota Press.

Desai, G., Nair, S. (Eds.) (2005) Postcolonialisms: An Anthology of Cultural Theory and Criticism. New Brunswick: Rutgers University Press.

De Saussure, F. (1959). *Course in General Linguistics* (W. Baskin, Trans.). New York: Philosophical Library.
De Young, K.L. (2009). *Just Do Something: A Liberating Approach to Finding God's Will.* Chicago: Moody Publishers.
Dhawan, N. (2005): Die verzwickte Position der Postkolonialen Feministin: Gegen eine Subalternisierung der intellektuellen Migrantin. In W. Müller-Funk, & B. Wagner (Eds.) *Eigene und Andere Fremde: Postkoloniale Kulturkonflikte im europäischen Kontext* (pp. 77–89). Wien: Turia+Kant.
Dhawan, N. (2007, April 25). Can the Subaltern Speak German? And Other Risky Questions. Migrant Hybridism versus Subalternity. Retrieved from: http://translate.eipcp.net/strands/03/dhawan-strands01en. Last accessed: 20 January 2019.
Digeser, P. (1992). The Fourth Face of Power. *Journal of Politics* 54(4), 977–1007.
Dirlik, A. (2001) Placing Edward Said: Space, Time and the Travelling Theorist. In B. Ashcroft, & H. Kadhin, (Eds.) *Edward Said and the Postcolonial.* New York: Nova Science.
Donaldson, A. (1996). *The Thought of Lucien Goldmann: A critical study.* Lewiston: Edwin Mellen Press.
Doty, R.L. (1996). *Imperial Encounters: The Politics of Representation in North-South Relations.* Borderlines, Vol 5. Minneapolis: University of Minnesota Press.
Doyle, M. (1997). *Ways of War and Peace.* New York: Norton.
Duden, B. (2002). The Quest for Past Somatics. In L. Hoinacki & C. Mitcham (Eds.). *The Challenges of Ivan Illich: A collective Reflection* (pp. 219–230). New York: State University of New York Press.
Duerr, G.M.E. (2018). Huntington vs. Mearsheimer vs. Fukuyama: Which Post-Cold War Thesis is Most Accurate? In Orsi, D. (Ed.). *The 'Clash of Civilizations' 25 Years On: A Multidisciplinary Appraisal.* Bristol: E-international Relation Publishing (pp. 87–97). Retrieved from: https://www.e-ir.info/publication/the-clash-of-civilizations-25-years-on-a-multidisciplinary-appraisal/. Last accessed: 02 December 2018.
Dupuy, J.-P. (2002). Detour and Sacrifice: Ivan Illich and René Girard. In L. Hoinacki, & C. Mitcham, (Eds.). *The Challenges of Ivan Illich: A collective Reflection* (pp. 189–204). New York: State University of New York Press.
Dürr, S. et al. (2016): Die Kölner Silvesternacht in Medien und Öffentlichkeit. Sexuelle Gewalt in der öffentlichen Debatte. *Communicatio Socialis* (49)3, 283–296. Retrieved from: http://ejournal.communicatio-socialis.de/index.php/cc/article/view/1316/1314. Last accessed: 15 December 2018.
Eagleton, T. (2005). *Figures of Dissent: Critical Essays on Fish, Spivak, Zizek and Others.* London: Verso.
Eagleton, T. (2007). *The Gospels: Terry Eagleton presents Jesus Christ.* London and New York: Verso.

El Masrar, S. (2010). *Muslim Girls: Wer wir sind, wie wir leben.* Frankfurt am Main: Eichborn.

El Masrar, S. (2018). *Muslim Men: Wer sie sind, was sie wollen.* Freiburg im Breisgau, Basel, Wien: Verlag Herder.

Elsner, L. & Lehmann, J. (1988). *Ausländische Arbeiter unter dem deutschen Imperialismus, 1900–1985.* Berlin: Dietz Verlag.

Extra, G., Spotti, M. (2009). Language, migration and citizenship: A case study on testing regimes in the Netherlands. In G. Hogan-Brun, C. Mar-Molinero, & P. Stevenson (Eds.). *Discourses on Language and Integration: Critical perspectives on language testing regimes in Europe* (pp. 60–81). Amsterdam, Philadelphia: John Benjamins Publishing Company.

Fairclough, N. (1992). *Discourse and social change.* Cambridge, UK: Polity Press.

Falbel, A. (2002). The Mess we're in: How Ivan Illich Revealed to Me that the American Dream is actually a Nightmare. In L. Hoinacki, C. Mitcham, (Eds.). *The Challenges of Ivan Illich: A collective Reflection* (pp. 129–139). New York: State University of New York Press.

Fasolt, C. (2004). *The Limits of History.* Chicago: Chicago University Press.

Favell, A. (2001). *Philosophies of Integration: Immigration and the Idea of Citizenship in France and Britain* (2nd ed.). London, New York: Palgrave Macmillan.

Feyerabend, P. (1975). *Against Method: Outline of an Anarchist Theory of Knowledge.* London: New Left Books.

Fink, C. and Schaefer, B. (2009). *Ostpolitik, 1969–1974, European and Global Responses.* Cambridge University Press, Cambridge: Cambridge University Press.

Fitzpatrick, J.P. (2002). Ivan Illich as We Knew Him in the 1950s. In L. Hoinacki, & C. Mitcham, (Eds.). *The Challenges of Ivan Illich: A collective Reflection* (pp. 35–42). New York: State University of New York Press.

Foucault, M. (1972). *The Archeology of Knowledge and the Discourse on Language* (A.M.S. Smith, Trans.). New York: Pantheon Books.

Foucault, M. (1984). The politics of health in the eighteenth century. In P. Rabinow (Ed.). *The Foucault Reader* (pp. 273–89). New York: Pantheon Books.

Foucault, M. (2002). Truth and Power. In J.D. Faubion, (Ed.) *Power: Essential Works of Foucault.* (*Vol.* 3, R. Hurley et al., Trans.), London: Penguin.

Foucault, M. (2010). *The Birth of Biopolitics: Lectures at the College de France (1978–9)* (G. Burchell, Trans.). New York: Palgrave MacMillan.

Foucault, M. (2011). *The Government of self and others: lectures at the College de France, 1982–1983.* Basingstoke: Palgrave Macmillan.

Freimuth, I. (2018). *Lehrer über dem Limit: Warum die Integration scheitert.* München. Europa Verlag.

Freire, P. (1996). *Letters to Cristina.* New York: Routledge.

Freire, P. (1996 [1970]). *Pedagogy of the Oppressed* (M.B. Ramos, Trans). London: Penguin Books.

Freire, P. (2000 [1997]). *Pedagogy of the heart* (D. Macedo, & A. Oliveira, Trans.). New York: Continuum.

Frigerio, G. (2005). À propos du "maître ignorant" et de ses leçons. Témoignage à propos d'une relation transférentielle *(M. Xufré, Trans.). Le Télémaque* (1)27, 57–62. Retrieved from: https://www.cairn.info/revue-le-telemaque-2005-1-page-57.htm. Last accessed: 09 December 2018.

Fuchs, M. (2018). Leitkultur, kulturelle Vielfalt und die Politik: Über Containerbegriffe? In O. Zimmermann & T. Geißler (Eds.), *Wertedebatte: Von Leitkultur bis kulturelle Integration* (pp. 45–47). Berlin: Deutscher Kulturrat. (Reprinted from Über Containerbegriffe, 2006, *Aus Politik &Kultur 2*).

Fukuyama, F. (2006). *The End of History and the Last Man.* New York: Free Press.

Gable, S.L. (2006). Approach and avoidance social motives and goals. *Journal of Personality* 74, 175–222.

Garcia, Jean-François (1997), *Jacotot*. Paris: PUF.

Gatrell, P. (2015). *The Making of the Modern Refugee.* Oxford: Oxford University Press.

Genova, N. de (2013). 'We are of the Connections': Migration, Methodological Nationalism, and 'Militant Research'. *Postcolonial Studies* 16(3), 250–258.

Germany: Basic Law for the Federal Republic of Germany [Germany], 1949, May 23. Retrieved from: http://www.refworld.org/docid/4e64d9a02.html. Last accessed: 08 October 2018.

Giddens, A. (1979). *Central Problems in Social Theory: Action, Structure, and Contradiction in Social Analysis.* Chicago: University of California Press.

Gil-Bazo, M. (2015). Asylum as a General Principle of International Law. *International Journal of Refugee Law* (27)1, 3–28.

Gogolin, I. (1994). *Der monolinguale Habitus der multilingualen Schule.* Munster/New York: Waxmann.

Goldenziel, J.I. (2016). The Curse of the Nation-State: Refugees, Migration, and Security in International Law. *Arizona State Law Journal*, 48, 579–636. Retrieved from: https://ssrn.com/abstract=2684903. Last accessed: 08 October 2018.

Goldmann, L. (1964). *The Hidden God: A Study of Tragic Vision in the Pensées of Pascal and the Tragedies of Racine.* (P. Thody, Trans.). London: Routledge.

Goldstein, J. & Keohane, R.O. (1993). Ideas and Foreign Policy: An Analytical Framework. In J. Goldstein, & R.O. Keohane, (Eds.) *Ideas and Foreign Policy: Beliefs, Institutions and Political Change (pp. 3–30).* Ithaca, New York: Cornell University Press.

Gordon, D.M., Richard R. Edwards, & Reich, M. (1982). *Segmented work, divided workers: The historical transformation of labour in the United States.* Cambridge, UK: Cambridge University Press.

Görtemaker, M. (1989). *Deutschland im 19. Jahrhundert: Entwicklungslinien* (3rd ed.). Opladen: Leske u. Budrich.

Gründer, H. (2012). *Geschichte der deutschen Kolonien* (6th ed). Paderborn: Schöningh.

Guha, R. (1982) (Ed.) *Subaltern Studies I: Writings on South Asian History and Society*. Delhi: Oxford University Press.

Guha, R. (Ed.) (1983). *Subaltern Studies II: Writings on South Asian History and Society*. Delhi: Oxford University Press.

Guha, R. (Ed.) (1984). *Subaltern Studies III: Writings on South Asian History and Society*. Delhi: Oxford University Press.

Guha, R. (Ed.) (1985). *Subaltern Studies IV: Writings on South Asian History and Society*. Delhi: Oxford University Press.

Guha, R. (Ed.) (1987). *Subaltern Studies V: Writings on South Asian History and Society*. Delhi: Oxford University Press.

Guha, R. (Ed.) (1989). *Subaltern Studies VI: Writings on South Asian History and Society*. Delhi: Oxford University Press.

Guha, R. (1997): *Dominance without Hegemony*. Cambridge: Harvard University Press.

Gutiérrez Rodríguez, E. (2000). *"My traditional clothes are sweat-shirts and jeans". Über die Schwierigkeit, nicht different zu sein oder Gegen-Kultur als Zurichtung. Für eine antirassistisch-feministisch-queere Internationale*. Retrieved from : http://eipcp.net/transversal/0101/gutierrezrodriguez/de. Last accessed: 09 February 2019.

Guzzini, S. (1993). Structural Power: the Limits of Neorealist Power Analysis. *International Organization* (47)3, 443–478.

G5 Sahel Sécurité et Développement (2018, February). Le Nouveau Collège Sahélien de Sécurité. *Revue Semestrielle d'Information du G5 Sahel*. Retrieved from : http://www.g5sahel.org/images/Docs/G5_SAHEL_revue_N4.pdf. Last accessed: 28 September 2018.

Haas, P. (1992). Introduction: Epistemic Communities and International Policy Coordination. *International Organization, 46*(1), 1–35. Retrieved from: http://www.jstor.org/stable/2706951. Last accesed: 09 February 2019.

Habermas, J. (1991). *The Structural Transformation of the Public Sphere: An Inquiry into a Category of Bourgeois Society*, (T. Burger, F. Lawrence, Trans.). Massachusetts: MIT Press.

Hafez, K. (1997). Der Islam und der Westen-Kampf der Zivilisationen? Einleitung. In K. Hafez (Ed.) *Der Islam und der Westen: Anstiftung zum Dialog* (pp. 15–27). Hamburg: Fischer.

Hailbronner, K. (1990). The Right to Asylum and the Future of Asylum Procedures in the European Community. *International Journal of Refugee Law* 2(3), 341–60.

Hailbronner, K. (1993). The Concept of "Safe Country" and Expeditious Asylum Procedures: A Western European Perspective. *International Journal of Refugee Law* 5(1), 31–65.

Halfmann, J. (2005). World Society and Migrations: Challenges to Theoretical Concepts of Political Sociology. In M. Bommes and E. Morawska (Eds). *International*

Migration Research. Constructions, Omissions and the Promises of Interdisciplinarity (pp. 129–51), Aldershot: Ashgate.

Hall, I. (2018). Clashing Civilizations: A Toynbeean Response to Huntington. In Orsi, D. (Ed.). *The 'Clash of Civilizations' 25 Years On: A Multidisciplinary Appraisal* (pp. 15–25). Bristol: E-international Relation Publishing. Retrieved from: https://www.e-ir.info/publication/the-clash-of-civilizations-25-years-on-a-multidisciplinary-appraisal/. Last accessed: 01 December 2018.

Hall, M. & Jackson, P.T. (Eds.) (2007). *Civilizational Identity: the Production and Reproduction of 'Civilizations' in International Relations*. New York, N.Y.: Palgrave Macmillan.

Halliday, F. (2001). The Romance of Non-state Actors. In J. Daphné, & W. Wallace (Eds.). *Non-state Actors in World Politics* (pp. 21–37). New York: Palgrave.

Halliday, F. (2005). *The Middle East in International Relations: Power, Politics and Ideology*. Cambridge: Cambridge University Press.

Hardt, M. & Negri, A. (2000). *Empire. Cambridge*. Massachusetts: Harvard University Press.

Hart, I. (2015). History Painting and Its Critics, ca. 1870–1910. *Nineteenth-Century Art Worldwide 14*(2). Retrieved from: http://www.19thc-artworldwide.org/summer15/hart-on-history-painting-and-its-critics-ca-1870-1910. Last accessed: 18 February 2019.

Hasenclever, A. (2001). *Die Macht der Moral in der internationalen Politik: Militärische Interventionen westlicher Staaten in Somalia, Ruanda und Bosnien-Herzegowina*. (Studien der Hessischen Stiftung Friedens- und Konfliktforschung). Frankfurt am Main: Campus Verlag.

Haynes, J. (2018). Huntington's 'Clash of Civilizations' Today: Responses and Developments. In Orsi, D. (Ed.). *The 'Clash of Civilizations' 25 Years On: A Multidisciplinary Appraisal* (pp. 52–62). Bristol: E-international Relation Publishing. Available online: https://www.e-ir.info/publication/the-clash-of-civilizations-25-years-on-a-multidisciplinary-appraisal/. Last accessed: 02 December 2018.

Herbert, U. (2001). *Geschichte der Ausländerpolitik in Deutschland: Saisonarbeiter, Zwangsarbeiter, Gastarbeiter, Flüchtlinge*. München: C.H. Beck.

Herzog, R. (1997). Unser Verhältnis zum Islam: Rede zur Verleihung des Friedenspreisees des Deutschen Buchhandels an Annemarie Schimmel am 15. Oktober 1995 in Frankfurt am Main (Auszüge) [Our relationship to Islam: Speech on the awarding of the Peace Prize of the German Book Trade to Annemarie Schimmel on October 15, 1995 in Frankfurt am Main (excerpts)]. In K. Hafez, (Ed.) *Der Islam und der Westen: Anstiftung zum Dialog* (pp. 223–228). Hamburg: Fischer.

Herzog, R. (2000). Das Gemeinsame Erbe westlicher und islamischer Kulturen (Ansprache vor dem Department of International Relations der Quaid-e-Azam-Universität Islamabad, 5. April 1995 [The Common Heritage of Western and Islamic Cultures (Address to the Department of International Relations of Quaid-e-Azam

University, Islamabad, April 5, 1995)]) (pp. 3–10). In R. Herzog, & T. Sommer, (Eds.) *Wider den Kampf der Kulturen: Eine Friedensstrategie für das 21. Jahrhundert*. Frankfurt am Main: S. Fischer Verlag.

Herzog, R. (2000a). Asien und der Westen (Auszüge aus einer Ansprache anläßlich eines Abendessens, gegeben zu Ehren des Präsidenten der Volksrepublik China, Jiang Zemin, 13. Juli 1995 [Asia and the West (excerpts from a speech given at a dinner given in honor of the President of the People's Republic of China, Jiang Zemin, July 13, 1995)]). (pp. 49–64). In R. Herzog, & T. Sommer, (Eds.). *Wider den Kampf der Kulturen: Eine Friedensstrategie für das 21. Jahrhundert*. Frankfurt am Main: S. Fischer Verlag.

Herzog, R. (2000b). Die Rechte des Menschen. (Artikel in der Wochenzeitung „Die Zeit", 6. September 1996 [Article first appeared in the weekly newspaper „Die Zeit", September 6, 1996]) (pp. 31–47). In R. Herzog, & T. Sommer, (Eds.) *Wider den Kampf der Kulturen: Eine Friedensstrategie für das 21. Jahrhundert*. Frankfurt am Main: S. Fischer Verlag.

Herzog, R. (2000c). Auszüge aus einer Rede anläßlich der Verleihung der Ehrendorktorwürde der Juristischen Fakultät der Waseda-Universität, Tokio, 7. April 1997 [Extracts from a speech at the ceremony of the Reception of the Honorary Degree of the Faculty of Law of Waseda University, Tokyo, April 7, 1997] (pp. 52–60). In R. Herzog, & T. Sommer, (Ed.) *Wider den Kampf der Kulturen: Eine Friedensstrategie für das 21. Jahrhundert*. Frankfurt am Main: S. Fischer Verlag.

Hess, S. et al (2018, August). Welche Auswirkungen haben „Anker-Zentren"? Eine Kurzstudie für den Mediendienst Integration. Retrieved from: https://mediendienst-integration.de/fileadmin/Dateien/Expertise_Anker-Zentren_August_2018.pdf. Last accessed: 29 September 2018.

Hirschman, A.O. (1970). *Exit, Voice and Loyalty. Responses to Decline in Firms, Organizations and States*. Cambridge: MA.

Hirschman, A.O. (1980). "Exit, Voice, and Loyalty": Further Reflections and a Survey of Recent Contributions. *The Milbank Memorial Fund Quarterly. Health and Society* 58(3), 430–453.

Hobsbawn, E. (1964). *The Age of Revolution, 1789–1848*. New York: Mentor.

Hochschild, A.R. (2016). *Strangers in Their Own Land: Anger and Mourning on the American Right*. New York, London: The New Press.

Hoffmann, F. (2008) In quite a state: trials and tribulations of an old concept in new times. In: R. Miller, & R. Bratspies, (eds.) *Progress in International Law. Developments in international law* (pp. 263–88). The Hague: Martinus Nijhoff Publishers.

Hogan-Brun, G., Mar-Molinero, C. & Stevenson, P. (2009). Testing regimes: Introducing cross-national perspectives on language, migration and citizenship. In G. Hogan-Brun, C. Mar-Molinero, P. Stevenson, (Eds). *Discourses on Language and Integration:*

Critical perspectives on language testing regimes in Europe (pp. 1–13). Amsterdam, Philadelphia: John Benjamins Publishing Company.

Hoinacki, L. (2002). Reading Ivan Illich. In L. Hoinacki & C. Mitcham, (Eds.). *The Challenges of Ivan Illich: A collective Reflection* (pp. 1–7). New York: State University of New York Press.

Hoinacki, L. & Mitcham, C. (Eds.) (2002). *The Challenges of Ivan Illich: A collective Reflection.* New York: State University of New York Press.

Holling, C. & Meffe, G.K. (1996). Command and Control and the Pathology of Natural Resource Management. *Conservation Biology* 10, 328–337.

hooks, bell (1993). Bell Hooks Speaking about Paulo Freire- The Man, His Work. In P. McLaren, P. Leonard, (Eds.). *Paulo Freire: A Critical Encounter* (pp. 146–154). London: Routledge.

Horner, K. (2009). Language, citizenship and Europeanization: Unpacking the discourse of integration. In G. Hogan-Brun, C. Mar-Molinero & P. Stevenson, (Eds). *Discourses on Language and Integration: Critical perspectives on language testing regimes in Europe* (pp. 109–128). Amsterdam, Philadelphia: John Benjamins Publishing Company.

Horsley, R., & Hanson, J.S. (1985). *Bandits, Prophets, and Messiahs: Popular Movements in the Time of Jesus.* Minneapolis, Chicago, New York: Winston Press.

Horsley, R. (1986). The Zealots. Their Origin, Relationships and Importance in the Jewish Revolt. *Novum Testamentum, 28*(2), 159–192.

Hume, D. (1986 [1739]) *A Treatise of Human Nature.* (L.A. Selby-Bigge, Ed.). Oxford: Clarendon Press. Retrieved from: http://oll.libertyfund.org/titles/hume-a-treatise-of-human-nature. Last accessed: 15 August 2018.

Hunter, D., Salzman, J., & Zaelke, D. (2002). *International Environmental Law and Policy.* New York: Foundation Press.

Huntington, S.P. (1993). The Clash of Civilizations? *Foreign Affairs* 72(3), 22–49.

Huntington, S.P. (1996). *The Clash of Civilizations and the Remaking of World Order.* London: Simon & Schuster.

Hurtz, S. (2015, 12. December). "Blanker Rassismus": Höcke und die Fortpflanzung der Afrikaner. Retrieved from: https://www.sueddeutsche.de/politik/afd-thueringen-blanker-rassismus-hoecke-und-die-fortpflanzung-der-afrikaner-1.2780159. Last accessed: 10 January 2019.

Hutter, B.M. (2006). The Role of Non-state Actors in Regulation. In Schuppert, G.F. (Ed.) *Global Governance and the Role of Non-State Actors* (pp. 63–79). Baden-Baden: Nomos.

Hutton, C. (1999). *Linguistics and the Third Reich.* London and New York: Routledge.

ICG [International Crisis Group] (2005, March 31). *Islamist Terrorism in the Sahel: Fact or Fiction? Africa Report N°92.* Retrieved from: https://d2071andvipowj.cloudfront

.net/92-islamist-terrorism-in-the-sahel-fact-or-fiction_0.pdf. Last accessed: 14 October 2018.

ICRC (2016). *Protracted Conflict and Humanitarian Action: some recent ICRC experiences. International Committee of the Red Cross, Geneva.* Retrieved from: https://www.icrc.org/sites/default/files/document/file_list/protracted_conflict_and_humanitarian_action_icrc_report_lr_29.08.16.pdf. Last accessed: 20 August 2018.

Illich, I. (1971). *Deschooling Society.* New York: Harper and Row.

Illich, I. (1973). *Tools for Conviviality.* New York: Harper and Row.

Illich, I. (1976). *After Deschooling, What?* London: Writers and Readers Pub. Cooperative.

Illich, I. (1976). *Medical Nemesis: The Expropriation of Health.* New York: Pantheon.

Illich, I. (1982). *Gender.* New York: Pantheon.

Illich, I. (1991). *In the Mirror of the Past: Lectures and Addresses 1978–1990.* New York: Marion Boyars.

Illich, I. (2002). Epilogue: The Cultivation of Conspiracy. In L. Hoinacki, C. Mitcham, (Eds.). *The Challenges of Ivan Illich: A collective Reflection* (pp. 233–242). New York: State University of New York Press.

Illich, I. (2008). Foreword. In M. Hern (Ed.) *Everywhere all the Time: A new Deschooling Reader* (pp. iii–v). Oakland: AK Press.

Initiative Kulturelle Integration (2017, May 16). Cohesion in diversity: Fifteen theses on cultural integration and cohesion. Available at: http://kulturelle-integration.de/wp-content/uploads/2017/11/Theses_english.pdf. Last accessed: 28 December 2018.

ISB. (2014). Berufsschulpflichtige Asylbewerber und Flüchtlingen: Beschulung von berufsschulphlichtigen Asylbewerbern und Flüchtlingen an bayerischen Berufsschulen. Staatsinstitut für Schulqualität und Bildungsforschung. Retrieved from: www.km.bayern.de/download/10538_handreichung_baf_beschulung.pdf. Last accessed: 10 February 2019.

Joffe, J. (2006). *The perils of soft power.* Retrieved from: http://www.nytimes.com/2006/05/14/magazine/14wwln_lede.html. Last accessed: 16 October 2018.

Josselin, D. & Wallace, W. (Eds) (2001). *Non-state Actors in World Politics.* New York: Palgrave.

Kampf, L., & Steinke, R. (2018, August 30). Wie deutsche Beamte Hoffnung auf Gerechtigkeit in Syrien wecken. Retrieved from: https://www.sueddeutsche.de/politik/kriegsverbrechen-wie-deutsche-beamte-hoffnung-auf-gerechtigkeit-in-syrien-wecken-1.4105397. Last accessed: 10 October 2018.

Kastrup, W. (2016) Zur Einführung. In Kastrup, W. & H. Kellershohn,(Eds.) *Kulturkampf von rechts: AFD, Pegida und die Neue Rechte* (pp. 10–13). Münster: UNRAST Verlag.

Kaya, A. (2009). *Islam, Migration and Integration: the Age of Securitization.* New York: Palgrave Macmillan.

Kellershohn, H. (2016). Nationaler Wettbewerbsstaat auf völkischer Basis: Das ideologische Grundgerüst des AFD-Grundsatzprogramms. In Kastrup, W. & H. Kellershohn (Eds.) *Kulturkampf von rechts: AFD, Pegida und die Neue Rechte* (pp. 14–28). Münster: UNRAST Verlag.

Kemper, A. (2016). Geschlechter- und familienpolitische Positionen der AfD. In Kastrup, W. & H. Kellershohn (Eds.) *Kulturkampf von rechts: AFD, Pegida und die Neue Rechte* (pp. 146–161). Münster: UNRAST Verlag.

Kennedy-Boudali, L. (2009). *Examining U.S. Counterterrorism Priorities and Strategy across Africa's Sahel Region*. Santa Monica. CA: RAND Corporation. Retrieved from: http://www.rand.org/pubs/testimonies/CT335. Last accessed: 10 February 2019.

Keucheyan, R. (2014). *The Left Hemisphere: Mapping Critical Theory Today* (G. Eliott, Trans.). London: Verso.

Kim, J. (1995). *Supervenience and Mind: Selected Philosophical Essays*. Cambridge: Cambridge University Press.

Kim, J. (2000, October). Interview Transcript (R. Howell, Interviewer). *Ephilosopher*. Retrieved from https://web.archive.org/web/20071017192900/http://www.ephilosopher.com/page.php?15. Last accessed: 15 August 2018.

Kim, S.H. (2004). *Max Weber's Politics of Civil Society*. Cambridge: Cambridge University Press.

Kimminich, O. (1972). Die Entwicklung des Asylrechts in der Bundesrepublik Deutschland. *JuristenZeitung* 27(9), 257–263. Retrieved from http://www.jstor.org/stable/20812631. Last accessed: 08. 10. 2018.

Koeppel, M. (1997). Die Öffnung der Berliner Mauer. Rede von Matthias Koeppel anlässlich der Übergabe des Triptychons an das Berliner Abgeordnetenhaus am 16. Januar 1997 (Auszüge) [The opening of the Berlin Wall. Speech by Matthias Koeppel on the occasion of the handover of the triptych to the Berlin House of Representatives on 16 January 1997 (excerpts).]. In U. Christoffel, (Ed.). *Matthias Koeppel: Neue Bilder von 1987 bis 1997* (pp. 70, 74, 75). Berlin: Kunstamt Wilmersdorf.

Kolb, H. (2010, March 25). Eckfeiler der Green Card-Verordnung. Retrieved from http://www.bpb.de/gesellschaft/migration/kurzdossiers/57444/green-card-verordnung. Last accessed: 26 September 2018.

Konno, H. (2004). *Max Weber und die polnische Frage (1892–1920). Eine Betrachtung zum liberalen Nationalismus im wilhelminischen Deutschland*. Baden-Baden: Nomos.

Koskenniemi, M. (2004). *The Gentle Civilizer of Nations: The Rise and Fall of International Law 1870–1960*. Cambridge: Cambridge University Press.

Kposowa, A.J., McElvain, J.P., & Breault, K.D. (2008). Immigration and suicide: The role of marital status, duration of residence, and social integration. *Archives of Suicide Research* 12, 82–92.

Krashen, S.D. 1982. *Principles and Practice in Second Language Acquisition*. Oxford: Pergamon.

Kross, K. (1991). Translator's Introduction. In J. Rancière. *The Ignorant Schoolmaster: Five Lessons in Intellectual Emancipation* (Kross, K., Trans.) (pp. vii–xxiii). Standford: Standford University Press.

Kuhn, T.S. (1962). *The Structure of Scientific Revolutions*. Chicago: University of Chicago Press.

Lakatos, I. (1968). Criticism and the Methodology of Scientific Research Programmes. *Proceedings of the Aristotelian Society* **69**(1), 149–186.

Lammert, N. (2018). Nachdenken über Leitkultur: Welche Verbindlichkeiten brauchen wir? In O. Zimmermann and T. Geißler (Eds.), *Wertedebatte: Von Leitkultur bis kulturelle Integration* (pp. 37–38). Berlin: Deutscher Kulturrat. (Reprinted from "Nachdenken über Leitkultur: Welche Verbindlichkeiten brauchen wir" *Aus Politik & Kultur 2*).

Lang, B. (2013) (Ed.). Traumapädagogische Standards in der stationären Kinder- und Jugendhilfe: *Eine Praxis- und Orientierungshilfe der BAG Traumapädagogik*. Weinheim, Basel: Beltz Juventa Verlag.

Lau, M. (2016, July 23). Dieser Mann hat für Angela Merkel den Flüchtlingsdeal erfunden. Nun will er die Katastrophe verhindern. *DIE ZEIT Nr. 27/2016*. Retrieved from: https://www.zeit.de/2016/27/gerald-knaus-fluechtlinge-eu-tuerkei-abkommen. Last accessed: 28 September 2018.

Lebow, R.N. (2003). *The Tragic Vision of Politics: Ethics, Interests, and Order*. Cambridge: Cambridge University Press.

Lennon, A.T.J. (2003). *The Battle for Hearts and Minds: Using Soft Power to Undermine Terrorist Networks*. Cambridge, Massachusetts: MIT Press.

Lewis, B. (2002). *What Went Wrong? The Clash between Islam and Modernity in the Middle East*. London: Weidenfeld & Nicholson.

Li, X.E. (2018, August 20) The Rise and Fall of Soft Power: Joseph Nye's concept lost relevance, but China could bring it back. Retrieved from: https://foreignpolicy.com/2018/08/20/the-rise-and-fall-of-soft-power/. Last accessed: 16 October 2018.

Lightbown, P. & Spada, N. (2006). *How languages are learned*. Oxford: Oxford University Press.

Lindblom, C.E. (1959). The Science of Muddling-Through. *Public Administration Review* 19(2) 79–88.

Lindner, J. (2015, July 29). Seit 15 Jahren wirbt Deutschland um Fachkräfte. In *Mediendienst Integration*. Retrieved from: https://mediendienst-integration.de/artikel/von-der-green-card-zur-blue-card-arbeitsmarkt-migration-von-fachkraeften.html. Last accessed: 24 September 2018.

López, J.S. (2003). *Télémaque* au coeur de la « méthode » Jacotot. In *Documents pour l'histoire du français langue étrangère ou seconde*. Retrieved from: http://dhfles.revues.org/1608. Last accessed : 10 February 2019.

Löwy, M. (1996). *The War of the Gods: Religion and Politics in Latin America*. London and New York: Verso.

Lupton, D. (2006). Risk and Governmentality. In J.F. Cosgrave (Ed.), *The Sociology of Risk and Gambling Reader* (pp. 85–100). London and New York: Routledge.

Luxemburg, R. (1964). *The accumulation of capital* (A. Schwarzschild, Trans.). London: Monthly Review Press.

Maas, U. & Mehlem, U. (2003). Qualitätsanforderungen für die Sprachförderung im Rahmen der Integration von Zuwanderern. In *IMIS-BEITRÄGE 21*. Retrieved from: https://www.imis.uni-osnabrueck.de/fileadmin/4_Publikationen/PDFs/imis21.pdf. Last accessed: 07 November 2018.

MacKinnon, M. (2016, December 2). The Graffiti Kids who sparked the Syrian War. Retrieved from https://www.theglobeandmail.com/news/world/the-graffiti-kids-who-sparked-the-syrian-war/article33123646/. Last accessed: 19 August 2018.

Mahnken, T.G. (2010). Bridging the Gap Between the Worlds of Ideas and Actions. *Orbis* 54(1), 4–13.

Mahoney, K. (2018, September 14). Bible Stories about Sibling Rivalry. Retrieved from: https://www.thoughtco.com/bible-stories-about-sibling-rivalry-712735. Last accessed: 07 January 2019.

Malcolm, W.N. (2008). *Terrorist Recognition Handbook: A Practitioner's Manual for Predicting and Identifying Terrorist Activities* (2nd edition). Boca Raton: CRC Press.

Martinovic, B., van Tubergen, F., & Maas, I. (2009). Changes in immigrants' social integration during the stay in the host country: The case of non-Western immigrants in the Netherlands. *Social Science Research* 38, 870–882.

Marx, K. ([1867] 2001). *Das Kapital: Kritik der politischen Ökonomie. Erstes Buch, der Produktionsprozeß des Kapitals*. In K. Marx and F. Engels: *Werke* (vol. 23, 20th edition). Berlin: Karl Dietz Verlag.

Matschke, C., & Sassenberg, K. (2010). The supporting and impeding effects of group-related approach and avoidance strategies on newcomers' psychological adaptation. *International Journal of Intercultural Relations* 34, 465–474.

Mazower, M. (2004). The Strange Triumph of Human Rights, 1933–1950. *The Historical Journal* 47(2), 379–398.

M'Bokolo, E. & Sabakinu, K. (Eds) (2014). *Simon Kimbangu, le prophète de la libération de l'homme noir*. Paris : L'Harmattan.

Mbembe, A. (1992). Provisional Notes on the Postcolony. *Africa* 62(1), 3–19.

Mbembe, A. (2001) *On the Postcolony* (A.M. Berrett, et. al., Trans.) California: California University Press.

McNamara, T. (2005). 21st Century Shibboleth: Language Tests, Identity and Intergroup Conflict. *Language Policy* 4(4), 351–370.

McNamara, T. (2009). Language tests and social policy: A commentary. In G. Hogan-Brun, C. Mar-Molinero, & P. Stevenson (Eds). *Discourses on Language and*

Integration: Critical perspectives on language testing regimes in Europe (pp. 153–163). Amsterdam, Philadelphia: John Benjamins Publishing Company.

Mearsheimer, J. (2001). *The Tragedy of Great Power Politics*. New York: Norton.

Mearsheimer, J. (2013). Structural Realism. In T. Dunne, M. Kurki, & S. Smith (Eds.). *International Relations Theories: Discipline and Diversity* (3rd edition, pp. 77–93). Oxford: Oxford University Press.

Mégret, F., & Hoffmann, F. (2003). The UN as a Human Rights Violator? Some Reflections on the United Nations Changing Human Rights Responsibilities. *Human Rights Quarterly* 25(2), 314–342. Retrieved from http://www.jstor.org/stable/20069667. Last accessed: 10 February 2019.

Merz, F. (2004). *Nur wer sich ändert, wird bestehen: Vom Ende der Wohlstandsillusion - Kursbestimmung für unsere Zukunft*. Freiburg, Basel, Wien: Herder.

Merz, F. (2000, October 25). Einwanderung und Identität. Retrieved from: https://www.welt.de/print-welt/article540438/Einwanderung-und-Identitaet.html. Last accessed: 27 December 2018.

Mishra, V. & Hodge, B. (1991): What is Post (-) colonialism? *Textual Practice* 5(3), 399–414.

Mitcham, C. (2002). The Challenges of This Collection. In L. Hoinacki, & C. Mitcham (Eds.). *The Challenges of Ivan Illich: A collective Reflection* (pp. 9–32). New York: State University of New York Press.

Mohr, R. (2000, 06 December). Operation Sauerbraten. *Der Spiegel 45*. Retrieved from: http://www.spiegel.de/spiegel/print/d-17757661.html. Last Accessed: 27 December 2018.

Moïsi, D. (2007). The Clash of Emotions. *Foreign Affairs*.

Moïsi, D. (2010). *The Geopolitics of Emotion: How Cultures of Fear, Humiliation, and Hope are Reshaping the World*. New York: Anchor Books.

Mommsen, W.J. (1984). *Max Weber and German politics, 1890–1920*. Chicago, IL: University of Chicago Press.

Montague, R. (1969). On the Nature of Certain Philosophical Entities. *The Monist* 53, 159–194.

Morgenthau, H. (1967). *Politics among Nations: The Struggle for Power and Peace* (4th ed.). New York: Knopf.

Mountz, A. (2003). Human smuggling, the transnational imaginary, and everyday geographies of the nation-state. *Antipode* 35(3), 622–644.

Münch, U. (1994) Vorgeschichte, Probleme und Auswirkungen der Asylrechtsänderung 1993. In C. Tessmer (Ed.), *Deutschland und das Weltflüchtlingsproblem* (pp. 103–36). Opladen: Leske & Budrich.

Münz, R., Seifert, W., & Ulrich, R. (1997). *Zuwanderung nach Deutschland: Strukturen, Wirkungen, Perspektiven*. Frankfurt am Main: Campus Verlag.

Münz, R., & Ulrich, R. (2000). Migration und zukünftige Bevölkerungsentwicklung in Deutschland. In K.J. Bade & R. Münz (Eds.) *Migrationsreport 2000: Fakten, Analysen, Perspektiven* (pp. 23–57). Bonn: Bundeszentrale für politische Bildung.

Mutua, M. (2001) Savages, Victims, and Saviors: The Metaphor of Human Rights. *Harvard International Law Journal* (42)1, 201–245. Retrieved from: https://ssrn.com/abstract=1525547. Last accessed: 15 October 2018.

Nandy, A. (1986) *The Intimate Enemy: Loss and Recovery of Self under Colonialism.* Dehli: OUP.

Nentwig, F. (2014). „Himmel, Berlin!". In Nentwig, F.; Bartmann, D. (Eds.). *Matthias Koeppel: Himmel, Berlin!* (p. 7). Berlin: nicolai.

Nentwig, F. & Bartmann, D. (Eds.) (2014). *Matthias Koeppel: Himmel, Berlin!.* Berlin: nicolai.

Norris, C. (2009). *Badiou's Being and Event: A Reader's Guide.* London: Continuum.

Nossal, K.R. (2018). The Kin-Country Thesis Revisited. In Orsi, D. (Ed.). *The 'Clash of Civilizations' 25 Years On: A Multidisciplinary Appraisal* (pp. 63–75). Bristol: E-international Relation Publishing. Retrieved from: https://www.e-ir.info/publication/the-clash-of-civilizations-25-years-on-a-multidisciplinary-appraisal/. Last accessed: 02 December 2018.

Nye, J. (2004). *Soft Power: The Means to Success in World Politics.* New York: Public Affairs, a member of the Perseus Books Group.

Nye, J.S. (2009, April 13). Scholars on the Sidelines. The Washington Post. Retrieved from http://www.washingtonpost.com/wp-dyn/content/article/2009/04/12/AR2009041202260.html??noredirect=on. Last accessed: 11 September 2018.

O'Connor, E. (2003). Preface for a Post-Postcolonial Criticism. *Victorian Studies* 45(2), 217–246.

Ognjenović, V. (2005). *Es Soll Dir gut gehen! 50 Workshops für die sozialtherapeutische Arbeit mit traumatisierten Kindern und Erwachsenen.* Weinheim und München: Juventa Verlag.

Orsi, D. (2018). The 'Clash of Civilizations' and Realism in International Political Thought. In Orsi, D. (Ed.). *The 'Clash of Civilizations' 25 Years On: A Multidisciplinary Appraisal* (pp. 5–14). Bristol: E-international Relation Publishing. Retrieved from: https://www.e-ir.info/publication/the-clash-of-civilizations-25-years-on-a-multidisciplinary-appraisal/. Last accessed: 01 December 2018.

Orsi, D. (Ed.) (2018a). *The 'Clash of Civilizations' 25 Years On: A Multidisciplinary Appraisal.* Bristol: E-international Relation Publishing. Retrieved from: https://www.e-ir.info/publication/the-clash-of-civilizations-25-years-on-a-multidisciplinary-appraisal/. Last accessed: 01 December 2018.

Ortner, S.B. (1995). Resistance and the Problem of Ethnographic refusal. *Comparative studies in society and history* 37(1), 173–193.

Pallasch, E., & Kölln, D. (2014) *Pädagogisches Gesprächstraining: Lern- und Trainingsprogramm zur Vermittlung pädagogisch-therapeutischer Gesprächs- und Beratungskompetenz.* Weinheim, Basel: Beltz Juventa.

Pasolini, P.P. (2014). *St. Paul: A Screenplay* (E.A. Castelli, Trans.). London: Verso.

Patton, P. (2009.) History, the Event and the Untimely. In H. Berressem & L. Haferkamp (Eds.) *Deleuzian Events: Writing History*, (Vol. 3. Paper presented at n-1| work-science-medium, Cologne, pp. 170–187). Berlin: Lit-Verlag.

Paul, J. (2016). Der Niedergang- der Umsturz- das Nichts. Rassistische Demagogie und suizidale Perspektive in Björn Höckes Schnellrodaer Rede. In H. Kellershohn, Kastrup, W. (Eds.) *Kulturkampf von rechts: AFD, Pegida und die Neue Rechte* (pp. 122–146). Münster: UNRAST Verlag.

Paulsen, P. (2018). *Deutschland außer Rand und Band: Zwischen Werteverfall, Political (In)Correctness und illegaler Migration.* Mühlenbecker Land: Macht-steuert-Wissen Verlag.

Pautz, H. (2005). "The politics of identity in Germany: the Leitkultur debate". *Race & Class* 46(4), 39–52. Retrieved from: http://polisci2.ucsd.edu/rabarrett/ps108/Pautz%20%28Germany%20Leitkultur%29.pdf. Last accessed: 27 December 2018.

Pezard, S. & Shurkin, M. (2015). *Achieving Peace in Northern Mali: Past Agreements, Local Conflicts, and the Prospects for a Durable Settlement.* Santa Monica, CA: RAND Corporation. Retrieved from: http://www.rand.org/pubs/research_reports/RR892.

Pianesi, F. & Varzi, A.C. (2000). Events and Event Talk: An Introduction. In J. Higgingotham, F. Pianesi, & A.C. Varzi (Eds.) *Speaking of Events*, (pp. 3–47). New York, Oxford: Oxford University Press.

Piore, M.J. (1979). *Birds of passage: Migrant labor and industrial societies.* Cambridge, UK: Cambridge University Press.

Politico (2017, June 16). Why Greece is Germany de facto 'Colony.' Retrieved from: https://www.politico.eu/article/why-greece-is-germanys-de-facto-colony/. Last accessed: 06 October 2018.

Price, M. (2009). *Rethinking Asylum: History, Purpose, and Limits.* Cambridge: Cambridge University Press.

Quine, W.V.O. (1960). *Word and Object.* Massachusetts: MIT Press.

Rancière, J. (1991). *The Ignorant Schoolmaster: Five Lessons in Intellectual Emancipation* (K. Kross, Trans.). Standford : Standford University Press.

Rancière, J. (2011). *Staging the People: The Proletarian and His Double* (D. Fernbach, Trans.). London: Verso.

Rancière, J. (2012). *Staging the People: The Intelelctual and His People* (D. Fernbach, Trans.). London: Verso.

Rancière, J. (2003, 24 January). L'actualité Du "Maître Ignorant": Entretien avec Jacques Rancière. Interview with Benvenuto, Andréa; Cornu, L.; Vermeren. *Le Télémaque* 27(1), 21–36. Retrieved from: https://www.cairn.info/revue-le-telemaque-2005-1-page-81.htm. Last accessed: 09 December 2018.

Rancière, J. (2016, [1987]). *Le Maître Ignorant: Cinq Leçons sue l'Émancipation intellectuelle*. Paris : Fayard.

Rehman, J. (2005). *Islamic State Practices, International Law and the Threat from Terrorism. A Critique of the 'Clash of Civilisations' in the New World Order*. Oxford, Portland: Hart Publishing.

Ringmar, E. (2018). Samuel Huntington and the American Way of War. In Orsi, D. (Ed.). *The 'Clash of Civilizations' 25 Years On: A Multidisciplinary Appraisal*. (pp. 26–36). Bristol: E-international Relation Publishing. Retrieved from: https://www.e-ir.info/publication/the-clash-of-civilizations-25-years-on-a-multidisciplinary-appraisal/. Last accessed: 01 December 2018.

Robinson, A. (2014, December 15). An A to Z of Theory | Alain Badiou: The Event. Retrieved from: https://ceasefiremagazine.co.uk/alain-badiou-event/. Last accessed: 22 August 2018.

Rosa, H. (2013). *Beschleunigung und Entfremdung - Entwurf einer kritischen Theorie spätmoderner Zeitlichkeit*. Suhrkamp, Frankfurt am Main.

Roth, C. (2018). Deutsche Begriffskrankheit? In O. Zimmermann and T. Geißler (Eds.), *Wertedebatte: Von Leitkultur bis kulturelle Integration* (pp. 58–60). Berlin: Deutscher Kulturrat. (Reprinted from: *Aus Politik &Kultur 2*).

Rubin, M., Watt, S.E., & Ramelli, M. (2012). Immigrants' social integration as a function of approach-avoidance orientation and problem-solving style. *International Journal of Intercultural Relations* 36, 498–505.

Russett, B., Oneal, J., & Cox, M. (2000). Clash of Civilizations, or Realism and Liberalism Déjà Vu? Some Evidence. *Journal of Peace Research, 37*(5), 583–608. Retrieved from http://www.jstor.org/stable/425280. Last accessed: 10 February 2019.

Said, E. (1978). *Orientalism*. New York: Pantheon Books.

Said, E. (2000). *Reflections on Exile and Other Essays*, Cambridge, MA: Harvard University Press.

Samers, M. (1998). "Structured coherence": Immigration, racism and production in the Paris car industry. *European Planning Studies* 6(1), 49–72.

Samers, M. (2001). "Here to work": Undocumented immigration in the United States and Europe. *SAIS Review* 21(1), 131–145.

Samers, M. (2002). Immigration and the global city hypothesis: Towards an alternative research agenda. *International Journal of Urban and Regional Research* 26(2), 389–402.

Samers, M. (2003). Invisible capitalism: Political economy and the regulation of undocumented immigration in France. *Economy and Society* 32(4), 555–583.

Schäfer, C. (2018, April 29) Jeder Zweiter scheitert am Deutschtest. Retrieved from: http://www.faz.net/aktuell/wirtschaft/mehr-wirtschaft/fluechtlinge-jeder-zweite-scheitert-am-deutschtest-15565140.html. Last accessed: 05 November 2018.

Schugurensky, D. (1998). The legacy of Paulo Freire: A critical review of his contributions. *Convergence* 31(1–2), 17–28.

Schuster, L. (2005). *The Use and Abuse of Political Asylum in Britain and Germany.* Portland: Frank Cass Publishers.

Scott, D. (1999). *Refashioning Futures. Criticism after Postcoloniality.* New Jersey: Princeton University Press.

SCPR [Syrian Center for Policy Research] (2016). Forced Dispersion, Syrian Human Status: The Demographic Report 2016. Retrieved from: http://scpr-syria.org/publications/forced-dispersion-syrian-human-status-the-demographic-report-2016/. Last Accessed: 19 August 2018.

Seehofer, H. (2018, June 22). *Masterplan Migration: Maßnahmen zur Ordnung, Steuerung und Begrenzung der Zuwanderung* [Masterplan Migration: Measures for the Organization, Control and Limitation of Immigration]. *Retrieved from: https://www.handelsblatt.com/downloads/22758182/4/masterplan-migration.pdf.* Last accessed: 27 September 2018.

Seliger, M. (2018, March 7). Mission Wüste: Darum kommt der Bundeswehr-Einsatz in Mali nicht voran. Retrieved from http://www.faz.net/aktuell/politik/ausland/bundeswehr-in-mali-mission-steht-vor-grossen-problemen-15481916.html?printPagedArticle=true#pageIndex_0. Last accessed: 14 October 2018.

Shaull, R. (1996). Foreword. In P. Freire, *Pedagogy of the Oppressed* (M.B. Ramos, Trans., pp. 11–16). London: Penguin Books.

Shoemaker, S. (1980). Causality and properties. In P. van Inwagen (Ed.), Time and Cause. *Essays presented to Richard Taylor* (pp. 109–35). Dordrecht: D Reidel Publishing Company.

Shohamy, E. (2001). *The Power of Tests. A Critical Perspective on the Uses of Language Tests.* London: Longman.

Shohamy, E. (2009). Language tests for immigrants: Why language? Why tests? Why citizenship? In G. Hogan-Brun, C. Mar-Molinero, P. Stevenson (Eds.). *Discourses on Language and Integration: Critical perspectives on language testing regimes in Europe* (pp. 45–59). Amsterdam, Philadelphia: John Benjamins Publishing Company.

Shor, I. (1993) Education is Politics: Paulo Freire's Critical Pedagogy. In McLaren, P. & Leonard, P. (Eds.) *Paulo Freire: A Critical Encounter* (pp. 25–35). London: Routledge.

Sieferle, R.P. (2017). *Das Migrationsproblem: Über die Unvereinbarkeit von Sozialstaat und Masseneinwanderung.* Waltrop: Manuscriptum.

Sieferle, R.P. (2017a). *Finis Germania.* Schnellroda: Verlag Antaios.

Singh, A. (2005). Four Challenges to Postcolonial Theory. Retrieved from : http://www.thevalve.org/go/valve/article/four_challenges_to_postcolonial_theory/. Last accessed 17 January 2019.

Slater, D. (2004). *Geopolitics and the Post-colonial: Rethinking North-South Relations.* Oxford: Blackwell Publishing.

Spiegel (2001, June 29). Süssmuth-Kommission: Pläne für 50.000 Einwanderer pro Jahr. Retrieved from: http://www.spiegel.de/politik/deutschland/suessmuth-kommission-plaene-fuer-50-000-einwanderer-pro-jahr-a-142315.html. Last accessed: 23 September 2018.

Spivak, G.C. (1994): Can the Subaltern Speak? In: P. Williams & L. Chrisman (Eds.) *Colonial Discourse and Post-Colonial Theory: A Reader* (pp. 66–111). New York: Harvester/Wheatsheaf.

Spivak, G.C. (1999): *A Critique of Postcolonial Reason: Towards a History of the Vanishing Present*. Calcutta, New Delhi: Seagull.

Spivak, G.C. (2014) Postcolonial theory and the specter of capital. *Cambridge Review of International Affairs* 27(1), pp. 184–198.

Steinbach, U. (1997). Nachwort. In K. Hafez (Ed.) *Der Islam und der Westen: Anstiftung zum Dialog* (pp. 214–219). Hamburg: Fischer.

Steinbach, U. (2003). German Foreign Policy and the Middle East: In Quest of a Concept. In H. Goren (Ed.): *Germany and the Middle East. Past, Present and Future* (pp. 85–113). Jerusalem: Magnes Press.

Steinbach, U. (2004). Die islamische Welt und der internationale Terrorismus. In: H. Vorländer (Ed.). *Gewalt und die Suche nach weltpolitischer Ordnung* (pp. 42–59). Nomos: Baden-Baden.

Steinbach, U. & Ende, W. (Eds.) (2005). *Der Islam in der Gegenwart* (5th Ed.). München: C.H. Beck.

Steinert, J.-D. (1995). *Migration und Politik. Westdeutschland – Europa – Übersee 1945–1961*. Osnabrück: sec Kommunikation und Gestaltung.

Steyerl, H. (2002). *Can the Subaltern speak German? Postcolonial critique in German context*. Retrieved from: http://translate.eipcp.net/strands/03/steyerl-strands01en. Last accessed: 10 February 2019.

Steyerl, H. & Gutiérrez Rodríguez, E. (Eds.) (2003). *Spricht die Subalterne Deutsch? Migration und postkoloniale Kritik*. Münster: Unrast.

Stiles, K.W. (2000). Grassroots empowerment. States, non-state actors and global policy formulation. In R.A. Higgot, G.R.D. Underhill, & A. Bieler (Eds.). *Non-State Actors and Authority in the Global System* (pp. 32–47). London and New York: Routledge.

Stölzl, C. (2014). Koeppel –ABC: Eine Huldigung. In F. Nentwig, D. Bartmann (Eds.). *Matthias Koeppel: Himmel, Berlin!* (pp. 11–18). Berlin: nicolai.

Straka, B. (2014). Die Himmel über Berlin: Horizonte der Begegnung von Romantik und Realismus im Werk von Matthias Koeppel. In F. Nentwig, D. Bartmann (Eds.). *Matthias Koeppel: Himmel, Berlin!* (pp. 19–39). Berlin: nicolai.

Sturrock, J. (1979) *Structuralism and since: from Lévi Strauss to Derrida*. Oxford: Oxford University Press.

Süssmuth, R. (2001). Zuwanderung gestalten- Integration fördern. Bericht der Unabhängigen Kommission. Zusammenfassung. Available online: http://www.fluechtlingsrat.org/download/berkommzusfas.pdf. Last accessed: 24 September 2018.

Süssmuth, R. (2006). *Migration und Integration: Testfall für unsere Gesellschaft.* München: Deutscher Taschenbuch Verlag.

Süssmuth, R. (2015). *Das Gift des Politischen: Gedanken und Erinnerungen.* München: Deutscher Taschenbuchverlag.

Süssmuth, R. (2015, September 11). 15 Jahre Zuwanderungskommission: Wir brauchen ein Einwanderungsgesetz. Available on: https://mediendienst-integration.de/artikel/15-jahre-zuwanderungskommission-rita-suessmuth-einwanderungsgesetz.html. Last accessed: 24 September 2018.

Süssmuth, R. (2016, February 5) "Es trifft nicht zu, dass Angela Merkel die Tür für alle öffnet" (L. Langenau, Interviewer) [Sueddeutsche Zeitung]. Retrieved from: https://www.sueddeutsche.de/politik/migration-es-trifft-nicht-zu-dass-angela-merkel-die-tuer-fuer-alle-oeffnet-1.2850761. Last accessed: 24 September 2018.

Tardy, T. (2015, February 06). Mali : Restaurer la paix dans un pays en guerre. Retrieved from: http://www.iss.europa.eu/uploads/media/Alert_8_Mali.pdf. Last accessed: 10 February 2019.

Tardy, T. (2013, December 06) Mali, Centrafrique: les contours d'une réponse multiforme. *European Union Institute of Security Studies* 47(6). Retrieved from http://www.iss.europa.eu/publications/detail/article/mali-centrafrique-les-contours-dune-reponse-multiforme/. Last accessed: 10 February 2019.

The Economist (2013, June 15). Europe's reluctant hegemon. Special Report. Retrieved from: https://www.economist.com/special-report/2013/06/15/europes-reluctant-hegemon. Last accessed: 06 October 2018.

The Economist (2018, April 14). The Somewhat Reluctant Hegemon: Germany has been Slow to reassess its place in the world. Retrieved from: https://www.economist.com/special-report/2018/04/14/germany-has-been-slow-to-reassess-its-place-in-the-world. Last accessed: 06 October 2018.

The Economist (2007, June 14). Africa and the "war on terror": Policing the undergoverned spaces. Retrieved from https://www.economist.com/middle-east-and-africa/2007/06/14/policing-the-undergoverned-spaces. Last accessed: 14 October 2018.

The Soft Power 30 (2018). A Global Ranking of Soft Power. Retrieved from: https://softpower30.com/wp-content/uploads/2018/07/The-Soft-Power-30-Report-2018.pdf. Last accessed: 07 October 2018.

Therborn, G. (2009). *From Marxism to Post-Marxism?* London and New York: Verso.

Thompson, E.P. (1978). *The Poverty of Theory and Other Essays.* New York: Monthly Review Press.

Thym, D. (2017). Einwanderungsgesetzgebung: Chancen und Illusionen (Teil 1). *ZAR Zeitschrift für Ausländerrecht und Ausländerpolitik* 37(8), 297–344.

Thym, D. (2017). Einwanderungsgesetzgebung: Chancen und Illusionen (Teil 2). *ZAR Zeitschrift für Ausländerrecht und Ausländerpolitik* 37(9), 361–370.

Tibi, B. (1992). *Die fundamentalistische Herausforderung. Der Islam und die Weltpolitik.* München: C.H. Beck.

Tibi, B. (1998). *Europa ohne Identität? Die Krise der multikulturellen Gesellschaft.* München: Bertelsmann.

Tibi, B. (2000). Internationale Moralität und kulturübergreifender Brückenschlag. In R. Herzog & T. Sommer (Eds.) *Wider den Kampf der Kulturen: Eine Friedensstrategie für das 21. Jahrhundert* (pp. 139–168). Frankfurt am Main: S. Fischer Verlag.

Tibi, B. (2001). *Krieg der Zivilisationen: Politik und Religion zwischen Vernunft und Fundamentalismus* (2nd ed.). Munich: Wilhelm Heyne Verlag.

Tibi, B. (2001a). Vorwort zur neuen Auflage [Preface to the new Edition]. In ibid. *Krieg der Zivilisationen: Politik und Religion zwischen Vernunft und Fundamentalismus.* (2nd edition, pp. xi–xvi). Munich: Wilhelm Heyne Verlag.

Tibi, B. (2001b). Vorwort zur Taschenbuchausgabe [Preface to the paperback edition]. In ibid. *Krieg der Zivilisationen: Politik und Religion zwischen Vernunft und Fundamentalismus* (pp. xvii–xxix, 2nd Edition). Munich: Wilhelm Heyne Verlag.

Tibi, B. (2001c). Einleitung- Erneutes Nachdenken über den Zivilisationskonflikt. [Introduction- Rethinking the Civilization Conflict]. In ibid. *Krieg der Zivilisationen: Politik und Religion zwischen Vernunft und Fundamentalismu* pp. 1–64, 2nd Edition). Munich: Wilhelm Heyne Verlag.

Tibi, B. (September 2006). Über Bürgerrechte und Bürgerpflichten Die Leitkulturdebatte ist wieder entfacht. *In Politik und Kultur* (5), 1–2. Available at: https://www.kulturrat.de/wp-content/uploads/2016/06/PK-05_2006.pdf. Last accessed: 27 December 2018.

Tibi, B. (2016, July 7). Diese Männer denken: Deutsche Frauen sind Schlampen (*B. Neff*, Interviewer). *Basler Zeitung.* Retrieved from https://bazonline.ch/ausland/europa/Diese-Maenner-denken-Deutsche-Frauen-sind-Schlampen/story/22916308. Last accessed: 29 August 2018.

Tijmes, P. (2002). Ivan Illich's Break with the Past. In L. Hoinacki, & C. Mitcham (Eds.). *The Challenges of Ivan Illich: A collective Reflection* (pp. 205–217). New York: State University of New York Press.

Toby, A. & Popovic, T. (2007). The Trans-Saharan Counter-Terrorism Initiative: The US War on Terrorism in Northwest Africa. *FIIA Report 16.* Retrieved from: https://www.files.ethz.ch/isn/32043/16_TransSaharanCounterTerrorism.pdf. Last accessed: 13 October 2018.

Todorov, T. (2010). Introduction: Between Fear and Resentment. In *he Fear of Barbarians: Beyond the Clash of Civilizations* (pp. 1–12), (A. Brown, Trans.). Chicago: The University of Chicago Press.

Todorov, T. (2010). *The Fear of Barbarians: Beyond the Clash of Civilizations* (A. Brown, Trans). Chicago: The University of Chicago Press.

Tonnelé, A. (2009). Joseph Jacotot, un coach au XIXe siècle. *Annales des Mines - Gérer et comprendre* 98(4), 78–80. Retrieved from: https://www.cairn.info/revue-gerer-et-comprendre1-2009-4-page-78.htm?contenu=article. Last accessed: 08 December 2018.

Torres, R. (1998). The million Paulo Freires. *Convergence 31*, 107–117.

Treibel, A. (1999). Current debates on integration and de-integration in Germany. In R. Münz & W. Seifert (Eds.) *Demographie aktuell: Inclusion or exclusion of immigrant—Europe and the U.S. at the crossroads* (pp. 56–59). Berlin: Bevölkerungswissenschaft, Humboldt-Universität.

Tritin, J. (2016). Fluchtursachen bekämpfen oder Flüchtlingsabwehr? Warum der öffentliche Konsens scheinheilig ist. *Speech Delivered as part of the Lecture Series of the Refugee Law Clinic at the University of Würzburg*. Rtrieved from: https://www.trittin.de/2016/12/12/fluchtursachen-bekaempfen-oder-fluechtlingsabwehr-warum-der-oeffentliche-konsens-scheinheilig-ist/#1_dominante_diskurse. Last accessed: 23 September 2018.

Tuck, R. (1999). *Rights of War and Peace*. New York: Oxford University Press.

UNESCO (1982, August 6). Mexico City Declaration on Cultural Policies World Conference on Cultural Policies Mexico City, 26 July–6 August 1982. Available at: http://www.culturalrights.net/descargas/drets_culturals401.pdf. Last accessed: 28 December 2018.

Van Avermaet, P. (2009) Fortress Europe? Language policy regimes for immigration and citizenship. In G. Hogan-Brun, C. Mar-Molinero, P. Stevenson (Eds.). *Discourses on Language and Integration: Critical perspectives on language testing regimes in Europe* (pp. 15–43). Amsterdam, Philadelphia: John Benjamins Publishing Company.

Van Dijk, T.A. (1987). *Communicating Racism: Ethnic Prejudice in Thought and Talk*. Newbury Park, CA: Sage.

Van Munster, R. (2009). *Securitizing Immigration: The Politics of Risk in the EU*. Palgrave Studies in International Relations. New York: Palgrave MacMillan.

Van Raden, R. (2016). Pegida-Feinbild "Lügenpresse". Über ein massenwirksames verschwörungstheoretisches Konstrukt. In H. Kellershohn, & Kastrup, W. (Eds.) *Kulturkampf von rechts: AFD, Pegida und die Neue Rechte* (pp. 162–179). Münster: UNRAST Verlag.

Walther, O. & Retaille, D. (2010). *Sahara or Sahel? The Fuzzy Geography of Terrorism in West Africa*. Luxemburg: CEPS/INSTEAD Working Paper 35.

Waltke, B. (1995). *Finding the Will of God: A Pagan Notion?* Grand Rapids: Eerdmans.

Watson, S.D. (2009). *The Securitization of Humanitarian Migration: Digging Moats and Sinking Boats*. London and New York: Routledge.

Weber, M. (1988 [1893]) 'Die ländliche Arbeitsverfassung', in M. Weber (Ed.) *Gesammelte Aufsätze zur Sozial- und Wirtschaftsgeschichte* (pp. 443–469). Retrieved from:

http://www.zeno.org/Soziologie/M/Weber,+Max/Schriften+zur+Sozial+und+Wirtschaftsgeschichte/Entwickelungstendenzen+in+der+Lage+der+ostelbischen+Landarbeiter. Last accessed: 28 August 2018.

Weber, M. (1988 [1894]) 'Entwickelungstendenzen in der Lage der ostelbischen Landarbeiter', in M. Weber (ed.) *Gesammelte Aufsätze zur Sozial- und Wirtschaftsgeschichte* (pp. 470–507). Retrieved from: http://www.zeno.org/Soziologie/M/Weber,+Max/Schriften+zur+Sozial-+und+Wirtschaftsgeschichte/Entwickelungstendenzen+in+der+Lage+der+ostelbischen+Landarbeiter. Last accessed: 28 August 2018.

Wehry, W and Ossing, F.J. (Eds.) (1997). *Wolken Malerei Klima in Geschichte und Gegenwart.* Berlin: Deutsche Meteorologische Gesellschaft.

Weiß, W. (2013) *Philipp such sein Ich*: Zum pädagogischen Umgang mit Traumata in den Erziehungshilfen (7th ed.). Weinheim, Basel: Beltz Juventa Verlag.

Wendt, A. (1991). Bridging the Theory/Meta-Theory Gap in International Relations. *Review of International Studies, 17*(4), 383–392. Retrieved from http://www.jstor.org/stable/20097273. Last accessed: 10 February 2019.

Wertheimer, J. (1987). *Unwelcome Strangers: East-Europeans Jews in Imperial Germany.* Oxford: Oxford University Press.

Wiermer, C. (2017). *Die Nacht, die Deutschland veränderte. Hintergründe, Fakten und Enthüllungen zu den dramatischen Übergriffen der Silvesternacht in Köln.* München: riva.

Williams, P. (1993). Problems of post-colonialism. *Paragraph 16*(1), 91–102. Retrieved from http://www.jstor.org/stable/43263394.

Wright, S. (2000). *Community and Communication: The Role of Language in Nation-State Building and European Integration.* Clevedon: Multilingual Matters.

Yasnitsky, A. & van der Veer, R. (Eds.) (2015). *Revisionist Revolution in Vygotsky Studies.* London: Routledge.

Yassin-Kassab, R., & Al-Shami, L. (2018). *Burning Country: Syrians in Revolution and War* (New edition). London: Pluto Press.

Zacks, J.M., & Tversky, B. (2001). Event structure in perception and conception. *Psychological Bulletin, 127*(1): 3–21. http://dx.doi.org/10.1037/0033-2909.127.1.3. Last accessed: 14 August 2018.

Zakaria, F., & Yew, L.K. (1994). Culture Is Destiny: A Conversation with Lee Kuan Yew. *Foreign Affairs* 73(2): 109–126.

Zantop, S. (2001) Europe's Occidentalisms. In B. Ashcroft, & H. Kadhin (Eds.) *Edward Said and the Postcolonial* (pp. 107–125). New York: Nova Science Publishers.

Zimmerer, J., & Zeller, J. (Eds.) (2003). *Völkermord in Deutsch-Südwestafrika. Der Kolonialkrieg (1904–1908) in Namibia und seine Folgen.* Berlin: Links Verlag.

Zimmerman, A. (2001). *Anthropology and anti-humanism in imperial Germany.* Chicago, IL: University of Chicago Press.

Zimmerman, A. (2006). Decolonizing Weber. *Postcolonial Studies* 9(1), 53–79.
Zimmermann, O. (Ed.) (2017). *Initiative Kulturelle Integration. Zusammenhalt in Vielfalt. 15 Thesen zu kultureller Integration und Zusammenhalt.* Regensburg: ConBrio.
Zimmermann, O. (2018) Leitkulturstandards. In O. Zimmermann and T. Geißler (Eds.), *Wertedebatte: Von Leitkultur bis kulturelle Integration* (pp. 37–38). Berlin: Deutscher Kulturrat. (Reprinted from "Leitkulturstandards", 2006, *Aus Politik &Kultur 2*).
Žižek, S. (2001). The Fragile Absolute: Or, why is the Christian Legacy worth Fighting For? London: Verso.
Žižek, S. (2006). *The Universal Exception: Selected Writings*, London: Continuum.
Zoungrana, W. (2017). *Method as Theory: Lakatos, Methodology, and Interpretive International Relations.* Berlin: wvb.

Index

Abazid, Naief   36–38
Abel (biblical figure)   187, 190
Abgeordnetenhaus (Berlin's state parliament)   1
Abram (biblical figure)   185
absenteeism (in integration classes)   113, 127, 129
Abwehrpolitik (anti-Polish defence policy)   59
acceleration (as in sociology)   178
acculturation   114n3, 168
Achcar, Gilbert   158n11
acquisition-learning-hypothesis   128
actionism (of the New Right)   171
Adam (biblical figure)   184n4
Adib-Moghaddam, Arshin   158
AfD (German political party)   86, 170, 193n7
affective-filter-hypothesis   128
Afghanistan   19, 86n26, 154n1
Africa   54, 87, 107n14, 108, 192n6
  scramble for   54
Africom   108
Agamben, Giorgio   21, 43
agency dependence   14, 15
agreement   4, 33, 48, 70, 77, 86n25, 106, 107, 109, 145, 170n20
  Algiers   107
  Dublin   30, 99
  EU-Turkey   86
  German-Italian   77
  Sykes-Picot   33
aid
  development   87, 109, 165
  humanitarian   109, 147, 165
al-Andalus   157n9
al-Assad (*see*: Baachar)
Albania   4
Algeria   19, 107n13
Algiers-Agreement   107. *See also* agreement
alien   8, 66, 70, 74, 144, 167
alienation   71
Aljazeera   30
Allah (in theocratic rule)   168
allegiance   21, 28, 108
alliance   40, 108, 157
Al-Mourabitoun   88n28

alphabetization   111, 112, 123, 134n13
Al-shami, Leila   32, 147, 188
Althusser, Louis   11
ambiguity   77
ambivalence   107n14, 114, 194n2, 195
amorous events   47. *See also* events
amorphous masses   20. *See also* Baudrillard
Ancien Régime   136
  Collèges in the   136
Anderson, Benedict   52, 55, 59, 64, 120
aneurysms   19
AnkER (arrival, decision, repatriation)   88–90. *See also* Seehofer, Masterplan
anti-decolonization   168
anti-feminism   170n20, 183
anti-immigration   7, 52
anti-Islam   170, 192
anti-migration   60, 64, 87, 88
antisemitism   6, 97, 189
anxiety   48, 120, 129, 191
apology   148
apostasy   161
Arabic   122, 124, 125, 128, 157
Arab-Spring-revolution   4
Arbeitnehmer   79
archives   24, 34
Aristotle   164
Arizpe, Lourdes   175, 176
Aron, Raymond   167
arrogance
  Eurocentric   171
  Western   155
Ashcroft, Bill   194, 195
Asian values   165n17
Assad (*see*: Baachar)
assemblage   26, 53
assimilation   114, 170
Asylsystem   88
asylum:
  asylum-admitting   103
  asylum-granting   101
  asylum-seeking   6, 8, 33, 86, 94, 106
Asylverfahrensgesetz   84
Aufenthaltsgesetz   111
Auschwitz   133
Ausländerforschung   49

Ausländergesetz 83
Ausländerpolizeiverordnung 79
Australia 155
Austria 29, 33, 36, 52, 86
Auswärtiges Amt 96
Ausweisungsverordnungen 58
autopoiesis 19, 20
Avermaet, Piet Van 121, 122, 136
Axioms (of the event) 16, 27 *See also* events
Ayatollah 162
Azawad 107

Baachar 32, 33, 36, 38, 40, 41, 103, 146
Baath Party 33, 146
Bach, Johann Sebastian 174
Badiou, Alain:
   abnormal multiples 21
   aleatory arrangements 21, 37
   aleatory combination 21
   aleatory elements 38
   amorous events 47
   count-as-one 32, 43, 47
   edge of the void 6, 20–22, 34, 38–43, 45
   evental site 21, 22, 28, 31–37, 39, 40, 43, 44, 46–48, 56
   fidelity to the event 21, 22, 28, 40, 183
   inconsistent multiples 33, 37, 39, 45
   interpretative intervention 22
   interventional capacity 44, 45
   sans-culottes 47
   transcendental laws 46
Bahr, Egon 163, 173, *See also* Willy Brandt
balance of power 76, 154, 157
Balkan route, the 30, 43, 86, 129
Balzacq, Thierry 53, 54, 56, 58
BAMF (Federal Office of Migration and Refugees) 29, 87–89, 111, 112, 127, 134 n13
ban
   Muslim 157
   Polish 62, 74
banking method (of education) 8, 116, 143, 144, 148, 149
bare life 21, 43
Barkhane (Military operation) 108n17
Barthes, Roland 11, 138
Bashaar (*see*: Baachar)

Basic Law, The (German Constitution) 84, 98–100, 104, 105, 109, 112, 173, 174, 176, 178. *See also* Grundgesetz
Bauder, Harald 61, 66, 70, 72, 73, 75, 78, 79n20, 81, 85, 114
Baudrillard, Jean:
   amorphous masses 20
   de-simulation 18, 28, 30, 31
   event strike 17
   fake events 6, 17, 18, 20, 28–30
   non-event 19
   terrorism as an event 18
   terrorism is the event 19
Beck, Ulrich 73
being-qua-agency 35
bell hooks 144n19
Berlin Wall, The 1–4, 17, 20, 92, 152, 153, 177
Bhabha, Homi 194
Bible 184, 185, 187, 190
biologism 171
biopolitics 113
bipolarity 167
birthright 190
Bismarck, Otto von 7, 51, 52, 55, 57–59, 66, 67, 73
Bloch, Ernst 181
BMZ (Federal Ministry for Economic Cooperation and Development) 96
Bommes, Michael 49, 50
Bouazizi, Mohamed 36
Bourdieu, Pierre 8, 70, 115, 117–120, 138, 174
brain drain 191
Brandt, Willy 2, 79, 162, 163
Brexit 94, 96
bridge, cultural 157, 162, 164, 165
British Empire 194n1
Broder, Henryk 46n25
Brutus 15, 16
Bundesrat 84, 99
Bundestag 99, 170, 172
Bundeswehr 109
Burkina Faso 108n16

Caesar 16
Caesarism 60
CAH (Contrastive Analysis Hypothesis) 128
Cain (biblical figure) 190

Caliphate, The   38, 162
Canada   46, 80, 114
cancer   75
capacity-building   107
capital   61, 66, 67, 77, 119
capitalism   9, 32, 50, 51, 62, 68, 154, 167, 176, 178, 182, 183, 188
Caracazo   31
Castelli, Elizabeth   183
Castells, Manuel   66
causality   25
CDU (political party)   76, 84, 104, 172, 189
ceasefire   109
CEFR (Common European Framework of Reference)   122
Celan, Paul   133
CFSP (Common Foreign and Security Policy)   109
Chad   88n28, 107n14, 108n15
chaos   2
charisma   60
Chemnitz   105
Chicago School   114
civilization   8, 133, 152, 153, 156–158, 161, 164–169, 176, 177
clash rhizome   8, 9, 151–153, 169, 171, 174, 176–178
classroom   115, 124, 127, 130, 132, 134
co-dependency   54, 56
cohabitation   165, 189
colonialism   155, 194n2, 195
commensurability   165
composition   57n4, 125, 156
compositional contiguity   40
compositional dependence   15, 30
compositional interrelation   40
confidence-building   109
Confucius   165
Congo   181
constitutionalism   161
contiguous events   14. *See also* events
contingency   36, 78
co-option   37, 93
co-proletarians   76
copula   57, 125
correspondence theory   17
corruption   32, 33, 107, 134

counter-acculturation   168
counterinsurgency   93, 107
counterrevolution   4, 146, 188
counterterrorism   19, 108
crime   100, 113
Critchley, Simon   182
crusades   168
CSS (Collège Sahélien de Sécurité)   87, 88
CSU (political party in Bavaria)   84, 104

Damascus   32, 183, 184
damma (Arabic vowel)   125
Dämonisierung (demonization)   169
Darwinism   64
Davidson, Donald   6, 16, 17, 28, 30
Dawkins, Richard   182
debt (Greek)   30, 95
decomposition   37
de-escalation   37
deficit   95
Deleuze, Gilles:
    conceptual personae   26, 28
    geophilosophy of the event   6, 23, 27, 28, 39
    incorporeal events   26
    pure event   19, 26, 28
    sense and event   26
demagogy   192
dependency   14, 76, 77, 79
depression   76
deprivation   9, 32, 75, 165, 185
deregulation   62
Derrida, Jacques   138, 202
Descartes, René   140
Deschooling Society   8, 115, 133–135
despair   19, 154
detainees   146
determinism   13, 15
deterrence   53, 84, 93
de-territorialization   159
detours   137
Deutschland   2, 63, 112
Deutschmark   95
Deutschtum (German identity)   52, 55
de-Westernization   168
dialect   124
dialogic solutions   169

dichotomies 10, 53, 71
dictators 3
differentiation 11, 13, 54, 130
differentiator 11
dilettantism 54
diphthongs 125
diplomacy 93, 94, 163, 164, 190
disadvantage 70
disagreement 82
discontent 120, 155, 182, 190
discrimination 146, 189
dishonesty 167
disobedience 37
disorder 166, 167
Displaced People (DP) (see: *Vertriebene* (displaced people))
dispositif 22, 57, 58, 62, 113
dissatisfaction 9, 185, 187, 191
dissemination 93
disseminators 69
divide-and-rule 66
Dohse, Knut 79
DTZ (*Deutsch-Test für Zuwanderer*) 111
Dublin 4, 30, 99
Dublin Agreements 4, 99

Eagleton, Terry 182
East-Germans 4
Écoles 136–137
Ecuador 103
Egypt 33, 42, 185, 190
Eibl-Eibesfeldt, Irenäus 71, 72
Eichberg, Henning 171
Einbürgerungstest 150
Einwanderungsgesetz (immigration law) 50, 91, 106
eliminativists 12
emigration 51, 64, 70, 76, 88, 191
emotions 53, 178, 179, 197
empiricism 5, 137
empowerment 7, 59, 202
emptiness 59
enforceability 88
enlightenment 50, 51, 137, 162, 169
enmeshment 158
entangled subalternities 9, 10, 194
Entwestlichung (see: de-Westernization)
Entwicklungsinvestionsgesetz 87
epistemic challenges 152

Erstaufnahmezentren 88
es (pronoun) 57, 198, 203
Esau (biblical figure) 190
ESI (think tank) (see: Knaus, Gerald)
EU, The (European Union) 43, 82, 83, 86–88, 90, 97–99, 110, 116, 117, 121, 147, 163, 170, 189, 205
Eurocentrism 169
Euro-crisis 6, 33
Euro-Islam 169
EUTM (European Union Training Mission) 109
evental site 21, 22, 28, 31–37, 39, 40, 43, 44, 56. See also Badiou
events
   discursive 6, 23–25
   fake 6, 17, 18, 20, 28, 29
   incorporeal 26
   Janus-faced 26, 27
   non- 6, 19, 29
   quasi- 44
   real 18, 28, 40
exodus 4, 42, 51, 54, 58, 86
expediency 60
expulsions 66, 74, 76
externalities 50, 170
extra-territorialization 87

Facebook 112
Fachkräfteeinwanderungsgesetz 91
faculty of speech 123, 133
faith 182n3 46, 102, 149, 182, 187, 188
fake events 6, 17, 18, 20, 28, 29
fallacy 21
fanaticism 147
Fanon, Frantz 148
Far East, The 156, 195
Far Right, The 7, 9, 152, 153, 171, 191–193
fatherland 9
fatwa 160, 162
FDP (German political party) 84
Feldarbeiter (field workers) 75
feminism 195
Fénelon, François 138n15
FIFA 18, 96
Flachdenker (shallow thinkers) 167
Flintlock (military exercise) 108
Fluchtursachenbekämpfung 86
folklore 173

INDEX 243

Foucault, Michel:
   archeology of discourse   28
   archeology of events   27
   archeology of knowledge   25
   corporeal objects   23
   discursive events   6, 23–25
   discursive formation   25
   incorporeal materialism   26
foundations   57
France   46, 52, 80, 86, 93, 95, 96, 110, 137, 140, 143, 171, 173, 192
Frankfurter Allgemeine Zeitung, Die   112
Frankfurt School   145
fraud   113
Freire, Paulo   8, 116, 135, 143–149, 200, 201
FRG (West Germany)   112
Friedenstrategie   164
Frisch, Max   81
Frontex   88
Fukuyama, Francis   18, 153, 154, 160
functionalism   114
fundamentalism   155, 161, 162, 166, 168, 169, 184

Galula, David   107
Gastarbeiter   2, 65
Gastarbeiterforschung   49
gate-keeping   116, 117
Gauck, Joachim   4, 113
GDP   95
GDR   2, 3, 112
GEAS (Common European Asylum System)   88
Gegenakkulturation   168
Geldleistungen   87
Gellner, Ernst   120
glasnost   32
globalization   17, 18, 20, 29, 53, 65, 85, 92, 168, 175, 179
Gogh, Theo van   173
Goldmann, Lucien   181, 187
Görtemaker, Manfred   50, 51, 55, 67
governance   33, 36, 83, 86, 108, 109, 163
governmentality   74, 113n1
grammar   31, 115, 117–119, 126, 130, 134, 140, 141, 145, 146
Grotius, Hugo   101–103, 105

Grundgesetz (*see*: Basic Law (German Constitution))
Guattari, Félix (*see*: Deleuze, Gilles)
Guattari's   151, 152
guest-workers (*see*: *Gastarbeiter*)

habitus   58, 174
Hafez, Kai   8, 153, 160–163
Hague Convention   69
Haliday, Fred   153
hard-power   7
heaven   2, 173, 185, 186
Hegel, Friedrich   158n11
hegemony   134, 167, 176
Heidegger, Martin   12
Heidelberg Manifesto, The   71
Heimat   9
Herbert, Ulrich   51, 52, 54, 56–59, 63, 66, 68–71, 74, 75, 77, 78, 84, 85
Herzog, Roman   8, 153, 163–166
heuristics   13, 15
Hirschman, Albert   190, 191
Hochkultur   177
Hochschild, Arlie Russell   191, 192
Höcke, Björn   192
Hoffmann, Florian   116
Hollywood   93
Holocaust   100, 173n25
homophobia   192
Hoyerswerda   105
humanitarianism   103
human-rights   86
human-trafficking   105
Hume, David   11, 13–15, 27
Huntington, Samuel   8, 154–157, 159, 160, 166, 168–171, 177, 179

ICG (International Crisis Group)   107
ICRC (International Committee of the Red Cross)   41, 42
Identität   171, 197, 204. *See also* identity
identity
   German   52, 55, 72, 91, 114, 123, 170
   asylum-seekers and   103, 104, 195
   language and   115, 116, 120, 123, 172
   politics of   159, 164, 170, 172, 177, 182, 195
ideology   70, 114, 137, 167, 170, 174
idiosyncrasies   39

ignorance   63, 167
Illich, Ivan   115, 133–135, 197, 204
ill-preparedness   30
ill-treatment   75
IMES (Institute of Middle East Studies)   163n16
immigration
    citizenship and   172
    country   2, 3, 7, 201, 205
    discourses on   7
    laws on   49, 50, 82–84, 86, 87, 89, 91, 99, 106, 114
    quota model and   106
    Polish   62, 66, 68, 76, 79–81
imperialism   60, 68, 70, 171, 183, 194, 195
impetuousness   36, 38, 44
incommensurability   20, 71, 149, 176
incompatibility   149, 162, 176
independence   115
indeterminacy   13, 15, 48
industrialization   50–52, 58, 67, 168
infrastructure   42, 44
insecurity   42, 52, 107, 149
insurgency   37
Integrationskursverordnung   111
intelligence   8, 37, 103, 116, 138–142, 145, 146
interdependence   53, 165
interpenetration   161
interpretation   4, 11, 17, 45, 98, 161, 183
interpretative intervention   22
intervention   19, 20, 22, 34, 35, 43–47, 58, 64, 88, 95, 109, 146, 182, 185
introspection   186
Iqbal, Muhammad   164
Iraq   19, 42, 86, 124, 129, 154, 184
iron-cage   178
ISIS   40, 184
Islam   33, 48, 49, 72, 104, 156, 157n10, 158, 160–164, 166, 167, 169, 177
Islamo-fascism   157n10
Israel   190

Jacotot, Joseph   8, 116, 136–146, 205
Jakobson, Roman   11
Janus-faced event   26, 27
Japan   35, 93
Jasmine revolution   31, 36
Jemen   33

jurisdiction   101–103
justiciability   41

Kant, Immanuel   165
kasra (Arabic vowel)   125
Keucheyan, Razmig   11, 23n15, 181, 182
Khomeni (Ayatollah)   162
Kim, Jaegwon:
    cambridge dependence   14
    compositional dependence   6, 13, 15, 21, 23, 27, 30, 33, 39, 40, 44, 56
    determination relations   15
Kim, Duk-Yung   60, 63, 64
Kimbangu, Simon   181, 196
Kimbanguism   181n1
kin countries   154, 167
KJV (King James Version)   38n22, 186, 187
Knaus, Gerald   86n25
Koeppel, Matthias   1–5
Kohl, Helmut   1, 2, 72, 81, 105
Koskenniemi, Martti   41
Krashen, Stephen   128
K-strategy   192
Kulturkampf   55, 56, 170, 199
Kulturkreis   170n20
Kulturpluralismus   171
Kurds   40, 146

Lacan, Jacques   11
Landarbeiter (farm workers)   61
language:
    acquisition   8, 111, 112, 116, 119, 121, 123, 124, 126, 130, 133, 140, 141, 146
    certificate   122
    courses   8, 123, 127
    instructors   148
    pedagogy   116
    proficiency   111, 120, 122, 123
    skills   128
    textbooks   8, 115, 127, 131, 134
Latin alphabet   111, 112
legalism   66
legislation   65, 67, 79, 91
Leitkultur   8, 153, 170–174, 176–178
Leitkulturstandards   173, 207
Lemkin   100
Lenin   68, 183
Leutenot (labor shortage in the 1880s)   7, 51, 52, 54–56, 60

Levantine dialect 124
Levi, Primo 133
liberalism 163, 195, 200
line-cutters 192
Lorde, Audrey 19
Lügenpresse 192

MacKinnon, Mark 36–38, 40
Maghreb 87
maître 136
Mali 88n28, 107n14, 108n15, 109, 110
map 127, 143, 178
Marx, Karl 51, 72, 196
Marxism 181, 194, 195, 203
Marzower, Mark 100, 101
Masterplan 86–90
Mauritania 88n28, 107n14, 108n15
Mbembe, Achille 194n2
Mearsheimer, John 92, 154n1, 160
meta-discourse 152
metahistory 158
metaphor 8, 75, 78, 102n12, 119, 151, 175n27, 176
method 8, 41, 131, 139–143, 146
migration policies
　Command-and-control, C2 3, 7, 50, 64, 65, 71, 86
　Muddling-through 7, 50, 64, 77–80, 82–85, 90, 91, 97
　Public-private-partnership 3P 7, 50, 64, 67, 74, 91
mnemonics 140, 146
modernization 168, 191
Moïsi, Dominique 179
Momper, Walter 2, 4
monoculturalists 173, 176
monolingualism 121
Morgenthau, Hans 92n2
Morocco 79, 108
Morsi, Mohammed 187
Mubarak, Hosni 187
Mukhabarat (Syrian intelligence agency) 37
multiculturalism 159, 171, 172
muntadiyat (forums) 32, 146
mysoginy 10
M'Bokolo, Elikia 181n1

nationalism 50, 55, 59, 60, 64, 116, 120, 123, 162, 170, 184, 194

nation-building 162
nation-state 51, 52, 55, 62, 73, 74, 168, 177, 206
NATO 95, 109
naturalization 76, 82, 150
Nazism 70, 98, 100
neocolonialism 194
neo-liberalism 66, 170
NGOs 36, 65, 86, 93
Nietzsche, Friedrich 158, 173
Niger 88n28, 107n14, 108n15, 110
Nigeria 108
nodal point 85, 153
non-believers 182, 184
non-causal relations 6, 13, 15
non-event 6, 17–20, 29
non-refoulement 99, 100
non-state 36, 37, 39, 65, 72, 74, 156, 176, 182
Nye, Joseph 61n7, 92, 93, 96, 97, 156n6

objectivity 22
occupation 2, 129, 195
Oka, municipality of 47
Omissions (historiographical) 6, 50
one-size-fit-all measure 121
Opium 167n18, 181
oppressors 147–149
Orbán, Viktor 43, 86
ordinance on foreign workers 79
Orient 160, 195
orientalism 60, 195
Orientierungskurs 150
Orsi, Davide 154, 156
Ostpolitik 2, 162n15, 163
over-didacticized textbook 141
overprotection 102
over-regulation 66

pacification 107, 109
painting 1, 2, 4
paix 167
Pakistan 164, 165
Pan-Arabism 33
parasitism, social 8
Paris Commune 31
Parlamentarischer Rat 84
Pascal, Blaise 181
Pasolini, Pier Paolo 182–184
pathology 144
patriarchal structures 10

Paul the Apostle   38n22 (*see also* St Paul)
PCI(Italian Communist Party)   183
Pegida   104, 170
perestroika   32
persecution   32, 85, 98, 99, 184
Pharisee   184
Pianesi, Fabio   12–15, 199
Pius IX (Pope)   55
plateaus   8, 151, 152, 177
Plato   12
Pluralistic postcolony   194
Poland   51, 70
Polanyi, Karl   72
Polensperre (Polish ban)   62
Polish workers   58n5 52, 56, 58, 59, 63, 66, 68, 69, 71, 74
Post-Algiers   109
postcolonialism   194, 195
poststructuralism   11, 23
presence-absence paradox   6
Preußen   51, 54, 56, 57, 59, 61, 63, 68, 69
primordialists   157–159
proto-securitization   60
Prussia (*see*: *Preußen*)
Pufendorf, Samuel von   102–104
pure event   19, 26. *See also* event
Putin, Vladimir   155

Québécois administration   47
Quinean theory   12, 13
Quran   157

race   60, 63, 99, 114, 152, 153, 157, 159, 160, 174
racism   31, 49, 71, 101, 146, 167, 170, 171, 192
radicalism   6, 35, 158
radicality   134, 143
radicles   152
RAF (*Rote Armee Fraktion*)   105, 168
Rancière, Jacques (*see*: Jacotot)
reactionary dogmatism   154
reactionary inventions   47
reactionary progressivism   51
reactions to the event   6
real events   18, 28, 40
Realism (in International Relations)   92n2, 154
recognition of an event   22, 43
Red Army Faction (*see*: RAF (*Rote Armee Fraktion*))
reductionism   117
refuge   8, 101, 103, 116, 179, 184

Régime, Ancien   136
regulation-school   72
Reichstag   173
reification   176
re-islamization   164
relativism   165, 167n18, 171, 182n3
religion   49, 55, 60, 99, 138, 166, 170, 181–184
re-traditionalization   168
revisionism   192
rhizome   8, 9, 151–153, 169, 171, 174, 176–178
right-wing populism   9, 48, 97, 185, 189
risk   114n3 19, 41, 67, 73, 74, 78, 79, 113, 114, 132, 158, 187
r-strategy   192
Rushdie, Salman   161, 162
Russia   41, 52, 59, 82n21, 103

Saarland   89
Sachleistungen   87
Sachsengängerei   62
Sahara   107n13, 108, 109
Sahel   7, 87, 88n28, 107–110
Sartre, Jean-Paul   11
Sassen, Saskia   108
Saussure, Ferdinand de   117, 118
savages   102, 198
scaffolding   145, 146
Schäuble, Wolfgang   95
Schengen   87
Schily, Otto   83
Schmidt, Helmut   105
Schoolmaster   136, 140, 199
Schröder, Gerhard   82
science   6, 77, 97, 133, 138, 140, 153, 162, 165
Scriptures, The   182
sectarianism   147
secularization   178
securitization   7, 19, 50, 52–56, 58–60, 71, 91
   audience and   54–56, 58, 172, 195
Seehofer, Horst:
   AnkER   88, 89
   Frontex   88
   Masterplan   86–90
Senegal   108
Serval   108
sexphobia   183
sexuality   159
Shibboleth   113, 196
Shiite   161
Silesia   56
Silvesternacht   113

INDEX

Singh, Amardeep   194n1
Snowden, Edward   102, 103
Socrates   14–16, 139, 185
Soft power   7, 91–98, 101–103, 105, 106, 108
Soft Power 30 Index   95, 96
Spiegel, Der   105
Spivak, Gayatri   194
Staatsräson   157
state actor   35–37, 39, 65, 66, 72, 74, 156, 176, 182
state-centrism   166
Steinbach, Udo   8, 153, 163, 164
St. Paul   4, 38n22, 182–184
structuralism   11, 23
subalternities   9, 10, 194
subclass   15
subversion   18, 59
Sudan   108
surveillance   19, 75, 102
Süssmuth, Rita   83, 84, 111
Süssmuth-Kommission   118n5
Sykes-Picot agreement   33
Syrian revolution   40, 44, 47, 147, 188

Tarski, Alfred   16
Tarsus, Saul of (*see*: St Paul)
Télémaque   137, 138, 141, 143
terrorism   17–19, 28, 57, 58, 92n1, 105, 107, 108, 153, 167n19, 176, 177, 184
Thym, Daniel   91, 106
Tibi, Bassam   8, 46, 159, 166, 167n18, 168, 169, 171–173, 177, 179
Todorov, Tzvetan   155, 157, 179
torture   32, 37, 38, 103, 165
transparency   32
triptych   1–5

Überfremdung   192
Ultramontanism   55
  Zentrum (a political party in the 1880s)   55
Umgangssprache   130
umlaut   125
uncertainties   29, 159
undecidability   22, 39, 48
un-securitization   57, 58
USA, The   9, 80, 82, 93, 95, 177
utopia   3, 39, 154, 156, 181

Varzi, Achille   12–15, 199

Vatican   55
Vattel, Emerich de   102, 103, 105
Verbindlichkeiten   173
Verfassungspatriotismus   8, 153, 171, 174, 176, 178
vernaculars   64
Vertriebene (displaced people)   78
visa   53, 67, 82, 89n30
voice (strategy)   9, 185, 189–191
Volkszeitung, Die Schlesische (Silesian Newspaper)   56
Vygotsky, Lev   131

wager   187
Washington Post, The   61n7
wāw (Arabic letter)   125
Weber, Max   7, 50, 59–64
Weimar Republic   64, 76, 77
Weizsäcker, Richard von   2, 4
Werterelativismus   165
Wilhelmine Germany   7, 60, 64–66, 73, 74, 77, 80
Wirtschaftsflüchtlinge   84
Wirtschaftswunder (economic recovery after WWII)   81
Wittgenstein, Ludwig   12
Wolff, Christian   102
WWI   7, 68, 71, 76
WWII   49, 76, 79, 81, 91, 93, 94, 97, 100, 101, 105

Xantippe   14
xenophobia   5, 9, 48, 60, 64, 97, 106, 113, 162, 189

Yarmouk   1
Yassin-Kassab, Robin   32, 146, 147, 188
Yugoslavia   79, 116, 162

Zeit, Die (German newspaper)   29
zeitgeist   140, 155, 160, 177
Zivilisationen   160, 169, 204
Zivilisationsbewusstsein   167
Žižek, Slavoj   158, 181, 207
Zoungrana, Wilfried   61
ZPD (Zone of Proximal Development)   131
Zurückdrängung   52
Zuwanderung   83, 86
Zuwanderungsgesetz (a 2004 immigration law)   49, 50, 82, 83, 91n1

www.ingramcontent.com/pod-product-compliance
Lightning Source LLC
Chambersburg PA
CBHW070917030426
42336CB00014BA/2453